COLLECTIVIZATION GENERATION

COLLECTIVIZATION GENERATION

Oral Histories of a Social Revolution in Uzbekistan

Marianne Kamp

CORNELL UNIVERSITY PRESS   ITHACA AND LONDON

Copyright © 2024 by Cornell University

All rights reserved. Except for brief quotations in a review, this book, or parts thereof, must not be reproduced in any form without permission in writing from the publisher. For information, address Cornell University Press, Sage House, 512 East State Street, Ithaca, New York 14850. Visit our website at cornellpress.cornell.edu.

First published 2024 by Cornell University Press

Library of Congress Cataloging-in-Publication Data

Names: Kamp, Marianne, author.
Title: Collectivization generation : oral histories of a social revolution in Uzbekistan / Marianne Kamp.
Description: Ithaca : Cornell University Press, 2024. | Includes bibliographical references and index.
Identifiers: LCCN 2024011164 (print) | LCCN 2024011165 (ebook) | ISBN 9781501777998 (hardcover) | ISBN 9781501779503 (paperback) | ISBN 9781501778001 (epub) | ISBN 9781501778018 (pdf)
Subjects: LCSH: Collectivization of agriculture—Social aspects—Uzbekistan. | Rural youth—Uzbekistan—Social conditions—20th century. | Uzbekistan—Social conditions—1917–1991.
Classification: LCC HD1492.U9 K367 2024 (print) | LCC HD1492.U9 (ebook) | DDC 338.109587/09043—dc23/eng/20240514
LC record available at https://lccn.loc.gov/2024011164
LC ebook record available at https://lccn.loc.gov/2024011165

Contents

List of Tables and Figures	vi
Acknowledgments	ix
Note on Transliteration	xii
Introduction: Collectivization Generation	1
1. Inedible Harvest: Cotton and Dehqons	21
2. Bosmachi Stories	37
3. Land Reform	59
4. Agitating for the Kolkhoz	83
5. Making Quloqs: Arrest, Exile, Escape, and Identity	104
6. Famine	132
7. Working	152
8. Orphans	179
Conclusion: A Generation, a Time, and Remembering	202
Appendix A: Oral History Interviewees	215
Appendix B: Questionnaire	221
Appendix C: Glossary of Uzbek Terms Used in This Work	227
Notes	231
Bibliography	269
Index	283

Tables and Figures

Tables

1.1. Cotton planting in Desiatin, Russian Empire / Early USSR, 1914–1924   34

3.1. Uzbek SSR population by province (*viloyat*), urban and rural, 1926   66

3.2. Uzbekistan's 1926 population by nationality and province (*viloyat*)   67

4.1. Expanding cotton planting and harvest in Uzbekistan, 1925–1936   86

4.2. Pace of collectivization in Uzbekistan   89

5.1. The dynamic of anti-collectivization actions in Uzbekistan, 1930s   111

6.1. Uzbekistan and Tajikistan populations in 1926 and 1939   138

6.2. Uzbekistan rural population by age group according to birth year, 1939 census   139

7.1. Tractors in the Uzbek SSR, 1920s   156

7.2. Tractors at Uzbek SSR machine-tractor stations, 1930s   156

7.3. Russian Empire / USSR silk textile production and export, selected years 1913–1937   175

8.1. End Illiteracy Enrollment, Uzbek SSR   183

A.1. Bukhara interviewees   215

A.2. Fergana/Marg'ilon interviewees   216

A.3. Namangan interviewees   217

A.4. Navoiy interviewees   217

A.5. Qashqa Daryo interviewees   218

A.6. Tashkent interviewees   219

A.7. Xorazm interviewees   220

A.8. Overall interviewees   220

Figures

3.1. Map of Uzbekistan in 1928   65

7.1. Photo of two women tractor drivers   155

7.2. Uzbek poster, man with horse and tractor   160

8.1. Primary schools, Uzbek SSR 1928–1939   186

8.2. Primary enrollments, Uzbek SSR, 1928–1939   186

Acknowledgments

This book, so many years in the making, began in a conversation with Russell Zanca (anthropologist, retired from Northeastern Illinois University), where we compared what we knew about agricultural collectivization in Uzbekistan—in my case, from interviews that I had conducted for a different project, on women and unveiling, and in his, from his anthropology fieldwork in a rural community near Andijon, Uzbekistan. Russell was my research partner on every stage of this project from conception through the end of interviewing. Together we submitted grant proposals, some failed and some successful. Russell opened doors for me in his fieldwork site, sharing his extensive network of contacts and friends, and we carried out the first set of interviews together, discussing and reworking as we went along. Russell and I cowrote a final report to the National Council for Eurasian and East European Research (NCEEER), the major funder for our research, and much later, we coauthored an article, "Recollections of Collectivization in Uzbekistan," that became the basis for chapter 5 in this volume. Russell has generously read and consulted on many of my conference papers, chapters, and articles that are based on this project, and he read and commented on the first draft of this book. Our interviews in Namangan were facilitated by Ortaqali, who hosted us and connected us with respondents. Alisher Ilkhamov facilitated transcription of those interviews.

Our third partner in this project was Elyor Karimov (historian, formerly of the Institute of History, Academy of Sciences of Uzbekistan). In a time when the Institute of History was allowed to pursue innovative projects, Karimov led a small group of history and social science researchers, the Young Scholars Society. This project would not have taken on such large dimensions and we would never have been able to collect interviews across so many provinces without the leadership of Elyor Karimov, the organizational work of Komil Kalonov, and the phenomenal, creative, dedicated work of so many of the Young Scholars (who are now mature scholars) who conducted interviews: Shahnoza (Gayupova) Madaeva, Ulfat Abdurasulov, Hurshida Jabbarova, Zavqiddin Gadoev, and Elyor Xalilov. Thanks as well to those who transcribed: Nigora Xalmuhammedova, A. Turdiyev, Asliddin Obidov, Sherzod Salaev, and others. My research in Uzbekistan was made possible by Dilarom Alimova, who mentored my dissertation work in the early 1990s and who, as director of the Institute of History in the 2000s, supported my visa requests and facilitated my access to archives and libraries. Her friendship and scholarly consultation continues to enrich my life and my understanding of Uzbekistan. Translation of interviews went very slowly when I worked on it alone. Everything improved when Donohon Abdugafurova and Rahimjon Abdugafurov came to the University of Wyoming for MA degrees. They completed translations into English for about sixty interviews, and Donohon also consulted with me about specific customs and colloquial terms related to farming life.

Oral history projects, especially those that involve international collaboration, are expensive. I am grateful to the institutions and organizations that supported this research: the University of Wyoming, which provided me with several grants that covered expenses for the pilot interviews in the Namangan region in 2001, with funds to purchase many necessary books, with a semester of leave and a sabbatical year, and with a supportive atmosphere. Zanca's interviews in Nurota (Navoiy Province) were supported by a grant from the International Research & Exchanges Board (IREX). NCEEER provided a collaborative research grant, "Collectivization in Uzbekistan: Oral Histories," for the period 2002–2004, that supported our collaboration with Karimov and the Young Scholars. A Kluge Fellowship from the Library of Congress (2006–2007) provided me with time to research and access to a rich collection of statistical and agricultural journals and published scholarship from Soviet Uzbekistan. A short-term residence at the University of Illinois Libraries Summer Research Laboratory for scholars working on Russian, East European, and Eurasian topics in 2011 and a workshop hosted by the same institution in 2018 were excellent venues for developing several of these chapters. A workshop on the family in Central Asia, hosted at Heidelberg University in 2014 by Sophie Roche, gave me the initiative to focus on respondent orphan stories. A workshop on women in Central Asia, hosted by Marlene Laruelle and Sébastien Peyrouse at George Washington University in 2018, prompted my focus on gender in stories about Bosmachis. Other workshops hosted by Julia Obertries at Freiburg University, and by Svetlana Jacquesson at the Max Plancke Institute in Halle, and Paolo Sartori at Martin-Luther University in Halle also stimulated work toward this book.

It would be impossible to mention every colleague whose insights helped me to develop this book, interacting at conferences and workshops and through email over so many years, but I owe particular thanks to Beatrice Penati, Tommaso Trevisani, Niccolò Pianciola, and Zulfiya Tursunova, all of whom have sharpened my understanding of the ways that changes in land use have shaped lives in Central Asia. The Central Eurasian Studies Society is the organizational home where I have presented work in development that eventually became articles, chapters, and sections of this book. Among the many who commented on my work in ways that sparked rethinking were Doug Northrop, Adeeb

Khalid, Shoshana Keller, Jeff Sahadeo, Ali İğmen, Adrienne Edgar, Svetlana Peshkova, and Mehmet Kesikçi. My 2018 presentation of a paper on famine and potatoes at the Institute of History in Tashkent provided me helpful insights from Nodira Azimova, Saidakbar Ag'zamxo'jaev, Alisher Sobirov, and many other Uzbek colleagues. Other friends shaped my understanding of wheat farming on dry land—Cole Ehmke and Brian Baumann—and about the labor involved in cotton picking, Saurjan Yakupov and Dildora Alimdjanova.

Although I worked with the materials for this book for many years while I was a faculty member at the University of Wyoming, joining the Central Eurasian Studies Department at Indiana University (IU) in 2017 pushed me into the serious labor of turning a mess into a book. Colleagues, especially Nazif Shahrani, and students provided critical and thought-provoking comments when I presented parts of this work. Generous research funds from IU and support from the Inner Asian and Uralic National Resource Center made travel to various conferences and workshops possible. Research funds from IU supported my work with the freelance editor Helen Faller, whom I have known since her time as an anthropology graduate student at the University of Michigan. Helen patiently consulted with me throughout a rewrite of this manuscript for a resubmission to Cornell University Press, and the improvements, which the reader cannot see (because the reader does not know what this looked like previously), are thanks to Helen's thoughtful recommendations and interventions, while the flaws remain my own. I owe thanks to the reviewers for this book manuscript, who do know what it looked like previously and who gave their time, attention, and thoughtful critiques that shaped my revisions. Thanks as well to Jim Lance, the editor who took over this project at Cornell University Press upon the retirement of Roger Hayden.

Note on Transliteration

In 1993 Uzbekistan (O'zbekiston) initiated a slow transition from a Cyrillic to a Latin alphabet. The younger generation, including those who transcribed the Uzbek and Tajik language interviews, produced transcripts in the O'zbek Latin alphabet. However, senior scholars from Uzbekistan who published most of the scholarship used in this work were more comfortable with either Cyrillic script Uzbek or with Russian. For any publications in Uzbek, whether they are in 1920s Arabic script, 1930s Latin alphabet, or the Cyrillic that began in 1940, I transliterate to contemporary Latin O'zbek. In doing so, I part ways with Library of Congress recommendations for romanization of non-Latin-alphabet Uzbek. Switching between two systems based on the publication year and alphabet of the source would be confusing, and O'zbek Latin has been in use long enough (thirty years) that it should be accepted as standard. But as I write this, there is uncertainty about that standard: Uzbekistan has mooted changing some letters that currently involve ', such as *o*', which will become *ö*. Given the decades it has taken to phase out Cyrillic Uzbek, it seems likely that the modifications to O'zbek Latin will also take some time, and in any case, they are not radical changes.

Russian transliteration follows the Library of Congress standard in its simplified form. Some city names are presented in the form that is best known in English, although they are based on transliteration from the Russian rather than the Uzbek pronunciation: for example, Tashkent rather than Toshkent, Kokand rather than Qo'qon, and Bukhara rather than Buxoro.

COLLECTIVIZATION GENERATION

Introduction

COLLECTIVIZATION GENERATION

In 2003, twelve years after the Soviet system of collectivized farming collapsed in a welter of proposals about privatization and land leasing, Qurbon A., a ninety-five-year-old former member of a kolkhoz near the city of Shahrisabz, Qashqa Daryo Province, Uzbekistan, shared his memories of collectivization with oral historians.[1] His account, one among 120 interviews from an oral history project described in this chapter, offers a glimpse into the changes that swept across Central Asia after the Russian Revolution in 1917 and the violence that divided rural Uzbek communities when the new Soviet Uzbek regime initiated land redistribution.

This book is a history of agricultural collectivization in Soviet Uzbekistan, but it is not focused on party decisions. It is instead a history of everyday life that relies on the voices of oral history respondents whom I call the "collectivization generation." Born between the early 1900s and the early 1920s, the collectivization generation were rural youth who, willingly or unwillingly, participated in this transformation of agricultural life in the early 1930s as teens or young adults. A top-down restructuring ruptured their predictable life trajectories and created new categories for understanding self and society. For many, the newly formed kolkhozes became their economic, social, and political milieu throughout their working years, shaping their identities and their material lives.

This book examines their stories of life in the 1920s and 1930s, before, during, and after collectivization, to answer the following questions. How did rural Uzbekistan become Soviet? How did those who lived through the process of collectivization and lived with its consequences throughout the entire duration of

1

the Soviet experiment come to identify with or against the Sovietized rural order? Collectivization produced immediate material changes in the lives of the collectivization generation. In their work of remembering, how do their recollections of those tangibly new things allow us to understand their identification with a Soviet order that became durable and entrenched in rural communities?

Histories of the Soviet Union have familiarized readers with collectivization's imposition of Stalinism in rural Russia and with collectivization as the catalyst for starvation in Ukraine and Kazakhstan. Is there anything distinctive to be learned from oral histories about ordinary rural lives in Uzbekistan? Uzbekistan's material conditions differed from those in the Soviet Union's grain and livestock zones; the primary crop, cotton, was inedible, industrial, dependent on irrigation, and oriented toward cash earnings, not subsistence. Most of Uzbekistan's *dehqons*, meaning anyone who tilled the land, owned their farmland individually, unlike Russia's peasants whose traditions of communal ownership underlay Soviet visions of collectivized agriculture. Two themes are at the heart of these dehqon stories: losing land and livelihood assets or gaining access to them through collectivization; and the resulting rise or fall of family security, influence, and status.

Uzbek dehqons were not victims of genocidal starvation like Ukrainian peasants nor of the total disruption of their way of life that resulted in mass starvation as was the case for nomadic herders in Kazakhstan. Sedentary Uzbek dehqons owned small holdings where they raised cotton, wheat, and other food crops. For them, collectivization meant joining lands, changing modes of working, and witnessing the violent shift in local leadership from traditionally influential men to a new set approved by the Communist Party. Some respondents experienced collectivization as a shattering of their family and fortune. Others found in the collective farm relief from poverty and an opening to a better future. Voices from Uzbekistan's collectivization generation enable us to see those ruptures and transformations through the eyes of dehqons whose life courses moved from precarious or marginalized to empowered and dehqons whose social capital was pulverized by Communism's arrival. Elderly oral history respondents who had a lifetime to weigh and to reevaluate collectivization's outcomes spent a surprising amount of time talking about the concrete elements of everyday rural life that were significant to them: getting paid, starting to farm with tractors, food and famine, experiencing violence, and being orphaned. They told stories that allow us to reconstruct some of the ways that Communist Party designs reconstituted rural identities. Respondents naturalized party discourses of class and nation within their own accounts of families joining or resisting the processes of agricultural collectivization.

Breaking the Relations of Dependence: Qurbon's Story

Qurbon A. was born near Shahrisabz, in the period when the Manghit Emir Muzaffar al-Din (1886–1910) ruled Bukhara as a not-quite sovereign despot, his lands having been conquered and made into a Russian imperial protectorate in 1873.[2] Qurbon A. was born in 1908 into a dehqon household and orphaned as a child. He vividly recalled episodes of mid-1920s land reform, wealthy landowners (*boylar*), the process of dispossessing the wealthy (making them into *quloqs*—the Uzbek version of the Russian *kulak*), and violent anti-Soviet resistance by the so-called Bosmachi (bandits or anti-Soviet rebels). Qurbon described himself as strongly supporting Soviet rule and collectivization. In this chapter, his narrative illustrates the ways that large-scale political and material changes impacted the lives of young men in rural Central Asia, creating moments for new self-definition.[3]

Oral history accounts tell us about details of life, about social structures, and about the materiality of human experience. They offer us a narrator's "interpretation of life events rather than a chronicle of the past."[4] Talking with Ulfat Abdurasulov, an interviewer from the Tashkent-based Young Scholars Society, and with two of Ulfat's colleagues, a local facilitator, and family members present in his guestroom, Qurbon A. portrayed his orphanhood, his relations of dependence, and his political awakening as an active supporter of the newly formed Soviet government. Through his interaction with a violent political process, he forged an identity with other hired rural laborers, called *novcha*, against the rural wealthy, the boylar.

> QURBON A.: My father and mother both passed away in 1915 or 1917, due to famine and an epidemic. I was left in the care of my father's mother, with my older sister and one younger brother remaining out of five children. The cattle died off after a drought, the lands dried up and so did the crops, and people were unable to get any kind of harvest from the dryland crops. And then prices for everything soared. I must have been ten, or seven or eight years old at that time. My grandmother talked to [the village head], and they entrusted me with grazing livestock from the village. After I had done that for a couple of years, my paternal aunt's husband took me into his care and made me his dependent. I would go out into the pastures to take food and bread to the novchas [hired laborers],[5] check the cattle's bellies, and I did that until I grew up.... In 1922 the Soviet government came here.
>
> ULFAT: The Soviet government came?

QURBON: While I was working looking after the herds, we heard that the Russians are coming; the Russians are coming.

Like many interviewees, Qurbon A. approximated years, ages, and sequences of events. Many respondents estimated their own year of birth and would differentiate between what was written in their passport and what they thought was the actual year. Qurbon A. was not sure when his parents and siblings passed away, but it is known that Russian Central Asia suffered a severe drought and famine in 1917.[6] His was a herding and grain-raising village, where the wealthier families owned large herds and hired the poor novchas to work as herders and tillers. Although revolution swept Russia in 1917, the Bolshevik Revolution arrived in Bukhara's rural districts far more gradually. In 1920, revolutionaries in Bukhara who opposed the emir's rule sought aid from the Bolsheviks in Tashkent, overthrew the emir, and created the Bukhara People's Republic. From 1918 through the 1920s, the Red Army fought an ongoing campaign against Central Asian militant groups whom the government designated, pejoratively, Bosmachi. In 1924, there was a geographical restructuring of Central Asia, whereby parts of what had been the Turkestan Territory were joined with the former Bukhara Emirate and the former Xorazm Khanate to form the Uzbekistan Soviet Socialist Republic.[7]

The new Soviet government first showed its face in Bukhara's rural communities in the early 1920s when administrators arranged for the election of village committees.[8] The village committee became a site of political contest where traditional local leaders sought positions and where Soviet government agitators tried to elevate locally powerless people who might become supporters of the revolutionary Soviet order. In addition to village committees, representatives of the new Soviet government created rural organizations called Qoshchi, or the Plowmen's Union, and Kambag'allar Uyushmasi, or the Union of the Poor. When the Uzbek Soviet Socialist Republic's Communist Party initiated land reform in the mid-1920s, activists in Shahrisabz District mobilized the Union of the Poor as their revolutionary force, challenging these dependent rural laborers to seize the lands and herds of the wealthy. Qurbon presents this as a dramatic episode in his own life, one that he linked to the protracted struggle between the Reds and the Bosmachis. As he began to recall events aloud, he shifted attention away from Russians and Soviet government toward conflict within his community between the novchas and the boylar, to illustrate what he meant by the establishment of Soviet government.

QURBON A.: In 1926, land reform began. A man named Rayimqulov came from Tashkent. He had a meeting, called everyone together, went into the rich people's houses. He said we will take the land from you rich and socialize it and give it to the poor people.

ULFAT: He gathered all the people?

QURBON: Not everyone, primarily the novchas. They got about five or ten of the smarter ones together, and the commission held a meeting. The commission then appointed the best talkers from among the novchas as the leaders. The commission had four or five of them, and they distributed land. For example: "To Qurbon goes so much land, so many hectares in such-and-such a location." ... And then they accused some people of being *quloq* [exploiters]. That was in 1926. No, it must have been later, in 1927 or 1928, because the Bosmachis came first. Bosmachis, who were made up of rich men from the city, came and hid themselves in the mountains.

As chapter 4 explains, during Uzbekistan's land reform, a commission comprising community members and Soviet government representatives collected data on every landowner's holdings, established a norm or average for the district, and seized land beyond that norm from the larger landowners. The seized lands were then distributed to dehqons who owned little or no land.[9] Qurbon began with this story about land reform but then backed up to tell about Bosmachis who asserted control and rallied support from some of the wealthy in his village against the Soviet Red Army and Soviet policies. Evident in the transcript is elderly Qurbon's control over his own narrative, as he pushed back against the much younger interviewer's line of questioning.

ULFAT: Let's come back to the Bosmachis later. What did that commission do?

QURBON A.: The commission had not come yet, and we will come to them later. The Bosmachis went to the mountains; they came and levied taxes on the dehqons; they took guns and items they needed. The Bosmachis were all those city people who were made quloq and who ran away and came here. The Bosmachis increased. From Mo'minobod—our village—Berdiboz, Jabbor Amin, and Sulton joined the Bosmachis and were called *amin*. You know what that is, like today's district head. ... [10] They took control of ten or fifteen villages and made people there serve as their soldiers.

And then one day a rumor went around the village that an *eshon* [a Muslim preacher] was coming from Sariosiyo. ... People gathered for prayers, and the eshon told them that everyone in the village who considers himself a man ought to take part in this [the Bosmachis' struggle].

Qurbon then explained his own low status in the community as a landless fieldworker who sharecropped and his resentment against the large landowners who used his labor and allowed him to keep only half of what he raised. In the context of Soviet land reform, he decided to act against the wealthy landowners.

> QURBON A.: This was 1926. At that time my older sister had married, and I was working for my brother-in-law. I was dependent on him.... We rented land, and we would pay [the owner] from the harvest. We would pay about half and keep the rest.
>
> At that time my brother-in-law and I were raising rice, and the rich men, who were getting richer all the time, were taking the water, and there was not enough for the rice. It was a drought. Then I came to my brother-in-law, telling him I will be late.... "I'll stay here until it is too dark for people to see.... Then I'll get my hoe, and I will cut off the irrigation water to all those quloqs, and I will water all of the rice. And then I'll gather the people who are close to us and go around to reveal who is a quloq. They don't know."... I watered every corner, and then I called my brother-in-law. "Hoji! Hoji! Are you done?" "I'm done." "Come quick." After we, together, cut off [the water to] the quloqs, then we headed off toward the village, singing that the novchas had risen up.... The novchas sang and danced. And then the two of us hurried to our village. When we came back into our village, everything in the direction of our house was on fire. They had set it on fire.[11]

Qurbon portrayed his own moment of revolution as a merging of his individual needs and those of people like him, the novchas. Accusing the rich men of unfairly controlling irrigation flows, he acted, inspiring other novchas to change their situation. Qurbon and the other novchas initially felt that they had triumphed over the rich by stealthily redirecting irrigation, but the boylar, whom he understood as working with the Bosmachis, retaliated. Qurbon recalled the emotional intensity of battling the fire that he attributed to nefarious boylar. He was injured, lost consciousness, and when he recovered, he learned that the struggle had resulted in murder.

> QURBON A.: After the fire had burned out, I heard my nephew calling, "The Bosmachis got together, took them [the village commission members] to the mosque, and killed them." I went to the mosque, and I saw nine men, all strung up at the neck by their own turbans.
> INTERVIEWER: Why? What had these men done?
> QURBON: As I said, there were Bosmachi leaders named Berdiboz, Jabbor, and Sulton Amin who attacked the people. The government sent soldiers village to village searching for them. We had gone out hunting for them. The boylar said, "We will kill them all [the village

commission members] when we find them and their children." . . . The commission members—the Bosmachis killed them all. The people who were made into quloqs were that angry. And then the Bosmachis set fire to [the houses of] those who participated.

The novchas' local revolution involved more than an afternoon of irrigation diversion. Qurbon and others from the village joined with Red Army soldiers to hunt for local men who opposed the new government, men whom Qurbon consistently called Bosmachis and identified by name as he recalled their use of murder to assert local control.

    ULFAT: What did that eshon say? What did your brother-in-law tell you?
    QURBON: The eshon only talked to the people inside the mosque whom he trusted, and he put others outside to guard the door. After the basic prayers, he said that they lived in the day of vengeance. After they slaughtered sheep, ate, and drank, the Bosmachis attacked [the commission members] and locked them up behind the gates. He [the eshon] said, "Don't let a single man go." . . . [The Bosmachis] went up to the mountains where they had hidden with their gold.
    ULFAT: So they had killed only those who had helped the Soviet government?
    QURBON: Those Bosmachis killed all the commission members. The members of the commission were all poor, and they killed all nine of them. There was one man named Abduqodir, who was a strong man, and they hanged him, but they only succeeded in killing him with a sword. They made him raise his hand, and they cut off his head with a sword. That is what they did to members of the commission who had exposed the quloqs.
    ULFAT: So explain land reform. The commission was formed and . . . ?
    QURBON: That was after 1926. In 1928 this man named Rayimqulov who came from Tashkent, he formed a commission, held a meeting, and he told us the conditions for who was a quloq, and he said so many hectares would be given to the village and officially to the poor.
    INTERVIEWER: Did they take all the land from the rich or just part of the land?
    QURBON: They took all the land from rich. They finished them off, so there were no more rich men. They took houses, land, and livestock. They distributed the land. They gave me six *tanobs* [about one hectare] and an official document for the land. The land is yours; the owner cannot take it back. I worked that land for two years. I planted rice. It was not much. But then in 1930 the kolkhoz was formed.

Perhaps not surprisingly, Qurbon A. was one of the first to join the kolkhoz, which he noted had plenty of land and considerable livestock due to confiscations from the wealthy. In the early 1930s, he attained literacy in the newly opened village school and eventually became a teacher and the director of a school.[12] Even the fact that someone whom he denounced turned the tables and denounced him in 1936 did not turn Qurbon A. into a critic of the Soviet version of rural revolution.

His narrative combines his memory of his own actions with community memory of a violent struggle precipitated by Bolshevik efforts to replace opponents with compliant new village leaders. He indicated learning about the perfidious eshon's words from his kin, and the Bosmachi murder of Abduqodir took on the tones of a local legend. Qurbon A. and others like him viewed their own role in this struggle as heroic and their opponents as treacherous and greedy. Portions of his story will be analyzed, along with many other accounts, in the following chapters, which are organized chronologically and thematically, both to understand the ways that the Communist campaign to change rural lives and livelihoods reshaped rural identities and to examine the interplay of individual voice with communal and public discourses in memories that respondents shared.

Oral Histories of Collectivization
Interviewing, Interviewers, and Respondents

In 2001, Russell Zanca (an anthropologist) and I initiated a project to conduct oral history interviews about Uzbekistan's 1930s collectivization of agriculture, seeking out elderly collective farmers who could tell us about the transition from individual farming to collective farming, based on their own lived experiences. We started in 2001 in Namangan and Andijon Provinces with ten interviews that included fourteen speakers, found through a network of Zanca's friends from his prior fieldwork in that region. Zanca followed that in 2002 with ten interviews in Navoiy Province, working with Komil Kalonov, a Tashkent-based sociologist. In 2003, we expanded the project in collaboration with Elyor Karimov (a historian from the Institute of History, Tashkent), who headed a research group, the Young Scholars Society, made up of Uzbek graduate students from various social science fields, all native speakers of Uzbek and some of whom spoke additional languages, such as Tajik and Kazakh. They worked in teams of three in Tashkent, Fergana, Bukhara, Xorazm, and Qashqa Daryo Provinces, adding one hundred more interviews. The respondents included ninety-six men and twenty-nine women. Most interviews were conducted in the Uzbek language with widely varied regional dialects; three interviews were in the Tajik language. I was present for some of those interviews, Zanca for others, but the interviewers for the 2003–2004 interviews were from the Young Scholars Society.[13]

The Young Scholars group found the 2003–2004 respondents by writing to district administrative offices, which assigned a local intermediary, usually the village committee member responsible for veterans and pensioners, to select respondents. Those intermediaries assembled lists of elderly men and women in their districts, choosing those whom they knew to be of sound mind and who were willing to talk with us. Their uncoordinated choices resulted in an overrepresentation of interviewees who were retired teachers, former kolkhoz directors, and narrators from families that were dispossessed as quloqs. The Young Scholars group transcribed the interview recordings, and I used their transcriptions to translate sixty interviews into English. My research assistants Donoxon Abdugafurova and Rahimjon Abdugafurov completed about sixty additional translations.

In the Western scholarly tradition of oral history interviewing, and for many other kinds of research as well, the privately conducted interview is the standard for ethical research, with assumptions that an individual will be more truthful if interviewed alone and that this format protects the interviewee's privacy.[14] By contrast, folkloric approaches to research understand the value of performance and audience.[15] In my first, untrained approach to oral history interviewing in Uzbekistan in the early 1990s, I learned from experience that the elderly women whom I was interviewing about the unveiling campaign were more comfortable telling their stories when family members and friends were with them; asking for a private interview was too close to interrogation. Timur Dadabaev, who similarly used semistructured interviews with family members present in a project on oral histories of everyday life in Central Asia, observes that their presence tended to make the interviews more interactive and prompted remembering.[16] Most interviews took place in narrators' homes—almost always in a private house in a rural community, not in an apartment—with five to ten people present: the respondent, family members, the local facilitator (described above), and the interview team that included a lead interviewer, an assistant, and the videographer. We asked narrators to talk about their early lives and the transition from individual household farming to collective farming. We did not expect them to reveal secrets but rather to tell accounts they had previously told their family and friends.

The criteria for inclusion in this interview project were that the respondent was born in rural Uzbekistan before 1925, making them members of the cohort who experienced the process of collectivization, and that they were willing to share their story. When one potential respondent on our list refused to be interviewed, we went on to the next. The age difference between elderly interviewees, who ranged from seventy-five to one hundred years old, and the interviewers, who were between twenty-one and forty, shaped the interview dynamics. Age-based hierarchy is a fundamental feature of Uzbek culture: that the young must accord respect and deference to those who are older is unquestionable. Deference is expressed in physical form, in elements of speech, and in what can and should not be said. Central Asians conceive of the layout of any room as having a place of honor farthest from and facing the door, and that is where the oldest, most honored person sits. Others recognize their own status relative to the occasion and their age and arrange themselves accordingly. In interviews, we followed these proxemic norms, with interviewee in the place of honor and interviewers in symbolically lower places.[17] Deference in speech means that a younger person addresses an older person with honorific kinship terms, such as *auntie, older sister,* or *father*; these appear in some of the interview excerpts. The social norms shaping the habitus of both interviewer and interviewee lead to a style of interviewing where the older respondent speaks with some authority, as in Qurbon's insistence on controlling the direction of his story about land reform. The younger interviewer must consider whether responding with a critical question will be perceived as ill-mannered. Occasionally, older community or family members who were present for an interview would challenge the interviewee's story by recalling other accounts that the interviewee had shared or by interjecting their own interpretations, as will be seen in some quoted interview selections.

In each province, our team interviewed between ten and twenty-four respondents in three or more villages. We also spoke with people in the cities of Tashkent and Margilon who spent their youth on a collective farm that was absorbed into the city or who moved to the city later.[18] We were looking for the ways that stories were similar across the seven provinces, even as respondents' judgments and attitudes about the process of collectivization diverged widely. Analyzing the repetition of similar accounts of mundane changes by unrelated people in some twenty-five different communities in seven of Uzbekistan's provinces constitutes a method of validating that the events and their impacts on rural life described by these narrators are not unique or exceptional, and neither were the narrators' views of those events. Cohort experiences underlie the stories that our narrators were able to tell about collectivization. The Russian sociologist Viktoria Semenova explores the dual implications of the term *generation*: the generations of a family, such as a father-daughter relationship, and the generations within a society, meaning the age cohort that experienced the same historical events and transitions. Her post-Soviet oral history studies undertaken in the 1990s and 2000s concern both aspects of generation: the ways that older Soviet generations transferred their stories and experiences to a younger generation, or did not do so, and the shared generational experiences of key Soviet events.[19] The research undertaken for this project relates to the latter aspect of generation, a cohort sharing a historical experience, though interviews were also an intergenerational transfer of stories.

Interview subjects represent two generational cohorts, those born before the Russian Revolution and those born after. Narrators who were born between 1904 and 1918 experienced collectivization as teens or as adults, and their memories came from their own direct participation in collectivizing processes. Those born between 1919 and 1925, whom the historian Seth Bernstein has called "the first Socialist generation," also experienced collectivization as it happened but did so largely through the lens of family, feeling the impacts of specific changes on their households, hearing older household members either enthuse or complain as collectivization unfolded.[20] They or their parents joined labor collectives or collective farms between 1923 (the very earliest) and 1936 (the latest). The two cohorts we were interviewing were recalling their lived experiences from the time when they were between the ages of about eight and twenty-five, a life stage of "intense memory formation."[21] Most of them spoke vividly and with surprising detail about the founding of collective farms and the social and political changes that accompanied that economic shift. Throughout most of their adult lives, they engaged in or were exposed to Soviet ideological discourses about social class, quloqs, and the value of the collective farm. The fact that interviewees were youths at the time of collectivization may have meant that they were less resistant to change than their elders and that they had less to lose in collectivization's redistribution of resources.

The collectivization generation was also the greatest generation, to borrow Tom Brokaw's moniker for those who fought in World War II. From 1941 through 1945, Soviet conscription included men ages eighteen to forty-three, born between the early 1900s and 1927. Among our respondents, more than half of the men referred to serving in World War II. The war was a topic that they raised voluntarily, the sort of thing that happens when an oral history interview is loosely structured, allowing both the respondent and the interviewer to drive the flow of topics. Unlike millions of Soviet soldiers in World War II, these respondents survived, returned home, and in many cases developed a career wherein their military service gave them a boost.[22] Although we asked no questions about the war, many told their war stories proudly, and they chose to don their medal-bedecked suit coats when being photographed. Interviewees strongly identified with the Soviet victory in World War II.[23] The brief stories about the war that our respondents wanted to impart were similar to the patriotic accounts that Central Asian veterans shared in a 2007 oral history project led by Timur Dadabaev.[24]

Interviewees clearly distinguished between what they recalled of their lives before collectivization and after the founding of the kolkhoz, with the war serving as a boundary in memory between early years on the kolkhoz and everything that transpired later. In responding to our questions about Bosmachis, land reform, and collectivization, interviewees were remembering episodes that had long since ended rather than events that were still underway. Archival sources on collectivization offer records of events that, when they were happening, would have seemed hopeless, unbelievably wasteful, cruel, shortsighted, and coercive. Since 1991, when many Soviet archives opened, historians who have researched Soviet collectivization or written about Central Asia in the 1920s and 1930s have documented the disastrous results of many Soviet policies, sometimes concluding that Stalinist transformations were maliciously and deliberately destructive.[25] Reading such work tells us much about the processes of Sovietization in Central Asia but leaves us wondering how people survived such turbulence and assuming that anti-Soviet attitudes must have been nearly universal in Central Asia.

The end-of-the-story perspective from oral history interviews with elderly people who survived that turbulence shifts attention from the lurching, cruel course of collectivizing to outcomes. Building an irrigation canal by hand was hard work, but the longer-term consequence was water for one's village and fields and an increase in crops and a better life. Hardships on the farm drove some to find off-farm work or education and sometimes into a Soviet version of upward mobility. Collective farms themselves were very diverse: some eventually brought prosperity to most of their members, while others saddled members with debt and provided a poor livelihood until they were consolidated into much larger entities in the 1950s. Any individual's memory of the collectivization years was reshaped through the vicissitudes of a long life and through repeated episodes of reevaluation, some of them stimulated by family or community events and others provoked by new political turns, such as the Khrushchev thaw or the end of the Soviet Union. Throughout this book, discussions frequently focus on the imbrication of government discourses with individual memory. As in the example of Qurbon A.'s life, class position shaped experience even before class was the focus of politicization, and the party language about class stimulated solidarities and actions, which then shaped life trajectories and the individual's memory about and interpretation of events.

Methods of Analysis and Multiple Standpoints

This project created a large data set: 120 interviews, each one recorded, transcribed, and then translated from its original language to English. A questionnaire resulted in interviews addressing a consistent set of themes. For this book,

I searched across interviews for sections where narrators told their stories about specific themes, such as tractors, the dispossession of quloqs, the role of agitators and outsiders in forming their collective farm, or famine. Mine is by no means an exhaustive analysis of the topics that narrators addressed as they recalled their own pasts. I focused on themes that seemed important for indexing social change in everyday life and for which respondents expressed contrasting views that could shed light on significant social divisions or where there was remarkable consistency in stories from across the seven provinces that could offer insight into the ways that Soviet processes created a strikingly uniform mold for rural life in Uzbekistan.

An oral history approach demands that an individual's words be associated with that individual's identity: it matters whether a narrator came from an impoverished household or a life of power and plenty, whether the speaker is male or female, and whether the individual experienced the Soviet system as providing opportunity or oppression. These positionings, or standpoints, generally correlated with very different and sometimes diametrically opposed narratives about the same events. Feminist, gender studies, and ethnic studies scholars use the term *intersectionality* to focus analytical attention on "the interaction between gender, race, and other categories of difference in individual lives, social practices, institutional arrangements, and cultural ideologies, and the outcomes of these interactions in terms of power."[26] Knowledge, as the feminist standpoint theorist Donna Haraway asserts, is always situated, and for many critical ethnic studies scholars, asking questions that emerge from the standpoints of marginalized people offers a way to challenge the bonds between knowledge and power by bringing forward multiple ways of knowing.[27] However, as Susan Hekman pointed out in her critique of feminist standpoint theory, "Foucault would counter that . . . all knowledge is necessarily from some perspective."[28] An a priori judgment as to who among the interview respondents should be understood as marginalized or oppressed would impose rather than elicit categorizations and identities that respondents themselves recognized and voiced as they recalled events and processes from the 1920s and 1930s that shifted their standpoints. Although intersectional theory provokes some of my questions, I am not looking for silences and omissions that result from intersecting marginalized positions. My efforts focus on understanding and analyzing what interviewees said in these interviews. I do not believe that I can know the many things that a respondent might have said but did not say, and I am more interested in how they categorized themselves than in whether I can find the truth about the degree of their oppression or marginalization.

In this book, my effort to listen to many voices does not result in challenging hegemonic narratives of the Communist years but instead highlights diverse perspectives that include support for and criticism of the hegemonic Communist narrative of socialist construction through collectivizing. Children of the rich had their common stories, men who became party members had theirs, as did women who focused on child-rearing and women who entered kolkhoz leadership. Many of them claimed a marginalized position at some point in their narrative: they were poor and had been oppressed by the rich, or they had been doing just fine until the Soviets repressed their families, or they were wrongly accused of something and were unjustly arrested or dispossessed. Almost all of them began their lives as peasants, and only a few of them ever attained any form of political power, and moreover, they were all Central Asians living under the dominance of an alien Soviet regime, Russian colonialism in a new form.[29] A focus on their own ways of identifying draws attention to what we may judge as complicity or as resistance, though I find both of those concepts problematic when thinking about Sovietizing processes in rural Uzbekistan. Qurbon A. told his story with an explicit theme of class-based resistance, as a novcha against the boylar, in an account that included elements of family and kin identification and loyalty, personal hostilities, and ideological agitation by an eshon, by boylar, and by party members, all of whom actively shaped the perceptions, solidarities, divisions, and events of a struggle for power over land and the local community. If we take seriously Qurbon A.'s self-identified position as an orphan fated to labor for the rich, his rebellion is a straightforward story of resistance against oppression. The same events, if they were recalled by others who were involved, might find the boylar and Bosmachis casting themselves as oppressed by the Soviet conquest of Bukhara (colonialism) and by the eradication of individual rights of ownership (Communism), and their narratives about people like Qurbon A. would interpret his actions not as resistance but as complicity.

Paying attention to the ways that wealth or poverty, status, gender, and ethnic belonging shaped Central Asian life trajectories provides insight into reasons that many supported the new Soviet rural order and its economic system, while others endured it, and some even challenged collectivization's implementation. My analysis highlights the differently positioned standpoints of narrators for social history goals, elucidating ways that collectivization empowered some who had previously been subordinate and disempowered others who previously had been dominant within a field where the Soviet state radically changed the bases for social power and where everyone was forced to live under terms set by the Soviet state.

Telling One's Story of a Soviet Life

Oral histories are unique: any individual's experience of collectivization, although shared in broad outlines by others of the same generation, was shaped by family and material conditions and is rendered through the individual's own personality. As the historian Julia Obertreis observes in her sweeping survey of the development of Central Asian agriculture and irrigation under Russian imperial and Soviet rule, studies of Central Asia in the early Soviet years usually concern the "history of the political, scientific and technical elites," not of the "peasants of Central Asia, at least not in regard to their mind-set, worldview or everyday lives."[30] This book is about Central Asian dehqons and their stories of the everyday aspects of collectivization. The frameworks of their lives changed rapidly, and while I may not use concepts like mindset, *mentalité*, or worldview in my analysis of changing everyday life, I highlight their contextualizations of identity, pointing to the ways that each drew on forms of belonging—to family, to the poor, to the activists, to an ethnic group, to Islam—as they interpreted the revolutionary transformation of collectivization as tragedy, as opportunity, as a hardship to be endured, or as the basis of improved everyday life. Rural Uzbeks who lived through the 1920s and 1930s are not lumped into a faceless peasant mass; instead, their stories—inflected as they are by identifications as Uzbek or Tajik or Kyrgyz; as male or female; as poor, middle, or wealthy; and as those who supported, opposed, or were indifferent to the Soviet system—are featured with their complexities, elucidating collectivization's processes while evaluating its transformations of their own lives.

In this book, I treat oral history interviews as individual memories of shared social experiences. Aleida Assmann, a scholar of cultural memory, writes: "Participation in social memory is always varied because it is based on lived experiences and linked to autobiographical memory, which is irreducibly specific in its position, perspective, and experiential quality."[31] Drawing on Pierre Nora's observation that memory evolves and Sue Campbell's more specific discussion of the social moments when remembering takes place and becomes coconstructed, I emphasize that these narrations were cocreated from the very moment new events transpired and that many of them have been retold and reshaped over decades, in interactions with friends, family members, and other less personal contexts as well.[32] During the Soviet period, everyone from the highest-level party member to the lowest collective farmer knew that he or she should say that collectivization was a success that improved the lives of all. During the final Soviet years, it became possible to criticize both the history and the current state of collectivized agriculture, and in the ten years between independence and the initiation of this project, Uzbekistan's official history of the Soviet period had pivoted toward a thorough rejection. The imbrication of ongoing memory processes with social and political discourses forms part of the analysis.[33] An oral history interview, Alessandro Portelli wrote, "tells us less about events than about their meaning." Much of the analysis in this volume concerns the ways that respondents made sense of their own world and their changing place in it.[34]

At the same time, one of the traditional goals of oral history is to document aspects of the lived past that were not written about, whether because they were deemed mundane and unimportant, because the people who lived them did not write about their lives, or because of fears that silenced their voices. Themes not previously found in scholarship on 1920s and 1930s Uzbekistan but that this volume documents because respondents talked extensively about them include rural experiences of orphanhood outside of Soviet institutions, new forms of child labor created by the kolkhoz, the significance of tractorization to the lives of dehqons, and the scope of Uzbekistan's 1933 famine.

Looking Ahead

Each chapter draws on the stories of multiple individuals to provide grounded views of a particular theme. I look for the multiplicity and recurrence of shared narratives, shared experiences, and the discourses and interpretations of collectivization that developed among Uzbekistan's collective farmers as the collectivization process unfolded. Many of the themes of chapters in this volume were those that we, the interviewers, asked them to talk about based on our already-formed understandings of collectivization, such as land reform and dekulakization. Some chapters focus on themes that respondents talked about with a level of detail that directed my attention to the material ways that collectivization distinguished this phase of their lives, through famine and recollections of eating cornbread, in their physical descriptions of tractors and the changes they brought about, or in the rates and modes of payment they used in their own assessments of the collective farm as fair or as exploitative.

Russian Turkestan was cotton country before the Bolshevik revolution came to Central Asia, but Bukhara and Xorazm were not. Chapter 1 uses archival and published historical works as well as interviews to describe dehqon livelihoods, labor, relationships to land, and relationships of dependency against the backdrop of the expansion of an inedible harvest in the Russian imperial and early Soviet years (1900 to 1925). Following Russia's conquest of Turkestan, new strains of cotton, amenable to modern manufacturing processes, were spread there, displacing the Central Asian native cotton, *go'za*, and turning Turkestan's agriculture into a commercially oriented cash economy. Many respondents in Bukhara, Qashqa Daryo, and Xorazm associated the arrival of the new-style cotton with collectivization. However, dehqon memories of precollectivization labor relations differed little, no matter where they lived or what their primary crops were. This chapter familiarizes the reader with the ways that dehqons described their laborer and owner roles, in terms that became politicized as the language of class when the Soviet state introduced land reform and collectivization.

The Soviet military conquest of Central Asia was violent, leaving those who lived through the early 1920s with stories of attacks, raids, and lasting fears. Chapter 2 outlines the struggle between Central Asian rebels, the so-called Bosmachi, and the Red Army. In remembering episodes of banditry and skirmishes that affected their families and communities, respondents recalled the past in starkly opposed terms, even defining the rebels differently. Most told of terrifying raids by Bosmachis, or bandits, who stole and murdered, and different narrators recalled such attacks taking place from 1920 through the mid-1930s. Some, however, identified with the rebels, referring to them as *Qo'rboshi* (commanders) rather than bandits. After many decades when state-controlled media depicted Bosmachis as vicious enemies, independent Uzbekistan's state-supported revision of this violent history regards Qo'rboshis as fighters for national liberation, giving the sons of rebels room to tell those stories with pride. Gender shaped these accounts: those women who told Bosmachi stories used emotional language, focusing on the threat of kidnap and rape. Not every respondent had a Bosmachi story based on personal or family experience, but for those who did, the terms with which they remembered Bosmachis corresponded more broadly to their supportive or oppositional attitudes on collectivization.

After declaring defeat of the Bosmachis in 1924, the Soviet state drew the boundaries of new republics based on nationality. Following the national delimitation, the newly constituted Uzbekistan's Communist Party initiated land reform in a political effort to win dehqon support, combined with an economic goal of increasing cotton production. Chapter 3 examines the ways that those two initiatives began to transform identities and to bring the language of revolution into the everyday interactions and perceptions of people in rural Uzbekistan. While questions about ethnic identity elicited little discussion from respondents who had lived for decades with the fixed Soviet nationality categories, their stories of land reform emphasized their active engagement with Uzbek versions of Bolshevik class categories, as local contests over land produced the identity groups required for a rural revolution.

Chapter 4 concerns mass collectivization of Uzbekistan's cotton regions, which began at the same time as mass collectivization of the USSR's core grain-growing regions, in November 1929. The rationale underlying rapid collectivization lay in the Soviet state's desire to control grain and the peasants who grew it, but that rationale was irrelevant to cotton. The chapter begins with an effort to understand why mass, rapid collectivization policies were applied in Uzbekistan. The chapter then turns to an analysis of remembrances of the moment when kolkhozes were organized. Those whose families joined first voluntarily and enthusiastically remembered that activists who were from similar circumstances claimed that the kolkhoz would offer them an improved living. Those who joined due to coercion and fear remembered threats that they would be barred from obtaining seed loans or would be denounced as quloq. The process of collectivization shaped and consolidated identities with politicized class-based categories. Part of this chapter was previously published as Marianne Kamp and Russell Zanca, "Stalinism as Collectivization in Uzbekistan: Stalinism and local activism," *Central Asian Survey* 36, no. 1 (2017): 55–72.

Chapter 5 examines memories of collectivization's brutality and destruction in the dispossession of the larger landowners, known in Soviet history as dekulakization. The making of quloqs, to use the Uzbek term, was both the force that drove frightened dehqons to collectivize and the economic transfer that provided newly formed collective farms with substantial land, as this chapter outlines, using published works of history and archival documents. Oral history respondents talked about the arrest, exile, or disappearance of the rural wealthy. They spoke as participants in making quloqs, as quloqs, and as mystified or fearful bystanders. Dehqons who were "made into quloqs" told of exclusion from their communities and of exile to land reclamation sites. Liberated somewhat from Stalinist-era fears both by the passage of decades and by Uzbekistan's independence, respondents told of quloq making in ways that echoed and contested state discourses from the 1930s and that revealed the lasting social impact of quloq making on identities and on the structure of rural communities.

Across the Soviet Union, hunger, the subject of chapter 6, accompanied collectivization. Unlike Ukraine and Kazakhstan, where dire starvation is evident in the historical record despite Stalinist efforts to hide collectivization's disastrous consequences, in Uzbekistan collectivization-related famine was severe enough to appear in interviewee accounts from every province, but it did not result in mass starvation. This chapter compares interviewee memories of hunger in 1933 with Uzbekistan's archival records that document famine. While party initiatives such as land reform, collectivization, and dekulakization produced pervasive and dominant public narratives, Uzbekistan's famine of 1933 was not a matter of public discussion, and there was no dominant, state-sponsored narrative that was shaping individual accounts. Respondent stories offer stark details of individual and community suffering with a wide variety of explanations for famine. Beyond documenting famine in Uzbekistan, this chapter analyzes memory of the Soviet past in an instance when the state was not consciously and actively directing Uzbek dehqons' consciousness. This chapter is a revision of a previously published article: Marianne Kamp, "Hunger and Potatoes: The 1933 Famine in Uzbekistan and Changing Foodways," *Kritika: Explorations in Russian and Eurasian History* 20, no. 2 (2019): 237–267.

Recollections of the early kolkhoz were not uniformly dark. Chapter 7 features the romanticism with which interviewees recalled the advent of tractors and, surprisingly, of working on Uzbekistan's mass canal-building projects. Many late-in-life evaluations described collective farm labor as a source of reward and pride, as interviewees linked their own efforts to state narratives of progress for the Uzbek nation. This chapter's analysis contrasts the enduring romanticism of canals and tractors with respondents' pragmatic and critical discussions of kolkhoz labor and payment.

Nearly a third of the respondents to these interviews lost their father during childhood. Chapter 8 examines orphans' stories, comparing the older cohort's recollections of kin care and child labor before collectivization with stories from the younger cohort of orphans, focusing on child labor, schooling, and widowed mothers who worked on the farm. The chapter highlights ways that Soviet collectivization restructured childhood and family life. Although the Soviet state emphasized rearing orphaned children in children's homes as its solution to a pervasive social issue, oral histories highlight the significance of collective farms as the source of livelihood for orphans and widows, breaking enduring patterns of precarity.

Ultimately, through this effort to see the wide spectrum of stories, I hope to answer a question that confounds us when reading accounts of Soviet destruction: Why did this system survive? The interviews from rural Uzbekistan show that, although there was resistance to collectivization, there were also many who believed that collectivization would improve their lives. The believers either passively or actively supported this radical transformation, securing from below the policies imposed from above. Oral history offers us the small truths of individual lives. As Donald Raleigh writes, even though respondents may tell us stories that are full of "errors, conscious silences, exaggerations, inventions, and the co-opting of other's stories," an individual's memory, their interpretation of life, can be "factually 'wrong' but nonetheless psychologically true, because people often act on the basis of how they understand life events rather than on the events themselves."[35]

1

INEDIBLE HARVEST
Cotton and Dehqons

Qurbon B. was born in 1906, in an area of Bukhara where farming was more important than herding and where his father owned and farmed a small tract. Qurbon B. praised the traditional Central Asian cotton, or g'oza, a strain of *Gossypium herbaceum*, contrasting it with *paxta*, the longer-fiber self-opening *Gossypium hirsutum* (American upland cotton) favored by Russian and later Soviet textile industries.

> [My father] had some land. I'll tell you that cotton [paxta] is what has saved the Uzbek soul and our living in the world. Our Uzbek history is tied up with cotton, but at the time we did not talk about paxta but about g'oza that saved us. On our plot of land we planted three basic crops. G'oza—g'oza is the kind of cotton that you pick without it opening up—we used to plant that. And second, maize: we made corn flour out of that for bread instead of wheat; I never saw wheat bread until I was fifteen. And the third was turnips and onions. At that time we did not have potatoes or tomatoes. But g'oza was what sustained us. Do you know why?
>
> We planted a quarter of our land in g'oza, and after it was ready, then we cut it down, and we would remove it from the husk, all of us, including the children, and our mothers and our fathers would gin it to separate the fiber from the seed. And our mothers would spin it into thread to weave cloth. In a week they could weave several lengths. On bazaar day our fathers would take it to the bazaar to sell it. And then

> we would eat sour milk and corn bread. And on bazaar days or holidays when our pot was full and we had plenty to eat and drink, we were happy.... We plowed the land with my father, but some people had oxen, and some did not. We did not have our own oxen; we borrowed them.¹

As Qurbon B. explained, harvesting g'oza was a separate process from extracting its fiber. Dehqon households harvested the cotton pods, dried them, and stored them. In the winter months, family members from old to young would do the work of breaking open the pods and removing seeds from the cotton fiber. After praising the resilience of poor dehqon families, subsisting on maize and homespun cotton and borrowing draft animals, Qurbon B. depicted his own adolescence in far darker terms. Even though his father owned some land, it did not provide the family with an adequate living, so he also worked on the land belonging to a rich man:

> Both my father and I did *mardikor* [hired laborer] work on the lands of the rich. I was a mardikor. In our village there were rich men named Mirolim and Mirxakim, and I went to work for them along with a group of active lads. At nights we would sleep in the barn, and if they brought an evening meal, we called it a false belt.... They would bring a big bowl, and it would be dry and full of dirt. And then we'd shout, saying, "What is this?" We had to fill our stomachs regardless of the dirt.
>
> They did not pay us a rightful wage. They gave food, and if there was wheat, they would give that, but if they provided anything else, I don't know about it; my father did. But because of this work, I went off to the city to study. One morning the rich man came and tried to wake me up before the sun rose. I couldn't wake up, and eventually he brought some water from the well and poured it on me. After that I said, "Let's run away to the city. I know of so-and-so who ran away and entered school; let's do that." I was fourteen or sixteen at the time. So then I ran away to the city to study.

Rejecting rural poverty and the oppression of mardikor work, Qurbon B. made his way to Bukhara and studied in a boarding school, "a new style school where they taught both religious and worldly knowledge. The teachers all came from Turkey."² Later, after Qurbon B. told of the formation of the kolkhoz in 1930, where his father was a founding member, the interviewer Ulfat Abdurasulov returned to the distinction between go'za and paxta:

> ULFAT: What did the kolkhoz grow?
> QURBON B: It raised paxta, sorghum, maize, and wheat....

ULFAT: Honored father, you said that before the kolkhoz, we raised g'oza, and did you change to paxta after the kolkhoz was founded?
QURBON B: It was not long after, but we gradually changed over to growing paxta.

This chapter concerns cotton growing in the region that became Uzbekistan and the people who grew it, turning to oral histories for respondent descriptions of their family identities in relation to land and to labor. Why did so many dehqons in Russian Turkestan turn to cotton (paxta) planting in the early twentieth century, and why didn't the same phenomenon arise in Bukhara and Khiva? The first section explains the transformation of Russian Turkestan into a land of cash crops and exploitative labor relations, conditions that shaped early Soviet developments. Next, I highlight the language of ownership, dependence, and status that elderly Uzbeks used when remembering their rural youth, comparing those terms with the Communist Party's language of class. In addition to words that can be thought of as expressing class relations, respondents from all parts of Uzbekistan, whether they were born in Russian Turkestan's cash-oriented cotton economy or in the less commercialized agricultural economy of Bukhara or Khiva, also identified themselves in status terms. A discussion of the words that respondents used to describe their family livelihoods and relationship to land ownership before collectivization lays a foundation for themes in subsequent chapters, wherein processes of land reform and collectivization politicized these terms and consolidated dehqons' class-based identities. The chapter ends with an account of 1917, a revolutionary year that brought upheaval to Uzbek dehqons, as cotton planting suddenly disappeared and violence spread across Central Asia.

Qurbon's distinction between g'oza and paxta was not a minor affair. By the early 1900s, American upland cotton had displaced g'oza in Russian Turkestan, meaning that interviewees from Namangan, Fergana, and Tashkent Provinces, formerly part of Russian Turkestan, were born into a different agricultural economy than those who were born in Bukhara. Dehqons who were born before the 1917 revolution in Russian Turkestan, especially those from the Fergana Valley, grew up in districts dominated by intensive, commercial cotton cultivation and a cash-oriented economy. Interviewees from Qashqa Daryo, Navoyi, and Xorazm Provinces, formerly belonging to the Bukhara Emirate and the Khiva Khanate, were born in districts that grew no cotton at all or grew g'oza. For dehqons in the western provinces of Uzbekistan, collectivization and its attendant expansion of paxta cultivation was a far more profound shift in the rhythms of agricultural life than it was for those from the Fergana Valley.

Cotton: Global Commodity

Uzbekistan's inedible harvest, cotton, is frequently described in political terms as the starkest form of Soviet colonialism and as an environment-destroying monoculture imposed by a rapacious state.[3] Uzbekistan's 1930s collectivization was designed to increase cotton production, as the Moscow-based leadership and economic planners sought to make the Soviet Union self-sufficient in raw cotton for its own needs, a cotton autarky. But cotton's rise to dominate Uzbekistan's production had begun long before Soviet economic planning, in response to global economic trends and due to decisions made by dehqons who calculated their own planting risks. The Central Asian zones of irrigated farming had been producing cotton for several thousand years before they became the Uzbek Soviet Socialist Republic in 1924. In the heyday of the Silk Road, Bukhara's weavers produced and exported fine cotton textiles.[4] In the seventeenth century, Bukharan merchants sold finished cotton cloth, articles of clothing, and cotton yarns from Astrakhan to Moscow and Siberia.[5] In his tracking of Russian trade statistics, the historian V. I. Iuferev pointed to a rapid rise in Central Asian cotton exports to Russia in the 1820s, a time when, as the historian Scott Levi notes, the Khan of Kokand dramatically increased irrigation works in the Fergana Valley. In the early nineteenth century, Central Asians exported more finished cotton fabrics than cotton fiber, but terms of exchange shifted after Russia's conquest of Turkestan (1860s to 1880s), and Turkestan's raw cotton flowed to Russia's textile mills.[6] In the 1840s, Russia's newly opened cotton textile factories absorbed raw cotton from far-flung suppliers in the Americas, Egypt, and India, as well as Central Asia and Persia.[7]

In the nineteenth century, increased supplies of cotton fiber and rapidly decreasing manufacturing costs popularized Western and European consumption of cotton textiles. The American upland cotton strain of *Gossypium hirsutum*, developed in the southern United States, produced longer fibers than did Central Asia's g'oza, and it became the standard for the mechanized spinning and weaving machinery of burgeoning textile mills in Europe.[8] The industry spread this seed globally, displacing other cotton strains.

Between 1865 and the early 1880s, Russia conquered the sedentary farming zones of Central Asia. Alexander Morrison argues that Russia did not conquer Central Asia specifically to capture a source for raw cotton but, rather, expanded imperial control southward to create a fixed and stable frontier.[9] Nonetheless, in the decades following conquest, the Russian Empire engaged in processes that the cotton historian Sven Beckert dubs "war capitalism." Beckert writes, "What happened was a swift transition from the older world of cotton—discontinuous, multifocal, horizontal—to an integrated, centralized, and hierarchical empire of cotton."[10] This process of colonial economic integration was swift in Russia, where Russian cotton textile output fed a Russian market, and Russian textile merchants began to sell their finished goods to customers in Central Asia, Persia, and other neighboring regions.[11]

Central Asian dehqons who farmed irrigated lands often raised go'za cotton for their own consumption as well as for sale, but after the conquest, Russian cotton manufacturers began producing textiles that were designed to appeal to Central Asian consumers and that commanded higher prices in the bazaars than locally produced fabrics.[12] The Nalivkins, a Russian family who lived in a Fergana Valley village in the early 1880s before the dramatic commercialization of cotton production, described g'oza as one of the foundations of household production. Hand spinning locally raised cotton still filled many of women's hours, and local weavers produced the simplest cotton cloth for everyday use. However, incomes for both spinners and weavers were extremely low; their hand-spun cloth could not compete with newly arrived, colorful cotton chintzes from Russia's mills.[13]

Within a decade after that 1880s description, Fergana Valley dehqons stopped raising go'za, switching to paxta for commercial production.[14] Upland cotton bolls opened on the stalk, all at once, and cotton fiber had to be handpicked shortly after opening to prevent yellowing and spoilage. Paxta was far more productive than g'oza, and this, combined with the need for immediate picking, meant that demand for farm labor soared. Seasonal laborers came to the Fergana Valley from as far away as Kashgar for the cotton harvest.[15] The slow pace of household production of g'oza that Qurbon B. described disappeared from Russian Turkestan before the revolution but continued in Bukhara, where he grew up.

Following Russia's conquest of Turkestan, the government facilitated a vertical integration between cotton growers in Central Asia and Russian textile mills through taxation, infrastructure, and credit. Russia placed tariffs on cotton fiber imported from lands outside its imperial territories so that cotton raised in Central Asia and transported by slow camel caravan could compete against cheaper cotton shipped from Egypt or the Americas.[16] In Turkestan, the imperial administration taxed cotton at the same comparatively low rate as grains, although cotton produced a much higher value per hectare than wheat or other grains; this low tax gave Central Asian tillers incentive to grow more cotton and less grain.[17] Russia's cotton industry leaders worked with bankers to introduce *hirsutum* strains, providing high-interest loans to Central Asian middlemen, who dispersed cotton seed advances to small landholders.[18] The Russian government supported railroad construction from the Caspian Sea to Samarkand (completed in 1888), from the Fergana Valley to Tashkent and Samarkand (1898), and linking Tashkent and Moscow via Orenburg (1908).[19] Railroads firmly oriented

Central Asia's trade toward Russia, stimulating more cotton production in Bukhara as well as in Turkestan.[20] Dehqons came to expect that they would be able to use cash from cotton sales to purchase wheat, imported by rail from other parts of the empire. In the Fergana Valley, loans, high productivity, low taxation, and immediate cash payments for cotton delivery drove dehqon decisions to plant more paxta and fewer food crops and to stop raising g'oza.

Industrial capital supported the opening of cotton-ginning factories in many cities in Russian Turkestan, with associated mills that rendered oil from cotton seeds. However, Russia banned factories using mechanized looms to produce finished cotton textiles in Turkestan, "on the grounds that this would be detrimental to the cotton textile industry in Central Russia."[21] Mechanized factories with gins to clean raw cotton spread throughout the Fergana Valley, which quickly became home to the most intensive cotton production in the Russian Empire. In 1916, when Central Asian cotton production peaked in response to Russian wartime orders, the inedible harvest covered 60 percent of all planted lands in the Fergana Valley. Meanwhile, Bukhara and Xorazm's cotton output expanded more slowly: cotton factory investments focused on machinery to crack open go'za pods and extract the fiber.[22] Before the revolution, dehqons from the Fergana Valley had adopted paxta to such a degree that cotton production and associated labor in the Fergana Valley was orders of magnitude larger and more intensive than anywhere else in Central Asia or in the Russian Empire.

Cotton and Landowning in Imperial Turkestan

While global trends and Russian administrative incentives stimulated paxta adoption, they do not fully explain why Turkestan's dehqons took up raising cotton on such a large scale. Although some Russian administrators imagined attracting wealthy Russian investors to colonize rural Turkestan with cotton-growing plantations, such experiments failed, and instead paxta increased due to the choices made by Central Asian dehqons.[23] Unlike the Americas, where cotton expanded when slave owners made the decision to raise it on plantations using a labor force who had no choice in the matter, in Russian Turkestan, dehqons expanded their own paxta plantings in response to incentives in the form of seed loans, with cascading consequences—namely, land consolidation that expanded the numbers of landless dehqons who were forced to sell their labor. The structural changes described below reshaped dehqon relations to land in Russian Turkestan, but those changes were only beginning in Khiva and Bukhara at the time of the Russian Revolution.

Although Russians were favored and Turkestanis were subject to discrimination, economic integration into the modernizing empire enabled many Central Asian merchants and dehqons to prosper.[24] In the Fergana Valley, land values increased as planting of paxta expanded. Russian rule gave dehqons an advantage over herders for legal claim to land.[25] In the oasis-based agriculture of Central Asia, Islamic law provided an incentive to extend irrigation, by deeming as the land's owner anyone who "improved" land by making it cultivable.[26] Imperial directives in colonial Turkestan recognized those who farmed lands as the owners of those lands and confirmed their rights to use and pass on land as inheritance, as well as to sell land according to local practice.[27] Unlike its practices in nomadic zones, where the Russian colonial administration seized land from nomadic Kazakhs and Kyrgyz and distributed it to Russian agricultural settlers, in Turkestan's oasis areas the Russian administration affirmed the land rights of indigenous sedentary farming people (Uzbeks, Tajiks, Sarts) and made only limited efforts to encourage Russian agricultural settlement through its Resettlement Directorate.[28]

Turkestan's dehqon population increased, and so did demand for land. Data from the 1917 agricultural census show that in the cotton-intensive Fergana Valley, where land prices soared, half of rural households owned less than one hectare of land.[29] Dehqons who owned little land sought out land to rent so that they could plant more cotton. Larger holdings combined a smaller proportion of irrigated land and a larger proportion of unirrigated farmland (*lalm-i kor*) and grazing land. Large landowners expanded their cotton plantings by offering sharecropping arrangements or by hiring mardikors to plant and harvest their lands. For example, Abduqodir, born in the Andijon region in 1916, said, "I don't know how much land we had . . . maybe ten hectares." In a region where average landholding size was 1.5 hectares, Abduqodir's family was wealthy. "We planted everything on it: melons for ourselves, not so many of those; rice and cotton, primarily. We had *chorikors* [sharecroppers] work our land. Now you would call them hirelings. There were ten chorikor households. They worked on contract, received one-third. They took the land for one year, and we gave them seed, oxen, horses."[30] Wealthy landowners took on sharecroppers whether or not they were raising cotton, but cotton's need for labor intensified this trend.

The rush for cotton did not distribute wealth equally. In the early twentieth century, many small landholders lost their lands; colonial officials regarded the rising numbers of landless farm laborers in Turkestan to be the result of usurious lending. Small landholders took out high-interest loans for cotton seed from large landholders or middlemen, and if their cotton crop was insufficient to repay the loan, they became overwhelmed with debt, and some were forced to sell their land.[31] Sven Beckert, in his global history of cotton, notes that in the late nineteenth century, the same pattern occurred in regions around the world where cotton was raised for commercial purposes: "Sharecropping, crop liens, and powerful local merchants in control of capital characterized the countryside in which they lived. These cotton farmers, the world over, were deeply enmeshed in debt."[32] Turkestan's wealthier landowners benefitted from small landholder problems by acquiring debt-forfeited lands. In 1912, it was estimated that 25 to 30 percent of rural Fergana families were landless. Families might send members to the cities to find work, but most of the landless earned their living either as sharecroppers or mardikors.[33]

In Bukhara and Xorazm, dehqons continued raising g'oza, with its less intensive labor demands and lower commercial value than paxta. Russian railroad construction brought Russian merchants, factories for g'oza processing, and Russia-oriented commerce to the Emirate of Bukhara. These spurred a rapid expansion in cotton production, an increase in the value of land, and a degree of commercially oriented land consolidation, but some of the factors that stimulated adoption of American upland cotton in Russian Turkestan were absent in Bukhara and Khiva.[34] The Khanate of Khiva, connected to Russian trade by boat on the shifting Amu Darya and the Aral Sea and by camel caravans, was less enmeshed in imperial commercial forces. But even there, Russia's seizure of the Amu Darya's right bank facilitated some settlement by agriculturalists from Russia.[35] N. I. Noskov, writing a report for the Russian Resettlement Directorate on prospects for Russian peasant settlement on land seized from Khiva, described landownership patterns and concluded that paxta would expand more effectively if Russian banks offered credit to dehqons for the new seed, as they were doing in Russian Turkestan, rather than by encouraging Russian peasant colonization. Noskov noted a decrease of go'za in the Shurakhan region, where paxta was taking over. "The reason for this is understandable. The poor are the overwhelming mass of the local agriculturalists.... They experience a great need for cash, and American cotton was the most marketable and most beneficial plant, despite its complex cultivation."[36]

Respondents who were born in the Khiva Khanate confirmed Noskov's images, that most of Khiva's dehqons owned very small plots or no land at all and that dehqons raised far more grain and fodder than cotton. Ibroyim K., born in 1917, explained that his father was a shoemaker who also sharecropped: "He would work on a section of irrigated land. Some rich man would give him some land ... and say, 'You will take half the crop.' ... The owner did not give him any seed or anything else, no support.... He planted what he wanted—mung beans, sorghum, rice ... wheat."[37] Sanamjon, born in 1913, said that her family of twelve raised millet, wheat, and melons. With too many people in the household for their small amount of land, Sanamjon's father sought additional income by working as a sharecropper. When asked about cotton, she said, "Cotton came later, between 1932 and 1937, and then we became collective farmers."[38]

Abdullo S. (b. 1921) was born into an elite Khiva family who served in the khan's administration. His father owned considerable land and hired sharecroppers. He told a story, passed down to him, of the coming of American upland cotton seed during the khan's rule. He was told that merchants brought the seed, and those who heard about it sold their livestock to obtain and plant paxta. "It was delicate, silk-like cotton. So much money came from that planting, and the price was so high that rich Russians came to buy it up.... Our uncles, our grandfathers obtained that seed from merchants, and they spread that kind of cotton around."[39]

Paxta, a crop for the era of mechanized factories, made inroads in Bukhara and Khiva before the 1917 revolution, but it had not yet displaced wheat or g'oza and transformed the economy, as it had done in Russian Turkestan. For most respondents from Qashqa Daryo, Bukhara, and Xorazm, the transformation wrought by paxta was part of living memory, and they associated it with collectivization rather than with prerevolution Russian capitalism.

Dehqons: Rural Relations of Dependence

Respondents from districts where grain growing was dominant and in those where cotton prevailed, in colonized and cash-oriented Russian Turkestan, as well as in the Bukhara Emirate and Khiva Khanate, described their family's precollectivization relationship to land, labor, and the means of production in details that alluded to the changing meanings of traditional terms. In the early twentieth century, the word *dehqon* was used in Central Asian Turkic and Persian languages to mean someone who tilled the soil and grew crops.[40] Among sedentary Turkic and Persian speakers, now known to us as Uzbeks and Tajiks, a widely read treatise, or *risala*, about *dehqonchilik* (farming) explained that Adam was the first farmer, and it depicted agricultural work as a human activity ennobled by God's attention and direction. The dehqon had to carry out specific rituals when planting food crops: recite the *Dehqonchilik Risala* at least once per season, pray before plowing or planting, and pay the one-tenth tax so that the crop would be *halal* (pure, in Islamic terms). The treatise names wheat, pumpkins, and melons as the crops requiring these moral interventions; it does not address cotton.[41] Dehqon actions might have equal moral status, but socially, they were not all equal. The term *dehqon* denoted a tiller, as opposed to a nomadic herder, but the tiller could own or rent or be a hireling, as explained below, and dehqon also had status nuances.

Although most respondents described their family's livelihood as dehqonchilik, not all of them used the term *dehqon* as their identity. Those whose families owned a lot of land described themselves as boylar (wealthy). Tillers who owned enough land for their own support called themselves dehqons. People who combined farmwork with a craft or trade, such as weaving or butchering, identified as artisans who also owned or worked on the land. Those who did not own enough land for subsistence described themselves with regionally specific terms denoting relations of dependence, as hired laborers. Categories of landowning and laboring became politicized in the 1920s. When collectivization began, those categories were important for establishing whether one could join a collective farm on favorable terms or whether one would be subject to dispossession. Collectivization made land relations into the core element of rural identity.

Sharecropping was a common form of dependence that many respondents discussed, either from the perspective of landowner or of sharecropper.[42] In addition to a plot of land, the landowner usually provided the sharecropper with such inputs as loaned draft animals, a plow and other implements, and the seed, and the landowner determined which crops to plant. For the poor and landless in the paxta zone, sharecropping may have seemed more advantageous than renting land because the landowner took the risk of obtaining credit for cotton seed. The landowner and the sharecropper divided the resulting crop. In much of what became Uzbekistan, the term for sharecropper was *chorikor* (quarter worker), meaning working for one-fourth of the crop. In Xorazm, the term was *yarimchi*, from the word for half. In fact, payment shares were not dictated by these names; landowners offered widely varying verbal contracts. Some sharecroppers were entirely dependent on the landowner, living on his land, but in many cases dehqons who owned small plots would sharecrop as an additional source of income.

A second form of dependency was short-term or seasonal farmwork. Across Uzbekistan, respondents used a variety of names for agricultural laborers who were hired by the day or seasonally. Respondents in Fergana, Namangan, and Tashkent Provinces said *mardikor*, a term that was also used in the Uzbek- and Russian-language press before and after the revolution. Respondents in Qashqa Daryo and Xorazm used additional terms, such as *novcha* or *korranda*. *Yetim* (orphan) emerged from interviews across Uzbekistan as a term for a hired herder. One Xorazm respondent indicated that a local term, *kullakchi*, indicated a worker who had lower status than a mardikor. In the Communist Party's Marxist analysis, the mardikor was an exploited and impoverished worker, equivalent to the Russian *batrak* (landless rural laborer), and therefore a rural stand-in for the proletarian.

In the 1920s, the Communist Party defined some traditional terms in newly politicized ways, a topic for a later chapter, but Uzbek respondents, who were telling us their stories in their language, not in Russian, had their own ways of describing the unequal socioeconomic relationships in rural communities. For example, Yo'lchiboy described his father as a landless dehqon who owned camels and earned his living partially through transportation and partially doing farm labor "in the gates of the rich," as a mardikor in the Fergana Valley.[43] "Working in the gates of the rich" (*boylarning eshigida xizmat qilib*) was a set expression, widely used by those interviewees who identified themselves or their fathers as sharecroppers, mardikors, or servants. G'anijon, born in 1920 in an area almost entirely devoted to cotton, said that his father, who planted cotton and wheat on less than one hectare, could not adequately provide for his family, so he also worked on the lands of the rich (*boylaning yerida mehnat qilgan ... xizmat qilib*).[44] Madqurbon, born in Khiva in 1914, said, "My father ... did not have enough land, and he would go with his two brothers to an eshon's land or someone else's land to plant as a *yarimchi*, and by working in their gates, he would raise wheat to earn a living."[45] Land reform commissions and, later, collectivization activists would ask sharecroppers and day laborers "in whose gates" they had worked, learning the names of the local wealthy landowners, whom they then dispossessed.

Bozorxo'ja, born in 1913 in a mountainous wheat-growing area southeast of Tashkent, became a convinced Communist activist during collectivization. He described his situation in this way:

> I was born into a totally impoverished dehqon family. We did not have livestock or anything. We worked in others' gates. We were servants in the gates of the rich, and that is how we survived. Mardikor work was by the day; chorikor was by year or two years. My father worked for the rich as a chorikor on one- or two-year contracts, and I did also. When I was thirteen, I worked in the gates of the rich.... We did not have land until 1926 or 1928.... In Parkent there were fifty-one boylar who owned all the land and water. The rest of us worked, two or three for each of them.... They paid me, for example, with three sacks of wheat for one year.[46]

Bozorxo'ja expressed resentment of the wealthy landowners in ways that were repeated in other oral histories of former hired laborers: they had performed the labor that brought wealth to the owner but little reward to themselves.

In the same district, Tojivoy, born in 1917 to a large landowner, described relations of dependence from the perspective of the boylar:

> In our village there were poor and landless people who had nothing and who really worked as slaves. The poor were those with no land, who fell

into the hands of others as slaves and ate what they were given.... There were three or four who worked on my father's lands as plowmen and guards, plowing and planting. They were paid from what was produced and from what was threshed. A reckoning was made: you worked for a year, and here are four kilos or fourteen kilos and your pay.[47]

Tojivoy's description of landownership and labor exploitation was mirrored in the accounts of others who came from families wealthy in land, though unlike some others of his class he expressed empathy for hired workers rather than disparaging them.

In between those who had nothing and those with large landholdings were the majority: dehqons who owned small amounts of farmland and relied primarily on family labor. In the Communist Party's lexicon, these were the middle peasants. Some interviewees used the Uzbek version of that term, *o'rta xol*, but most described their precollectivization farming in terms of land and modes of earning a living. Aliqul, born in 1916 in the Fergana Valley, said that his father owned three hectares, on which they planted sorghum, wheat, rice, and cotton. He said: "We earned good money from cotton, but it all had to be picked by hand, and there was a lot of land and cotton. People were hired, mardikors, so that it could be harvested quickly, and they were paid with money. Some just did cotton picking: they had no land, no work at home, and they picked to earn money."[48]

Perhaps because hiring a mardikor became the sine qua non for defining the rich who were stripped of their land during collectivization, many who identified their families as "middle" stressed that their fathers did not hire strangers, even if they occasionally relied on the labor of kin. Hojimurod, from Bukhara, explained that his father was a silk weaver and a dehqon. "He had ten *tanobs* of land.... Four tanobs was one of today's hectares, so two and a half hectares. He farmed.... There were a lot of us. On the land we planted wheat, g'oza, melons, and everything. Some of our own relatives helped, our close relatives. They were paid from the harvest and in money. We did not have others to work on it."[49]

In Qashqa Dayro Province, a region that formerly belonged to the Bukhara Emirate, and where grazing and dryland wheat farming were dominant, there were individual farms, but there was also a form of shared landownership, the *paikal*. The Soviet historian Lidiia Kunakova describes the paikal as a "land society" whose members had to be male, married, and native to the village, and they usually belonged to an extended family or kin group. A paikal typically included eight to fourteen member households that annually allotted land for planting.[50] Halil, born in 1905, described such an arrangement: "My father was a dehqon. He did not have a hectare, maybe half a hectare of land. He planted melons, vines, and trees on his land. We planted wheat in the field in a paikal of eighty and divided it by ten and by eight.... I worked in the gates of the rich. I worked as a mardikor, as a hired herder.... I was paid a share in money or wheat."[51] Halil was remembering his youth: he did not hold a share in the paikal, perhaps because he was not yet married or due to family poverty. Soviet-era historians like Kunakova equated the paikal with the Russian mir to argue that Central Asia had its own indigenous form of communism, but the Communists of the 1920s interpreted the large holdings of a Central Asian paikal as belonging to the household patriarch who exploited family members and deserved dispossession.

Although the Communist Party viewed the peasant/dehqon as an economic identity defined by relations of production, respondents saw dehqon as a hereditary status. Melivoy (b. 1918) observed: "Dehqonchilik was handed down from generation to generation; otherwise, who would have done it?"[52] Some who identified their fathers as dehqons who worked in the gates of the rich as sharecroppers or mardikors reflected the fact that dependency could change: they spoke of fathers who started sharecropping in response to loss of their own land and others who stopped doing mardikor work when they gained land of their own. Olmajon (b. 1903), whose mother died when she was very young, was raised by her father, who took her with him to work in the gates of the rich, driving a cart. "After we increased our lands and built our house, then we no longer worked in the gates of others. We lived on our land."[53] But not everyone who worked in the gates of the rich was recognized as belonging to the status of dehqon: some identified their families as *xizmatchi* (servants); others described those who depended on them as *qul* (slaves).

War, Revolution, and Cotton's Sudden Demise

Dehqons in Russian Turkestan who were owners of land responded to incentives from Russia's textile industry and chose to plant more and more land in cotton. Until 1916, cotton's expansion was unrelenting. In 1913, Russia's cotton textile mills met 51 percent of their supply needs from Russian Turkestan. During World War I, importing raw cotton became difficult, even as the Russian military's demand for cotton rose. Under new pressures from taxation and fixed prices, Turkestan's cotton output reached a peak in 1916. Individual dehqons decreased the proportion of land planted with food crops, relying on government and industry promises that grain shipments would arrive.[54]

In June 1916, the tsar issued a conscription order requiring that 250,000 indigenous Turkestani men join the empire's war effort as unarmed workers behind

TABLE 1.1 Cotton planting in desiatin, Russian Empire / Early USSR, 1914–1924

	TURKESTAN	KHIVA AND BUKHARA	CAUCASUS	TOTAL
1914	469,505	128,573	135,500	724,528
1915	523,559	139,999	92,250	755,808
1916	533,771	147,050	93,500	774,321
1921/22	88,642	19,000	2,500	109,542
1922/23	51,423	12,000	980	64,403
1923/24	50,000	23,000	27,300	103,300

Source: A. I. Fedotov, *Tekstil'naia Promyshlennost' SSSR* (Moscow: Tentral'noe Upravlenie Pechati VSNKh SSSR, 1926), 89–90. One desiatin equals 2.7 acres or 1.09 hectares.

the lines. Turkestanis had never previously been subject to conscription; the 1916 order reflected both the empire's dire state due to repeated battle losses and its deep distrust of Central Asians, who were not to be trained in use of weapons.[55] Turkestan exploded with demonstrations against conscription and, in some places, with violent attacks on representatives of the colonial authority and on settlers from Russia.[56] Russia declared military control over Turkestan, diverting a division of soldiers from the front to quell the uprising. By late fall 1916, the Russian governor-general of Turkestan again ruled supreme in Turkestan's southern provinces, while in the Kazakh and Kyrgyz regions, the uprising grew into a war between indigenous peoples and Russian settlers.[57] The uprising disrupted planting and cut railway lines, and Kazakh attacks on Russian grain planters included burning their harvested grain.[58] Even before Russia's February 1917 revolution, Russia's wartime controls on grain prices had reduced peasant incentives to grow grain, and grain shortfalls were raising political tension in Turkestan.[59] In 1917, wartime railroad bottlenecks exacerbated grain shortages in Central Asia.

In the oasis lands of Turkestan, Bukhara, and Khiva, dehqons planted a significant proportion of their wheat on *lalm-i kor* lands, unirrigated fields dependent on rainfall. However, the spring rains apparently failed in 1917 and, with them, the wheat crop.[60] Faizulla R., who was born into the family of a mardikor in Shahrisabz, Bukhara Emirate, in 1909, said, "I remember several famines. The first was in 1917 when I was eight years old. At that time, the mosques would make porridge and serve it to the people. Each of us would take a bowl to fill it. It was a time of inflation, and there was nothing to be found."[61] Qurbon A., the novcha whose story appeared in the introduction, explained that his parents died in the 1917 drought, leaving him orphaned.[62]

Russia's February 1917 revolution changed some of the personnel in Turkestan's Russian administration, but it did not improve either the cotton economy or the food situation in Turkestan. "By late April, district authorities were urging farmers to grow food instead of cotton to avoid a severe crisis."[63] As of summer 1917, the wheat harvest in Turkestan was one-fourth of what it would be in a normal year.[64]

Just as the cutting of railway lines meant that grain could not be shipped to Turkestan, neither could cotton be shipped out of Turkestan. The bumper cotton crop of 1916 piled up in warehouses, the price dropped, and incentive for planting cotton in early 1917 was almost entirely absent.[65] The February Revolution increased economic instability in Russia, and in Central Asia one result was that banks could not provide cotton seed loans. Turkestan's cotton-cleaning factories shut down "one after another."[66] A commission in Moscow had established a fixed price range for cotton in 1915, and as of 1917, when the price of grain rose rapidly in Turkestan, many dehqons recognized that planting cotton, which now had a low fixed price vis à vis grain, would bring a loss. Rather than plant a cash crop, dehqons turned toward planting food that they could sell or consume.

In an episode of agricultural imperialism, paxta (American upland cotton) nearly annihilated g'oza (Central Asian short-fiber cotton), a crop that dehqons had grown for several thousand years. In Russian Turkestan's core cotton region, the Fergana Province, as well as in much of Syr Darya and Samarkand Provinces, dehqons who owned their own land and who were under no coercion to do so replaced g'oza with paxta, responding to the many incentives that the Russian textile industry provided. In Turkestan, Russia's preference for farmers over herders was nearly absolute.[67] In the Fergana Valley, where the Kokand Khan's pro-agriculture policy had expanded irrigation and encouraged dehqons from surrounding regions to settle, the sedentary dehqon population continued to increase following Russian conquest, displacing nomads. Unlike in the Kazakh Steppe, the Russian administration discouraged settlers from Russia acquiring farmland in the cotton zone, declaring that dehqons were the rightful owners of the land they farmed.[68] The massive expansion in Fergana's rural population due to natural increase and regional migration provided an ever-increasing pool of labor for paxta, a crop notorious for its high labor demands.

Central Asian dehqons in Russian Turkestan increased their cotton planting not because they had some cultural affinity for the work or the product but because it was more lucrative than other crops, had tax advantages, and they could obtain seed loans. Raising cotton was not necessarily an individual dehqon's free choice, though: banks and merchants offered cotton-related loans to large landowners who acted as local middlemen, proffering land for rent, sharecropping arrangements, seasonal labor contracts, and small loans to small landholders and landless farm laborers, who could only repay their debts or fulfill their contracts by raising cotton. This process was not universal among Central Asian dehqons. Those living in Bukhara and Khiva felt the impact of cotton capitalism far less than those in Russian Turkestan, and even in Russian Turkestan, cotton could only be grown in lowland zones that had well-developed irrigation systems. Dehqons who lived in higher lands, such as interviewees from Parkent or Hojakent in Tashkent Province, continued to raise grain.

From the time of Russian conquest until the 1916 uprising, the farming regions of Central Asia became increasingly tied to cotton and to Russia's imperial economy. Dehqon life was similar across the lands that would become Uzbekistan. Whether they lived in the emirate, the khanate, or under the rule of the "white padishah," as some of them called Tsar Nicholas II, most dehqons farmed on individually owned lands, and they were differentiated by status, by wealth, and by relations of dependence. Whether one's father had been one of the boylar, had been self-sufficient, or had worked as a chorikor was of profound importance before revolutionary changes swept Central Asia and became even more significant, through inversion, when the Bolsheviks brought class warfare to rural Uzbekistan.

2

BOSMACHI STORIES

Ninety-year-old O'g'ilxon was full of stories about the Bosmachi struggle, the war between the Red Army and Central Asian militant groups that began in 1918 and dwindled to scattered attacks by the mid-1920s.¹ She was born in 1914 in the Fergana Valley city of Marg'ilon, the hometown of Madamin Bek Qo'rboshi, one of the most storied anti-Soviet rebels.² All of the Marg'ilon interviewees from the cohort born before the revolution told stories about him. O'g'ilxon spoke of Bosmachis, meaning bandits, using the Communist Party's delegitimizing term for their Central Asian opponents. For more than six decades, Soviet Uzbekistan's press, films, literature, and textbooks defined Bosmachis as enemies of the state and of ordinary, peace-loving dehqons. In contrast, O'g'ilxon's son, who participated in the interview, sometimes repeating questions for his partially deaf mother, talked about Qo'rboshis, or commanders, a term emphasized in postindependence Uzbekistan's discourse that legitimizes Madamin Bek and other anti-Red Central Asian fighters as heroes of a failed movement for national liberation.

O'g'ilxon's Bosmachi stories, told below, illustrate an episode that had been the touchstone of early Soviet history making in Central Asia and that continues to figure large in Uzbekistan's public history. This chapter focuses on respondents' stories about their own lived experiences of Bosmachis. Following O'g'ilxon's story, this chapter provides a brief sketch of the Bosmachi conflict, explains why Bosmachi became a messy and contested label, and then examines groups of stories about Bosmachis for themes of gender, victimization, and sympathy. The competing Soviet period and post-Soviet public histories intersected with narrators' memories of lived experience in ways that were both surprising and consistent. Respondents who had not been victims of attacks and who were convinced that Bosmachis only attacked "the Soviets" supported a narrative about Qo'rboshis as liberators, while those who experienced raids and robbery remembered Bosmachis as enemies. Gender stands out as a dividing line in analysis of Bosmachi stories: elderly women, who were young girls at the time of these events, emphasized their fear of kidnapping, which would have led to rape or forced marriage. Men's memories diverged between those who recalled fearful episodes of armed robbery, murder, and shooting and those who depicted violence as resistance to Soviet rule.

O'g'ilxon and Her Son: Gender, Ethnicity, and Generation in Bosmachi Accounts

When Shahnoza, the interviewer, asked whether O'g'ilxon's father, a dehqon, had lost his land to the state, O'g'ilxon responded by blaming Bosmachi raiders, not the state, for her family's losses: "It was around 1919. The turmoil began in 1917, and by 1919 everything all around was being seized and destroyed, and that was after my father was shot and killed.... Nothing was left because the children of one of my father's other wives took it all and destroyed it." O'g'ilxon's father came from a wealthy and important *xo'ja* lineage; some of their kin joined the Bosmachis, others were exiled during collectivization, and others fled. When she asked about the Bosmachis, Shahnoza seemed to expect that O'g'ilxon would take their side, but the respondent did not.

> O'G'ILXON: The Bosmachis? I was young back then. They would come; we would be frightened. I was taking lessons from an *otin-oyi* [a Muslim woman teacher]. My teacher told me that if I pray a certain prayer when I lie in bed, then they won't come.... She said that the Throne verse is the strongest.[3]
> SHAHNOZA: Did the Bosmachis come?
> O'G'ILXON: They came. Shermat and Madamin were against each other.... My father fled to Turkestan, and then my older brother also fled. And out of my two older sisters, one of them was kidnapped; she was my cousin.[4]
> SHAHNOZA: And what was her fate? Did she return from the Bosmachis?
> O'G'ILXON: They murdered Nurxon [her cousin]; they killed her.

O'g'ilxon knew who had kidnapped Nurxon, and she cursed them: "They were children of Kyrgyz dogs.... They were the sons of my father's Kyrgyz wife. My father had taken a Kyrgyz wife. None of them are still alive, and I give thanks to the Lord for that. They destroyed our gates." The Bosmachis of O'g'ilxon's childhood experience carried out an act of gendered violence that robbed a high-status xo'ja family of honor. Her way of talking about this internecine incident reflects the fact that *Bosmachi* became a capacious term. As explained throughout this chapter, victims of violence used the term *Bosmachi* to denote anyone who carried out any kind of raid or robbery, regardless of whether the violence was politically motivated.

O'g'ilxon, who was married in 1932, spoke admiringly of her brother-in-law, Muxtor, who had told her his Bosmachi stories. Bosmachis killed Muxtor's father while he and his younger siblings hid, after which fifteen-year-old Muxtor offered his services to the Cheka, the Bolsheviks' first security agency, to track down the Qo'rboshi—the rebel commander—who had murdered his father. O'g'ilxon related Muxtor's story of learning that the Qo'rboshi was having a wedding and of bribing two of the children at the wedding to point him out and then shooting him. "He said, 'This was the service that I did, and thanks to the Lord, I was able to restore my honor.'" O'g'ilxon added, "Those [Bosmachis] who were our enemies were afraid of my brother-in-law."

Shahnoza asked: "What did you hear about Madamin Bek Qo'rboshi, what kind of a person was he, what did he look like, and was he cultured?"[5] O'g'ilxon answered, "He harmed everyone; he killed horses; he kidnapped girls. He oppressed even his own soul. Those were remarkable times." O'g'ilxon's assertion contradicted a new assessment that had turned Madamin Bek into a fighter for freedom and the pride of Marg'ilon.[6] O'g'ilxon's son, who had been born after the Bosmachi struggle ended, preferred the newer version of the Bosmachi struggle as national liberation, and he immediately tried to correct O'g'ilxon's statement: "It has been two years since they made new discoveries in Marg'ilon and they cleared him. He [Madamin Bek] was a very cultured man." Her son also redefined the Kyrgyz men who had kidnapped and killed O'g'ilxon's cousin: "They were not Qo'rboshis; those four were more likely to have been close to the government's investigators . . . giving aid to the [Soviet] militia."

O'g'ilxon, like almost every other woman respondent who recalled individual or family encounters with Bosmachis, regarded them as a gendered threat. In the years of their fight against the Red Army, Bosmachis earned a reputation for kidnapping women and forcibly marrying them.[7] The image of Bosmachis as kidnappers endured in individual women's memories and in stories that families told their daughters for the purpose of controlling their behavior. In the early 1920s, Women's Division activists attributed the early marriage of Muslim girls in the Turkestan Autonomous Soviet Socialist Republic (ASSR) to family fears of violence, rape, and kidnapping.[8] O'g'ilxon, the granddaughter of an elite regional leader, a xo'ja who had probably taken the side of the Bosmachis, saw the Bosmachis through an ethnic and gendered lens, as Kyrgyz enemies who kidnapped young Uzbek women. Some Uzbek respondents from other provinces identified Bosmachis as Kazakhs or Turkmens or Tajiks.[9] Her son, through a lens of nation, defined the Uzbek Qo'rboshi Madamin Bek as a hero and, in using the word *cultured*, implied a shared class identification, while he excluded the Kyrgyz attackers from the name Bosmachi by associating them with the Soviet government.

Bosmachis vs. Reds: War in Turkestan

Bosmachi incidents and stories originated in the war that swept across Turkestan, Bukhara, and Xorazm from 1918 to 1924. The February 1917 revolution unleashed calls for "freedom" across Central Asia. Members of the indigenous intelligentsia debated a variety of trajectories for Central Asia, with some envisioning full liberation from Russian colonialism and others a redefined relationship with the empire.[10] Meanwhile, Russia's provisional government in Turkestan wavered between supporting the interests of Russian settlers versus those of anticolonial indigenous representatives. In November 1917, self-declared Bolsheviks drove the remaining provisional government leaders out of Tashkent, asserting their unity with the Petrograd-based Bolshevik government, while declaring that Turkestan had no indigenous proletariat, and thus Central Asian peoples should not take part in Communist government.[11]

In December 1917, a multiethnic group of Central Asians gathered in Kokand, in Turkestan's Fergana Valley, to declare their own government, the Turkestan Autonomy. Participants included local militia heads such as the Uzbek Ergash Bek, whose title as a militia leader was Qo'rboshi. Other Qo'rboshis, Central Asian men who had served as the Russian administration's militia leaders in towns and cities throughout the Fergana Valley, brought their *yigits*—armed men on horseback—to join Ergash Bek's forces in Kokand. Tashkent's Bolsheviks, comprising primarily Russians, sent newly formed Red Army units to attack the Turkestan Autonomy. In February the Red Army shelled Kokand, killing many people in an attempt to destroy the attempt at autonomy and dispersing its political leaders and the Qo'rboshis. The Qo'rboshis returned to their communities to recruit more men for their fight, while the Tashkent government raised its own competing Central Asian militias in the Fergana Valley. Both sides lured militia units to defect, making it difficult for people who suffered violence to be certain whether they were being attacked in the name of the Qo'rboshis or in the name of the Soviet government.[12]

War expanded, and by 1920 the Red Army faced guerilla opposition groups across Turkestan, Bukhara, and Khiva. In one important case, the Fergana-based Qo'rboshi Ko'r Shermat (Shermuhammad Bek), whose name respondents frequently recalled, attempted to coordinate with militant leaders from Bukhara, but his forces could not match the Red Army; he left Soviet territory for Afghanistan in 1923, when the Red Army defeated the Fergana Valley Qo'rboshi-led groups after five years of intense fighting.[13] In Xorazm in 1918, a Turkmen warlord, Junayd Khan, overthrew the Khan of Khiva and seized power, until he was defeated by Red Army forces in 1920, and the Xorazm People's Republic was announced.[14] Some interviewees from Xorazm recalled that episode as an assault by Turkmen nomads against sedentary Uzbek farmers. In 1920 the Red Army defeated the Emirate of Bukhara, putting Emir Alimxon to flight and creating the new Bukhara People's Soviet Republic, but groups aligned with the emir continued to fight the Reds. In the mountain regions of what became Tajikistan, this struggle continued into the early 1930s.[15]

The Red Army leadership referred to the Qo'rboshi-led forces with the term *Bosmachi* (bandits, attackers), as a propaganda of de-legitimization, depicting opponents of the Bolsheviks not as politically motivated rebels who sought a different sort of government but as organized thieves. They had a point: the Qo'rboshi commanders acted as local warlords, demanding food, goods, livestock, and people from rural communities, frequently using force and theft to support their mission, while asserting that their actions were in service of Islam.[16] Red militias also forced rural communities to feed them. The Tashkent government angered dehqons by following War Communism measures pioneered in Russia and by declaring the nationalization of all cotton in 1918. Politically organized and armed requisitioning brigades were to supply Tashkent and the Red Army with wheat for bread, and they collected it by force.[17] Those who were coerced to give up grain saw Red Army actions as theft.

Who Could Be Called a Bosmachi?

Among 125 interviewees, 60 recalled that between 1917 and 1937, Central Asian raiders committed some violent attack on their community and family. Interviewees who were victims of such attacks called the attackers *Bosmachi*, even when younger relatives present during the interviews proposed that these were not thieves but *Qo'rboshi*, legitimate opponents of the Soviet government. Long before the 1917 revolution, the word *Bosmachi*, from the verb *bosmak*, "to tread on or strike," was used by Central Asians and Russians in Central Asia to mean armed, mounted bandits or raiders.[18] After quelling most of the Qo'rboshi-led militant groups, the Soviet government continued to use the term *Bosmachism*. From the early 1920s through the late 1930s, horse-riding Central Asians who joined in groups to commit robbery, assault, and murder could be charged with the crime of Bosmachism.

In the 1920s, the limits on what could be considered Bosmachism were unclear, even to judges in the Soviet legal system, which deemed Bosmachism a crime against the state, deserving of the death penalty. In 1926, the Uzbek politics and culture magazine *Yer Yuzi* published an account of the trial of raiders who had attacked a cotton-purchasing station near Bukhara and, in the process, murdered someone there. The reporter noted the details that raised questions as to whether the attackers could be tried for Bosmachism. Usually, those accused of Bosmachi attacks were Uzbek and other Central Asian men; they were not Russians, workers, or women, as the raiders were in this case:

> The attackers were not Bosmachis who come and go, murdering and extorting; they were employees of the cotton [purchasing] station, including a 19-year-old man named Ra'utof. He and his men planned the attack and the murders. The judges in the Zarafshan Court said that the crime had political coloration; it was not just a robbery. The men working at the cotton station all seem to be enemies of the Soviets and they extort the dehqons. That made this Bosmachism against the government. But the investigation did not find that they were defrauding the dehqons. This was determined to be just a robbery, but because they caused turmoil among the dehqons at the cotton purchase station, shooting guns and killing someone, the sentence is the highest, death by shooting.[19]

The attackers were identified as three men, Ra'utof, Qatashof (two non–Central Asian surnames), and Shamsiddinov (a Central Asian surname), who had three women partners in the crime. These included Shamsiddinova (possibly Shamsidinnov's wife) and Bogdanova (a Russian surname). According to the Zarafshan court, not every case of mounted, armed people engaging in plunder and murder could be designated Bosmachism: gender, ethnicity, and class set limits on the term's use, even when actions used the same violent modes as Qo'rboshi-led raids that involved murder and plunder.

As soon as fighting between Reds and opponents broke out in Central Asia, Bolshevik military leaders associated Bosmachism with raiding, with the influence of the boylar (the wealthy), and with Central Asian masculinity. The Soviet government and the press continued to use this term when armed gangs attacked collective farms in the 1930s. In the 1937 "Kulak operations" that accompanied the mass Communist Party purge in Uzbekistan, 430 of the 3,627 people who were arrested in the month of December were charged as Bosmachis, accused of having taken part in bandit gangs and committed murder.[20] Most interviewees spoke of Bosmachis in similarly broad ways, not limiting the name to anti-Soviet militants of the early 1920s. Their expansive use of *Bosmachi* confirms one of the Soviet government's strategies: the Soviet government consistently framed its Central Asian opponents as bandits, encouraging all victims of violent attacks to associate their own victimization with opposition to Soviet power that stemmed from greed and exploitation.

Reds and Bosmachis: Politics of Memory

Muqimjon (b. 1902), the son of a small shop owner in Marg'ilon, was familiar with the argument that the Qo'rboshis led a liberation struggle, but drawing on his own experience, he questioned that view.

> The one called Madamin Bek was from here, and we knew about him quite well, but we couldn't tell what their purpose was: Was it to separate Uzbekistan from the state, or was it to steal from the people? Madamin Bek organized a government, and he led Ko'r Shermat, Soli Mahsum, the Qo'rboshis.... Madamin Bek was a very capable man.... They did not have any income, so they would go to a place, attack quickly, extorting and robbing the people. You could call it raiding.

But Muqimjon was also critical of the early Red Army's effort to take control of Marg'ilon: "At that time, the government was newly formed and had no resources. Wherever there was a rich man, they seized his land, in my view, so that they could survive." He described fighting between Reds and Bosmachis in Marg'ilon. He recalled confusing rumors that spread concerning Madamin Bek's betrayal and death, and then he said, "I saw Bosmachis in our streets. If you had a cow, sheep, horse, or anything else, you would take them to the station and leave them there until morning [to prevent theft]. Everyone was afraid and went up on the rooftops to sleep.[21] The next morning there would be wailing and rumors about someone's death. And now they have been exonerated because the government discovered their true purpose: Was their goal to take control of Central Asia?" Shahnoza asked Muqimjon whether the Bosmachi movement grew during collectivization, but he continued with his thoughts on this period of violence: "[People] became so tired of struggling for survival that they fled. The government squeezed them from one side, and they squeezed from the other; for the unfortunate people in between, there was oppression. At night the rich and the thieves went about extorting, and during the day the soldiers did. The soldiers would demand things for their own survival, taking money or livestock if people had them."[22]

Muqimjon did not indicate whether his family took a side; throughout his interview, he maintained a critical and ambivalent position. Unlike Muqimjon, other respondents did not limit the term *Bosmachi* to the period that is usually thought of as the Bosmachi struggle (1918–1923). They used the term *Bosmachi* as it was framed for them by the Soviet state, describing rural violence that took place any time between 1917 and 1937.

Women's Voices: Bosmachis as Kidnappers

Women interviewees spoke of Bosmachis as kidnappers, whether they were recalling Qo'rboshi attacks of the period up to 1923 or remembering attacks associated with 1930s opposition to collectivization. Umriniso M., born in 1914 in Fergana City (formerly Skoblev), told of her father's role as a Soviet militiaman and her mother's efforts to negotiate with Bosmachis from her village. Umriniso's father, a Uyghur man from Qashgar, had moved to Russian Turkestan before World War I and had signed up for the militia under Russian administration. During the years of the Bosmachi struggle, he stayed on the government's side, and as she put it, he "killed seven Beks," the term she and her family used for Qo'rboshis or Bosmachis; the term *Bek* was also used in the Uzbek press of the 1920s.[23] Umriniso's close encounter with Bosmachis took place when she was a little girl visiting her maternal grandparents in the village of Oqariq.

> When we were sleeping outdoors on the platform, Beks came, looking for militiamen. The Beks were from the neighborhood, and my mother knew them. My uncle told my mother that they [the Beks] would kidnap her, so she should hide under a flower bush. My sister said they would shoot that bush, so she should hide inside the house. They hid my mother inside the house. When I was lying beside my mother, two of them leaned on the door of the house and shot the bush. When they shot, a spark came out from the bullets.
>
> They were Bosmachis who were from the neighborhood; out of respect for my grandfather they did not seize my uncle. . . . Men were looking inside. They knocked at the door and said, "Uncle, open the

door." They were our people, and my mother opened the door then and asked if they were hungry. She brought bread made with onion. One said he would not eat onion, and my mother brought plain bread. That was how I witnessed the Beks.

I had a very beautiful sister. Every time that the Beks came, we made her run away to hide. Once she was sleeping on the flat house roof when the Beks came. My mother worried that they would find her, and she pushed my sister off the roof to the neighbor's side. She fell down into a tree and broke her left rib. . . . That was the Beks' fault. Everybody ran away from them. They would kidnap young girls, and they took young boys to work for them. Many young people joined them forcibly. Bosmachis came from places like Yolmozor and Oqariq. . . . Ko'r Shermat came from Joydon.[24]

The names of Fergana Valley Qo'rboshi leaders—Madamin, Ko'r Shermat, Halho'ja, and others—were well known. They entered the stories of Fergana Valley interview respondents, both those who were old enough to have formed their own memories of the Bosmachi struggle and those who learned these stories from their parents or from later social discourses. Did Umriniso know Ko'r Shermat's name when she was nine years old, or did she cite his name because he was the most famous Qo'rboshi from the area, a man whose name had been reiterated by her father, by Soviet historians, by independence historians, in the local press and museums, and in popular discourse? Umriniso's father participated in battles against the Bosmachis, but Umriniso saw Bosmachis when they raided homes. She vividly remembered the threat of kidnapping, a topic that she indicated was discussed repeatedly by both men and women in her family.

Unlike O'g'ilxon, who knew the raiders who kidnapped her sister and identified them as ethnic others, Umriniso said that the Bosmachis were "our own," men from the village whom her mother knew. Umriniso recalled that her father stressed his pro-Soviet credentials as a militia member, reminding her that he held a document certifying his heroism in killing Bosmachis and pointing out that such documents might be useful for the family. Umriniso also remembered her mother providing bread to the Bosmachis, the sort of detail that could have been used politically against her family, had someone chosen to denounce them as Bosmachi supporters. Umriniso's telling of that episode, and of the whole Bosmachi encounter, emphasized that her family members were at the mercy of violent men who were hunting militia members like her father: she depicted providing them with bread as survival under threat, not as support.

Other women from Umriniso's cohort, from Marg'ilon and from other provinces, recalled similar childhood experiences of the threat of kidnapping and of hiding from Bosmachis.²⁵ Zulayho was old enough to remember Bosmachi attacks: they would come, raiding houses. She said that everyone from her village in Xorazm fled over a canal and into the desert; and three or four days after the Bosmachis shot things up and left, her family returned home.²⁶ A Tajik-speaking woman from Nurota, Bozorova, talked about local men who joined the Bosmachis: "Some people who joined from here kidnapped young girls from the places where they went. And then they would carry out a *nikoh* [religious wedding] for those men. For example, there was an old woman in our village who was kidnapped from Sentob. She died recently. She was kidnapped and forcibly married here." Interestingly, Bozorova then pointed out that everyone has seen these things in the movies, where the Bosmachis raided, stole things, killed people, and kidnapped girls. She, like other women of her generation, emphasized that, for her, these were not just tales: she knew women who were kidnapped by Bosmachis.²⁷

The consistency of the themes of kidnapping and hiding in women's recollections indicates that these collective fears shaped the lives of young girls around Marg'ilon and across Uzbekistan, not only when the Qo'rboshis were active in the early 1920s but for a long time after that. A Marg'ilon women from a younger cohort, Hidoyatxon (b. 1919), recalled her own Bosmachi encounter during collectivization. Hidoyatxon's pro-Soviet, divorced mother sent her to Soviet school, where she joined the Komsomol. In 1932, she went with a group of Komsomol members to agitate for collectivization in a village near Marg'ilon. She said, "On the way back there were Bosmachis, and by that time we were not afraid of them, and we said, let's just return at night, but the Bosmachis shot at our cart. We got covered with the horse's blood, and we all jumped into a ditch." Hidoyatxon referred to those who violently opposed collectivization as Bosmachis, saying that when dekulakization, meaning the dispossession of wealthy landowners, began, "the Bosmachi movement really strengthened. It became so bad that you couldn't even go out into streets because there was crossfire. The sons of those rich men were shooting; it was turmoil." The effects of their violence lingered. Hidoyatxon said, "They [the Bosmachis] have all died, but sometimes when I go to feasts, there are still a few old women who sit there weeping, old women who had been carried off by those Bosmachis. They sit there crying, saying, 'We saw them from behind the curtains, we saw their feasting, and they abducted us.'"²⁸

O'ktam, born in 1919 in Qashqa Daryo, was told about the Bosmachis by her parents. She said:

> The times were worst when the Bosmachis attacked. I didn't see it because my mother was pregnant with me. When my mother was giving birth, she went to the city with me. Those Bosmachis seized many good women and children. My father, fearing them, sent my mother to

the city. One woman who had not yet given birth had been seized. We returned six months later. My mother would tell me about this; I heard it from my mother's and father's mouths.... That was a very bad time, when people would hide their daughters underground or other places. If they were taken, they [Bosmachis] would keep them ten or twenty days and then discard them.[29]

Other women respondents, too young to have experienced any of this violence directly, told stories from their mothers of fleeing their homes so as not to fall into Bosmachi hands.[30]

Embedded in all these accounts are the anxieties that parents felt and impressed on their daughters, a feeling of a specific, gendered vulnerability of unmarried girls and young married women. Rumors about Bosmachis kidnapping girls and women shaped family strategies for protecting girls by restricting their movements, influenced how and when parents decided to arrange marriages, and remained a topic that could arise at women's gatherings when Bosmachi victim-brides told their own stories. The Soviet government's discourse about Bosmachis as raiders and bandits interacted dialectically with women's own lived experiences. Moments of public remembering, whether stimulated by solemn political speeches or by lighthearted Soviet films, had provided respondents with many occasions for retelling their own Bosmachi encounter narratives. In these interviews, women emphasized that their Bosmachi accounts were not simply tales about bogeymen: they knew of kidnappings, and those incidents spread terror within their families.

Men as Bosmachi Victims

Men's accounts also emphasized fear of Bosmachis, focusing on shootouts, home invasion, and theft of goods and horses. Several interviewees described their fathers or grandfathers being murdered by Bosmachis.[31] Men's stories included remembrances of fleeing or hiding from Bosmachis by donning a *paranji* (women's veiling robe), concealing themselves in the cemetery, heading into the hills to hide, or hiding in a clay oven. One man mentioned digging holes, hiding the children in them, and covering up the hole with blankets or ashes.[32] One spoke of being beaten by Bosmachis, and others talked of being robbed of horses.[33] Ahmad (b. 1921), whose father became a kolkhoz director and whose uncle was dekulakized, said that from 1917 to 1937, Bosmachis continually threatened his village near G'ijduvon, gathering en masse to plunder, extort, and kidnap, "until 1937, when they were all finally captured and exiled and we lived in peace for two years until the war started." He said that Bosmachis would start their raids after evening prayer and that they frequently demanded girls be given to them as brides. "Eight of them came, Bosmachis, and they seized my bride when she was bathing and carried her away on their horses. Do you understand? I'm left standing, shouting for help, and she was also screaming for help.... That was the way that they oppressed the people."[34]

Eminjon (b. 1920) was born in Joydon, the same Fergana Valley village as the Qo'rboshi Ko'r Shermat, and his stories of Bosmachis began with the fact that Madamin Bek had seen Eminjon when he was a baby—a story told to him by someone in his family. Although his family members knew those famous Qo'rboshis, Eminjon spoke of them as violent men. He mentioned specific girls and women in his community whom Bosmachis had kidnapped and forcibly married. He then turned to a family story of men's victimization: "My uncle was forced to join. Madamin Bek tied his hands and legs and said that if he refused to join, he would be shot. Then he joined. Later he ran away and died in Marg'ilon. Bosmachis kidnapped daughters, stole goods and livestock, and killed people. They targeted people who were rich in the village. I do not know of rich people who joined voluntarily."[35]

Rustam (b. 1912) recalled a time when Bosmachis and soldiers fought in his neighborhood in Navoiy District: "I was a small child then, and I needed to go to the toilet. My mother put an old robe over my head to protect me from the bullets. Imagine that! I went out [to the outhouse] and saw the bullets flying and went back in." Red Army soldiers who were chasing Bosmachis entered his family courtyard to rest, and men in the community, including one of Rustam's older relatives, approached the soldiers for help in retrieving some male youths who had been abducted. "Some of the boylar had sold the sons of seven of the poor men, sending them away to Bukhara... so those seven men came to the soldiers, and they all went together. A little later they heard that Ko'r Shermat and his Bosmachis were at Jo'sh. The soldiers fought the Bosmachis there, and my maternal uncle was among those who were shot."[36] Rustam did not finish the story of the sons of the seven poor men, but the sequence of his narrative implied a connection between boylar, Bosmachis, and abduction. While other interviewees condemned the Bosmachis by associating them with kidnapping girls, Rustam's story hinted that the rich and the Bosmachis colluded in the sexual exploitation of young boys. Rustam filled his whole interview with references to local history: he was not at Jo'sh himself, but it was known locally that the famous Qo'rboshi commander Ko'r Shermat fought there, and Rustam linked the account he had heard about his uncle's death to his role in aiding the Red Army in this documented battle.

Halil (b. 1905) told of encountering Bosmachis in 1922, while he was working "in the gates of a rich man" as a hired herder. Bosmachis came to his Qashqa Daryo village: "They shot Rashid and a certain old man.... Then later they went into the deserts, about twenty or thirty mounted men. No one from our village joined the Bosmachi, but we paid them *haq* [tax] because if we did not, we would have been killed. There were only about twelve or thirteen Bosmachis left when they were defeated."[37] While men who were little children during episodes of Bosmachi attacks remembered terror and hiding, Halil's account adds an adult observation, noting a key method of Bosmachi control over villages: violence and its threat, leading to extortion of a "tax," something that the Bosmachis may have understood as demonstrating popular support.

Abdurashid (b. 1905) grew up in Baliqchi District in Andijon Province, a place that suffered significant depopulation due to the conflict in the early 1920s. He told of ongoing battles in his village, Xo'jaobod:[38]

> They [the Bosmachis] attacked somebody's house at night.... Later at night they started their attack with six to ten horsemen. When we were living in Xo'jaobod, "the fourth" [government forces] came. There was a small river. On the other side of the river, there was an ambush. They let half of the Bosmachis go and then opened fire. Our house was on that side. There was chaos. Half of the people ran that way; the other half ran to the other side. One Russian [soldier] hid in the mosque. He did not have a horse. He fired on the Bosmachis until night from that mosque. When his bullets ran out, he came out of the mosque, and the Bosmachis captured him. I witnessed that.[39]

Abdurashid was orphaned as a child, grew up making a living as a herder and a felt maker, and then returned to the house his father left to him around the time the Bosmachis were dominating the Fergana Valley. The Qo'rboshi commanders, he said, usually had fifty to seventy *yigits*, or young fighters, in their military units. Five or ten of these units attacked Xo'jaobod, took over the *saray*—the walled trade depot—and from there went raiding in all directions. His house was on a street higher than other parts of town, and he said he watched as the Bosmachis would return to the saray in the evenings, bringing the livestock that they had acquired. The Russians, he said, sent the "fourth division" from Andijon, made up of several Russian soldiers and many more Central Asian militiamen, whom he called Beks. Having later served in the military during World War II, Abdurashid applied his soldier's knowledge to his description of the 1922 battle in Xo'jaobod, noting how the Reds held their fire before springing their ambush on the Bosmachis.[40]

One woman respondent, Qimmat (b. 1906), whose husband was dekulakized, combined an emphasis on Bosmachis as ethnic others with a story of male victims from her family. She lived in an ethnically mixed Kazakh and Uzbek district north of Tashkent. The interviewer Zavqiddin asked whether Bosmachis came to her village.

> QIMMAT: The Bosmachis rose up from among the Kazakhs and came here.
> ZAVQIDDIN: The Bosmachis were only Kazakhs?
> QIMMAT: They were Kazakhs and our own also; the Bosmachis were everywhere.
> ZAVQIDDIN: Did some of our own [Uzbeks] also join the Bosmachis?
> QIMMAT: Yes, some joined them. They attacked and carried off both of my older brothers, To'raqul and Orzu.
> ZAVQIDDIN: Why did they abduct them?
> QIMMAT: Who knows why? But when they were carried off, their crops were abandoned.

Later in the interview, Qimmat added more detail to this story. After Zavqiddin asked whether Bosmachis joined the boylar in opposing collectivization, she said, "No, the Bosmachis here came from the Kazakhs of G'ilva Soy. The Bosmachilik was when those Kazakhs rose up and migrated here. They found this place for themselves and seized it." Like O'g'ilxon, Qimmat depicted Bosmachis as ethnic others; like Eminjon, Rustam, and Abdurashid, she focused on their male victims, her older brothers whom the Bosmachis carried off in an effort that she interpreted as seizing crops and land.⁴¹

Sharafutdin (b. 1911), from a landless agricultural worker's family in the Fergana Valley, joined the Soviet military in 1933 and was involved in tracking down and killing Bosmachis in the 1930s, in the mountains south of the Fergana Valley. He said that during collectivization:

> There was a lot of fighting with the Bosmachis, but it did not reach the army. They would hide in the mountains and consume the kolkhoz's cattle, shoot at their own people, and continually go raiding. Then the people from So'x, which is very far from the regional center of Fergana, wrote letters, all the way to Moscow: "Our party members cannot go out into the streets to work because of the Bosmachis," and they wrote this to [Uzbekistan's political leaders] Usmon Yusupov and to Oxunboboev. And then the army was sent from Tashkent. At that time, I was sent to So'x; I searched for a month but could not capture anyone; it was very difficult. I would say it was because I did not know the territory.

And then they sent the soldiers, and the search went out in every direction.... On the sixth day, their group [the Bosmachis] ran into us. There was shooting. I was afraid that those Kyrgyz would come here, shoot, and then get away without being arrested, but no. They really were Sulaymon's Bosmachi group. We shot at them. Some were killed, including a man from our side.... When the dawn came, we saw that one of the dead was Sulaymon, but we could not identify him.... We brought his mother and wife from Batken to identify him.... He was Kyrgyz, on our territory.... He had killed some Komsomol lads. Sulaymon had ten or fifteen men in his group, some from that village.... I am Uzbek.[42]

Sharafutdin told another story of tracking and capturing other Bosmachis in the ethnically mixed zone south of Uzbekistan's Fergana Valley border. In each episode he portrayed his forces as bringing peace to rural villages troubled by violent raiders who were ethnic Kyrgyz Bosmachis. Sharafutdin's father's given name, which had become Sharafutdin's surname, happened to proclaim identification as Kyrgyz. This fact makes his assertion of his own identity as Uzbek seem a very intentional, political declaration.[43] Like other anti-Bosmachi respondents, he recalled the names of the Qo'rboshi commanders, but as a militia member, he also recalled political details that provided his actions with moral authority: letters from beleaguered sedentary villagers and orders from some of Uzbekistan's leading political figures, Oxunboboev and Usmonov.

From their own recollections of such violence, many of the men whom we interviewed would have agreed with Sharafutdin's version of the Bosmachi struggle: they applied the term Bosmachi equally to the civil war–period rebels against Red control of Central Asia, to those who took up arms to disrupt collectivization, and to any violent opportunists who preyed on rural communities. Violence was pervasive in rural Uzbekistan, not only during the civil war period but well into the 1930s. Both the men and the women who fell victim to bandit-style aggression would have been comfortable retelling their stories when moments of public remembrance of the Bosmachis occurred, in ways that linked their own lives to a government narrative that explained the violence: rebels and bandits fought against Soviet power and harmed ordinary dehqons, but the government forces defeated the bandits and brought peace.

Qo'rboshi Defenders

Among the respondents, there were also men who presented a different standpoint: they told of Qo'rboshi commanders or of the Bosmachi rebels as defenders of the people, as nobly aspiring for Islamic government, or as simply misunderstood. O'rozboy (b. 1908), the son of a man who was dekulakized and who himself engaged in sheep stealing, was arrested and accused of being a Bosmachi. "I was imprisoned in Nurota, but then they let me go because they could not make the case. I was exonerated, but Xasil Podsho, Rasulboy, and Jabborboy were sentenced and shot in the evening. They were Bosmachis and rich men. Then I was exiled."[44] His story continues in a later chapter; he and his father opposed collectivization.

Ravshan (b. 1920), from a village near Bukhara, had been told by other family members that "my father, two brothers, and two uncles all died in the fight against the Russians. My mother died of a heart attack after hearing that my brothers and father died. I was in the cradle at that time."[45] Saidalixon (b. 1921) related what his uncles and father told him: his maternal uncles were close to Madamin Bek, the Qo'rboshi commander. When other Bosmachis stole from Saidalixon's merchant father, Saidalixon's uncles were able to negotiate the return of the stolen money. However, Saidalixon's father was then threatened with arrest for his associations with the Bosmachis; he went into hiding for a few years.[46] Abdullo (b. 1919) spoke of his relative Mullomirzo, who joined the Bosmachis and eventually fled to Afghanistan in the early 1930s, taking his family and his wealth to avoid dekulakization.[47]

Yusupboy (b. 1917), who came from an ethnically mixed Kazakh and Uzbek region north of Tashkent, had an uncle who was accused of being a Bosmachi and who disappeared. Yusupboy said that in his district, there were "twenty or thirty men" who tried to take the land back from the Soviet government. "They came chanting that God gave strength to the religion of Islam. I know that because I was playing in the streets. They hoped to develop the religion of Muslims... but the Red Army annihilated them all." The raiders' actions included killing the assistant to the district Communist Party leader and dumping his body in a river. But, Yusupboy said, they did not attack the poor, and they were trying to build a different kind of country. When he was asked about Bosmachi identities, a topic that had been discussed by previous interviewees from his district, Yusupboy, who identified himself as Uzbek, depicted them as a multiethnic movement: "They were mixed. There were Kazakhs and Kyrgyz and Uzbeks and Tajiks. Uzbeks from over there mixed in with Kyrgyz who came on foot, and the same for Tajiks; that is what I heard."[48]

A few interviewees who did not claim any connection to the movement empathized with the Bosmachis. Faizixon (b. 1917), a woman from Shohimardon, in the same mountainous region where the above-mentioned Sharafutdin hunted down the Kyrgyz Qo'rboshi Sulaymon, said that the Bosmachis in that area never attacked dehqons; they only attacked Russians.[49] Qurbon B. (b. 1906) was a consumer of Uzbekistan's new, pro-Qo'rboshi interpretation of history, and he sought to balance his view of the Bosmachis, arguing that their recent historical rehabilitation was the right way to see them, despite what he knew of their crimes. "Maybe they were forced to carry out all of that extortion and theft.... A person has to struggle for a living and fill his stomach." A group of Kazakh Bosmachis had asked permission to cross Qurbon's uncle's field, but when the group came into the village, soldiers shot at them, chased them out into the desert, and killed them. "I saw this with my own eyes," said Qurbon.[50] He stated that the Bosmachis did not steal from or bother ordinary people; they were only opposed to Soviet power. Avez, who came to an Uzbek kolkhoz when his Turkmen father left for Afghanistan during dekulakization, argued that those who opposed collectivization or opposed the Soviet government should not be called Bosmachis. "They judged that in collectivizing them, the state was exploiting and harming the people.... Those who did not understand them called them Bosmachi," and because important people used that term, everyone did. Avez said that none of these attacks took place in his village.[51]

Some of those who identified with or empathized with the Bosmachis were victims of the Red Army's actions or witnessed those actions; some were related to Bosmachis and were telling family stories that had become acceptable, even celebrated, after 1991; and some approved of the Qo'rboshis' anti-Soviet or anti-Russian stance. Most were men, though there was one woman among respondents with this view, and not all of them came from wealthy or dekulakized families. They were not identical in their gender, ethnicity, or class, but they shared one piece of good fortune: none claimed to have suffered violence at Bosmachi hands.

Individual Experience and Standpoints

Standpoint matters profoundly in these narratives. Victims called their attackers Bosmachis. Every act of rural violence could be explained as a Bosmachi attack, and when the topic of Bosmachis came up, victims of that violence spared no time on political discussion: goods were stolen, and lives extinguished, regardless of whether the raiders were interested in loot or in autonomy. Women focused on the threat that raiders posed to the female body: kidnapping, rape, forced marriage. Many of the men spoke as victims of plunder, of beatings, or loss of family members. Anti-Bosmachi stories were often told by people who viewed their pre-kolkhoz lives as oppressive, but some had come from families that were comfortable or wealthy before collectivization. Victimization, rather than social condition, was the thread that united their standpoints and was the factor that directly connected to their favorable views of the Red Army and of Soviet power.

A contrasting standpoint can be seen in the stories of those who were connected to Bosmachis but whose families had apparently never been subjected to violent raids by nonstate actors. The exception was Saidalixon's story of Bosmachis robbing his merchant father, who was a close associate of Madamin Bek, but in this case, the Qo'rboshi commander righted that mistake, restoring Saidalixon's father's goods.[52] Their defense of Bosmachis was not as extreme as what the anthropologist Sergei Abashin heard in Tajikistan, where oral history interviewees praised their local hero, Rahmankul the Qo'rboshi, even justifying his kidnapping and murder of a young girl by telling it as a tale of Bolshevik insertion of a dangerous young female spy into his ranks.[53] The pro-Qo'rboshi accounts include details that mirror some of what emerged in anti-Bosmachi stories: for example, pro-Qo'rboshi Sayidabdullo claimed that young men only joined the Reds because they were forced, just as anti-Bosmachi Umriniso asserted that young men only joined the Bosmachis because they were carried off.[54] Qo'rboshi supporters viewed Red Army defeats of rebels as slaughter, directly contrasting with Qurbon A.'s remembrance, told in chapter 1, of Bosmachis slaughtering village committee members. The interviewees who were most ready to defend Bosmachis as Qo'rboshis were themselves people who had suffered at the hands of the Soviet state, with family members dekulakized.

In one exceptional case, status as a victim of the Red Army did not determine loyalty. Bekmurod (b. 1907) was about fifteen years old when Bosmachis attacked his village near Shahrisabz.

> In 1922, my father was killed when a Bosmachi group entered our village. When they were fleeing, Soviet soldiers trailed and hunted them. . . . If someone shot at them, they named all of the people who were outside as Bosmachis, and they shot eighteen people, some of whom were riding donkeys, some on foot, some going to the bazaar. Among those eighteen people, there was only one Bosmachi, named Qilich. The rest of them had not been in the Bosmachi ranks or run with them. They were just unfortunate people minding their own business. Among them, my father too was shot and killed.[55]

This incident, his father's execution for misattributed association with the Bosmachis, did not turn Bekmurod into a supporter of the Bosmachis. Because his family was left without a provider, he went to work "in a rich man's gates" as a novcha, a hired worker, and eventually he became a strong supporter of collectivization.

Boltaboy (b. 1914), whose father came from a high-status lineage but who died, leaving Boltaboy orphaned as a child, consciously differentiated between the

Bosmachi movement and other perpetrators of violence. Boltaboy said, "I don't know anything about Bosmachism, but at that time, we were raided." He told of a time in his childhood when thieves broke into the house while he and his sister were alone. They stole a carpet and the sewing machine and told them, in Turkmen, to stay inside until morning, after which the children also discovered that sheep had been taken.[56] Like many others, Boltaboy had experienced a frightening raid, but he was unwilling to assume that what might have been just a petty criminal act was associated with the politically loaded idea of Bosmachism.

Memory and History

The post-Soviet historians R. Abdullaev and S. Agzamkhodzhaev offer an astute argument on the construction of anti-Bosmachi memories: "Over the course of many years the image of the enemy in the form of the face of so-called 'Bosmachis' formed in the consciousness of the people. The huge Bolshevik propaganda machine worked from the very first appearance of the movement: special cultural-educational trains, agitation brigades . . . actors, poets, playwrights."

They highlight the fact that propagandists spread anti-Bosmachi ditties, which historians later referred to as evidence from folklore that ordinary people associated Bosmachis with the "pillaging and theft that proliferated with the uprising movement, terrorizing people. Undoubtedly, such things did take place. War was going on, a cruel, lengthy war that left its mark on people's psychology and morality. . . . But placing the blame for all similar evildoings on the entire movement contradicts the truth. . . . Hundreds of thousands of rebels . . . carried on a courageous and honest fight."[57]

The stories that respondents told attest to Soviet ideological success in choosing to call the rebels Bosmachis: the Central Asian men who joined the Qo'rboshi leaders in a fight against Russian colonialism's Bolshevik continuation were merged in popular imagery into prerevolution bandits and into every act of rural predation and murder through the late 1930s. However, I am less persuaded by Abdullaev and Agzamkhodzhaev's argument concerning the might of the Soviet propaganda machine. The Red Train was an innovation in 1918, carrying a pro-Bolshevik acting troupe led by the playwright Hamza Hakimzoda Niyazi to cities and towns along the rail lines, but most dehqons lived in villages remote from urban centers and rail lines, and few would have had access to that form of propaganda. The Uzbek-language newspapers that spread the Bolshevik interpretation of Qo'rboshis as Bosmachis had small print runs and were distributed in major cities; they had little presence in dehqon villages where illiteracy prevailed and where, until the Bosmachi conflict died down, no one yet had joined the Communist Party. For the early postrevolution years, 1918–1924, we can believe an image of rural Turkestan, Bukhara, and Khiva where there was extensive and unpredictable guerrilla warfare, with thousands of skirmishes and some pitched battles between a Red Army whose numbers swelled beyond a hundred thousand and hundreds of Qo'rboshi-led groups that could range in size from just a few men to several thousand, a war that disrupted planting and that drove hundreds of thousands of people to leave their homes temporarily and repeatedly. Alternatively, we can believe that the nascent Soviet government was in control of that same countryside and capable of spreading propaganda to the masses. The first image is consistent with documented evidence; the second is not.

However, violent action is its own form of propaganda. Even if only a few members of a raiding band plundered, kidnapped, or murdered, that memory remained with the living victims, who would have taken very little persuading to associate such a raid with the Qo'rboshi-led uprising. The news of even one rape could terrorize a neighborhood, convincing families to flee. Plundering was not an occasional incident. It was the main means by which the Qo'borshis supported their struggle. One of the oldest respondents, Muqimjon, who was age sixteen and living in Marg'ilon, where the war began in 1918, remarked about the Qo'rboshi Madamin and his followers, "They did not have any income, so they would go to a place, attack quickly, extorting and robbing the people."[58] Until 1920, both the Red Army forces and the rebels supplied themselves by taking grain and livestock from dehqons. After 1920, the Soviet government more consistently supplied the Red Army and expanded its numbers. The Qo'rboshis continued to rely on seizure or voluntary contributions to resupply themselves with horses and food. Abdullaev and Agzamkhodzhaev downplay Qo'rboshi violence against noncombatants, for example, when depicting the struggle as it spread across Bukhara in 1922: "In Western Bukhara in the district centers and larger villages—Shafirkan, Talisafed . . . G'ijduvon and other places—military garrisons were sent to intensify the fight against the rebels. There started to be robbery of the peaceful population, burning of villages, and rape of women. Tens of documents from the time attest to this."[59] The authors do not mention who was doing the robbing, burning, and raping; but the Qo'rboshis were documented and remembered by their victims as using those modes to achieve their ends, while the Red Army forces usually used artillery and heavy gunfire. Red Army violence was destructive and terrorizing but usually in a different way: the same authors attribute the Bolshevik government's triumph over the guerrilla forces to its use of massive military strength, harsh repression, and such policies as show trials that induced fear in ordinary people.

Among the 130 respondents in this oral history project, sixty told Bosmachi stories. Many of the 70 who had no such accounts came from the younger cohort, and they responded to our question as did Sharofat (b. 1922): "There were Bosmachis, but we did not see them; we were too young."[60] Like many others, Muhammadjonov responded to the question about Bosmachis by saying, "I heard about Bosmachis, but I don't know anything. They did not turn up at this village or this neighborhood.... People say a Bosmachi is anyone who comes at nighttime to commit theft."[61] Interviewers asked about Bosmachis after many other topics; respondents had been consistently talking about their own lives, families, their family's land, and events that they had experienced directly. The Bosmachi stories that they told were about things that they experienced directly or that parents or other relatives had told them about family experiences, whether of victimization at the hands of raiders, of support for Qo'orboshi-led rebels, or of no direct experience whatsoever.

Every story, whether of terror, victimhood, or noble opposition, concerned an episode in Uzbekistan's history, the Bosmachi struggle, that had been saturated with political meaning. As the political scientists L. E. Bliakher and I. F. Yarulin observe, the term *Bosmachi* carries with it an entire mythology that defies attempts at "objective analysis."[62] Throughout the Soviet decades, the Communist Party celebrated the Red victory over the Bosmachis as liberating ordinary Central Asians from the depredations of the wealthy and their henchmen. Those accounts focused primarily on government and military action, while occasionally referring to instances where Bosmachis harmed communities. Accounts featuring ordinary people harmed by Bosmachis and featuring the kidnapping of young women were prevalent in the 1920s Uzbek-language press and in film and literature, but those themes were not the focus of the military and political archival documents that historians used in writing formal Soviet-period or post-Soviet histories. After independence in 1991, people whose parents or grandparents had been Qo'rboshis or members of Bosmachi groups, including many who went into exile abroad, wanted their stories included in Uzbekistan's nation-making narratives. The historical establishments in Central Asian countries were very open to a reexamination of the past that focused on anticolonialism, showing Central Asians as having struggled, in vain, for national liberation against the all-powerful Soviets. Those accounts drew on the words and writings of exiles who had been on the Qo'rboshi side, who, by definition, were not the victims of Bosmachi violence and who made what I consider unsustainable claims that the Qo'rboshis never harmed ordinary people.[63]

By and large, the octogenarians whom we interviewed had not subscribed to post-Soviet reinterpretations of the Bosmachi struggle. Most of their individual stories came from standpoints that supported the Soviet-period hegemonic narrative: that raiders on horseback, wielding weapons, harmed ordinary Uzbek dehqons. Some told accounts in line with the new nationalist hegemonic story, that Qo'rboshis resisted Soviet oppression and never harmed ordinary people. Qo'rboshi defender stories were the minority among our accounts, and Bosmachi victim stories dominated. Indeed, over the course of two decades, many ordinary people suffered harm from raids, whether those were politically motivated or were just lawlessness. Participation in anti-Soviet actions or in raids on rural communities tended to result in the perpetrators' eventual flight, arrest, death, exile, or efforts to move and hide identity. Those who lived through the violence of this period and remained in their villages were more likely to be or to become Soviet supporters, precisely because known Bosmachis were not allowed to join a kokhoz, and if they were found among kolkhoz members, they were arrested. Armed detachments led by Qo'rboshis and raiding thieves were few in number, compared with the eventual numbers of the Red Army forces in Central Asia.[64] A gendered lens offers a somewhat different insight. Men's standpoints divided along the lines of those who had experienced Bosmachi victimization and those who had not, while women's standpoint was unified: the very existence of groups of armed raiders who would not honor the boundaries of the courtyard home but would invade and carry off women posed a gendered threat, shaping the ways that an entire generation of women apprehended their own world.

3

LAND REFORM

Land reform, which started in 1925, turned Hayitboy into a strong supporter of the Soviet government, a point that he reiterated many times during his interview.[1] His interview serves to illustrate the ways that an intersection of factors—in his case, class, ethnicity, age, and family status—shaped his lifelong identity as a supporter of Communism in Uzbekistan. Russell Zanca and I interviewed Hayitboy in 2001, when he was ninety-one years of age. He wore a loose traditional Uzbek men's shirt, loose pants that revealed his missing lower leg, and a Soviet-era men's suitcoat covered in medals. He was a World War II veteran, about which he remarked, "I did not make it all the way to Berlin, because I was wounded on the way to Berlin." He talked about the many ways that the government's radical programs to transform the rural economy and class relations changed his life.

> MARIANNE (MK): You were born in 1910; is that right?
> HAYITBOY (HM): I'm from 1910.
> MK: And what is your name?
> HM: I am M. Hayitboy. I was born here, in this courtyard house. My father was a dehqon here and a butcher. My father had died in the year of *vabo* [epidemic].[2] My father and mother both became ill and died within twenty days. I was left along with the other children in our family trying to fend for ourselves within our gates. I was my father's only son. We became poor, and I worked in the gates of the rich.

After they died everything was sold off. I was young at that time. My older relatives sold their things for the funeral rituals; they took care of that, and they contributed their own money. When I was orphaned, I had a grandmother, my mother's mother. I was in her care for two years, and then after that I went to work in the gates of the rich. I herded the livestock; I did household chores, as I grew older. That was from age ten to twelve.

In this place there was only a religious *maktab* [school]. The *domla* taught there; that was what we called the teacher. After that kind of studying, then the Soviet government school came into existence, and then they [the domlas] fled to Qashgar.... And then after that, somewhere around 1926 or 1927, I went off to study, and I became a teacher. I studied in the technical school in Namangan. I ... returned and opened the school. The government gave a free education to children of the poor. The Union of the Poor chose me and sent me off to school to get educated.

My father left three *tanobs*, or thirty *sotixs* [three-tenths of a hectare]. That land was along the side of the irrigation canal, by the water; that is where we lived. Our father was one of the poor. What did we plant? Maize, mung beans for food, this and that. It was the time of individual farming. There was no *artel* [farm labor collective]. My father ... was a butcher who butchered sheep to sell.

B [HM's SON]: They made a good living. They had enough, but then they died when he was a child.

RUSSELL: Before collectivization, were there problems with water or conflicts?

HM: There was water stealing. A fight, and they would cut off the water and steal from each other, and the crops would dry up, or else the rich men would refuse water to the poor, when the rich were planting. They wouldn't give the poor water or land. The poor worked in the gates of the rich and planted their land.

And then the artel started in 1927, and they invited the poor to join. They took in the poor, including me. They did not accept the rich into the kolkhoz at first.... I entered the artel when I was fifteen years old. We planted paxta [cotton] ... as well as rice and other crops, but cotton was the primary crop. It was the artel's own cotton. The poor took land from the rich, and having seized that, the poor created the artel.

At that time, I was asked to sign a letter to become a member of the artel, and then they made me into the secretary for the artel. I would write down who had worked. After some time, there was a director for the artel, and twenty-one people worked for it. It was called Kengash Kolkhoz, which . . . formed by inviting in all the poor. The artel was formed with the leadership of Communists. The Communists came from among our own Uzbeks. I also joined the Communist Party. After the war, I joined in 1946. I hadn't joined before that.

Between the years 1925 and 1927, the government of the newly delineated Uzbek Soviet Socialist Republic carried out land reform in the Fergana Valley, where Hayitboy lived, in a process that changed some aspects of landownership before mass collectivization began. In land reform, the government set a norm for landowning in each region and seized land beyond that norm from the boylar (the rich/wealthy, explained later), redistributing the seized lands to poor and landless dehqons like Hayitboy.

> HM: The rich were the owners of the shared-use lands. In collectivization, when we said we will take their lands, of course the rich were—well, what can you say?—but the poor were happy. And they even said they would give us a bit of their land, dividing it out to the poorest. They gave me three hectares from that land, for the poor who had no one to rely on. They took the owners away in train wagons and sent them off to Siberia. Those lands that now had no owners were distributed to the poor, including me. The poor were happy, and the rich were angry. The rich and whoever was an old-style mullah—they were exiled to Siberia and Ukraine. I was happy. The state gave me a lot of help, it educated me, and I entered the artel to work. If it had not been for the state, I would have kept on working in the gates of the rich.
>
> The rich had really worked the poor hard as servants in their gates; they could have five or ten working for them, but after the artel formed, they were afraid. If something like one hundred fifty people were accepted into the artel and this [land] was given to the poor, then they had to fear the poor.

Hayitboy telescoped events that happened between about 1925 and 1932. He clarified he joined the artel when he was fifteen, in 1925, at the beginning of land reform. Hayitboy, as one of the poor and landless, was given land to call his own. He joined a planting collective whose members received seed loans from an agricultural purchasing cooperative to plant cotton in their united fields. He studied at the teacher's training school from 1928 to 1931, returning to his community to open a school. Dekulakization, which meant the total dispossession of those who were deemed to be rich, began in 1930, after which the state sent the dispossessed rich men into exile.

Hayitboy was politicized first by his association with the Union of the Poor and then through his education in the teacher's training school. He strongly asserted his identification as poor, even attributing poverty to his father, the butcher, an image that his son intervened to correct. Haytiboy recognized that his standpoint differed from that of the boylar: his gain was their loss. He continually alluded to the class consciousness that agitators fostered among the poor, linking state programs to his own improving fortunes: joining the artel, being granted land, being provided with education, becoming a teacher. Consistent about his support for the government's dispossession of the rich throughout his interview, he conceded that there were "excesses"—using an expression from collectivization-era discourse. He recalled another young man from his community who joined him in Namangan: "When we were entering the teacher's training school, someone here wrote a letter saying he is the son of a rich man, so don't admit him. I was called to respond about him, and they told me that they had sent him off. At that time, the rich were really blackened. They accepted me because I was poor; they even gave me clothing, a jacket, shirt, pants, and boots all for free, and I stayed and studied."

The triumph of the poor over the rich was Hayitboy's refrain, but his newly created class advantage and approval of the Communist government did not correspond to any love for Russians or Russia; he associated the changes with Uzbeks like himself. Russell asked him about changes in everyday life, such as in foodways or in dress. He responded:

> My shirt was always this kind of shirt [the open-necked traditional Central Asian men's shirt]. I wore a shirt like this when I went to study, but when I went, I took this off and put on the clothing that the government gave me, the jacket. And when I returned here, I threw that off and put on my own robe, my own shirt, because here they would say, 'You have become a Russian.' If I had worn those clothes at home, they would say I had become Russian, and they would think of me as a bad person. They taught in Russian, but I had not learned Russian. Later, Uzbeks were made into Russians by studying Russian. I learned some, superficially, never seriously.

Hayitboy gained the opportunity to become a teacher because he was a poor, young Uzbek dehqon who happened to be literate, during a time when the state's program to open Soviet primary schools in rural communities created a demand for even slightly literate young Uzbeks to become teachers. The political and economic upheaval that destroyed the fortunes of older, wealthier Uzbek men opened doors for Hayitboy: "If the government had not done these things for me, what would I have done? I would have gone on working in the gates of the rich."³

Class and Nationality in Uzbekistan

In October 1924, the Soviet government announced Central Asia's new map and new governmental structures, setting in motion processes that gave everyday life importance to new forms of identification based on class and nationality. Class and nationality became sources of social capital or categories of exclusion. Being identified as poor, middle, or rich took on fundamental importance in the everyday life of Uzbekistan's dehqons, something that Hayitboy and many other respondents highlighted as they told of the ways that political decisions shaped their lives. In terms of nationality, Russian dominance in Central Asia operated through different modes than in imperial times. Nationality was defined in ways that maintained colonial difference and privilege for Russians and other Europeans and that simultaneously created new hierarchies among Central Asians, privileging "titular" nationalities—like Uzbeks in Uzbekistan—over others.⁴ During land reform, Uzbeks and other indigenous Central Asians constituted only half of the membership of the Uzbekistan Communist Party, even after the 1924 Lenin levy initiated a swift rise in indigenous membership. Russians and others whom Central Asians referred to collectively as "Europeans" dominated the state security forces who backed land reform with threats of arrest.⁵ Although the equality of nations that the Communist Party platform promised did not materialize, within the new boundaries of Uzbekistan, identifying as Uzbek became associated with rights to landownership during land reform, claims to seats in burgeoning teacher training courses, and recruitment into party and rural leadership roles.

As explained below, the 1926 census clarified boundaries on identification for members of the collectivization generation. The sociologist Maya Marx Feree emphasizes structuration and ongoing dynamic processes of identification that make race- or ethnicity-based identities meaningful. She writes: "When the dimension of 'race' is constructed and 'fixed' in national censuses, it generates meaningful and contestable categories (such as 'Asian') that can always be further decomposed, but which serve to distribute real resources and recognition in response to which identities and activities become oriented."⁶ In the newly formed Uzbek SSR, the census, the daily-life use of nationality-based categories, and class-instilling events such as land reform produced the categories within which dehqons claimed resources and recognition or that defined their exclusion. The new government of

Uzbekistan sent Communist Party activists to rural communities to propagate class-based divisions. Those Uzbek dehqons who had lacked security and been dependent on the wealthy for their livelihoods were recognized as *kambag'allar*, "the poor." They felt their own oppression ease as they gained access to land. When those whose ownership of extensive lands had provided them not just with a livelihood but with a comfortable life and power over others were politically identified as *boylar*, the state deprived them of the sources of their security and their social influence.

The Soviet Commissariat for Nationalities promoted the idea that the larger national groups within Soviet domains should be allowed to develop within territories where their languages and cultures would dominate, but this was an autonomy that precluded the possibility of independence. The Soviet Union created a new map of Central Asia, in a process that progressed from ethnic surveys, to Communist Party decisions about which smaller groups could be subsumed to larger ones, and then to negotiations over specific boundaries among the most mobilized of Central Asian Communist Party members—the Uzbeks and the Kazakhs.[7] The process of creating political boundaries that were linked to nationality made stating one's national self-identification into a necessary action, articulated in everyday life.

As declared late in 1924, the new Uzbek Soviet Socialist Republic consisted of the most densely populated cities and rural areas and the most intensively irrigated farming zones of the former Turkestan ASSR, that is, Russia's Turkestan Territory, plus the most populated and intensively farmed areas of the former Bukhara People's Republic and of the former Khiva People's Republic.[8]

The nomadic and core grain-raising areas of the Turkestan ASSR became part of the Kazakh ASSR and the Kyrgyz Autonomous Oblast (AO), both subordinate to the Russian Federated Soviet Socialist Republic. Importantly for Uzbekistan, most of the rural Russians who had settled in Central Asia to farm lived in land designated as the Kazakh ASSR or Kyrgyz AO. In contrast, Russians constituted less than 1 percent of the rural, farming population in Uzbekistan, although they outnumbered Uzbeks in Tashkent and several other cities.[9] The chart in table 3.1, based on the 1926 census, illustrates population distribution by province (*viloyat*) in the Uzbek SSR, in its collectivization-period borders (1930–1935).[10] Uzbekistan's 1926 population, minus the Tajik ASSR and minus Khujand Province, was 4,217,000, among whom 76 percent lived in rural areas.[11]

Representation of ethnic or national categories in the 1926 census has repeatedly been subject to critique.[12] Like any modern census, the All-Union Population Census provided a list of category choices for national identity, from which the respondent who answered on behalf of a household could choose only one. The 1926 census was designed to consolidate under the category "Uzbek" not

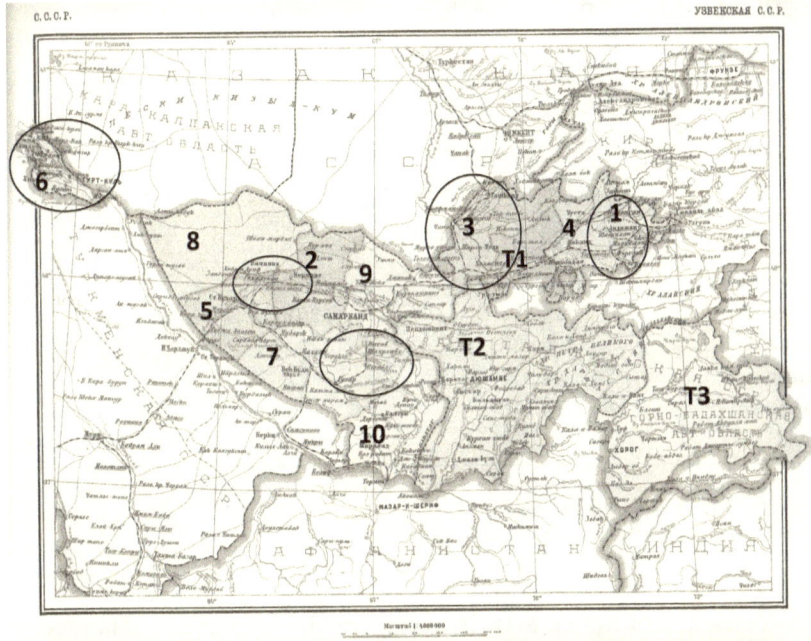

FIGURE 3.1. 1928 map of the Uzbek SSR and Tajik ASSR, with *viloyats* (provinces) and research sites. Number key: 1, Andijon (now Andijon and Namangan Provinces); 2, Zarafshan (now Navoiy Province); 3, Tashkent; 4, Fergana; 5, Bukhara; 6, Xorazm; 7, Qashqa Daryo. Other provinces of the Uzbek SSR in 1928 are shown as 8, Kanimex; 9, Samarkand; 10, Surhon Daryo; T1, Khujand, transferred to Tajik SSR in 1929; T2, Tajik ASSR; T3, Gorno-Badakhshan Autonomous Oblast, part of Tajik SSR. Karakalpak ASSR is shown as part of the Kazakh ASSR; it was transferred to the Uzbek SSR in 1936. Source: *Atlas Soiuza Sovetskikh Sotsialisticheskikh Respublik* (Moscow: Izdaniie TsIK SSSR, 1928), 101.

only those who already identified as Uzbeks but also those who spoke Turkic dialects and identified themselves with such terms as *Sart*, *Turk*, or *Kuruma*; and there are records of pressure on Tajik speakers to identify themselves as Uzbek.[13] Table 3.2 shows nationality by province; Uzbeks were the majority everywhere except in tiny Kanimex.[14]

In each interview, respondents offered their nationality out of long-established habit, or they responded to our question, "What is your nationality [*millatingiz nima*]?" Interviewers sometimes asked about belonging to tribe or other concepts of group identity. Some respondents, especially xo'jas, emphasized their status-group belonging. Those who identified as Uzbek usually stated that without any comment or qualification, while those from minority groups within

TABLE 3.1 Uzbek SSR population by province (*viloyat*), urban and rural, 1926

	URBAN	RURAL	TOTAL
Andijon	182,631	611,641	794,272
Bukhara	59,801	330,031	389,832
Fergana	158,734	515,372	674,106
Kanimex	–	22,692	22,692
Qashqa Daryo	39,038	304,321	343,359
Samarkand	131,735	394,298	526,033
Surhon Daryo	16,308	185,905	202,213
Tashkent	339, 106	333,183	672,289
Xorazm	29,358	284,848	314,206
Zarafshan	34,346	243,654	278,000
Total	991,057	3,225,945	4,217,002

Note: This table excludes data for Khujand Province and Isfara District, which were transferred to the Tajik SSR in 1929 before collectivization began.
Source: Vsesoiuznaia Perepis' Naseleniia 1926, 15:13–17, table 4.

Uzbekistan drew attention to their non-Uzbek identity. Uzbek had become an unmarked category, the definition of normal, against which others were obligated to define their own difference. Two interviewees described themselves as Turkmen, one as Uyghur, two as Kyrgyz, and two as Kazakh. Several who came from northern Tashkent Province asserted Uzbek identification but described nomadic herding lifestyles; in the 1920s, their families may have identified themselves as Kurama or Kipchak. Three identified unambiguously as Tajik, but there were more who blurred Tajik and Uzbek identification. Respondents mentioned contexts when their nationality had significance: when the Party conducted propaganda for land reform; when state organizations recruited dehqons into schools, into collective leadership, and into the Party; or when they lived in mixed or border-zone communities.

The process by which diverse possibilities for group identity narrowed into the five nationalities deemed worthy of their own socialist republics was at least in part shaped by Russian and Soviet census taking. Benedict Anderson cogently pointed out that colonial governments categorized subjects through censuses and, in so doing, aggregated groups according to various rationales: racial, linguistic, but always hierarchical.[15] Sergei Abashin details this process in Central Asia, showing the choices that imperial administrators made in choosing the categories for Russia's 1897 census in the Fergana Valley, which included Sart as one among numerous names for sedentary speakers of the Uzbek language, and the different choices made in the Soviet 1926 census, such as using Uzbek and not Sart. He demonstrates that identification, at least for state purposes, changed

TABLE 3.2 Uzbekistan's 1926 population by nationality and province (viloyat)

	ANDIJON	BUKHARA	FERGANA	KANIMEX (NAVOIY)	QASHQA DARYO	SAMARKAND	SURHON DARYO	TASHKENT	XORAZM	ZARAFSHAN (NAVOIY)
Uzbek	593,140	321,595	542,987	4,266	300,239	429,272	145,645	328,359	302,776	246,620
Tajik/Persian/Irani	28,249	33,849	63,543	–	21,984	35,245	38,340	14,875	–	10,476
Russian	15,844	–	26,554	111	4,769	31,245	7,153	133,171	2,364	3,737
Kazakh	–	–	–	9,688	–	–	–	84,874	3,020	2,908
Kyrgyz	46,274	–	12,686	–	–	–	–	3,175	–	3,014
Karakalpak	14,023	–	4,477	5,938	–	–	–	–	1,305	–
Turk	18,473	–	1,742	–	–	–	–	–	–	–
Tatar	2,476	2,614	2,397	–	–	2,751	991	12,398	1,135	1,398
Kurama	2,639	–	–	–	–	–	–	47,388	–	–
Uyghur	30,757	–	–	–	–	–	–	–	–	–
European Jew	2,066	1,408	3,849	–	–	1,434	–	9,498	–	–
Central Asian Jew	–	3,367	1,379	–	–	7,766	–	1,611	–	2,290
Turkmen	–	3,426	–	–	4,094	1,751	5,376	–	1,776	4,722
Arab	1,722	5,849	–	2,308	7,947	1,589	1,189	–	–	4,088
Armenian	1,798	–	2,609	–	–	3,760	5,317	5,317	–	–
Kipchak	27,857	–	4,431	–	–	–	–	–	–	–
Kashgari	3,000	–	–	–	–	–	–	–	–	–
Ukrainian	–	–	–	–	–	–	–	15,222	–	–
Belorussian	–	–	–	–	–	–	–	1,843	–	–
Polish	–	–	–	–	–	–	–	1,862	–	–
German	–	–	–	–	–	–	–	3,049	190	–

Note: Data from the census include nationalities that had at least one thousand representatives in at least one province.
Source: *Vsesoiuzniaia Perepis' Naseleniia 1926*, 15:13–48, table 4.

over the course of three decades; Qashgaris became Uzbek, while Galchas disappeared, emerging as either Tajik or Uzbek.¹⁶ In a recent study of ethnic identification in Uzbekistan's border zones, the ethnographer Peter Finke notes that Uzbek identity has low barriers, making assimilation to Uzbekness easy; one's self-ascription as Uzbek is accepted by the surrounding society.¹⁷

A few interviewees mentioned assimilation to Uzbekness. Ahmed, who was born in a village called Arablar, said, "Since long ago, our *millat* was Arab, but now it is Uzbek." His parents had called themselves Arabs, a group that in some places had retained a distinct dialect of Arabic and that elsewhere spoke Uzbek but told of Arab ancestry.¹⁸ In Bekabod, a district in the southern Tashkent region bordering Tajikistan, Xusenboy responded to the question about his millat by saying, "It was written down that the nationality for us is Uzbek. I am Tajik and officially Uzbek, so Uzbek." He noted mixed marriages in his community: "Everyone who comes here calls us Tajiks. The truth should be told. Our women are Tajik, and our men are Uzbek. My old lady [*kampir*] is Tajik as can be. But as for me, I became Uzbek. If you ask her, she will say Tajik."¹⁹ Half of the ten interviewees in Nurota spoke of themselves as Tajik-speaking Uzbeks, Uzbek-speaking Tajiks, or some other mix that defied the simple state categories.²⁰ Zanca's partner for those interviews came from Navoiy viloyat, spoke both languages, and conducted interviews in the language chosen by the interviewee, giving them latitude to link themselves to more than one identity category. One interviewee first rejected national categories altogether in favor of religion. Lutfullo U. said that he was from the Muslim millat but then added the Uzbek millat and the Ming *qabila* (tribe).²¹

With the 1924 establishment of an Uzbek SSR, there was state encouragement for and personal benefit in identifying oneself as Uzbek and, conversely, little reason to claim a less-entitled Central Asian identity. The 1926 census reflected this new political reality, and it also reinforced government policies whereby claiming identity as Uzbek opened some doors. In other words, official nationality became a form of social capital. As official nationality became important in everyday life, brief statements of belonging to one or another of the state-recognized nationality categories became habitual, requiring no additional explanation.

Policy differences among newly delineated Central Asian republics meant that those living in Uzbekistan between 1925 and 1929 experienced a different effort at the Communist mobilization of peasants, through land reform, than did their counterparts in the neighboring Kazakh ASSR, where, as Sarah Cameron describes it, the Party's 1928 Little October campaign drove many of the wealthiest Kazakh herders into exile.²² Awareness that policies differed across these internal Soviet borders instigated movement: we heard stories of Muslim religious leaders who, fearing dispossession as rich men or in Uzbekistan's anti-Islam campaign, left for the Tajik ASSR, and we heard stories of Turkmen wealthy families, facing dispossession in the Turkmen SSR, choosing to move to the Uzbek SSR to reinvent themselves.[23] We also heard many stories of kin who left Soviet territory entirely by crossing the border into Afghanistan.

Property Relations and Class Identities

Although newly formed SSRs were national in form and delineating nationality played a significant role in constructing Soviet forms of identity, the Bolsheviks thought in terms of class. In Marxist thought, class conflict is the engine of social transformation, and the proletariat's challenge to the old dominant social classes would ultimately result in a Communist society.[24] There was only a small urban proletariat in Russian Turkestan in 1917, made up of railway and cotton factory workers, but cotton processing nearly disappeared when the revolution erupted. Cotton processing plants were reopening in 1923 and 1924, but their employment rolls were miniscule compared to the masses of dehqons who raised cotton and other crops.[25]

As in Russia, where the Party had quickly recognized its need to use a revolutionary peasantry to seize and maintain control of rural regions and agriculture, in Central Asia the Party sought ways to make part of the peasantry into its rural arm.[26] In Russia, beginning with the February 1917 revolution, peasants themselves initiated anti-ruling-class actions, burning down manor houses, seizing parcels of land that had belonged to elite families, and driving out the noble families.[27] In Russian Turkestan, rural change came about somewhat differently but no less violently. Starting with the 1916 uprising, Kazakhs and Kyrgyz attacked Russian colonial settlers, driving them off some of their land. In 1918, much of the newly formed Turkestan ASSR's administrative action on land focused on recognizing Kazakh and Kyrgyz ownership or control and limiting the return of Russians and other colonists.[28] In the Turkestan ASSR, the Bolsheviks nationalized properties belonging to former imperial servitors, as well as unused agricultural lands they deemed to be abandoned. The lingering war against Bosmachis prevented the Soviet state from enacting any systematic land reform until 1925.

Around the time that the new SSRs and ASSRs were proclaimed (late 1924), government commissions carried out an economic region-defining project within each of the Central Asian SSRs and ASSRs. In Uzbekistan, newly defined and mapped regions included a central town where a Regional Committee (Raykom) of the Communist Party was established, surrounded by rural land with multiple villages and a population from 12,000 to 60,000.[29] The Raykom recruited rural members for the Communist Party from among Central Asian dehqons. Villages that previously had various forms of governance were told to form village soviets (councils). As Qurbon A.'s story about novchas who rose up against the boylar illustrated, village councils became a field of contest between those who wanted to hold on to their lands and their local power and those who hoped to gain by challenging and disrupting that order.[30] Agitators speaking in Bolshevik terms provoked the poor to recognize that the rich were not interested in their well-being.

We asked interviewees about what their family had owned during the period of individual farming (*yakka xo'jalik*—a term by which many retrospectively designated the rural order before collectivization). They responded by explaining how much land their family owned and what they raised, and they talked about livestock and revenue-producing assets, such as a mill. Respondents who came from families that owned more than their neighbors, who hired chorikor and mardikor labor, and who owned hundreds of head of livestock, described their families as *boy*, meaning "rich." Interviewees who said their families supplied for family needs without hiring chorikors and without seeking off-farm employment referred to themselves as "middle," *orta*, or as "satisfied," *o'ziga toq*. Those who owned little or no land and made their living by working for others sometimes called their families "poor," *kambag'al*, but more often used a traditional concept of dependency: they or their fathers had "worked in the gates of the rich," as sharecroppers, hired laborers, or servants. Fifteen respondents described their households as earning a living primarily through artisan work rather than farming. Twenty-one said that before collectivization their families owned extensive lands, with some declaring they had been rich, while others described wealth but asserted an identity as middle or poor. Thirty claimed they were middle or satisfied. Forty-seven described being poor or landless, and these usually mentioned that a family member had worked as a chorikor or a mardikor. Among the forty-seven poor or landless, fifteen said their family obtained land during land reform.

Aliqul (b. 1916), from a Fergana family that he described as middle, said that in the process of collectivization, the government's organizers and agitators held meetings separately for the rich and the poor.

> They found out in which rich person's house the poor people worked by questioning them. In the meetings, when they questioned poor people by asking where they worked and how long they worked, they made a list of people to make quloqs and made people sign. They wrote down a rich person's last name and the years people worked for him like five years, six years, or one year. They told poor people that they

should tell how long they worked for rich people and how much the rich owe them, so they would take away the rich peoples' belongings and give them to the poor.³¹

This articulation of difference, with corresponding claims to land and seizures of land, began during land reform. By the time collectivization started, dehqons had seen that identifying as poor or as rich carried immediate economic consequences.

Land Reform: Finding the Rural Proletariat

When the Peoples Commissariat for Land (NarKomZem) and the land provision committees in Uzbekistan were laying plans for land reform in 1925, the critical question was who should be thought of as a poor peasant. The results of the Bosmachi struggle, including significant disruption of rural communities, depopulation, and collapse of agriculture, meant that data on Central Asian agriculture collected in the 1910s had very limited value for new plans in the mid-1920s. Economists and administration members proposed several ways of accumulating the knowledge necessary for evaluating property relations in rural Uzbekistan and then using that knowledge to appeal to the poor and to dispossess the rich. In the three provinces where Uzbekistan first initiated land reform in 1925, namely Fergana, Tashkent, and Samarkand, regional committees were tasked with listing every household and the amount of its landholdings and then coming up with local norms for landholding. This was a rough and very personal process.

The other mode, favored by economists, was to carry out in-depth statistical studies of representative farming districts, including not only measures of land owned but the specific uses of that land, kinds of crops raised, other household assets, and the roles of various family members in working their own land and working for others. In 1924 researchers working for the Statistical Division carried out these studies in nine Central Asian regions.³² Resulting articles, published in Uzbekistan's economics journals, shaped Party instructions to local land committees who were supposed to evaluate dehqon classes.

Studies of Fergana Valley districts from 1924 and 1925 showed that dehqons who had abandoned their land during the years of the Bosmachi war were returning and that with support from the government for seed loans, dehqons were rapidly increasing their cotton planting.³³ The Soviet cotton and textile trusts wanted the economists to provide information that would encourage more cotton growing, and for this, the economists provided some answers that influenced land reform decisions. They noted that those who owned very little land planted the highest proportion in cotton, while those who owned the most land were able to make that land fully productive only by hiring labor power and, even so, planted a lower proportion with cotton.[34] Taking land from the rich and distributing it to those who worked it thus made sense for maximizing cotton planting.

Although the Communist Party wanted clear definitions for poor, middle, and rich dehqon households, the economists suffered from the academic affliction of nuance. One of them, K. A. Shuliak wrote: "The main socio-economic groups of poor, middle and well-off, into which we divided all the households in the villages under study, naturally do not all represent that group in every particular; they are not all the same with others in the group. If we regard differentiation in the village as a process, then it is clear that in every socio-economic group we should include a series of temporary groups, which in their own socio-economic nature are expressing a tendency to move toward a different group."[35] A household head with several unmarried or recently married sons was at the peak of his earning power, as more adult labor meant more intensive cropping on lands owned and possibly also on lands rented or sharecropped. Division of land and aging could mean that within a few years that same household head relied on a sharecropper to keep his remaining lands in use.

Several interviewees illustrated such household shifts from wealth to poverty or from poverty to wealth. Temir (b. 1920), from Qashqa Daryo, said:

> My father had thirteen older brothers. But then one year an epidemic broke out, and a big death came. My father, one younger brother, and one sister—three of them were left; there had been eighteen children. It was 1916 or 1917. In that epidemic, in the first fifteen days, six older brothers died, and in the next fifteen days, six older brothers died, and then only three of them were left. In those days there were no doctors to take care of you. We had a lot of land. There were about thirty hectares for the brothers. My father did his own work, except for watering and harvest. In the harvest he used mardikors. He paid them a share: five out of ten.[36]

By the time that land reform started in Qashqa Daryo, Temir's father controlled enough land to be regarded as one of the boylar.

Olmajon told of the ways that accumulation changed her family's economic conditions. She was born in Xorazm in 1903, to a father who worked in the gates of the rich as a cart driver. Her mother died when she was six years old, and her father took care of her by including her in his work. As a teen, before the revolution, she too worked in the gates of the rich as a driver. One of those wealthy employers "gave us a pair of oxen as our labor earning. After we extended our lands and built our own house, then we no longer worked for others." Her father and his brothers acquired thirteen hectares that they farmed together in the 1920s. When land reform came to Xorazm in the late 1920s, Olmajon might have claimed to be poor, referring to her earlier work in the gates of the rich, or her father's household may have been regarded as middle dehqons; she did not say whether they acquired their land prior to or due to land reform.[37] Hayitboy's account illustrated swift change in the opposite direction: butchers were generally among the more prosperous artisans, and Hayitboy's father also owned some farmland. However, upon the death of the butcher and his wife, the orphaned Hayitboy became impoverished and took up working in the gates of the rich.[38]

A Marxist definition of class avoids this sort of nuance by focusing on ownership of the means of production. For Communist Party activists the deciding factor in categorizing dehqons was not long-term household trajectory based on maximizing labor power but ownership of plowed lands—most importantly, irrigated lands—at a specific moment in time. Political decisions enacted locally by land reform committees were far more peremptory than the nuanced points raised by the economists. Hiring workers for more than five days per season, something that almost any cotton-growing dehqon might do, sufficed to designate an owner as wealthy (boylar) or oppressor (*mushtumzo'r*). Party declarations defined what proportion of boylar lands were above the norm and should be redistributed and, additionally, that land expropriation applied to former government servants, qazis, imams, merchants, middlemen, usurers, and those who made their living from something other than farming but owned land and rented it out. Abandoned land belonging to absentee owners and lands belonging to *waqf* (Islamic foundations supporting mosques or madrasas) would also become part of the fund for redistribution. On the other hand, dehqons who farmed their own land would keep it, and a three-year exception was made for those who owned some farmland but made their living as drivers, in construction, as factory workers, or as small shop owners. "For widows and orphans who are of the working people, lands will be preserved until the orphan reaches maturity."[39]

The Party's pronouncement established categories for dispossession and laid a foundation for defining classes and stimulating class conflict. While Party leaders in Moscow promoted voluntary collectivization as a strategy for creating a revolutionary peasantry, until November 1929 the Uzbek SSR's land reform policy fostered an increase in numbers of dehqons who owned land and farmed individually. This was exactly the outcome that the state-owned Cotton Trust's leaders wanted to see, as individual owners of small holdings were the most likely to expand cotton growing. Uzbekistan's Party leadership repeatedly declared land reform a success, because the numbers of landless dehqons decreased, households owning minimally sufficient land within a local norm increased, while cotton production rose.[40]

How to Deny Being Rich

Some wealthy landowners facing expropriation materialized a new status as poor by rapidly dividing land among sons, wives, mardikors, and chorikors. In family narratives that some respondents shared, this voluntary division was evidence of beneficence or canniness, and in Party critiques, these voluntary redistributions were efforts by the rich to maintain their influence and control over grateful subordinates. Temir (b. 1920), whose father had gained control of thirty hectares on the swift demise of his twelve brothers, explained that his father avoided confiscation by voluntarily redistributing his land.

> Land reform was when they raised the red banner over so-and-so's land and said it is now socialist property, and so-and-so gives his land to the collective; I saw how they would raise this red banner. That happened in my village. It must have been around 1926 or 1927. It was the poor that raised the banner. They did not take excess land, but they did not take all of the land—they took perhaps one-third or one-fourth, not all of it. They did not touch my father's land because he had joined the poor, the Qoshchi [plowman's union]; he led the poor in this village.... He gave his land to the collective. He was the administrator of the collective. After land reform started the collective of the poor took land from the rich, and at that time there were a lot of landless men in the village. The large landholdings taken from the rich were given to those landless men who united, who planted them, and who restored the economy.[41]

Through voluntary redistribution, Temir's father successfully transitioned from owning a lot of land and controlling hired workers to leading a collective of the poor on that same land, directing the members. In the 1930s, the collective became a kolkhoz.

Tojivoy's father, a wealthy man who owned one hundred hectares in a hilly area near Parkent, also took action to reidentify as an ordinary dehqon. He was an organizer of the local Qoshchi union, but he had three or four landless laborers working his own land. Tojivoy's father was on the land reform committee that distributed half of his land, about fifty hectares, to the poor and landless. Tojivoy remembered his father saying that his decision to join the Qoshchi union, work beside others as a plowman, and treat his hired hands well eventually saved him from being declared a quloq. When others who were similarly wealthy were arrested and exiled, Tojivoy's father joined the kolkhoz, surrendering the rest of his land. Tojivoy related his father's words: "Son, among quloqs I was a quloq, but the working people cleared me, because I did what I said, and if I had something to eat, I fed those who worked for me the same thing. If I had eaten *plov* while giving them leftovers, they would have hanged me. But because I did good, they cleared me."[42]

Reports came to the Land Reform Commission detailing strategies that the wealthy used in several districts near Tashkent. "A wealthy man with 277 desiatins gave them out to rent to an artel, but the artel did not exist. Instead, the owner and his relatives claimed it." In some places, the Qoshchi union was weak, a judgment that no doubt could have been made about Parkent, if a wealthy man who owned one hundred hectares, like Tojivoy's father, was a key member and used his membership to retain half his land.[43]

Ahmad T. (b. 1920), from Marg'ilon, identified his parents as poor dehqons, even though his evidence flatly contradicted that designation: "They had five hundred to six hundred tanobs; that was perhaps twenty-five hectares [in fact, one hundred hectares]. Our lands were in a village called Qirg'iz mahalla and Garmdon and in Honariq, all over the place. But we were considered poor, not quloqs. We did not hire people to work on the land. Or maybe we did, but I don't know. All of it was used by God's servants." They also had extensive livestock. Ahmad's grandfather was later designated as quloq: "He was exiled to O'ratepe, Kazakhstan, and then went to Tajikistan, here and there, in exile."[44] If either of Ahmad's assertions about lands owned were accurate, his family was very wealthy compared with most others in the Fergana Valley. Every aspect of his description of family property equaled the definition of boylar, but Ahmad reiterated his father's claim of belonging to the poor, an assertion that came up in other wealthy family narratives as well (chapter 7).

Hidoyat-xon (b. 1919), whose mother became a Communist and a Women's Division activist, and who herself joined the Komsomol and the Party, wanted to soften the association between wealth and exploiting others. Her father was a wealthy merchant in Kokand who also owned land, but the Soviet government took it all, and no land was left.

> They took it sometime around 1927 or 1928, before 1930. It was in land reform. My father's land in today's measure was about three or four hectares. The dehqons planted and gave to us and also provided for themselves. They were just called dehqons, not mardikor. They would turn over whatever was in their heart; there was no contract. They did what they thought best in their hearts, for reasons of purity, giving from

their own earning, as a sort of gift given for good fortune. Yes, there also must have been those who gave a third or a fourth. After the land was taken away, then my father was noticed, there were rumors, and he fled to Qashgar.[45]

Hidoyat-xon's mother had been the third wife, and elsewhere in her interview, Hidoyat-xon had little that was positive to say about her merchant father, who divorced her mother, but in this recollection, she echoed his self-defense. She shared her family's discourse that her merchant father had not exploited his sharecroppers or renters at all: they were not even paying him but were providing him with a share of the crop out of their own goodwill.

Much was at stake in land reform, both for the wealthy and for the poor, and those who recognized this strove to shore up their own interests. There were many reports about the strategies that wealthy landowners took, which included simple dissimulation as in Hidoyat's account or limiting their land use, as in a report that focused on areas with Russian settler farmers: "There are villages of Russian colonizers who still live in their old colonial ways, and they hire local laborers at the lowest possible rates. Native landless laborers, having learned about Soviet law, are aware that the land they are hired to work could, in land reform, become theirs. Russian kulaks who own eight desiatinas thus often choose to plant only four desiatinas so that they do not wind up having to give away that land [to the laborer]."[46]

Abduqayum lived in a mountainous region north of Tashkent, where his father owned land in several locations for farming and herding. He said:

> Land reform began in 1927. It was after the Soviet government was founded, and the rich all abandoned their lands and left. It was taken away from them. A commission formed and they divided it out to the poor. They measured it out in 1.5-meter strips and gave it out. People who owned land in two or three places had it taken away, and some was even taken away from the poor, and if the middle dehqons had more than two or three hectares, the excess was taken and given to the poor.

Abduqayum's father lost several of his scattered land parcels, but their family was not severely affected. However, Abduqayum said that redistribution was not very fair and that, in his district, the process stimulated violence. "Land reform was very bad. People killed each other, and they beat up people from *mahalla* [neighborhood] to mahalla; they didn't have guns but clubs; they would cut them up, and one of the *oqsoqols* [village elders] would come out with accusations, and everyone would raise a club and fight, and that was land reform."[47]

During land reform, many of the wealthy tried to redistribute their own land to family members or sharecroppers, hide their holdings, reduce their plantings, resist being labeled as rich, and limit their own dispossession. The newly delineated republic borders suddenly had tangible meaning, as Uzbekistan launched land reform first in the Fergana Valley, while the wealthy who owned land in parts of the valley that belonged to the Kyrgyz Autonomous Oblast were unaffected. The Land Reform Commission received a report from the Uzbek-Kyrgyz border region: "A conflict has arisen in the Isbaskent volost of Andijan between Uzbek dehqons and chorikors against the Kyrgyz boy Lelmen, whose land has been partly seized in land reform. The Kyrgyz rich are calling for uniting Isbaskent volost with Kyrgyzstan, because Kyrgyzstan has not had land reform. Kyrgyz rich men are having influence among Kyrgyz landless workers in Uzbekistan." The border, which, as the author of this report noted, had not yet been delineated precisely, took on meaning for both the wealthy and the poor. "Following land reform, some of the rich and *manaps* [Kyrgyz lineage group leaders] from Uzbekistan have migrated to Kyrgyzstan, united with the rich and manaps, and are carrying on a campaign among the landless and poor against allowing land reform in Kyrgyzstan."[48] Differences in policy among the Central Asian republics stimulated the wealthy to protect their wealth by crossing borders and in this case also provoked ethnic tension, pitting Uzbek dehqons against Kyrgyz landowners.

Yolchivoy (b. 1922) was the son of a Kyrgyz transportation worker from a Fergana Valley village that bordered Kyrgyzstan. His father, he said, owned one camel that he used to convey goods to market; he also worked as a mardikor and did not own land. "My father was poor, and he did not have his own house; we lived in our relatives' houses." The interviewer asked whether Yolchivoy's father followed a nomadic or sedentary lifestyle. "He lived in one place, doing that kind of work for a living, staying in one place to earn something to eat. That was the life he knew." Then another relative who was present at Yolchivoy's interview provided a different image of their Kyrgyz kin in Quvasoy, telling of parents who owned ten to fifteen hectares: "My father and mother were made quloqs and driven out [of Quvasoy]: they came here [to Shahrixon] to hide until things calmed down, but things here were very poor."[49] Yolchivoy's father came from the same household but claimed no land or wealth, instead identifying as a mardikor.

In the Namangan region, where land reform was initiated early in 1925 and moved quickly, there were complaints of improper land seizure. In February 1926, the local land commission undertook review of more than one hundred claims from those who said their land had been seized illegally. In a collection of documents on thirty-eight land claims in Sardob District, ten plots were registered in the names of women. It was unusual for women to own land, as the norms of inheritance around Fergana usually provided land to sons, while daughters were given moveable property such as house furnishings or livestock. The ten women claimants from this small region all had names that included a status reference, such as xo'ja, *tura*, or mullah, suggesting that they came from families of men who owned land and had religious status or positions. The women's land reform claims could be seen as evidence that the women capitalized on a Women's Division effort to put land into the hands of women, but the fact that land reform directives explicitly targeted mullahs and other male religious leaders for expropriation makes it seem likely that their land registrations were the result of a husband or father's attempt to protect property that otherwise would be seized from imams or qazis by transferring it to family members.[50]

Successfully Claiming Poverty

Working for others became the key criteria for recognition as an exploited member of the rural proletariat. Dehqons who earned a substantial portion of their living as sharecroppers or mardikors asserted that as their class identity, even if they also owned land. During land reform, this could result in gaining redistributed land, and later, during collectivization, identifying as a sharecropper or mardikor guaranteed that a dehqon could enter a kolkhoz and would not be declared a quloq. Yoqubjon, who was raised in Shahimardon, said:

> My father had no land. My paternal uncle had some, not much. My father's father was a poor man who worked in the gates of the rich as a chorikor, a servant. They called him "Ermat the mardikor." He worked all the time as a mardikor, even when he went to Tashkent. On the rich man's land he had an agreement to work from early spring until fall. He was paid with a percentage of the crop that he grew, not in money. On the rich man's land they planted cotton but mostly wheat.

Hamza Hakimzoda, a well-known Uzbek poet who was famously murdered, or martyred, in 1929, initiated land reform in Shahimardon in 1927: "He went to Shohimardon and founded the Ortoq kolkhoz. They took the lands of all xo'jas and religious people in Shohimardon." Rather than distribute land as individual holdings, Hamza established several collective farms, and Yoqubjon's father joined immediately.[51]

During land reform, government aid to those newly endowed with land and to those who owned small amounts of land came with strings attached: to obtain seed loans, they were supposed to agree to some form of cooperation, such as forming a *shirkat*. A shirkat might be a temporary association of men working together in planting or harvesting or a group that was granted land for reclamation on condition they worked newly irrigated fields together.[52] Incentives to join a shirkat included favorable access to reclamation lands, to newly distributed farm implements, to low-cost draft animals, and to seed advances. Xoji (b. 1920) told of his father, who had no land of his own and worked for the rich as a mardikor in Bukhara Province. In 1928 he received redistributed land, but Xoji perceived that this was no gift from the government. His father and other landless dehqons were each given half a hectare, on the condition that they turned it from wasteland into productive farmland. "They opened that land themselves. It was unused, and they dug it up, corrected it, scattered seed, and planted it themselves. They planted cotton and sold it, filling one or two sacks, loading them on a donkey, and taking them to Bukhara to earn money for bread."[53]

Ibroyim (b. 1917) described his father as a brickmaker and sharecropper who gained land during land reform. When asked about land reform, he said:

> Before collectivization, there started to be shirkats. There was a little yellow notebook [to record member contracts], and if you had five tanobs of land, we said we would plant two tanobs with cotton, and on the rest we planted other things. When you took the cotton to the factory, someone would weigh it and take it and give you money for what you brought in on your cart. After that, in 1928 or 1929, collectivization started. Other than that, the shirkat did not tell you what to do, but you had to plant two of the five tanobs in cotton.

Zanca tried to clarify: "So you were forced to grow cotton?" Ibroyim replied, "You had to plant it and turn it in or else pay the tax by some other means. The Qoshchi union helped, planting cotton in exchange for money and selling seed."[54]

Land was usually distributed to those who already worked as dehqons, but Umriniso said that her father, a militia member in Fergana City, obtained nine hectares that were taken from the rich in land reform. "He wanted to plant cotton on that land, and he gathered people." He received financing from the government and from the cotton oil factory and used that to purchase oxen, horses, and carts and to start a cooperative to plant cotton. After several years, they turned it into a kolkhoz.[55]

In the Fergana Valley, land was redistributed in one- or two-hectare plots, but in other regions, norms of landowning were higher, especially in regions lacking in irrigation. Umrqul, from the Bekabod region, where there was a dearth of irrigation in the 1920s, said: "Before the revolution, he [my father] did not have land. Not all people have land. From our Begavot to Qiyot, all the land belonged to a Tajik man whose name was Umar Zavod. After the revolution, they took his land and gave it to people as individual property." Umrqul's father and grandfather worked on Umar Zavod's land as chorikors, "for one-fourth of what they raised." When Umar Zavod's lands were seized, Umrqul's father received fourteen hectares, as did each of his brothers: "A group of people came at that time and divided the land. I was a child at the time. After they gave us the land, my father planted apple and apricot trees on three to four hectares. To'ra's family started raising livestock. Yoqip planted all his land using a shovel. At that time, they did not have a pair of oxen or tractors. . . . Then they bought an ox, and someone else did as well. They all helped each other, and using a pair of oxen, they were able to plow each other's land."[56] Umrqul's father and his uncles formed a shirkat, joining efforts to plant cotton, and they also became members of a purchasing cooperative run by the Qoshchi union.

During land reform, a successful claim that one was poor and landless could lead to gaining land from the state land fund or directly from the wealthy. Some land was distributed to dehqons who already owned land, and some of it went to people like Umriniso's father, who previously had not farmed but who was enthusiastic about starting a cotton-growing collective. Receiving land frequently was tied to joining some sort of cooperative and to growing cotton. The cooperatives or collectives did not own land collectively. They did take out loans together, perform work together on their individual land and on land belonging to the rich, and make contracts for cotton production. These collectives convinced their members of the state's goodwill toward the poor and turned the members' discourse of dependency (working in the gates of the rich) into the basis for identification with a social class: the poor. Land reform thus opened a cleavage between the poor and the rich, laying the foundation for collectivization's harsher forms of class warfare.

Hayitboy's telescoped story of land reform, like many others cited in this chapter, passes over events that may have involved local hostility and violence, of the kind that Abduqayum alluded to, saying that people beat each other, or that Qurbon A. told of, with the rich burning down the houses of the activist poor. The historian Bakhtiyar Babajanov, examining fatwas endorsing land reform that were issued by pro-Communist ulama in the mid-1920s, posits that Uzbekistan's Party leadership commissioned these new interpretations of Islamic law on land because land reform was not producing revolutionary results. Babajanov attributes dehqon reluctance to seize land from the rich to their respect for Islamic law, which he sees as standing clearly on the side of private property.[57] That reluctance is nowhere in evidence in interviewee accounts, but reports from the time of land reform showed that the newly designated poor did not immediately embrace taking land from the rich. The casualness with which Hayitboy related the expropriation and exile of the wealthy and his repeated differentiation of his interests from theirs may reflect a generational perspective. He was a teenaged, orphaned farm laborer who had nothing to lose and everything to gain in land reform: in other words, the perfect recruit for a rural revolution. Older sharecroppers who had houses, children, and long-standing relationships of dependence on their richer neighbors may indeed have been deterred from radicalism by those relationships or by their Islamic convictions, or they may not have believed that joining in land reform seizures served their self-interest.

Reports from the 1920s give mixed impressions of land reform as a successful step toward mobilizing a rural proletariat for revolutionary ends or as a tepid half measure that did not generate mass enthusiasm. A 1920s effort to measure the effects of land reform offered numbers of rural households who became owners of land or added to their holdings by noting, for example, that in 1925 36,000 households in the Fergana Valley received land. This seems a small number, some 5 percent of the rural households. But that was in one area, in one year, while land reform continued in the Fergana Valley and across all of Uzbekistan until 1928 with thousands more redistributions of land every year. The same report cited 252,270 members of land reclamation societies, whose new farms were the product of their own labor on state-owned lands allotted to them in land reform.[58] The politicization of rural identity in land reform also drove some of the wealthy to preemptively reregister lands to family members or dependents.

Dehqon lives changed in the mid-1920s due to Soviet policies that created new republics with new boundaries and that established new categories for belonging and exclusion by nationality and by social class. Land reform was a process that depended on the state's ability to reach into the countryside and reorganize local government. Regional centers organized land committees that assessed individual holdings, stripping the wealthy of land above the local norm and redistributing it those who owned little. The process turned what had been simple descriptions of a household's resources and relationships into class and national categories through which to make claims. Those who could validate their own belonging to the poor and landless stood to benefit by becoming owners of a hectare or two of land, while those who could not escape community identification as wealthy by such means as voluntary redistribution or who were landowning merchants or imams faced confiscation of some or all of their land. These politics of economic inclusion and exclusion left out the middle dehqons, but everyone was affected by national-territorial delimitation and the creation of an Uzbek SSR, which made ethnicity into nationality and national differences into forms of social capital that Uzbeks could employ to more effect than non-Uzbeks, establishing a lasting rural hierarchy.

The Moscow-centered USSR fostered colonial economic policies to reinforce Uzbekistan's position as a cotton-producing periphery, but our questions focused on what interviewees saw and felt in their own daily lives, not on macro-level analysis of colonial economics. In the selected narratives about gaining or losing land in land reform, each narrator spoke from a standpoint that reflected the economic conditions of his or her family in the 1920s, the changes they experienced, and the discursive battles that the Communist Party launched. Those who had worked as mardikor and who benefitted from state seizure and redistribution of land stressed their own service or exploitation in the gates of the rich as the factor that animated their support for this Party-led reversal of fortunes. Those who had owned more land than their family could utilize asserted a disposition of kindness and generosity toward their dependent workers, the sharecroppers and mardikors, saying that they had not really exploited others but had treated the less fortunate with kindness. These standpoints developed much sharper contours after mass collectivization began, when those who had been called wealthy were named as quloqs, dispossessed, arrested, and exiled. The contrasting standpoints of the sharecropper versus the landowner preexisted the revolution. In land reform, the Party's activists cultivated those differences, turning sharecroppers into state supporters though redistribution of land, provision of credit, support for cooperatives, and by politicizing identity.

4
AGITATING FOR THE KOLKHOZ

Agricultural collectivization came to Uzbekistan not because Uzbek dehqons thought that joining lands and production regimes would be a better way to farm but because, in November 1929, Stalin and the Communist Party of the USSR declared mass collectivization. Yet in practice, collectivization demanded many agents to convince dehqons that their futures would improve, to collect their signatures or thumbprints, to provide loans and goods, and to organize farmwork in new ways. As some scholars emphasize, the Soviet experiment materialized through mass participation and mobilization.[1] Respondents who remembered collectivization's first moments talked about agitation in their communities and, in a few cases, their own mobilizing actions. Many of the oral history respondents said that their families joined collective farms voluntarily, in response to incentives and to invitations to join made by agitators with whom they identified, "our Uzbeks."

One of those agitators, a man named Pirmuhammedov, was the author of a handwritten report I found in the Central State Archive in Tashkent. Handwritten documents in Arabic script Uzbek are not abundant among collectivization-related archival collections; if the information was deemed important, such reports were retained in their Russian translation. The document is a mundane day-to-day diary of his activities in November 1930, when he traveled around Kermina (today's Nurota), Katta Qurg'on, Jizzax, Narpay, and Juma-Ikramov Districts, holding meetings in regional centers with Raykoms and with the Kolkhoz Union and meetings in rural communities with kolkhoz members. A typical description of his actions went like this: "On 13 November, we went to Bahrin

Village, where we posed the issue of collectivizing, and twenty-seven people from that place submitted their petitions to enter. On 14 November, Qizil Boqcha kolkhoz was organized in the necessary way, and then I showed a movie.... On November 21 . . . we uncovered three Bosmachi/boy/*mushtumzo'r* [oppressor] and expelled them from the kolkhoz. Then I showed a movie." The odd phrasing "Bosmachi/boy/mushtumzo'r" was Pirmuhammedov's own, and it is indicative of the mixed ways that activists identified opponents and enemies, as rebels or rich men or oppressors. The word *quloq* had not yet become the standard exclusionary term, as is explained in the next chapter. Pirmuhammedov laconically lists excluding oppressors from the kolkhoz beside showing films in villages. In many of the interviews cited in this chapter, interviewees were similarly laconic, or even ironic, in their stories of the ways that agitators invited the poor, pressured the middle dehqons, and excluded the wealthy from newly formed kolkhozes.

Pirmuhammedov wrote: "When the necessary supplies are provided, organizing kolkhozes takes place quickly. Therefore, leadership must be shown in providing those supplies. Right now, there are kolkhoz sections that are not working, and help must be sent quickly. On November 15 after looking over the supplies, we returned from Kermina for a day." What were these necessary supplies? From the stories of interviewees, they were food, oil, seed loans or advances, and such goods as cotton fabrics that served as rewards for joining and pay for working in a newly founded kolkhoz. Pirmuhammedov repeatedly noted that the lack of delivery of supplies deterred sign-ups and slowed work on kolkhozes.

The agitator listed the topics that he discussed in his meetings with dehqons:

> We held a meeting on speeding up cotton picking and forming kolkhozes and about fall planting.... On November 18 we were at the regional kolkhoz union, and because there were people who knew Uzbek in every village, I was able to carry on every kind of work with the kolkhoz members.... On November 24 we held a meeting right at 9 o'clock, where we talked about kolkhozes finishing the cotton picking quickly and starting fall planting, and we made a declaration that those who had stolen from the kolkhoz would be sent to trial. After the meeting we showed a movie and then immediately returned to the city.

Pirmuhammedov noted that thousands of petitions were coming into Raykom offices; in addition to petitions to form kolkhozes, there were denunciations of opponents and calls from kolkhoz directors for supplies. However, these petitions sat, unread, on Raykom office desks:

> My overall view is that many issues are lying unaddressed in the Kermina, Narpay, Katta Qurg'on, Juma-Ikromov, and Jizzax regions

because of lack of knowledge of the Uzbek language. Only in the Narpay and Jizzax regions are the first secretaries Uzbeks. Except for the directors, everyone else who is supposed to read petitions and act on them is someone who does not know Uzbek. The papers that come in from the kolkhozes therefore are lying there. They are not acted on because the secretaries who are from among the European comrades do not know Uzbek.[2]

Recent studies of collectivization focus heavily on dekulakization and opposition to the kolkhoz, arguing that collectivization was state violence against peasants, who joined kolkhozes out of fear.[3] Coercion, threats, and making dehqons into quloqs all were important factors in collectivization, addressed in a subsequent chapter, but coercion does not fully explain how collectivization came about. As the historian Mary Buckley writes, peasants had interests, "varied ones at that, and ... they might act accordingly," in ways that changed their circumstances, regardless of whether they understood the Communist Party's ideology of rural transformation.[4] This chapter explores interviewee remembrances of the agitators who organized their kolkhozes, focusing on what narrators recalled about promises, incentives, and persuasive discourses, as well as about threats against holdouts and the division of communities into kolkhoz joiners, refusers, and the excluded.

Land reform had turned identification as "the poor" into something of a category of practice. "The poor" were no longer so poor, having become owners of several hectares each, a result of land reform; instead, "the poor" were those who eagerly joined a kolkhoz at the first opportunity. Many of them had previously joined groups that they referred to as artels or shirkats, for the purpose of obtaining seed loans, making cotton contracts, reclaiming land, or working on land owned by the rich. The rich were no longer so rich, either; dehqons who previously had owned forty hectares might have retained a fourth or a half, but some still relied on hiring labor. One argument that emerges from interviewee recollections about the process of organizing a kolkhoz is that identification with those agitating for collectivization, "Uzbeks like us," played an important role in early decisions to sign up to join collective farms. Respondents talked about identifying with the agitators due to class, nationality, locality, and shared language. They also emphasized their family's interests at the time of collectivization and what they felt they were giving up or gaining by joining a kolkhoz. Many who remembered their families as early opponents of collectivization associated the process with outsiders and with incomprehensible Russians in particular.

Mass Collectivization

A grain crisis in the Soviet Union in 1928 became the catalyst for forced mass collectivization in 1929. Stalin used a shortfall in the amount of grain that peasants sold to the state to create a politically driven, violent campaign of grain requisitioning.[5] According to Stalin, "emergency measures" of forced grain extraction were required to feed factory workers in the expanding industrial sector and so that the state could sell grain internationally to purchase industrial machinery, build tractor factories, and modernize the economy. In November 1929, after purging Communist Party members who had supported a mixed economy that provided peasants with incentives rather than forcing them to increase production, Stalin initiated mass collectivization in the USSR's primary grain-growing regions. Peasants were told to join collective farms and to seize land, implements, and livestock from the wealthier peasants in their midst. Henceforth, through the kolkhoz, peasants were coerced to plant crops according to government plans and to turn the kolkhoz harvest over to government collection points at government prices.[6] The first pronouncement of mass collectivization targeted the Soviet Union's core grain-growing regions, did not mention cotton, and indicated that collectivizing other sectors was not an immediate priority.

If the purpose of rapid collectivization was to give the state control over grain, what was the reason that forced mass collectivization in cotton-producing Uzbekistan began at the same time as in the core grain growing regions? The historian Christian Teichmann writes that the 1928 Five-Year Plan set aggressive targets for increasing cotton production so that the Soviet Union would command its own supply rather than rely on imports. The plan called for more than

TABLE 4.1 Expanding cotton planting and harvest in Uzbekistan, 1925–1936

YEAR	1925	1926	1927	1928	1929	1930	1931	1932	1933	1934	1935	1936
Thousand hectares planted in cotton	371	409	483	599	639	883	1,010	1,027	989	952	954	944
Cotton harvest, raw weight, thousand tons	375	358	474	543	575	744	755	804	860	855	1,107	1,549

Source: V. A. Bektimirova, ed., *Narodnoe Khoziaistvo Uzbekskoi SSR za 50 let* (Tashkent: Izdatel'stvo Uzbekistana, 1967), 102–103.

doubling the area of land planted in cotton in the Central Asian republics and southern Kazakhstan.[7]

The Cotton Committee, economic planners, and the Politburo exaggerated the degree to which the USSR imported raw cotton, framing import dependence as a problem demanding a fast solution.[8] The First Five-Year Plan for Uzbekistan anticipated vast increases in cotton based on individual farming, cotton contracts, and credit to cooperatives and planned for 10 percent of the dehqons to join kolkhozes and *sovkhozes* [state farms].[9] The president of Uzbekistan's soviets, Yo'ldosh Oxunboboyev, gave a speech in early autumn 1929, referring to the goal of cotton autarky for the Soviet Union:

> Not just thousands but millions are paid into the hands of the rich in Egypt and America for raw materials, especially for cotton. Our gold, our money, is flowing into their pockets. By producing our own raw materials to build our heavy industry and increase light industry, we can become successful on our own, rather than obeying the commands of the capitalists. Central Asia, including Uzbekistan and the republics of the Caucasus, should provide our cotton and raw materials for the Union's industries.[10]

Although he championed increasing cotton production for the greater good of the Soviet economy, Oxunboboyev made no mention of mass collectivization. Nor did he emphasize that small-scale collectivization efforts were underway in Uzbekistan. The leadership in Uzbekistan followed the line of thinking that informed the Five-Year Plan, that strengthening small-holding deqhons would achieve the USSR's cotton goals and bring prosperity to Uzbekistan.

In November 1929, in a speech known as "The Great Break," Stalin declared that collectivization was becoming a mass movement. Several weeks later, the Central Committee voted to increase collectivization's pace, calling for total (*sploshnaia*) collectivization in regions of intensive grain production. Stalin followed this with a December 1929 speech calling for "the liquidation of the kulaks as a class."[11] Liquidation was a change from prior policy: every wealthy peasant was to be entirely dispossessed. On January 5, 1930, the Central Committee published a decree titled "The Speed of Collectivization," which listed core graingrowing regions of Russia and Ukraine but did not name Uzbekistan as a site for rapid, mass collectivization.[12]

Following the Central Committee's November meeting at which Stalin called for rapid collectivization, Uzbekistan's Communist Party Executive Committee, feeling the pressure of an early November purge of Communist Party members, put forth its own similar declaration: "The UzSSR's agriculture, which is distinguished by its high marketability and commercial nature, heavy labor costs and high costs of capital input, and producing a crop that is primarily going straight into industrial supply, is an especially auspicious base for collectivization, all the way up through complete socialization of the labor process, of means of production, and processes of distribution."[13] By the end of the First Five-Year Plan, kolkhozes and sovkhozes should produce 60 percent of Uzbekistan's cotton crop, and other sectors would not yet be collectivized. New kolkhozes were to be organized "so that all of the lands in regions of *mass land provision*, carried out in 1929–1930, are fully used by kolkhozes, and so that kolkhozes will be founded on lands newly opened to agriculture."[14] By "regions of mass land provision," the committee meant the districts where poor dehqons had obtained land through land reform, redistribution, and land reclamation. Even in those districts, only a few kolkhozes had been organized. However, there were several hundred thousand beneficiaries of land reform who thought of themselves as "the poor" and of the boylar as their enemies. The Communist Party relied on these self-identified poor to be favorably disposed toward dispossessing the boylar and incorporating their lands into collective farms.[15]

Uzbekistan's Communist Party activists immediately began organizing kolkhozes in Uzbekistan, even before the party officially declared which districts would become the focus of "total" collectivization. In these districts a collectivization campaign was to take place quickly, as opposed to lower-priority or remote agricultural districts, where collectivization would occur later. As the historian Sheila Fitzpatrick notes in her study of collectivization in Russia, in regions where peasants had traditionally belonged to a peasant commune (*mir*) and where privately owned land was the result of recent separation from those communes, "mass collectivization" meant collectivizing whole villages in a single decision: "The kolkhoz became in effect . . . the successor to the peasant land commune as the possessor and custodian of village lands."[16]

But in Uzbekistan there was no preexisting commune; instead, collectivization, as respondents told us over and over, proceeded through agitation and active recruitment of individual dehqons. Even the poor who participated in artels or shirkats owned land privately and made individual decisions to join immediately or to hold out. Multiple tiny kolkhozes would form within one community, usually made up of households who owned the smallest plots of land, while those with more land continued farming individually until they succumbed to incentives, pressures, or threats. Mass collectivization was a challenging, contested process that demanded repeated agitation drives, such as the one Pirmuhammedov was leading in November 1930.

In late December 1929, attention in Moscow turned to cotton, with Grigorii Kaminsky, director of the All-Russia Kolkhoz Center, speaking for the commission that determined the speed of collectivization, proposing that cotton-

TABLE 4.2 Pace of collectivization in Uzbekistan

DATES	1928	1/20/1932*	1932	1937
Number of kolkhozes	867	9,653	10,300	9,201
Number of households in kolkhozes, in thousands	10.1	870.7 (of 936.1)	726.9	687.7
Average number of households per kolkhoz	14	90	60	75
% of peasant households collectivized	1.2	69.2	81.7	95
% of agricultural land collectivized	1.2		68.1	99.4

Source: Rizaev, *Sotsialisticheskoe sel'skoe khoziaistvo Uzbekistana*, 29; * column source, "Svodka o khode kollektivizatsii po raionam UzSSR na 20/1 32g," O'zRMDA, f R-95, op. 2, d. 186, ll. 21–23.

growing regions should be 75 percent collectivized within five years.[17] On January 1, 1930, Uzbekistan's Executive Committee decreed that private trade in cotton was forbidden, criminalizing dehqons who stored their harvest in hope of selling at the bazaar for more than the state contract price.[18] As happened elsewhere in the USSR, the speedy creation of kolkhozes stimulated open, violent opposition. Uzbekistan's Communist Party envisioned rapid collectivization in cotton regions and a much slower transition in Qashqa Daryo, Bukhara, and Xorazm Provinces, which were primary grain-producing regions. In fact, collective farms were rapidly organized among cotton and grain producers. Party activists did seem "dizzy with success," so determined to demonstrate their loyalty that they signed up members for kolkhozes in a mad scramble, not content to just meet the state's overblown plan for rapid collectivization. Hastily and nominally organized kolkhozes fell apart in the spring of 1930 but then were more carefully reestablished. By late 1931, Uzbekistan had far exceeded its goals for mass collectivization. In the expanded list of districts slated for total collectivization, more than 85 percent of households were enrolled in a kolkhoz.[19]

Defining what collectivization meant and did not mean for dehqons in Uzbekistan will help to explain why collectivization could occur so rapidly. An image of resettlement or forced sedentarization may dominate our understandings of collectivization in Central Asia. Collectivizing Kazakhs began with expropriating their livestock so that impoverishment, starvation, and mass deaths forced the surviving nomads to settle.[20] Entire regions of Tajikistan were developed through large-scale water engineering projects and mass resettlements, bringing highlanders down to river basins and turning herders into cotton farmers.[21] And in the better known aspects of collectivization, collectivization meant forced seizures of grain in Ukraine, in the Volga region, and in the North Caucasus, producing mass starvation in what the historian Lynne Viola calls a "war on the peasantry."[22] However, most of Uzbekistan's dehqons stayed in their homes and on their lands: they were not resettled.[23] When collectivization began, less than 2 percent of dehqons belonged to a kolkhoz or worked for a sovkhoz, but 78 percent of dehqons lived and farmed in districts that already produced some cotton; 9 percent lived in wheat-producing districts.[24] Collectivization did not change the kinds of crops that dehqons raised, although the proportion of irrigated land planted in cotton swelled, at the expense of other crops. Collectivization changed dehqons' modes of working, taking away their decision-making. It was a proletarianization: working for the kolkhoz was a poorly paid job.

Dehqons in the cotton zones designated for mass collectivization were not assumed to be grain producers, and unlike what happened to the peasants of Russia or the herders from Kazakhstan, collectivization agents did not seize their grain. Instead, as many interviewees stressed in their recollections, collectivization meant receiving goods: wheat, oil, seed, sugar, and cloth. Dehqons from a village were called to a meeting where activists told whoever came that they should form a kolkhoz and asked them to sign a petition either with a signature or a thumbprint. Those who signed up agreed to join their fields and farm together, not their houses or personal garden plots, and contribute draft animals if they owned any. Those who did not sign up kept farming individually, but by 1935 the constant pressures, increasing taxes, and threats drove almost every individual farmer to give up and join a kolkhoz.

Learning about Collectivization

Although party documents held in archives and published decades later reveal that the Communist Party of Uzbekistan followed the Stalinist line, made swift decisions for rapid collectivization, and instructed party organs at the Raykom level to initiate collectivization, those decisions were not made evident to the Uzbek public at the time. The leading Uzbek-language newspaper, *Qizil O'zbekiston*, covered the Uzbekistan Central Committee's meetings and speeches in late November but did not mention rapid collectivization; instead there were comments about creating the right economic and social conditions for kolkhozes.[25] A December 8, 1929, article decried weak efforts at awakening the party's rural allies, the chorikor and the poor, and called for striking a hard blow against the mushtumzo'r (oppressor), but Uzbekistan's press had featured those sorts of ideas throughout 1929.[26] December issues of the newspaper included reports that an attentive reader might have understood as a policy change: kolkhozes were being organized in name only; boylar were deviously joining kolkhozes. Articles denounced the boylar and mushtumzo'r for holding back their cotton. "The quloq, boy, and mushtumzo'r must be clearly understood, and they and their hangers-on must be decisively and mercilessly marginalized from the kolkhozes."[27] On January 28, 1930, more than a month after mass collectivization started, *Qizil O'zbekiston* published the USSR Central Committee's declaration of mass collectivization.[28]

In Uzbekistan's villages, word of collectivization spread swiftly, not by official proclamations or the press but via party members in Raykoms, local Komsomol members, leaders of village soviets, and Unions of the Poor. When we asked respondents how they first learned about collectivization, they made clear that it was by word of mouth. Most of them mentioned the rumors that swept across Uzbekistan and elsewhere in the USSR that collectivization would mean everyone would have to live under one roof, sleep under one blanket, eat out of one pot, and even share wives. We asked about agitation and about who first organized their kolkhoz, questions that led to responses with detailed memories of meetings, early kolkhoz leaders, threats, and promises.

Agitating

> INTERVIEWER HURSHIDA: Were there agitators at that time who held a meeting and told people if they joined the kolkhoz, it will be good?
>
> RESPONDENT OLMAJON (B. 1903): Yes, they had a meeting, and everyone held up their arm and said we will become a kolkhoz.
>
> HURSHIDA: Who were they, Uzbeks or Russians?
>
> OLMAJON: No, they came from Tashkent. They said if you will become a kolkhoz, we won't force you. When they asked who will join, everyone said, 'We will.' They gave out a lot of flour, oil, cotton cloth, and rock sugar to everyone. They gave thirty-five kilos of oil to each person.
>
> HURSHIDA: Thirty-five kilos of oil to a family?
>
> OLMAJON: Yes, not to a family but to every single individual.
>
> HURSHIDA: How long did they give that out for? A month? A year?
>
> OLMAJON: When this kolkhoz was founded and when we entered, then they gave out fifteen kilos and twenty kilos of oil. They brought flour and gave it out and cotton cloth that was worth sixty or seventy *tiyin* [kopeks] a meter. High-quality cloth was worth a ruble a meter at that time.

Olmajon (b. 1903) was a talkative one-hundred-year-old woman, a proud dehqon who had earned prizes for her kolkhoz labor. She had grown up working with her father as a cart driver in the gates of the rich. However, she was not poor when collectivization started: "Working with my father that way, we became people who had livestock." They owned land that her father and a group of eighteen men had reclaimed. She ambiguously identified the agitators as "from Tashkent," but she spoke as someone who attended the meeting, listened, and signed up, and she knew no Russian, so it is likely that her Tashkent agitators were Uzbeks, not Russians. Hurshida, the interviewer, found her claim about being rewarded with oil for joining the kolkhoz so excessive that she repeated her questions, checking to see whether Olmajon had merely misspoken. Olmajon stayed with her story, reinforcing the impression that she and her husband felt rewarded for joining the kolkhoz. Nothing that she said in the rest of the interview made her seem to be a teller of tall tales, but the fact that her father became the kolkhoz's first director suggests that her household may have received more favors than others.[29]

Like Olmajon, oral history respondents from across Uzbekistan recalled attending organizational meetings. They talked about the agitators from their own communities and from the Raykoms who told them about collectivization; and they remembered the community members who were enthusiastic and signed on immediately. They analyzed motives: Who joined early, and why? Who tried not to join, and why? Through their words, we see the ways that rural Uzbeks fitted themselves into class categories (poor, middle, rich), judged whether to join according to their material interests, and identified with the agitators who promoted collectivization or viewed the agitators and the whole collectivization scheme as a foreign imposition.

The Enthusiasts

Umrinoso (b. 1914) told about how her father acquired about nine hectares of land in the Fergana Valley from a dispossessed landowner during the 1926 land reform; he then sought out state support in exchange for planting cotton. She said: "We planted cotton; we formed an artel. When the cotton was ready, they put it on a cart.... They put a red flag on it and announced that a caravan was coming and brought it to the factory." Umriniso's father was a Uyghur member of the Communist Party who served in the Red militia against the Bosmachis. He recruited dehqons, and in 1928, before coercive pressure from above to collectivize, he turned the artel into a kolkhoz. Umriniso said: "Nobody wanted to join. Very poor people were selected, and when they worked five days on the kolkhoz, they were given a sack of flour, a bucket of oil, and a bucket of sugar per family. Then people became accustomed to that.... They gave a cow to the poor families. It supported the poor. Some poor people who got cows sold them and then had problems with their livelihood.... When other people learned about the flour, oil, and other things, they decided to enter the kolkhoz." Umriniso's father persuaded poor dehqons to join by offering goods. Although Umriniso's father and the poor entered the kolkhoz willingly, "people who were middle dehqons did not want to join" and did so only after the government "took their belongings" so that "they did not have a choice."[30]

The contours of Umriniso's account are echoed in many others: the poor were drawn into the kolkhoz by abstract and tangible benefits, but better-off individual farmers joined only under duress. Rural supporters of collectivization included Uzbek Communist Party members like Umriniso's father and Komsomol members. More important, however, were the large numbers of beneficiaries of two 1920s rural initiatives: land reform, discussed in the previous chapter, and credit. In 1929, approximately one-third of Uzbekistan's nearly 600,000 cotton-planting households received credit designated for the poor.[31] The cooperatives distributed credit in the form of advances at the beginning of the planting season, in kind (80 percent) far more than in cash (20 percent): cotton seed for planting and grain or flour to feed co-op members' families.[32] Individuals and groups (artels) signed contracts to obtain credit, in exchange for planting and raising cotton and selling it to the Cotton Committee for a set price at the end of the season.[33] Patterns established between 1925 and 1929—taking land from the rich, offering credit through cooperatives to artels and individuals to plant cotton under contract, and providing food advances—constituted the essential foundation for mass collectivization. Many respondents remembered the distribution of food advances as a key incentive for joining the kolkhoz. Indeed, Uzbekistan's Communist Party leaders, facing antikolkhoz demonstrations and rapid dissolutions of kolkhozes in February and March 1930, used the immediate distribution of food advances to maintain and reorganize kolkhozes.[34]

Sharofutdin, born in the 1910s near Fergana, belonged to a family that identified as poor and joined the kolkhoz at its founding:

> There were no Russians among the activists, only our people. There were no agitators, but the Komsomol carried out that work.... The kolkhoz here was established as an artel, by a man named Isayev, a partisan.[35] He invited people to the teahouse and said, "Comrades, I'll make you a kolkhoz. Let's become a kolkhoz. We'll collect everything." And some people said they would join, while others would not. They gave flour and oil to those who entered. And they got used to that. They gave each one a bag of flour and a kilo of oil. And they said to the others: "Why don't you join? They are giving out flour and oil."

The rich people who were invited to the first meeting joined, but those who were not invited did not. And some who were invited would not join. They said it openly when it was being organized. There were about ten rich men in the village. All of their lands were seized by that time. They took fifteen or twenty hectares from the rich. They had good lands, livestock, seized by mardikors and the poor.

Those who tried to continue as individual farmers eventually could no longer hire workers to pick cotton, and "they were forced to join."[36] According to Sharofutdin's recollection, for his family, a distribution of flour and oil and the ability to work lands taken from the rich were sufficient inducement to join the collective farm.

Musaxon (b. 1910) was the son of a butcher who had owned some land, but Musaxon was orphaned young and inherited nothing. During collectivization, he became a kolkhoz agitator in his own region, near Rishton in the Fergana Valley. "The activists for the collective farm were all local people; no one else participated—no Russians or Tatars. There were none in Rishton.... The people who entered were those who lived there, and so were the agitators.... I would go around door-to-door gathering people. There were people who wouldn't let you in, who would say, 'What are you doing here?' There were people who opposed collectivization and those who swore their allegiance to it."[37] Attempts to persuade individuals to attend a collectivization meeting might succeed or fail, and merely sharing an identity and a community with the agitator was not enough to persuade everyone.

Berdiqul (b. 1920), whose family lived in a remote mountain village in Nurota District, recalled collectivization as beneficial to the poor and coercive only to the rich: "Then we witnessed that all. The rich people's belongings were taken for the kolkhoz.... There were meetings that announced kolkhoz formation.... Poor people did not have anything to give to the kolkhoz; the kolkhoz was formed for their good fortune.... In the meetings people talked about the hardships that rich people gave to ordinary people. Poor people gained many rights because of the kolkhoz."[38] Berdiqul's father died just as collectivization began, and his mother, who identified with the poor and joined the kolkhoz, told him about meetings where agitators promised that the kolkhoz would improve members' lives. In Berdiqul's assessment, the kolkhoz provided security for his family.

Turdiboy (b. 1921) was the child of a man who was landless and who moved his family from Kokand to a place near Andijon, where community members said: "'These people have children but no place to live, so let's divide up the waqf lands to them,' and they gave us two-tenths of a hectare." Their poverty led to social exclusion: "When we went to our neighbors to ask the children to play, they shouted at my older sister and me, 'Go away, go away—my child won't play with you.'" In 1930, Turdiboy's father, a mardikor, joined a small kolkhoz made up of about fifteen men. Turdiboy was too young to have cared what was said to convince his father to join, but he was impressed with the rewards for joining: "When people formed a kolkhoz, those who entered were given bags and bags of flour, sugar, and oil and filled up with other food products. There was no paperwork either. If so and so said, 'I'm a kolkhoz member,' he was given a bag of flour, a bag of sugar, two or three buckets of oil. They took all of the best land from the rich and gave them the worst land."[39]

Nonviolent Coercion

In his Navoiy Province village, Rustam (b. 1912), the son of a merchant who also owned land, recalled: "Collectivization was forced, though not for everyone. They would invite people to join, but told them, 'If you don't join, we will make you a quloq and drive you out.' It was forced. They gave their water, land, oxen, sheep, and camels. Before that, Nurota's people were rich." Rustam was a teenager when the first wave of dispossessions started, affecting his father:

> My father had a chest for tea, and they came and searched it, seeing whether it was good or bad, and they took it away. They searched around father's things and found a gold coin or two. . . . A couple of Russian-looking youths took down notes of what was brought in, sheep, goats. . . . I sat there listening while they counted up sheep and goats. . . . Rajab o'g'li collected five thousand sheep in 1927 and formed the first sovkhoz at Qizilcha, with sheep taken from the rich. This was a good outcome for the poor. At that time, the kolkhoz did not pay money, and those who went to work there received wheat. . . . All of my relatives joined the kolkhoz, and so did I.

Although Rustam remembered Russian-looking youths as the officials who seized property from the rich, he named collectivization's organizers as Uzbeks: Rajab o'g'li and another Rustam, who was a local organizer of the kolkhoz in 1929, induced the poor to join by distributing wheat and livestock. Things became violent immediately. "And they [opponents] killed the [state's] leading representative, Rustam, in 1929, killed him and dragged his body to the irrigation channel and dumped it there. My father, uncle, and older brother were out irrigating the crops when the water stopped flowing. They searched and saw this man's body lying in the channel, head missing." Village soviet members called in the militia, which arrested numerous opponents of collectivization, sentencing some to death.[40]

Temir (b. 1920), whose story was told in the previous chapter, was the son of a wealthy dehqon who voluntarily redistributed his own land and joined a collective to which he contributed part of his land and one of his horses. The collective, which Temir described as not yet a kolkhoz, had eighteen households, and his father was put in charge of collecting the wheat from members to fulfill their wheat contract. In 1934, an Uzbek man came from the regional center and held a meeting to convince the collective's members to join a nearby kolkhoz. "My father was the executive member of the village committee, and he had no choice but to participate in that meeting. A government representative, he could not have said he wouldn't join." Later the interviewer, Ulfat, asked, "Did the state punish people who refused to join?" Temir responded: "No, but this is what they did.... First they raised their taxes. If a kolkhoz had a contract that took five or six large sacks of wheat per hectare [as their tax], then from the individual farmers, they took ten large sacks, and nothing was left for them to eat. And that forced them to join the kolkhoz."[41]

Halil (b. 1905), who had worked as a mardikor in the gates of the rich, recalled joining a kolkhoz as soon as he was called to a meeting, where taxation was part of the discussion. "A man named Islomov came from Tashkent to investigate seven people and take their land. They held a meeting.... They took their land and made it into the kolkhoz.... At the meeting they said, 'Join the kolkhoz. There won't be any taxes and everyone will live in peace.' Taxes were set appropriately. Before that, taxes were very high.... We decided not to punish those who refused to join, and they quickly ... joined because they were told, 'You won't pay taxes.'"[42]

Taxation rates were one of the key points of pressure on dehqons who tried to continue farming individually. Village soviets collected taxes in kind. Although in 1930 there were complaints about regressive taxation that seemed to punish kolkhoz members, by 1933, Uzbekistan's government was using taxation to keep members from withdrawing, by retroactively charging anyone who quit the kolkhoz with taxes dating back to 1931.[43] June 1933 rules declared that kolkhoz plantings of cotton, flax, hemp, and lucerne (alfalfa) would not be taxed, and neither would kolkhoz-owned livestock. However, members of kolkhozes and artels were taxed on vegetables and fruits raised on their personal plots. Meanwhile, individual farmers paid substantial graduated taxes on their agricultural earnings, while quloqs were charged rates of 50 to 70 percent.[44] Agitators may have spoken about many topics, but their audiences paid close attention to announcements that kolkhoz members could escape taxation, while nonmembers' taxes would rise.[45]

Uzbek Agitators

In Qashqa Daryo, Bukhara, Tashkent, and Xorazm, interviewers consistently asked about the identities of kolkhoz agitators and organizers. In those provinces, forty-nine interviewees out of eighty had something to say about the identity of collectivization's agitators. All but five identified them as "ours," "our Uzbeks," "local," or Uzbeks from the region. Among those in this subset who identified their agitators, thirty-four also said that their families joined willingly, and thirteen said their families were forced to join.

Collectivizing Uzbekistan's thousands of villages demanded effort from thousands of Uzbek-speaking activists. In 1929 and 1930, Uzbekistan's Kolkhoz Center announced training courses for 25,000 activists who would become agitators and kolkhoz workers, mirroring the target number of collectivization activists called for by Moscow in its 25,000er campaign. The Kolkhoz Center's announcement for a course to train kolkhoz instructors offered stipends to potential registrants between ages eighteen and thirty-five who already had general and some political education, giving priority to those from the "native nationalities," of "worker, poor, or middle dehqon origins," acquainted with agriculture and collectivization, and speaking the Uzbek language. There were also some non-Uzbek activists for collectivization, including 438 volunteers from the 25,000er movement who came to Uzbekistan from Russia and elsewhere in the USSR.[46] Activists who could not speak native Central Asian languages were useless in all but a few rural communities, and in fact and memory, Uzbeks played the role of kolkhoz organizers, even though Russians were dominant in the personnel of the directing institutions.[47] In the accounts that follow, elderly dehqons remembered Uzbek agitators by name because those activists were their neighbors and relatives or because organizers from elsewhere in Uzbekistan stayed on in their communities.

In Qashqa Daryo, Bekmurod, born in 1907, was a poor dehqon who had been granted four to five hectares during land reform. He became director of a shirkat with a contract for wheat production. He said that the kolkhoz formed

> in 1929 when a man named Muhammadi Eshonqulov was sent to Qayrag'och as a delegate, to establish the kolkhoz.... He invited us all, addressed us one by one, wrote down who had what land. He drew on

> the ground and said, "On this side, it is Soviet government, and if you go that way, it is Afghanistan." Then a bunch of our big heads said, "So let's cross over to Afghanistan. But those of us who stay in the Soviet side should sign up." And so the kolkhoz was formed. Everyone said they would join the kolkhoz; not a single person said, "I'll never be in the kolkhoz; I'll go to Afghanistan." We all said we'd join the kolkhoz under Soviet government, and we became a kolkhoz. There were people who did not agree, but they couldn't speak. Even if they thought it, they weren't permitted to say they did not agree. They were told, "We'll call the militia immediately and arrest you." So they said, "I'll be in the kolkhoz," and they even raised two hands to show they would join.[48]

Bekmurod and his fellow shirkat members responded favorably to agitation, but others in the community succumbed to Eshonqulov's threats. But their kolkhoz soon broke up, and everyone returned to farming individually. "Taxes on individual farming were high. Some people didn't pay them but instead fled or were arrested. Gradually people were unable to meet their contracts or pay their taxes. And they gradually began to reunite." Bekmurod joined a kolkhoz for the second time in 1932.

Abdullo (b. 1917), an orphan, was taken in by his relatively wealthy uncle and grandfather—they owned fifty tanobs and hired laborers. He said:

> I was young when the kolkhoz was formed. Of course there were meetings.... They said, "The old government has disappeared; a new government appeared in its place. We are now building a socialist state in accordance with Lenin's revolution; there is supposed to be collective agriculture," and they explained it that way. "You should give your land."... The meetings were led by people who came from the regional center and from our own community. I remember that there was O'taqaym; he has passed away. My father and grandfather participated in the meetings. They gave oxen, a pair of draft animals, and an oil press.
>
> Those were times of hardship.... People were so poor, so when they were told about socialist agriculture, they trusted that.... The mullahs, boylar, qazis, administrators, eshons, property owners—they did not join at first.... They fought it with tongues and weapons; a few even fired shots, as in Bosmachi times.... Agitation was just in the form of explaining. They said, "The dehqons at Beshkent did this; now you should unite." There were poor people who seized each other's things and who fought and some who were in their right minds also refused to join. The first to refuse were the middle dehqons, those who already had a good life. Then they were forced to join.[49]

Fayzi (b. 1915) was the son of a dehqon who owned enough land that he had sharecroppers, "but at the time of collectivization my father wrote his own petition and joined all of our land and livestock to the small kolkhoz." When asked about how the kolkhoz started, he recalled: "Davlat Nazar was one of the activists who formed the kolkhoz, someone who knew everything about the village.... Ten or fifteen people from the village gathered and said let us form a kolkhoz, and they gave their agreement.... Davlat Nazar, being a little bit literate, wrote it up.... After the kolkhoz formed there were lots of rumors; nothing happens without rumors. They said, 'They are all eating out of one pot,' and so forth." According to Fayzi, Davlat Nazar became the first of many kolkhoz directors. As a Komsomol member, Fayzi was active in village meetings and in dekulakization, providing reports to the OGPU [Soviet secret police, previously known as Cheka and NKVD, and later as KGB] on which of the local people were hiding livestock. He brought up the agitators' identities again, later in his interview, when explaining how they tried to make life difficult for the dehqons who wanted to keep farming individually. "They were local, but they had some instruction. They were invited to a course, and then they came back and mixed with the people. They worked hard, went to meetings and to other villages. They were all men, no women. People joined the kolkhoz through their agitation, not in other ways."[50]

Remembering Russian Agitators

Only a few stories mentioned Russians leading collectivization agitation campaigns, but those whose families were critical of collectivization were likely to remember outsiders as the instigators and to name local actors as incompetent illiterates who did the bidding of those outsiders. In Rajab's Qashqa Dayro village, everyone was forced to join the kolkhoz. "They had meetings to tell everyone to join the kolkhoz." He was a young teenager (b. 1917) when the kolkhoz first formed, and he said, regarding the poor: "People were happy. Why? Well, people had a little bit of land, and then twelve households each got [1.2 to 1.8 hectares] and joined together; who wouldn't be happy? The Russians came and gave me land, and the rich didn't get any land. And they didn't have much water. Now everyone was equal." Although he was orphaned, Rajab identified his family as middle dehqons; he worked for his brother-in-law, and they held out against joining the kolkhoz. Rajab did not remember who came to his village to organize the kolkhoz, but his language reflected that people in his village associated collectivization with Russian initiative.[51] Archival documents show that, in 1930, the 25,000er campaign, providing *shefstvo*, or "leadership," from urban Russia's textile factories for the spring cotton-planting season, sent twenty workers from

Serpukhov, in the Moscow region, to the district where Rajab lived, Guzar and Kitob in Qashqa Daryo.⁵² One of those Russian activists wrote a lengthy report on March 15, 1930, explaining that nearly everything they tried in their two months in the Kitob region had gone badly, concluding, "The thing that stops our work turns out to be our lack of knowledge of the Uzbek language."⁵³

Ahmad, from a village near G'ijduvon, said that Russians were deeply involved in the founding of his kolkhoz:

> At the beginning there was explanatory work, agitation, and propaganda. After they carried out those explanatory lectures every day, then gradually people understood and began to join the kolkhoz. The agitators came from the regional center and from the village.... Russians first came to our village in 1929 to keep the peace, to form kolkhozes, to form the village soviet, to form the government offices, to open schools. Russians came to show leadership. Russians came to our village every day. They brought a translator, so the people could understand them. They came from the province level to the regional center and then to our village soviet.... Then people joined the kolkhoz.⁵⁴

Ahmed was only eight years old in 1929 when those Russians came; but as the son of the first kolkhoz director and grandson of the chairman of the village soviet, he was close to the action and had opportunities to hear his father's discussion of organizing the kolkhoz reiterated many times. Although some of his relatives were exiled as quloqs, and he criticized arbitrary arrests, Ahmed's family approved of the kolkhoz, and he spoke as a supporter of the system: "In the time before the kolkhoz, other than the rich, people's life was not good.... People worked like slaves in the gates of the rich. After collectivization, development really began in 1953 to 1955 ... and after Brezhnev became the king, then the people had abundance."

The Russian agitators in Ravshan's Bukhara Province village left records of their efforts.⁵⁵ A committee of the poor organized meetings for collectivization. Ravshan (b. 1920) said: "They all came from different places. They were Uzbeks. If the director was Uzbek, then the vice director was certainly a Russian. If the chief of the police was an Uzbek from somewhere else, the second in command was a Russian."⁵⁶ Archival documents confirm that Russians were fulfilling all sorts of roles in Bukhara Province villages in 1930 as agronomists, finance managers, and regional directors.⁵⁷

The interviewee who knew the most about Russian agitators was Boltaboy (b. 1914), who came from a village near Khiva. His village formed two small kolkhozes around 1930, when he was a teenager, under local leadership: "The director of this one was Olloyor aka, and that one was Hayitboy aka.... The director of each of these kolkhozes was local. They did not bring in strangers, although they did bring in one experienced person from Fergana. That was in 1933," after the kolkhozes had fallen apart.[58]

> KOMIL (INTERVIEWER): Who took part in seizing land, buildings, and oxen: Russians or local people?
> BOLTABOY: Of course, there could have been Russians involved in seizing land and animals. You know that they promoted leaders from the local people; there was a policy of promotion from below. If they had not acted, things would have stayed the way they were.

Because he had a little more education than other people in his village, Boltaboy worked as the kolkhoz *tabelchi*, recording daily labor:

> We heard that the 25,000ers had a special Central Asia group. They were at the MTS [machine tractor station], where they carried out propaganda as the government ordered. As an activist from the kolkhoz and a tabelchi, I would go to the meetings. I sat in that meeting for two hours and did not understand anything, because they spoke Russian. That was in 1931, 1932. They were called the 25,000ers, Communists sent to explain the government's policies in the political division and to work in the MTS. They went and fulfilled the government's degree to do propaganda, whether or not anyone understood them. There was no translator.... Those meetings took place once a month.... They would gather the kolkhoz leaders.[59]

Although the interviewer Komil Kalonov had prodded Boltaboy to see Russians as directly involved in collectivization, Boltaboy identified people from his own community as the makers of the kolkhoz and the Russian 25,000ers as performing propaganda.[60]

While Uzbeks were dominant among the plenipotentiaries or agitators, Russians, who constituted half the Communist Party members in Uzbekistan, dominated the Raykom offices that implemented collectivization orders. A certain Tajiyev, who worked for the Uzbek Khleb (grain) Center, provided a lengthy report about several villages in the Tashkent region where kolkhoz members forcibly seized livestock and land from middle dehqons and then slaughtered the livestock to sell the meat or used the draft animals on their personal plots. Tajiyev ended his report with the complaint that he had sped from Samarkand to Tashkent to visit kolkhozes and file this report, but when he went to the district office in the Tashkent region, "I could not find a single person who could speak in Uzbek," and they were speaking so fast in Russian that he gave up and returned to Samarkand with his report.[61] Russians were present in Uzbekistan during collectivization and were involved in the effort at the level of the Raykom, but most of our interviewees did not see them or associate them with collectivization.[62]

At a macro level, no one in Uzbekistan chose collectivization, the quintessential Stalinist transformation of agriculture and of rural lives. Mass collectivization was imposed on Uzbekistan's leaders and on ordinary dehqons so that the state could take control over what dehqons would produce, ensuring that the USSR could order them to plant more cotton. Turning proclamation into reality was a project that was grounded in mass mobilization, drawing Uzbeks into the work of persuasion and organization. Oral history interviewees who recalled the formation of kolkhozes and who, at least in retrospect, supported the radical transformation of agrarian society, said that they responded to agitators with whom they identified as fellow Uzbeks and neighbors. Agitators were the face of the mass collectivization campaign, and they included trained activists like Pirmuhamedov, who traveled to rural communities from a regional center, as well as local activists, who could be members of the Committee of the Poor, Komsomol members, dehqons who had been awarded land in land reform, members of land reclamation societies, and others who had become the Party's rural allies. Interviewees included a few who had agitated for the kolkhoz, and many who remembered agitators by name because the agitators became members of the newly organized kolkhoz. In contrast with Kazakhstan, where as Sarah Cameron shows, there were deliberate efforts to send Kazakh Party and Komsomol members as plenipotentiaries to communities distant from their own, so that they would lack any local connections, collectivization came to Uzbek *qishloqs* [villages] through "our Uzbeks," who conducted agitation meetings conducted in the local language.[63] This, I argue, meant that those dehqons who were already favorably disposed toward the state's agricultural initiatives identified with the agitators and began to see kolkhoz creation as their own project.

Conceptualizations of their socioeconomic worlds based on class became convincing because agitators used class-based claims to offer poor dehqons the promise of a better living, telling those who had worked in the gates of the rich that the boylar were mushtumzo'r, oppressors who deserved to lose their land to the newly formed collective farms. Agitators were sometimes able to provide new joiners with immediate, tangible benefits, leaving members of the collectivization generation with images of carts loaded with sacks of wheat, buckets of oil, and lengths of fabric. These interviewees associated their own or their families' attraction to the kolkhoz with hearing this message from other Uzbeks, with distributions of food, promises of lower taxation, and with inclusion in the group that would benefit from land seized from their wealthier neighbors; this was the result of Stalinist agitation.

While articulating their own experiences and evaluations of collectivization, almost every individual pointed out the diversity of experiences in their communities: we joined because we wanted to, but others were forced to join; or we were forced to join, but the poor joined happily. Some interviewees strongly approved of, even reveled in, the arrest and removal of the large landowners. Others who joined their kolkhoz early and willingly nonetheless criticized this aspect of collectivization. Mass mobilization turned collectivization, a radical policy of economic and cultural transformation, into a process that found extensive and enduring support from below; but collectivization could never have become dominant nor taken place so swiftly without pervasive violence and designating certain people as quloqs.

5

MAKING QULOQS
Arrest, Exile, Escape, and Identity

Mass collectivization, declared at the end of November 1929, was inextricably linked to a second measure that Stalin announced in December of that year: there should be an attack on the kulaks, "breaking their opposition, liquidating them as a class, and replacing their production with the production of kolkhozes and sovkhozes."[1] Dekulakization was the Soviet government's dispossession and removal of ostensibly wealthy agriculturalists from their communities. A wealth of recent scholarship on the dispossession and removal of kulaks shows that dekulakization was the lynchpin of collectivization. Many historians concur with Moshe Lewin's view that, without violence against kulaks, Soviet peasants would not have joined or remained in kolkhozes, and so did one of the respondents quoted in this chapter, Avez, who said, "If they had not made quloqs and exiled people, there would be no kolkhoz."[2] Before detailing the events of this violent episode and the ways that respondents remembered them, this chapter differentiates between the Russian ideas of the kulak, in relation to Russian ideas of the peasant, and the term that was borrowed in Uzbek as *quloq*, in relation to the Uzbek dehqon.

Rather than using the terms found in most scholarship—*peasant* and *kulak*—I reflect the language of interviewees, using the terms dehqon and quloq. The typical Russian peasant was not an individual landowner. In Russia, a commune (mir) was made up of peasants who owned land collectively—the result of the Great Reforms that ended serfdom—and that commune became the basis for forming a kolkhoz. The Russian *kulak*, a term that predated the 1917 revolution, was a peasant who had left the commune and established an individual farm.[3]

Kulak, a word that means "fist," became a political slur, a label that the Communist Party used to stoke resentment and class warfare by accusing prosperous individual peasant farmers of oppressing other peasants. Dekulakization, or the removal of the kulak from his home community, was dependent on understandings of Russian peasant landowning and deviation from its communal norm that were foreign to Uzbekistan.

Uzbekistan did not have kulaks, in the Russian sense of the term. *Boylar* was a term that interviewees used to refer to the wealthy whether they were rural or urban and whether their wealth involved exploiting others, or not. The boylar were wealthy for reasons of historical descent and inheritance or due to combinations of power, luck, savvy, and work in trade or in the pre-Soviet cotton boom. When respondents who came from these families talked about being boylar, rarely did they explain why their household was wealthier than their neighbors.

The Communist Party undertook the work of turning the boylar into a political equivalent of the kulak. As the historian Bahtiyor Rasulov details in his work on kulak exile, the Bolsheviks first spread the terms *mushtum* and *mushtumzo'r* in the 1920s. *Mushtum*, or "fist," was a direct translation of *kulak*; combined with *zo'r*, it meant "one who beats others with fists," or an abuser. Rasulov writes that *mushtumzo'r* was the preferred term in Uzbek party discourse and in the Uzbek-language press for painting the boylar as an abusive rural ruling class. In 1933 the party decided to use the Russian term *kulak* but with Uzbek pronunciation, *quloq*.[4] However, I note that both *mushtumzo'r* and *quloq* appeared occasionally in the Uzbek-language press and in Communist Party documents in the late 1920s, before collectivization began. An overview of articles in the Uzbek newspaper *Qizil O'zbekistan* from late 1929 and early 1930 shows that the editors used *mushtumzo'r* more frequently than *quloq*. *Mushtumzo'r* and *quloq* were usually paired with *boylar*, as though to explain the political terms to an audience of readers who knew *boylar* but were unfamiliar with the new words. For example, an article on bringing kolkhozes to life declared that "the quloq, boy, mushtumzo'r must be clearly understood, and they and their hangers-on must be decisively and mercilessly excluded from the kolkhoz."[5] Pirmuhammedov's 1930 report about agitating for the kolkhoz shows a similar pattern, pairing the political term with the more common Uzbek word: "We uncovered three Bosmachi/boy/mushtumzo'r and expelled them from the kolkhoz."[6] He, along with thousands of other Uzbek-speaking agitators, spread the new terms as they excluded and arrested dehqons.

As agitators headed to Uzbekistan's regions of total collectivization to sign up dehqons for kolkhoz membership, the Communist Party's Central Asia Bureau issued its dekulakization directive. According to the Central Asia Bureau's director, Isaak Zelenskii, mass activism by the poor and landless was supposed to deprive the "*kulak-bai* [he used the same doubling in Russian as we find in the Uzbek texts of the period, kulak/quloq followed by bai/boy] exploiters of their land, implements, and means of production." Uzbekistan's quloqs were to be excluded from kolkhozes, and their property transferred to kolkhoz ownership. Quloq households would then either be sentenced to exile outside of their home region or prosecuted if they actively opposed collectivization. Quloqs who were excluded from kolkhozes but retained some rights were to be allotted land "in the amount of a labor norm on dryland, or on the worst quality irrigated land outside of the area of total collectivization, and that is not designated for cotton-planting this year." Zelenskii presented this order as redress for colonialism: "The malicious colonizer elements among the Russian kulaks, whose properties will be liquidated, will be subjected to exile outside of Central Asia."[7]

Making Quloqs

Collectivization generation interviewees did not speak of quloq as a recognized social category; for them quloq making was an activity. Quloq making meant that a community's revolutionary leadership designated certain dehqons as enemies, arrested them, stripped them of their land and goods, and sent them off to prison or exile. The constant threat that one might be made a quloq, a threat that continued through the 1930s, shaped the lives and identities of many respondents. Soviet political discourse that connected the quloq to subversion and oppression but also to wealth and savvy resounded in their accounts. The accounts at the heart of this chapter show that many distanced themselves from the label quloq, stressing that their families should not have been considered boylar, or at least not oppressive boylar. Some focused on the deprivation of rights that kept them out of school or limited their work opportunities. A few of them claimed the quloq label proudly, as an indication of their superior abilities as farmers. Most interviewees recalled the making of quloqs from their perspective as children or teenagers. Among the oldest interviewees, those who were in their twenties during collectivization, one was arrested as a quloq, one was investigated but not arrested, and one played a significant role in making quloqs.[8]

We, the interviewers who had learned about the past through books and schools, used the term *quloq* as a noun: "What did you hear about quloqs? Was anyone in your family a quloq?" Our respondents responded using both *mushtumzo'r* and *quloq*, but usually they spoke about boylar. In their phrasing, boylar became quloqs when they were singled out for political attack, arrest, and dispossession. In the interviewees' use, *quloq* was not a preexisting category; instead they used a verb, *quloqlashtirish*, or *quloq kilish*, literally, "turning someone into a quloq," or "making quloqs."

At the time of these interviews, revised understandings of collectivization were emerging that shaped our questions, but the impact of those revisions on respondent stories is unclear. During Stalin's lifetime (d. 1953), praise was the only acceptable speech about collectivization, and talking about kin who were repressed or exiled was done only within families. In the late 1950s and early 1960s, official histories began to discuss collectivization in greater depth, including mention of "mistakes." Long-term prisoners of the Gulag were released, and rehabilitation of some of the 1930s political victims expanded the limits on what people could say about former quloqs.[9] In the 1980s, Soviet glasnost, the policy of openness, stimulated new public discourses in Uzbekistan: the Soviet cotton program was colonialism, and journalists eagerly published accounts of people who had been arrested, exiled, or shot during the 1930s. By the late 1990s, Uzbekistan's official histories no longer presented the quloq as an enemy; Uzbek historians denounced collectivization, dekulakization, and the entire Soviet period as colonial tyranny.[10] Uzbekistan's historians highlighted the lives of a diverse set of historical actors, from Bosmachis to Uzbek party members who were accused of nationalism and repressed, weaving them into a national narrative of suffering, and quloq stories were also welcomed in public discourse.

The changed political environment may have enhanced interviewees' willingness to talk about experiences of victimization, something that is demonstrated through most of the narratives in this chapter. One reluctant interviewee offered a contrast, hiding his story of that threat only to have his son reveal it. Not every member of the collectivization generation felt that 1991 and independence had done away with Soviet-era censorship and self-censorship. This chapter also includes accounts of some respondents who participated in the making of quloqs and who adhered to the earlier judgment of quloqs as enemies. The chapter alternates between historical narrative to lay out the events of dekulakization in Uzbekistan and examples of interviewees relating those events from their own standpoints. The historical narrative and the interviews describe how quloqs were made, resistance to collectivization and quloq making, and what became of quloqs as they were arrested or escaped arrest. Finally, the chapter focuses on the subjectivity of interviewees: How did members of the collectivization generation make sense of quloq making and its impact on their own lives?

Remembering Making Quloqs

Bozorxo'ja (b. 1913) participated in forming the kolkhoz and in making quloqs in his qishloq in Tashkent Province. Like his father, grandfather, and uncles, he worked from the age of thirteen in the gates of the rich as a mardikor and chorikor. In 1927, they formed a Qoshchi Union, a collective of poor and landless dehqons farming for themselves. But he said, "We were poor, and we continued working in the gates of the boylar as servants right up until collectivization.... I remember the names of those whom I worked for: the father of Mirodil and Jomolov and Tillaxo'ja and Sulton Boyvachcha and Rasulboy in Qumariq."[11] His father and brothers became activists for collectivization: "The rich men's land was divided out, and a kolkhoz was formed on it. They elected a director and then brigade leaders. The activists did all of this. Someone came from the center to make sure this was begun in an orderly way. It was Hakimboy, who was shot here. The Bosmachis under Shermat shot him. They came here in April 1931. They shot Hakimboy and also quite a few people from the village, including the teachers. They said 'Qo'rboshi' at that time rather than 'Bosmachi.'" Bozorxo'ja associated boylar and opposition to the kolkhoz with Bosmachis. The interviewer asked exactly how the activists had formed the kolkhoz. He said:

> In order to form the kolkhoz, if I was director of Taraqqiy [Progress, the name of his kolkhoz], I would call together all three hundred households in the territory, and I would make them members of the kolkhoz, through the activists. It was through agitation. They went around house to house, inviting people. But if there were two hundred fifty or three hundred men in the territory, they managed to gather only ten or fifteen of them. These things are not accomplished in one day. There were those who did not want to join, but they were forced. If you did not want to join today, they would force you after five days.

Bozorxo'ja said that his older brother Zokir organized the Qoshchi union committee and gave them orders for making quloqs, and he listed names of a dozen members of the Qoshchi union who created the kolkhoz and who seized property from the boylar. He described his own actions:

> For example, I entered Tillaxo'ja's home and Ahmadjon Akramov's home and Toxtaxo'ja. I worked for Tillaxo'ja the butcher for three years. I was a Qoshchi member, and so was my younger brother Ibrohim. We served him for three years, earning one large sack of grain for twelve months, sleeping in the barn, looking after the livestock, butchering, and we did this for three years. In the making of quloqs, they found all sorts of things hidden in his house: wheat, barley, chickpeas. He hid them, but they were seized, and he was sent off as a quloq. The wheat was divided out to the people, to the members of the kolkhoz. He left and went to [Tashkent] and died there.

Both Komil, the interviewer, and the mahalla committee veterans' representative, who was present during the interview, protested that many people were wrongly dekulakized and asked if Bozorxo'ja did not know that. Bozorxo'ja rattled off a list of men who were made quloqs: "I saw what happened. In this area, there was Miraziz Xojibuva, who had land in Boyqazon and at Qayrag'och Spring and also in Qizilsuv. There were also Kukko'zboy, Soltonboyvachcha, Eshboy the felt maker.... They each had fifteen hectares or even more, and it was divided up, and they were sent away."

Bozorxo'ja defended the process of making quloqs and the decisions that the Qoshchi union made about the boylar in their community. From his perspective, the boylar were oppressors, partnering with Bosmachis, and the victims whom he remembered were the pro-collectivization activist Hakimboy and the teachers. "Those who were made into quloqs could not join the collective or the kolkhoz as members, and under all of that harsh treatment, they took their whole families and left for good."[12] Active participation in the process of making quloqs sealed Bozorxo'ja's identity as a kolkhoz supporter and his view that quloqs deserved their fate.

Rashid (b. 1917), the son of a sharecropper in Bukhara, recalled the making of quloqs very differently, and critically:

> There was a directive from above about putting an end to the rich men as quloqs. I heard about it, even though I was young at the time, and they came and took the boylar lands and divided them among the poor.... They formed a quloq-making commission here, at the village soviet. They had the idea that everyone should be poor. But maybe poor people are poor because they don't have enough wit to achieve more.... The fate of someone with a lot of land was in this commission's reckoning.... Someone could be a rich man even though he wasn't very rich. Asad Boy had thirty or forty hectares. He was judged to be a large landowner, and he was made a quloq. The commission would meet in the village soviet in the evenings. It was formed from among the poor of the village soviet. They were all local people. They did not say, "Let's have smart people like you." They said, "Let them be poor people." They carried things out according to their own grievances.
>
> We had this fellow villager named Mirzo Jo'ra ... who had seven children and one cow.... The director of the village soviet at the time was a very young man named O'roq Yaxshiyev, who dressed in military clothing with a belt. They would come into a quloq house and seize their property. He came alone, once. Mirzo was not at home, so he made

a thorough investigation of all the property and found nothing to seize. This person was poor, but he made him a quloq anyway.... We were young children, but we went to watch while they took Mirzo away to be shot as a quloq, and his wife was left wailing.[13]

Rashid came from circumstances similar to those of Bozorxo'ja, but his family did not participate in dispossessing the rich. Instead, he spoke of witnessing the arrest of a man whom he knew. Like Bozorxo'ja, he remembered the commission members and quloqs by name, with the sort of detail that suggests this episode had lasting emotional impact, but in Rashid's judgment the village commission and its leader were capricious and stupid, and Mirzo was a victim in the unjust destruction that was collectivization.

Resistance

In late January 1930, Raykom offices received lists of boylar, and party activists formed groups to carry out swift dispossession. A lengthy archival report on the Yangi Yul region in Tashkent Province provides details of this process that show why panic and resistance spread rapidly to other provinces. Party activists made plans for coordinated nighttime raids on January 29, confiscating the property of boylar households in one fell swoop and "arresting those who resisted." Committees of Komsomol members, village soviet members, cotton factory workers, and militia members spread out to villages, in some cases carrying precise lists of those to be dispossessed; others had only target numbers. In the middle of the night, they entered houses and confiscated livestock, grain, cotton, household furnishings, and valuables. In Chinaz District, for example, they arrested 120 people, sometimes confiscating their personal goods and sometimes allowing community members to carry off their neighbor's household goods. The sweep continued across Tashkent Province through February 5, 1930.[14]

The report on the Tashkent region quloq operations listed what its writers called mistakes. They noted that those who were made into quloqs included "eight households that had their excess lands taken away in land reform, and who since that time had not exploited hired labor."[15] Many arrests were overturned by higher authorities. Many wealthy households, anticipating raids, had sold off livestock and hidden goods or redistributed them to relatives and thus rendered fewer resources than kolkhoz leaders had anticipated acquiring. The report's writers deemed the nighttime arrests to be a mistake because they ignored the

TABLE 5.1 The dynamic of anti-collectivization actions in Uzbekistan, 1930s

MODES OF COLLECTIVE ACTION	1930	1931	1932	1933
Total mass actions (demonstrations)	235	164	10	–
Total number of participants	77,200	13,908	1,085	–
Acts of political terror	333	391	133	76
Of those, murders	157	242	119	–

Source: Rasulov, *O'zbekiston kollektivlashtirish jarayonidagi siyosi*, 174.

political value of having new kolkhoz members publicly name their oppressors as quloqs. Making arrests based on target numbers rather than lists of names was deemed a mistake, as the middle dehqons who were wrongly arrested would turn others of their class against collectivization.

On the day after Uzbekistan's first nighttime sweep, Stalin, the master of confusing political signals, sent a directive to party organizations across the USSR saying that he had been notified that various regional party organizations "had dropped the task of collectivization and had focused their power on dekulakization. The Central Committee explains that such a policy is wrong at its core. The Central Committee declares that its policy does not consist in naked dekulakization, but in developing the movement of collectivization."[16]

Isaak Zelenskii, the chairman of the Communist Party's Central Asia Bureau, immediately echoed Stalin's point, noting that there were as yet no laws about ending the kulaks as a class and that dispossessions should be conducted in an orderly way by party-sanctioned organizations. Directly contradicting his own prior communication, Zelenskii declared that dekulakization should not become a movement carried out by the masses.[17]

The deliberately disorderly nighttime raids and arrests in Tashkent Province continued for several more days, and anti-collectivization demonstrations and uprisings erupted across Uzbekistan. They were heavily concentrated in the Fergana Valley. By March 15, 1930, the OGPU recorded 105 demonstrations with a total estimated 33,873 participants.[18] Considering that Uzbekistan's rural population comprised some 3.2 million people in 770,000 households, the scope of anti-collectivization uprisings seems small, but they produced a political panic.

Demonstrator demands in Fergana Province communities were widely varied, but the most common was to break up the kolkhoz. The OGPU report included incidents of protesters killing, beating, or driving out kolkhoz agitators, members of the village Soviet, or other kolkhoz enthusiasts. In other incidents, kolkhoz members demanded a breakup but then were persuaded to drop their demands, as in an instance when Fayzulla Xo'jaev spoke to a crowd of five hundred in Chust-Pap District. In some cases, village soviets destroyed the lists of kolkhoz members, effectively ending the kolkhoz.[19]

In an early March 1930 speech known as "Dizzy with Success," Stalin attempted to reel in the chaos of mass collectivization, blaming the excessive enthusiasm of Communist Party members for all "mistakes." He asked whether proper conditions for collectivization existed in "areas where there are still backward nationalities, such as Turkestan." He singled out "Turkestan" for "attempts to 'overtake and outstrip' the advanced areas of the USSR by threatening use of armed force, by threatening peasants who are not yet ready to join collective farms with deprivation of irrigation water and manufactured goods."[20] While protests mounted across Uzbekistan, the Uzbekistan Communist Party's Central Committee tried to respond to Stalin's direct criticisms and to tamp down turmoil. Their declaration echoed Stalin's criticisms of an excessive pace of collectivization and use of force, stating: "In the future, collectivization should be conducted at a slower tempo." Poor and middle dehqons needed assurance that they could continue farming individually and still receive the kinds of advance loans that had been provided through cooperatives.[21]

Demonstrations succeeded in breaking apart many newly formed kolkhozes in Uzbekistan, and pressure for extremely rapid, total collectivization dropped off. Following violent demonstrations in February and March, regions in Fergana Province that had been slated for total collectivization encompassing 90 to 95 percent of all rural households and farmed lands were assigned much reduced goals. For example, in late March, the Chust-Pap region, a site where uprisings provoked anxiety among the Communist Party leadership, had its collectivization goal reduced from 90 to 47 percent.[22]

Although Uzbekistan's Central Committee stressed that kolkhoz formation should be voluntary and tacitly allowed kolkhoz members to leave and kolkhozes to dissolve, it did not turn away from the idea that party-led groups of the poor should continue to make quloqs. The committee proposed limits to dekulakization in the zones of mass collectivization, so quloqs—those who would be exiled far away and those who were to be deprived of their lands but remain—"should not exceed 2 to 3 percent" of all dehqon households.[23] Between February 1 and March 17, at least 1,195 people in Uzbekistan were arrested as quloqs; among them, 469 were identified as boylar and 59 as mullahs.[24] Some were arrested for leading demonstrations or murdering local activists, and others were arrested just because they were on the quloq list. They were not sent directly into exile; instead, some of the arrested were transferred to prison, and others were released. The making of quloqs slowed down, while fear drove more boylar and mullah households to flee to neighboring republics or to Afghanistan, to hide, or to redistribute their wealth in the hope of averting arrest.

Abduqodir told about his father, one of the Fergana Valley demonstrators who was arrested and sent into exile as a quloq. Abduqodir estimated that his father, Matsayidip, owned about ten hectares of land, planted primarily in cotton and rice. Matsayidip had two wives and sixteen children, but, as Abduqodir said, the children did not work. "At the time, we were dependent on our father, and we spent the days enjoying ourselves, riding horses, racing."[25] Rather than rely on family labor to deal with so much land, Abduqodir said, "We had chorikors work our land. Now you would call them hirelings. There were ten chorikor households. They worked on contract, received one-third. They took the land for one year, and we gave them seed, oxen, horses. Our father would make a spring agreement with them, like the government makes now."[26] Abduqodir's father Matsayidip matched the definition of the quloq: he owned more land than he and his immediate family could farm, and he hired workers to farm it.[27] In a recollection that was common among the children of boylar, Abduqodir spoke of his father as deeply concerned about the chorikors, providing them land, seed, draft animal power, and equipment. "And we did not go and take it [two-thirds of their harvest] from them. . . . They themselves brought it to the granary." Matsayidip fed the tenants every day in springtime, when food was scarce, and even provided food for their children and pregnant wives.[28]

In the first phases of land reform, between 1925 and 1929, large landowners like Matsayidip faced forcible dispossession, loss of rights, and perhaps arrest. Under this pressure, Matsayidip carried out his own "voluntary" version of land redistribution: "A year before my father was exiled, his land had been reformed, and they gave it all, by document, to others, freely. My father gave the land by document. . . . I do not know how many people he divided it out to, but the chorikors who worked all over were very smart people, and they immediately became poor, and he divided the land to them without money. Otherwise, he would have been driven off to Ukraine."[29] Abduqodir's view of land reform events differs significantly from the ideas expressed by respondents who were children of chorikors. Abduqodir regarded his father as exploited by clever tenant farmers: those chorikors suddenly understood that they could take advantage of the rich man's distribution of his own lands, and they quickly reidentified themselves as "the poor" to make their claims.[30]

Abduqodir's father was no longer the owner of extensive land when total collectivization began in the Oyim region, but from the perspective of the Communist Party, he was still one of the boylar. Having divided his land among his former chorikors, Matsayidip could influence them. The collectivization campaign began, and dehqons were persuaded to form a kolkhoz. Abduqodir said, "It was a 'millionaire' kolkhoz. But then many of them quit and left it.... They paid by the labor day, whoever worked more. The lazy people like us, we received less, we boylar, but those who wielded the hoe earned more."[31]

Rejection of the kolkhoz took dramatic form. "In 1931, people had an uprising.... The boylar were not happy with the collective farm and rose up." Abduqodir explained that his father, Matsayidip, and other wealthier dehqons who were deprived of their lands gathered, held a meeting, and set off as a group toward the city of Andijon, but they were stopped by the militia. "Most of them were imprisoned and exiled, sent to Ukraine and places like that [Ukraiyina-*pukrayinalarga*]."[32]

Matsayidip's participation in an anti-collectivization uprising led to his exile but not immediately. Even after joining a kolkhoz, a dehqon could be revealed as one of the boylar, as a former Bosmachi, as a former servitor of the khan or the emir, or as one of those with a role in religious leadership, a mullah or imam, and denounced as a quloq. Merely transferring the bulk of his land to chorikors had not been enough to protect Matsayidip from becoming a quloq. He was arrested in 1931, imprisoned for four months, and then exiled with his family, including the teenager Abduqodir, to Dalvarzin, a story that illustrates a later section of this chapter concerning the Gulag in Central Asia.

Quloq Stories: Arrest

Abdurasul's father was arrested as a quloq; he was imprisoned rather than exiled. Abdurasul (b. 1922 in Qashqa Daryo) described his father as a poor dehqon who owned a hectare of land. Abdurasul had attended an organizing meeting for the kolkhoz when he was nine or ten. "We went because we were curious; we kids were listening from outside wondering what they were talking about." The Communists called on people to join and then went house to house, threatening and persuading. His mother joined the kolkhoz and participated in picking cotton. Having first described his father as poor, Abdurasul changed his depiction, saying that rich men were owners of fifty to a hundred head of livestock, and they hired herders:

> Our father owned sheep and cows... fifty sheep and three cows and oxen.... There were hired herders who looked after the livestock. We would send them out to graze, and in the evening when they brought them back, we would give them some of the wheat, or if we had money, we paid that, or if not, they would get some *non* [bread] every week for herding.[33]

The kolkhoz began between 1929 and 1931. Then those who had not joined were forced to join and to turn over horses, cows, and oxen, gradually. In 1932, because we had livestock, my father was made a quloq and was arrested. My father did not join the kolkhoz right away. He thought about it. Then [after he joined], the leadership of the kolkhoz made him a quloq, and he was sent away for three years.

Directors of this kolkhoz and representatives from the regional center and the head of the militia put on a trial and sentenced my father to two years.... It was a closed trial, and they didn't let anyone know about it.... He served time in Qarshi Prison [in Qashqa Daryo Province], and then he was sent to the fields to work on a prison brigade.... We would go and take bread to him and visit him. Of course, our lives changed. We were children, and our mother, a woman, worked.

> INTERVIEWER HURSHIDA: Did they call you quloq child? And were you unable to go to school for that reason?
>
> ABDURASUL: No, when I was old enough, nine or ten, I went to school at the village school.

Released before his term ended, Abdurasul's father returned home and joined the kolkhoz. Abdurasul compared his father's relatively light sentence to the five-year sentence of another man, and Hurshida asked why there was such a difference. His explanation, likely based on what his father had told him, was that compared to his father, the other quloq "Abdusamat was very rich, and it seems that is why he was sentenced to a longer term."[34]

Some arrested quloqs returned home, but others did not. Ernazar's father belonged to a herding community where there was no individual landownership; instead the clan leaders distributed fields for planting grain to members of the paikal. Ernazar (b. 1923), also from Qashqa Daryo, a herding and wheat-growing province, said that his grandfather owned more than a thousand head of sheep:

> My father did not have so much. He had two camels, he did not have much other livestock, and he made his living with those camels.... In 1929, we were dispossessed. Some of the people from the mahalla got together and said he was a boy because of those two camels, and my mother's father was a boy, so he was made a quloq, and all of the livestock were seized.... I came home one day, and all of our things were taken out of our two houses and left in the open air.... The slander was made that we were quloqs, and after that, nothing could be done about it. Later a commission came around to check on the facts, and they showed that many non-quloqs had been slandered and had been made quloqs.

The kolkhoz, as he told of it, was badly organized. The founders belonged to the village soviet, and he described them as "mardikors from the village who had worked in someone else's gates. . . . If they had anything, they could not turn it into anything. They were people with no skills." Kolkhozes fell apart; in its first years, Ernazar's village's kolkhoz simply distributed land to each of its members to farm on their own. "My father died after he was imprisoned, and I was left with my mother and my grandmother. . . . My grandfather and father did not join the kolkhoz; they were arrested, made quloqs, and our possessions were taken, right down to the quilts." The family learned of Ernazar's father's death a few years after it happened, when another man who had been arrested with him was released.[35]

O'rozboy (b. 1907) tried to escape dekulakization by moving or fleeing. He was born in a village called Oq Qula in the northern part of the Bukhara Emirate, today's Navoiy Province. He said that his father owned 1,700 head of sheep, 80 oxen, cows, and extensive land. When collectivization began, his father's livestock was transferred to the Qizilcha sovkhoz. O'rozboy's uncle turned over an additional 640 head, and when they had no more livestock, or at least none that the authorities could find, O'rozboy said, "We removed ourselves to this village [Chuya]." O'rozboy said that his father was made a quloq, and he went to Kazakhstan, but O'rozboy did not clarify whether his father was hiding from dekulakization or was exiled. O'rozboy rode to Kazakhstan and brought him back home, but his father was again arrested and imprisoned. O'rozboy then told of his own arrest:

> I came riding back, and here Aziz's father said, "They will arrest you." I said, "Let them arrest me! Qo'ldoshvoy is turning over ten or twelve sheep to me!" He said, "You take them to the kabob maker Qurbon and sell them to him," and I went directly there to make them into kabobs. It was bazaar day, and there were six people waiting for me there [at the bazaar]. A couple of them approached me, asked what I had done, and sentenced me to sixteen months. I was about twenty-three or twenty-four, and I was imprisoned in Nurota. Then they let me go because they couldn't make the case. They charged me, it went to court, and I was exonerated. But Xosil Pasha, Rasulboy, and Jabborboy were sentenced and shot in the evening.

O'rozboy took possession of some sheep, an incident that he did not thoroughly explain but indicated was illicit; the sheep belonged to the sovkhoz. Charges of theft from a sovkhoz or kolkhoz show up frequently in OGPU records of quloq making, often with harsher sentences. After O'rozboy was released, he joined a kolkhoz in Chuya; he did not mention whether his father survived or returned.[36]

O'rozboy, though quite forthcoming about the fact that his *oqsoqol* (village elder) father had been arrested as a quloq, and he himself spent time in prison for stealing sheep, began his interview with open suspicion of the interviewers, Russell Zanca and Komil Kalonov. When he learned that Russell was from the United States, he told Komil, "I won't talk with a person from America. I have nothing to do with them." Komil said, "He speaks Uzbek, and he came here from Tashkent." O'rozboy: "I won't talk to a person from America." Komil: "Fine, I will record this myself." The interview proceeded, and later O'rozboy answered some of Russell's questions. Given his background, one might imagine that O'rozboy would have expressed criticism of the kolkhoz, but he did not. He praised Lenin and Stalin for having cleared away the "boylar, mullahs, oqsoqols like us, and the servants of the boylar.... They [Lenin and Stalin] made things prosper." Komil, surprised, asked, "Even if they killed people, you would still say that they did good things?" "It was good. Stalin and Lenin brought about good things; we even say our lights are Stalin's." Discourses that pervaded their lives in the 1930s, such as a requirement to praise Stalin or a defensive need to deny being boylar, were still part of the stories that some respondents told us, seemingly without irony, more than ten years after the Soviet Union had ended.

Quloq Stories: Flight

Ahmad (b. 1920) first said that his parents were poor dehqons and then that his grandfather lost his lands, was deprived of rights, was exiled, but was not made a quloq.[37] Later, he said that the family did not live on a kolkhoz; they were city people. He described extensive landholdings (six hundred tanobs) spread across numerous villages and ownership of plenty of livestock, but he claimed not to know whether his father or grandfather hired mardikors or chorikors to work that land. Pulling the various threads of his story together, it appears that his grandfather was a wealthy urban man from Marg'ilon who was deprived of rights and whose extensive landholdings were taken from him during land reform and collectivization. Or, perhaps, as Ahmad put it, "he turned over his land" under pressure. He said, "My grandfather was exiled to Oratepe in Kazakhstan, and then he went to Tajikistan, here and there, in exile. He returned from exile in 1936, and I came with him." The interviewer tried to clarify: "Because you had a lot of land, he was made a quloq and sent to Kazakhstan?" For Ahmad, a quloq was a more distinctive category: "No, he was exiled as a person deprived of rights, not a quloq. Stalin sent quloqs to Ukraine.... Some of us were arrested and sent off to Ukraine.... But later, see, those who had been deprived became rich again; they are all rich. There are some who have come back now, with their children and grandchildren. They were arrested and sent off—my older brother Maxsum was one of them, and my older brother the herder Askarxon."

After Ahmad's grandfather returned from Tajikistan to the Marg'ilon area, "he lived well.... When he was in O'ratepa they did not take his house away; they gave it back to him." Ahmad's story, confusing though it is, illuminates the varied and unpredictable fates of Uzbekistan's boylar. His own strategy during the interview for distancing himself from the label quloq was to call his parents poor dehqons and to link his grandfather's exile to the somewhat less opprobrious category "deprived of rights." His grandfather may have been exiled for a short time in Kazakhstan, but after that, he followed a pattern about which we heard of from others: many said that boylar and mullahs fleeing for fear of being made into quloqs went to Tajikistan.[38]

Abdullo (b. 1920) came from the social class of those who were likely to face dekulakization and other forms of repression: the boylar who were associated with the Khiva khan's administration. Abdullo told stories of numerous members of his xo'ja lineage group who moved to escape dekulakization. "We had a house in Khiva, Yusupxo'ja's house, the one who worked for the Khan. Yusup [Abdullo's grandfather] would come here in the summer to live. Then he built a house, seven levels, near where we lived," in Hadra, the village where they owned land and where they all moved permanently in the late 1920s, just before collectivization began. "The Soviet government found those who were from families of the rich, those whose families served in the government, and said, 'You are all opponents of the government.' So, in the 1930s, Salimboy [an uncle] and his sons, together with other people, were named as quloqs and were taken away to be shot ... but they did not talk much about it, because if you came from the khan's lineage, they would confiscate everything."

Abdullo's grandfather "had three sons, Komil, Veiz, Said. They said, 'If you give up half of your land, then we will not make you a *mushtum*.' A mushtum is a quloq.... After that, my grandfather came here and opened a school." Abdullo noted that those who had studied or taught in madrasas took short literacy courses to learn the Uzbek Latin alphabet and then transformed themselves into Soviet teachers. "Then the smartest ones said we need to form a kolkhoz. So the middle dehqons joined with about five or six boylar to form the Namuna Kolkhoz." Members of Abdullo's extended family joined, calling themselves middle dehqons. "The middle dehqons did not give much to join. They took half of our land for the school. The landless laborers who worked in our grandfather's gates were given the orchard when it was divided up." At first, the wealthy and the poor in Hadra Village formed separate kolkhozes, and Namuna Kolkhoz, with its wealthy founders, "belonged to my grandparents." Namuna Kolkhoz, according to Abdullo, worked well and prospered and did not follow the usual kolkhoz labor practices.

Abdullo's relatives first escaped repression by moving from the city to a village where they owned significant property. They then avoided being named as quloqs by giving up part of their lands and then again by strategically forming a kolkhoz with other boylar families. However, dekulakization was a repeatable enterprise, and the state launched another round of rural dispossession in 1936. "In 1936 . . . a man named Sharipov was sent here as a representative. He came from Khiva to ascertain who were quloqs and make them quloqs. . . . At that time we had livestock farms, and on them every dehqon was owner of his own land, planted his own land, but then had a plan for turning over the harvest. They raised cotton for the government, and there was a plan for wheat." In other words, Namuna was a kolkhoz in name only. Members had agreed that each would work his own fields, possibly with the ongoing aid of hired workers, and they combined enough of their harvest to meet the kolkhoz quota.

The district enforcer, Sharipov, began to ask questions about the cotton harvest:

> "Whose cotton is this?" "This is Ismoilboy's cotton." "Who picked it? Why, old man, did you not have your cotton picked? Why is it not harvested?" "It is my own. What business is it of yours?" . . . They made him a mushtum; they turned people into quloqs. They clarified; they investigated, made them quloqs, shot them. It was not in the plan. . . . They captured them at night. Three days later, a decision came from the regional administration. "Let Ismoilboy be arrested; and anyone over sixteen years may be arrested. Do not touch their wives, and their property is joined to the kolkhoz." So the kolkhoz was formed at that time. They were all imprisoned, and they passed away in prison.

Abdullo stressed that members of the kolkhoz had continued to farm as though the land was still private property. "They wasted a lot of time trying to unite their lands," he said, but after 1936, they finally were forced to operate as a normal kolkhoz, and Namuna Kolkhoz was merged with the kolkhoz that had been founded by the poor. Abdullo's father was arrested: "As I watched, he was taken away to prison, in 1937. I did not know why he was imprisoned. After six months he was released." Abdullo's relative who had built a large house in the village managed to escape dekulakization by moving. "That relative, whose name was Said, had an old mate in the village soviet. He told Said their decision early, that he would be reduced if he did not flee. They would make him a mushtum. One night he fled that palatial home and went to Turkmenistan and stayed there. The kolkhoz directorate appropriated his lands, and they made the school there.... In 1940 he came back from Turkmenistan. They said, 'This son of an oppressor returned,' but there was no directive against mushtum anymore. He returned and reclaimed his land and then sold it to the kolkhoz."[39] Abdullo's father was finally made a quloq in the 1937 wave of dekulakization, after many efforts within his extended family to avoid this fate.[40] Unlike some other respondents who described coming from objectively wealthy households but claimed their parents had been poor, Abdullo took pride in his family's illustrious past and seemed to relish telling the various ways that they tried to thwart dispossession and collectivization.

Avez's family had moved from Turkmenistan to Qashqa Daryo Province, Uzbekistan, to escape the quloq-making process. Avez's father was not wealthy: he and his brothers owned three hectares. "The kolkhoz took all of our land at some point around 1930.... They did not take the cattle." Avez (b. 1915) thought that his family had fewer than fifty head of cattle. "We did not hire others. But the really rich boylar all disagreed with collectivization and went to Afghanistan." Avez described the founding of the kolkhoz in their clan's village: "About thirty or thirty-five households unified, and three or four who did not like it opposed it and left." Avez's father did not meet the usual definition of the quloq, but he chose to flee collectivization. "He did not join the kolkhoz because he was an oqsoqol [village elder], and he was also religious. The Soviets hated oqsoqols and mullahs." Avez described meetings where the poor mobilized against the boylar and the mullahs:

> Whether it was good or bad, in their gates they had slaves, mardikor. My father did not have mardikors, but the Soviets took the side of the mardikor. "You are the rich person who exploited me, and I have nothing, not even clothing." There were village representatives, a group of three. The three [troika] would hold a meeting. They would say, "That Jumaev is rich, and in his gates are two mardikors. We have to exile him right away." And the three would make that decision. If they chose you, they arrested you unless you fled to Afghanistan or elsewhere.

Avez's father and older brothers left for Afghanistan, while Avez's maternal uncle took him, his mother, and other family members to join a kolkhoz in Qashqa Daryo, Uzbekistan. Avez mentioned poor dehqons who were wrongly made quloqs: "The quloqs were those who had a lot of sheep or who had been mullahs. But there were some people who had two to three sheep in their gates and had been mardikors, but they were judged to be quloqs. The troikas did this. If they had not made quloqs and exiled people, there would be no kolkhoz." In Qashqa Daryo, Avez's relatives joined a kolkhoz that he said had been "founded by the rich" and that owned many sheep, where he attended the new village school. After he was taken away from his natal village in Turkmenistan by his maternal uncle, Avez suffered none of the limitations that were described by other children of quloqs; by moving, his family shed their association with the boylar and the mullahs, but he was permanently separated from his father.[41]

Sa'dullo (b. 1920) said that his father was an Uzbek shop owner in Chorjoy, Turkmenistan, and that he was arrested.

> Until 1934 or 1935, my father stayed in Chorjoy. Then three people including him were sent to Krasnovodsk [to prison in Turkmenistan]. Then we moved to this village [in Uzbekistan]. . . . My uncle brought us here. Although some people beat us, we did not go back. It was not possible. Everything was confiscated, and my father was made a quloq. In 1935 or 1936, my father came here from Krasnovodsk in bad health. The kolkhoz did not admit him. . . . He went to Bukhara, where there was land designated for people like him to farm. My father worked there as a brigade leader with my two brothers. In 1937 or 1938–39 Stalin issued a decree stating that quloqs could join the kolkhoz.[42]

Official records do not capture the full scope of the ways that dekulakization impacted dehqon families. Knowing that they were likely to be named quloqs, some dehqons changed their fate by leaving their home communities to resettle elsewhere, crossing the borders between republics, heading for Afghanistan, or relocating to a neighboring village. The making of quloqs changed the lives of families that dispersed, abandoning their communities and moving to places where they would not be recognized as boylar. Interviewees who came from quloq families recalled relatives who were arrested and shot, who were imprisoned for short or long periods, who were allowed to return home and join the kolkhoz, or who were permanently excluded. Being named a quloq led to many possible outcomes, although the deepest impact came from sentences of exile.

Quloq Exile and the Proud Quloq

In summer 1931, the OGPU gave each republic a quota for arrests and deportations of kulaks. The Uzbek historian Rustambek Shamsutdinov details the unfolding of these orders in Uzbekistan, the distribution by region of quotas, the arrest of quloqs, their delivery to transfer points, and their embarkation to destinations in Ukraine and the North Caucasus. Some of the arrestees were sent to Kazakhstan, and some were resettled elsewhere within Central Asia. Over two weeks from the end of August 1931 until mid-September 1931, 3,795 households from Uzbekistan, totaling 17,839 members, were dispatched into exile in Ukraine, the North Caucasus, Kazakhstan, and within Uzbekistan.[43] After that large operation, troikas continued arresting quloqs in smaller numbers, sending some to prison in Uzbekistan and others to exile in Siberia or in the Urals.[44]

Lists of those found by anti-quloq operations in 1932 and slated for exile included the head of household and accompanying family members by name, age, and whether they were capable of work; in other words, the family's work-capable members became unfree labor in their place of exile.[45] By mid-1932, 29,555 quloq households with 90,090 members had been sentenced to exile in twelve such "special settlements" across Uzbekistan. In 1935, an agreement with the OGPU led to the return of many of the quloq families from their places of exile in Ukraine and the North Caucasus. Some had finished their sentences and were allowed to return home, while others were sent to Uzbekistan's special settlements.[46] Dalvarzin, in Bekabod, southern Tashkent Province, was the largest of those special settlement sovkhoz (state farms), with 5,034 exiled quloq households.

In 1931, Abduqodir's father, Matsayidip, had been arrested as a quloq for participating in a demonstration in the Fergana Valley, and the family was exiled to Dalvarzin.[47] Our question about whether he remembered the Qoshchi union prompted Abduqodir to contrast his family's hardships after they were made quloqs in Oyim with life in the special settlement of Dalvarzin. He said: "Because we were boylar, the Qoshchi [in Oyim] did not let us go to school, saying, 'You are boylar children.' They also did not accept us for work, so our lives were very difficult. We moved here [Dalvarzin], and it saved our lives." His father was imprisoned while the family remained in Oyim, and for the six months or so that they remained there, they were deprived of their land, their possessions, their livelihood, and their status. Exile to Dalvarzin relieved some of those hardships, though it imposed others. "We were not sent to Ukraine but exiled here, for twenty years. In 1952, after Stalin died, we were freed. It was called being under *komindantura*; I had to report every month. I could not travel five kilometers from here, and if I went anyway, I would be called to account; it was like being a slave. At first, I had to report every week, and they wrote about me every day. Then it became once a month. That continued until the war when I was drafted into the army."

In May 1932, Abduqodir's family—his parents and two of their sons—and twenty-four other prisoners boarded the OGPU's "red train cars" and were sent off, not knowing where they were going.[48] Ultimately, Abduqodir said, 1,400 people from quloq families were dispatched from the Fergana Valley to Dalvarzin, a special settlement sovkhoz in southern Tashkent Province, just outside the city of Bekobod, bordering Tajikistan. Arriving at Dalvarzin, they joined a large group of Russians who had been exiled from Streten, a colonial village near Jizzax, Uzbekistan. Abduqodir referred to the Russians as *muzhik*, by which he meant capable, prosperous farmers. At Dalvarzin, Russian and Uzbek quloqs were all placed together in the special settlement section of a state farm where they were to reclaim land for cotton planting. Dalvarzin's special settlement for kulaks was one of the outposts of SAZLag, the Central Asian division of the Soviet Gulag.

According to the *Instruction on Dekulakization*, internally exiled kulaks who were sent to develop new collective or state farms were supposed to be provided with materials for building houses before winter, but the exiles from the Oyim region were put into barracks.

> In 1932, it was cold for us here, and there was a lot of malaria. They treated it with "Akrizin." In this small place, among 150 families, up to sixteen people died.[49] It was a desert, and every year we reclaimed land, after mechanization.[50] If we had not reclaimed so much land, we could not have fulfilled the cotton plan. There was plenty of water but no drinking water. The bookkeeper lived next to us, and every day my father would go and make a fuss. My father would say, "What are we supposed to do? There is no well here, no drinking water, nothing to boil for tea—what are you doing?" ... Every day they brought one or two buckets of water to our door.

The OGPU reported that out of 31,000 people who were transported to Uzbekistan's special settlements in 1932, 4,156 died, and 7,333 escaped.[51]

He said, "We lived like chained prisoners," forced to plant cotton, and at times his parents were given two hundred grams of bread per day. "We lived in barracks at first, and then gradually we began to plan for houses. There was a collective for construction workers, and they were given what was necessary to build houses. This was in 1935. At first, I had a one room house. We do things gradually, Muslim style. Houses were built of mud bricks."

In addition to being a node in SAZLag, Dalvarzin was a showplace farm, one that the state provided with extra resources and that was favored in the distribution of tractors. Abduqodir attributed improvements at Dalvarzin to the efforts made by resettled quloqs from the Fergana Valley, saying: "When we came here, there was not a single tree like this. We brought all of them from the valley, cuttings; we brought trees, fruit trees." He described with pride Dalvarzin's extensive tractor base and how carefully they planted varieties of "silky cotton." When we asked about famine and hunger, Abduqodir associated hunger only with the time when his dekulakized family was still living in Oyim, not with the famine of 1933 or World War II, suggesting that Dalvarzin, as a showplace, may have been well provided with food. Abduqodir presented his experience of dekulakization as a dramatic change in the course of his life but not as tragedy.

Confined to Dalvarzin, he seemingly developed a quloq identity, one in which quloqs were successful, hardworking agriculturalists who had previously been assaulted by the jealous poor but who, when separated from their persecutors, created a prosperous state farm and established good lives for themselves. He even joined the Communist Party in 1963, and "no one asked anymore who I had been."[52]

Making Sense of Dekulakization

The making of quloqs had impact in every rural community, in part because the randomness of selection and the modes of arrest created fear; to borrow Teichmann's phrase, this was the power of disorder.[53] No male dehqon could be entirely certain that he would not be labeled a quloq and punished in some way, and even men who owned very little land could be made quloqs. Wives and children of quloqs shared the consequences of dekulakization, but women's names are not found in the lists of those that dekulakization committees singled out, put on trial, and sentenced.[54] Fear and the threat of being made a quloq drove many male dehqons to join kolkhozes, where they might secure their status as supporters of the state, and where they had collective access to the crop advances, payments, and investments in farm equipment that were denied to boylar who were excluded from kolkhozes. The same fear drove others to flee.

The randomness and irrationality of quloq making is reflected in stories told by respondents who came from boylar families concerning family discussions in which they tried to make sense of their fates. Abdullo F. (b. 1919) learned about his deceased parents from other family members; he came from the sort of family that was most likely to be made quloq. His grandfather was "Mullo Abduvahab, who was mirzo for Guzor To'ra." That is, Abdullo F.'s grandfather was a madrasa-educated local official, subordinate to a nephew of the Bukharan emir. Abdullo F.'s father was killed "in a bombardment" in 1920, when the Red Army invaded Bukhara. His mother died soon after, and he was taken to be raised by his maternal uncle, whom he referred to as his father. The maternal uncle, who farmed but also was an artist who carved decorative wood, also came from a family of high position. "It was my grandfather who was deprived of rights because he had been a mirzo. But he hadn't been arrested or exiled to Siberia." Abdullo F.'s maternal uncle was also deprived of rights, and this redounded to Abdullo, who was attending the village school.

> There was this boy who had been drawn into school, the son of a poor man; he did not even have a donkey, and he'd come and ask for a donkey,

so he could go to the bazaar. Sometimes he would drive the animals for Mullo Mirzo's [Abdullo's grandfather's] mill—that mill was still there, the government hadn't taken it yet—and he would say, "Who is the son of a quloq? Who is the son of a mullah-eshon? Who is the son of someone without rights? Bosmachi, son of a scoundrel, admit it!" We studied at the same school, but then they drove me out, saying, "He is an artist's son." I was a little child, six or seven, and it hit me hard: "His father is a mullah; he recites namoz; he gives the call to prayer; he is a cattle thief." . . . And they pointed at me; then they got together and drove me out, and then I wandered around for a month or two.[55]

After quloq making infected schoolchildren's interactions, Abdullo F.'s life changed for the better when Uzbekistan's president of the Soviets Oxunboboyev made a speech in their village, and his artisan uncle took the opportunity to seek restoration of his rights. According to Abdullo F.:

Oxunboboyev said, "You all say, 'This one is poor, this one is a middle peasant, this one is a quloq, and this person is deprived of rights; this person is a mullah-eshon and so on.' You all are making a muddle of one another, you Revolutionary Committee, but this is so antirevolutionary; this person is not against the government." My father drew a pretty picture of Oxunboboyev in his light robe and his [Fergana] valley skullcap, just in the time since he arrived. . . . He had drawn a picture and had made two busts, one of Lenin and one of Oxunboboyev, painted the Lenin bust with black and the Oxunboboyev one in white. . . . A petition was written in my father's name, given to Oxunboboyev, saying he had been deprived of rights. "My son cannot study in school. I am a middle dehqon, and they took my land and my mill, and now I am a member of the kolkhoz, but they deprived me of rights." That was in essence what he wrote, and he asked for pardon and requested that his case be investigated. Then he showed Oxunboboyev's picture to the people. . . . My father [uncle] said, "Look at this picture. Should my child be without rights? His father died. If he cannot call me his father, whom can he turn to?" Oxunboboyev agreed about his deprivation of rights, and I was allowed to return to school. . . . He removed some names from the quloq lists. Oxunboboyev was a man of justice, a dehqon, not very literate, just a little bit literate, as was appropriate. That evening there was a concert and a feast for Oxunboboyev, and he got on his horse and rode away.

Abdullo F.'s account of resisting quloq status was more elaborate than the stories of those who could not cite intervention from on high to explain their quloq sentencing or escape from that fate. The class warfare struggles in his village's collectivization shaped the elements that his family highlighted: Abdullo F. was an orphan and therefore could not be the son of a quloq; Abdullo F.'s uncle was a kolkhoz member who gave up his property and proved his loyalty through his art; therefore, he did not deserve deprivation of rights. The discourses that agitators spread to stimulate the poor to form kolkhozes and to attack the boylar made their way down to the actions of children in schools, and Abdullo F. blamed his own brief exclusion from school on the malicious son of a poor man.[56]

Abdullo F.'s family story about Yo'ldosh Oxunboboyev as an empowered dehqon who brought justice was consonant with the official image of Oxunboboyev in Uzbekistan's press. Respondents occasionally mentioned either Oxunboboyev or Fayzullo Xo'jayev, almost always in positive terms. The local committees might be full of stupid or vicious neighbors who wanted to despoil the boylar, but Uzbekistan's leading Uzbek politicians, if they were truly informed about mistakes, could step in and rectify problems. Stalin was rarely mentioned by our respondents, the generation who had become adults during the high Stalinist era, but there were those who criticized him openly and one or two instances of praise.[57]

Although many respondents talked openly and seemingly without hesitation about being made quloqs or about the defensive strategies that their families employed to avoid being made quloqs, the heavy impact of dekulakization fear still seemed to weigh on 102-year-old Abdullo Q. His family were among the boylar in the Parkent region. He explained that his parents owned ten hectares and that they were forced to turn it over to the kolkhoz that they joined, but his uncles were made quloqs. Abdullo Q.'s son and grandchildren were with him in this interview, often repeating our questions loudly to overcome Abdullo's deafness, and his son really wanted Abdullo to share his account as he had previously told it to his family. Abdullo Q. was quite lucid, describing his family's individual farming in detail. He kept insisting that the kolkhoz was good and that things were fine there, and his son finally intervened: "Tell them that you worked day and night without coming home! You worked as the warehouse manager. They imprisoned many people like you." The son recalled his father's story of an incident when the grain shipment that Abdullo sent from the warehouse was short by "a few hundred grams." "The NKVD gave you hard times, as you told me. They came and inspected your work for a month. Twenty-seven others who worked on kolkhozes in the same position were imprisoned!" Abdullo Q.'s eyes filled with tears while he insisted, "I don't remember that." His son persisted: "You are repeating, 'It became better, and we joined the kolkhoz.' What was better? You shivered from fear, because you worried that some time they might come for you, too."[58] His son repeated Abdullo Q.'s own explanation as to why he had escaped arrest: "They inspected my father for a month and could not find any error. He always urged us to live justly and honestly. He said honesty was 'the sword of Ali.'"

Xorazm resident Sidiq was the son of an *oxun* (a preacher from a Sufi lineage) who had served as a qazi (Islamic judge) in the city of Khiva.[59] After the Soviets took over and began repressing Islamic institutions and arresting mullahs, "he returned to his home village, and they did not tell anyone. He could not practice his profession any longer. He had five or six tanobs of land, and he farmed it." When asked whether the village people reported his father, Sidiq responded that his father was called in for questioning: "'Tell the truth: Were you formerly an oxun?' They just killed those who did not tell the truth. He said, 'I was a xo'ja, an oxun.' He didn't hide it. They killed everyone who tried to conceal themselves."[60] Knowing that most similar religious leaders were arrested, Sidiq tried to make sense of his father's survival, attributing it to his honesty. I understand this kind of explanation to reflect the respondent's desire to find some logic or justice in the state's incomprehensible decisions about who deserved repression.

The threat of being made a quloq instilled a very rational fear. Those male dehqons who owned enough land to satisfy their family needs, or more than enough, and who therefore could not believably claim to be chorikors or mardikors became aware that they might be designated as quloqs even if they joined their land to a kolkhoz. Some were made quloqs, while others were threatened but not harmed. This drawn-out, repeated process shaped their actions, and it shaped their identities. I understand their stories as reflecting their struggles to make sense of their fate. Some blamed the envious poor for their family's downfall; some attributed their family's avoidance of the worst outcomes to their virtuous or astute actions; or in rare cases, someone stepped in to save them.

Dekulakization and Social Change in Rural Uzbekistan

The Communist Party's goals for dekulakization were multiple. Dehqons who continued farming individually but who feared being made quloqs could be forced to produce cotton or grain at high tax rates, giving the state control over most of their labor and production. Alternatively, they would become convinced that remaining outside of the collective system was pointless. Making quloqs meant taking lands into kolkhozes where state-enforced plans would determine how those lands were used. Exiling quloqs removed their political influence over others in their community, preventing them from organizing resistance to collectivization. Exiling quloqs within Uzbekistan turned them into an unfree labor force that could be used for land reclamation efforts. Exiling quloqs outside of Uzbekistan was a severe form of distancing them from their communities, making them into unfree agricultural producers in Ukraine, Kazakhstan, or the North Caucasus. Quloqs and mullahs who fled their villages in anticipation of arrest sometimes went all the way to Afghanistan, but our interviews suggest that many went to neighboring republics, joining kolkhozes that ignored their questionable political status and becoming part of the proletarianized rural labor force.

Researchers who have tried to calculate numbers of the dekulakized, Shamsutdinov and Rasulov, focus on the total numbers of quloqs and household members who were exiled externally or internally. About 3,500 quloqs and a total of 18,000 in quloq households were exiled outside of Uzbekistan in 1931. In 1932, the NKVD sent at least 4,866 quloq households into exile in special resettlement nodes of SAZLag within Uzbekistan. In 1932, some 29,000 individuals—prisoners and their family members—were living in Uzbekistan's SAZLag nodes, though some may have been sent there from outside Uzbekistan, and some were political prisoners rather than quloq exiles. As Rasulov states, in the early 1930s, a little more than 1 percent of Uzbekistan's 716,000 dehqon households may have been exiled to places distant from their home communities.[61] Shamsutdinov offers a higher estimate, that between 1930 and 1933, more than 40,000 boylar were dispossessed, and most of these were exiled or resettled.[62] Of those, about 10,000 were designated "second category" kulaks, who were exiled within Uzbekistan.[63]

In addition to those numbers, as interviewee stories show, there were less visible quloqs: people who were excluded from the kolkhoz and deprived of rights but who continued living in their own communities. There were quloqs who were sentenced to death, and there were those who spent time in prison but who were released to join the kolkhoz. The process of making quloqs instilled fear and caused broader ripples of change. People who fled in fear of being denounced as quloqs abandoned their land, which was then joined to kolkhozes, benefiting those who stayed. Fleeing quloqs went to other communities where they reinvented themselves, going to cities to find work or hiring on with a kolkhoz or sovkhoz. Formerly well-off dehqons who joined kolkhozes lived in the fear that they would be denounced and excluded, a fear that drove them to join and then also served to silence them. Some who were exiled returned to their own communities after a few years, while, for others, exile was a permanent migration that they did not reverse even after their sentence ended.[64]

Old community leaders disappeared, and the process of kolkhoz formation allowed dehqons who formerly lacked any power, such as the mardikors, to assert themselves. The result was a Communist Party–guided revolution in the countryside, promoting a new group to rural leadership in the kolkhoz, in the Komsomol, in the party, and in regional administration: dehqons who did not come from the web of families that had formerly dominated their communities. Although much has been written about "clans" in Central Asia, with the assumption that late Soviet leaders of large collective farms represented continuity with prerevolution leading rural households, this assumption should be questioned.[65] Exiling quloqs, while inventing a new form of collective ownership and a new structure to agricultural life and economy, produced new rural leaders from the activists, the formerly marginalized mardikors and chorikors, or from among the middle dehqons. In the views of those whose fathers were made quloqs, the new leaders were both feared as instruments of terror and scorned as incapable of creating any rural prosperity.

One interviewee talked about his own involvement in tracking down quloqs who tried to escape. Fayzulla R. (b. 1909) was a Communist Party member and a local enforcer of party policies. He noted that quloqs often tried to leave the village:

> I was a party representative sent from Samarkand; I went to villages where we found them out. We would hold the quloqs, search their property, and turn them over to the appropriate organization; then try them, then make them answerable through imprisonment, and there were instances of seizing their livestock, too. I was not in the court; I wrote up accusations; I was entrusted with that. . . . There were occasions when we made mistakes and wrote up middle dehqons rather than only the rich. . . . We would arrive in the evening, and if there were quloqs who had fled, we would hunt them down. I wasn't NKVD, but we went out with them, with the head guard. When they found them, the state sent some into exile; I don't know where—many places. Some of them were exiled, and their families went too; in other cases, only they were sent, and their families stayed.[66]

Fayzulla R., whose mardikor father sent him to the Hydrology Institute in Samarkand to earn a Soviet education, viewed dekulakization through the lens of the poor, using the party's discourses on class struggle. He had served as secretary of his village soviet during collectivization and said, "I went to take land from one of the boylar and give it to the kolkhoz; those were my orders." Fayzulla was forthright in stating the interests of the poor who formed a shirkat, a labor collective, to farm on lands taken from the rich: "The state did not give them equipment or oxen; that was later, with the kolkhoz. They took it from individual farmers and from the hands of the boylar." Like Bozorxo'ja, the former mardikor who participated in dispossessing quloqs in Parkent, Fayzulla justified arresting and exiling quloqs as providing a benefit to ordinary dehqons.

In contrast, when Ravshan H. (b. 1920) was asked about quloqs in his Bukhara Province community, he exclaimed: "I was one of them, and I have a right to tell about them. In 1933, there was the making of quloqs. Wherever the political deputies found information, they invaded. They lay low during the day and worked like snakes at night. Whomever they listed, that person's possessions were confiscated." Ravshan's father had been a local administrator during the emirate period. "In his house twenty-eight people ate from one pot, because he was a rich man." Ravshan's father joined the Bosmachis, and in 1922, "My father, two brothers, and two uncles died fighting against the Russians." Ravshan was an orphan whose formerly wealthy relatives became ordinary dehqons; they were forced to join a kolkhoz out of fear. Ravshan was far too young to have been made a quloq, and though he knew people who were dekulakized, he gave no indication that any of his household members was made a quloq. His self-identification as a quloq meant something else to him: that if his wealthy, Boshmachi father had lived, he certainly would have been made a quloq and arrested.[67]

Between Fayzulla's and Ravshan's accounts can be found many different ways of remembering boylar and the making of quloqs. According to what we saw in the interviews, rural agitators successfully spread the party's version of class relations, adapted to an Uzbekistan context. Respondents' accounts, after the passage of seven decades and after six decades when this version of class relations was the official discourse, demonstrate that Communist Party members and agitators convinced mardikors and chorikors that they had a right to the lands on which they had labored and that the wealthy landowners were exploiters who should be dispossessed. Although after independence, historians no longer wrote of the making of quloqs as a heroic and necessary undertaking, and even in the 1960s, the Communist Party had allowed criticism of the "excesses" of collectivization, Bozorxo'ja and Fayzulla continued to interpret their own quloq-making actions as righteous and necessary.

Constraints on discussing repression and dekulakization began to fade during last few years of the Soviet period, and after independence, accounts of those who had suffered political repression or had left the country to escape dekulakization received continued attention. Those who came from quloq families were not reticent in remembering names and episodes of suffering. However, collectivization generation interviewees who came from boylar families and whose fathers were made quloqs or somehow escaped arrest spoke in counterarguments that were still couched in frameworks of the 1930s. Having been forced to live with the label quloq, some responded that their fathers were not very wealthy and were mistakenly made quloqs, or they were wealthy but not oppressors. They judged those who had joined in the effort to make quloqs and create kolkhozes as greedy and unfit for leadership, while seeking explanations for their family's fate. A few interviewees embraced the quloq label with some pride, among them O'rozboy, who told of stealing sheep and being arrested.

In Uzbekistan, as occurred across the Soviet Union, the Communist Party deputized local actors comprising village soviet members, committees of the poor, and Komsomol members, who, with the backing of the NKVD, attacked peasants wealthier than themselves, stripping them of land, goods, and freedom. The process used nighttime raids, public meetings, personal attacks, and rapidly changing laws and was designed to terrorize peasants into submission. Dehqons who joined kolkhozes as a result of persuasion, incentives, and promises of a better future often benefitted when local committees made quloqs because the kolkhoz acquired the land, livestock, and farm implements of those so indicted. For many of Uzbekistan's boylar, the ramifications of dekulakization went beyond the exile far from home of at least 8,300 quloq families: they also included uncounted numbers of boylar families deciding to flee their communities and establish new lives elsewhere in Central Asia or abroad, boylar households being excluded from kolkhozes to farm on their own while paying extraordinarily high taxes, and thousands of boylar who were deprived of all civil rights for five years.[68] Most of those who were made into quloqs remained in Uzbekistan. Whether and how they reintegrated into rural communities that had so demonstratively excluded them remains an open question, one that I wish we had asked about. Accounts from members of the collectivization generation who recalled making quloqs or being made into quloqs reveal some of the broad impacts of this policy and the ways that the activity of quloq making divided dehqon communities and consolidated class-based identities, both for the mardikors who became supporters of the new rural order and for dehqons who were long forced to silence their opposition.

6

FAMINE

In a 1984 short story, the Uzbek writer O'tkir Hoshimov related his father's account of the 1933 famine in Uzbekistan. As a young child, Hoshimov had asked his father why Uzbeks were taught to handle bread with respect.[1] His father told of his 1933 visit to the Parkent region, where "the famine was worse in the mountains than in the city." In Parkent, Hoshimov's father had witnessed the death of a starving six-year-old boy who had been begging for bread and heard the child's father wish for his own death, saying, "Now my child is released from this suffering; three days ago, his mother died, and I could not find people to carry her to the cemetery, so I buried her at home." The writer, Hoshimov, commented, "I did not know whether I should believe all of this," noting that his own visit to Leningrad's cemetery for World War II blockade victims had brought this story of famine in Uzbekistan to mind.[2]

The interviewee M. T. was a young teenager in Parkent in 1933; he recalled the famine when the interviewer Komil asked him, "Overall, after collectivization happened, did life become harder, or did conditions improve and life get easier, or did it get worse?" M. T. responded: "When did it improve? There were a lot of children who died from hunger."[3] Like most others in the collectivization generation, he began working as a child, not only on the collective farm. His father and uncles had owned a three-hectare orchard and more than twelve hectares of farmland. M. T.'s father, who tried to stay on the right side of Soviet power, formed an artel of farm laborers and became its director. In 1930, the artel transformed into a small kolkhoz, and M. T.'s father signed over their oxen and land to the kolkhoz, but as M. T. put it, his father, upset that he was not chosen to be director of the kolkhoz, decided to quit. He took back his livestock, regained some of his land, and farmed individually for several years before rejoining the kolkhoz. "You were forced to collectivize. If you said, 'I will remain on my own,' the kolkhoz would say, 'We won't give you any water.'" In the story he told about struggling for food during the famine, it is not clear whether his family belonged to the kolkhoz or was farming individually.

> KOMIL: What do you remember about *ocharchilik* [famine] years, and when did that happen?
>
> M. T.: It was during the famine, in 1933, when I was what—fourteen? Thirteen? There was an alfalfa bazaar, and horse carts would come from Tashkent to obtain bundles of alfalfa and salt. Every day, I carried twenty kilos of salt to the bazaar. I was a small kid, but I was selling salt, a four-hundred-gram bowl for one *so'm*, but then a kilo of flour rose to ten so'm. I would get four little bowls of flour. I would make food from that and eat once in the morning and use the rest of that flour to make food in the evening.[4]
>
> SHAHNOZA: How long did that ocharchilik last?
>
> M. T. (ignores her question, continuing his narrative): At that bazaar, bread sellers would come, and every man who had a family would struggle among them trying to grab bread to eat. Even if it was dirty, they would fight over it; men hit each other and tried to grab the rest—that was how those days were. When you went into the bazaar, there was a line of twenty or thirty men, begging, saying their sons and daughters were crying for bread.
>
> SHAHNOZA: Did people die of hunger?
>
> M. T.: So many people died from hunger. In our distant fields, things were just emerging a tiny bit . . . and all at once, the people, who were all starving, people came out in that grain field in springtime like sheep, tearing out every tiny grain—that's what they did to survive.[5]

M. T. did not explain where he acquired the salt that he sold to obtain flour. Amartya Sen, whose studies of the economy of famines shape the analysis in this chapter, would say that M. T.'s family used its endowments, which may have been stored salt or access to a salt mine or warehouse, enabling survival during a famine.[6] Interviewees from the Parkent region and elsewhere in Uzbekistan recalled surviving by drawing on their endowments, foraging, and consuming things that they previously judged to be inedible or haram (impure, according to Islam).

This chapter defines famine, examines some archival and statistical indicators of famine for Uzbekistan in 1933, and raises Amartya Sen's question about entitlements: Who eats and who starves during a famine? Based on repeated narratives that emerged in interviewee accounts, two arguments emerge that are not evident in known archival records: the first is that Uzbekistan's rural communities experienced ocharchilik (famine, defined below) in 1933. Respondents from across Uzbekistan spoke of drought and subsequent grain shortfalls, about deaths from starvation and typhus, and about struggling to obtain food; and some contrasted their own food security with the famine around them.

The second argument emerging from interview evidence is that food shortages convinced some Uzbek dehqons to plant and eat potatoes, a food they regarded as foreign. With the instigation of mass collectivization, the primary quandary for Uzbekistan's heads of government was how to increase cotton production while feeding the producers, in an economy dependent on grain imports. The final section of this chapter turns to potato resistance and potato adoption, pointing to common threads across many oral history accounts asserting that Uzbeks rejected the potato as a Russian thing and only gradually accepted it as an ordinary element in Uzbek soups and stews. Many interview respondents remembered adopting the potato to grow and eat following the 1933 famine, or in the 1940s, during wartime food scarcity. Oral history accounts show that collectivization's dramatic impact on rural livelihoods also was a catalyst for change in consumption.[7]

Terms: *Famine* and *Hunger*

We included a question about ocharchilik in our interview protocol, using an Uzbek word that indicates something beyond what the economist Amartya Sen, in his seminal study of famine, called "regular starvation," the predictable shortfall that affects farming families when food stocks are depleted and new crops are not yet ripe. *Ocharchilik* refers to a dramatic decline in food availability, due to drought, war, or other unexpected circumstances. This term corresponds to Sen's definition, "a sudden collapse in the level of food consumption," which leads to deaths from starvation and from famine-related epidemic diseases, typhus in particular.[8] In talking about ocharchilik, respondents from grain-producing regions associated a severe shortfall in their own supplies of food in 1933 with drought. Respondents from cotton-producing provinces associated ocharchilik with a sharp decline in wheat deliveries and soaring food prices.

We asked respondents questions about survival: What did they eat, and how did they find food? Their responses offer an intersection with Sen's analysis of differential entitlements, an explanation as to why in famine-struck regions in the capitalist world, some people continued to have food, while others starved to death. Sen uses "entitlement failure" to analyze the condition that occurs when food production fails and those who produce thus starve. He notes that "most people acquire food by trade, and their starvation can arise from failure of their trade entitlement either because of endowment loss [that is, loss of property and assets or loss of position] or because of worse terms of trade."[9] Felix Wemheuer, counterintuitively applying Sen's analysis of capitalist contexts to the Soviet collectivization famine and China's Maoist famine, argues that in Communist systems political entitlements shaped food distribution: these states prioritized some workers over others, and party members over nonparty members.[10]

Interviewees included grain producers, who expected to be able to meet their own food needs, and cotton growers and other agricultural workers, who expected to meet their food needs by exchanging cotton, money, or labor on a kolkhoz for grain. In Uzbekistan, endowments and entitlements changed with the formation of the kolkhoz: boylar families, who always expected to eat well, lost land and livelihood, while the kolkhoz director, the tractor driver, and various others gained positions that allowed them to "command food through the legal means available in the society."[11] Some interviewees pointed out that their families had better access to the most desired staple food, namely, non (flat wheat bread baked in a clay oven); but most described surviving by consuming things they previously deemed inedible and by leveraging what Sen would call their "exchange entitlements," selling off their personal goods or hustling for a living in the bazaar.

Grain Imports, Shortages, and Famine

In Uzbekistan's cotton intensive regions, dehqons planted most of their irrigated fields in cotton and purchased most of the wheat that they consumed, a pattern that was established before the 1917 revolution, that continued when cotton production rebounded in the 1920s, and that collectivization reinforced. In the 1920s, as cotton production increased, so did grain imports to Central Asia from Kazakhstan and Russia.[12] However, in 1929, a shortfall of grain imports prompted Uzbekistan's leadership to seek ways to increase grain production, even as the Five-Year Plan demanded expanded cotton planting.[13] In the 1920s, dehqons planted more wheat in irrigated fields than on *lalm-i-kor* (rain-watered or dryland fields). Beginning in 1930, plans for the zones of mass collectivization demanded that cotton be planted on almost all irrigated lands and that previously untilled, unirrigated pasturelands be plowed and planted with grain. In Uzbekistan's arid climate, lalm-i-kor fields offered only about 40 percent of the per hectare productivity of irrigated wheat.[14] Even the vast expansion in hectarage planted in grain did not mean that Uzbekistan could fulfill its own needs for grain. Per capita annual grain consumption in Uzbekistan was estimated at 186 kilos, and with a population of about five million in 1930, Uzbekistan would have required about 930,000 metric tons, a target consistently not met from within Uzbekistan, where wheat was produced largely in Qashqa Darya, Buxoro, and Samarkand Provinces.[15]

The 1932 and 1933 grain harvests in Uzbekistan were considerably lower than usual, and problems affected both winter and spring wheat production.[16] On about the same amount of lalm-i-kor land, Uzbekistan's dehqons produced 670,000 tons of grain in 1932, 700,000 tons in 1933, and 1,400,000 tons in 1934.[17] Data from weather stations in Uzbekistan showed lower than average precipitation, especially in late fall 1932 and winter 1933, at Guzar and Shahrisabz in Qashqa Daryo, in Kokand, Urganch, and Tashkent.[18] While production declined in grain-growing regions in 1932 and 1933, Uzbekistan's cotton-growing regions also experienced shortfalls in grain import. The Central Asian organizations, such as Aziiakhleb, that were responsible for purchasing grain and sending it to grain-deficit regions could not guarantee delivery; some of the grain loaded onto trains in Russia was diverted before reaching Central Asia.[19]

Another way to feed Uzbekistan was to produce other food crops for local consumption. Uzbekistan's Communist Party Chairman Akmal Ikramov sent a telegram to Stalin in April 1931, discussing Uzbekistan's plan to ban exports of vegetables: "The Central Asia bureau and the Uzbekistan TsK are consciously expanding food plantings with the goal of expanding cotton planting. We consider that in the conditions of intensifying cotton, cabbage and potatoes are essential."[20] Ikramov's attention to potatoes, a crop that before collectivization was rarely raised outside of Tashkent Province, merits further discussion below.

From 1930 through 1932, most of Uzbekistan's leadership's complaints to Moscow regarding shortfalls in grain imports stressed economic consequences: grain had been promised to kolkhoz members, and if it could not be delivered, kolkhozes would fail to produce the desired cotton, or they might disintegrate. In May 1932, Uzbekistan's first year of falling grain production and the year when famine reached a deadly level in Ukraine and Kazakhstan, the Soviet state made a large purchase of grain from Persia. From May through July 1932, there were rapid exchanges of requests for that Persian wheat, including proposals for taking wheat from areas of Central Asia to provide to Kazakhstan and then replacing the Central Asian shortfalls with the Persian wheat.[21] But in 1933, the tenor of the missives from Uzbekistan's leadership changed when Uzbekistan experienced a springtime famine. In March, Ikramov sent Stalin a telegram asking for seed wheat: "In those regions that did not meet harvest goals due to drought . . . the conditions of kolkhoz members and individual farmers is extremely bad, and there are cases of death from starvation."[22]

Official Accountings

Studies of collectivization have paid little attention to famine in Uzbekistan. Collectivization-related famine was catastrophic in Ukraine and Kazakhstan, resulting in starvation and the death of millions.[23] The historian Viktor Kondrashin has documented that famine was widespread in the Soviet Union beyond those better-known famine sites in 1933. Records of epidemic diseases associated with famine offer a way to document where famine was occurring. In April to June 1933, "an epidemic of typhus struck the industrial zones of Ukraine, the Central Black-earth oblast', lower and central Volga, Northern Caucasus, Ural, Kazakhstan, Central Asia, and also Gorkovskii Krai, Tataria, Bashkiria, Yakutia."[24] Kondrashin documents sharp declines in food availability and increased mortality rates in many Soviet cities and provinces.

There was no public discussion of famine in Uzbekistan's newspapers at the time, and archival documentation appears to be scant, for reasons explained below. The Uzbek historian Rakhima Aminova did not discuss famine in her multivolume comprehensive history of Soviet-period agricultural transformation and collectivization in Uzbekistan, though she did present statistics on the rapid decline in livestock numbers. In a 1989 article, she mentioned famine in a general way: "A direct result of collectivization in Central Asia was the mass hunger [*golod*] of 1933."[25] The leading post-Soviet historian of Uzbekistan's collectivization, Rustam Shamsutdinov, writes that "it should be remembered that in 1933, due to crop loss and famine, thousands or hundreds of thousands of people perished from hunger."[26] Shamsutdinov exhaustively researched dekulakization, which he calls the "tragedy of collectivization," but he does not focus on the sorts of documents that reveal conditions on kolkhozes, productivity, food supply, or the ways that collectivization affected the lives of the majority of Uzbek dehqons and does not examine famine. A comprehensive history of Uzbekistan offers a brief mention of the 1933 famine: "According to the recollections of people in Tashkent and other cities in Uzbekistan who saw these things with their own eyes, 'the bodies of countless people who had died lay in the streets and alleys.' On 'death carts,' as the people called them, and trucks, 'they were laid exactly like wood . . . and they were taken away and buried in common pits.' . . . The rural population, pulled into hunger's whirlpool, were forced to steal wheat and potatoes and other food from fields."[27]

Direct statistical evidence on population growth or excess deaths is lacking for Uzbekistan for the famine year. The Soviet Statistical Commission (TsUNKhU), in a secret report on the USSR's population losses for 1932–1933, explicitly excluded Uzbekistan because they had no foundational data, as registry offices opened in some rural communities for the first time in 1933, but in most villages

TABLE 6.1 Uzbekistan and Tajikistan populations in 1926 and 1939

POPULATION BY MAJOR ETHNIC GROUP	1926 CENSUS UZBEK SSR, INCLUDING TAJIK ASSR	1939 TAJIK SSR	1939 UZBEK SSR	REASONS FOR INCREASE/ DECREASE IN UZBEKISTAN
Total	5,267,658	1,484,440	6,271,269	–
Uzbeks	3,475,340	353,478	4,081,096	Natural increase
Tajiks	967,728	883,966	317,560	Tajikistan separated, many Tajiks moved there
Russians/Europeans · Of these, rural	303,508 · 47,000	175,738	987,069	Immigration
Kazakhs	106,898	12,712	305,416	Immigration
Koreans	–	43	72,944	Forced resettlement
Karakalpaks	26,563	–	181,420	Karakalpak ASSR joined UzSSR in 1936
Kyrgyz	90,703	27,968	89,044	Tajikistan separated

Source: 1926 census, *Vsesoiuznaia perepis' naseleniia 1926 goda*, Demoskop Weekly, http://www.demoscope.ru/weekly/ssp/ussr_nac_26.php?reg=6; 1939 census, *Vessoiuznaia perepis' naseleniia 1939 g.*, Demoskop Weekly, Tablitsa f.15a, http://www.demoscope.ru/weekly/ssp/sng_nac_39.php?reg=8.

they did not yet exist.[28] Rashid (b. 1917) mentioned this lag in rural recordkeeping, saying, "In 1940, I was elected the secretary of the village soviet, and I did the reports. Until that time, no one recorded birth dates."[29] The Statistical Directorate complained that "there is no recording of births and deaths in villages in Georgia, Azerbaijan, Turkmenia, Uzbekistan, Kirgizia, Kara-kalpakia, that is, in those regions where in 1933 matters with births and deaths were more positive than in Ukraine and the North Caucasus."[30] Kondrashin's review of mortality data, which exist only for Uzbekistan's largest cities, shows a higher death rate in 1933, at 22.8 per thousand, than the 16 to 18 per thousand that might have been expected in a nonfamine year.[31]

While the kind of direct data on famine-related deaths that can be produced for other parts of the USSR did not exist for rural Uzbekistan, indirect measures show that famine had no impact that can be measured in population numbers, other than, perhaps, on very young children. The 1939 census, compared with the 1926 census, indicates that Uzbekistan's total population grew significantly in those thirteen years.

TABLE 6.2 Uzbekistan rural population by age group according to birth year, 1939 Census

YEAR OF BIRTH	1930 (AGE 9)	1931 (8)	1932 (7)	1933 (6)	1934 (5)	1935 (4)	1936 (3)
Cohort size	105,171	130,616	122,313	112,890	103,850	111,847	131,262

Vsesoiuznoe perepis' naselenie SSSR 1939 g., table showing rural population in Uzbekistan by age cohort, http://www.demoscope.ru/weekly/ssp/sng_age_39.php?reg=8&gor=2&Submit=OK.

During that period, there were known, recorded decreases in Uzbekistan's rural Uzbek and Tajik population: tens of thousands left for Afghanistan; thousands of quloq families were exiled to Ukraine and the North Caucasus; and tens of thousands resettled to Tajikistan voluntarily and to flee dekulakization. Even considering those losses, which may have amounted to several hundred thousand, the population of Uzbeks and Tajiks increased.

Data on age cohorts for Uzbekistan from the 1939 census, during which household heads were asked the ages of their living children, provide an indirect indicator of famine's impact. These cohort data are retrospective, based on a parent's report, in a society where birthdays were not celebrated; and any child born in this cohort who died before the year 1939 was not reported. The data, showing substantial declines in cohorts for 1933 and 1934, suggest a correlation between the famine period and reduced live births and/or reduced infant survival rates.[32]

To sum up the statistical data, while increased mortality can be shown for Uzbekistan's cities in 1933, and there may have been a famine-related decline in infant survival rates, there is no glaring trace of famine-related death in Uzbekistan's population statistics. A famine that did not produce mass deaths nonetheless remains in memory and may have other physical impacts on populations.[33] One of the lasting impacts of famine in Uzbekistan was to shape attitudes about food, seen in shifting popular evaluations of the potato.

Eyewitnesses to Famine Deaths

While historical studies have been silent on famine in Uzbekistan, and searches in archives reveal only scattered indications of food scarcity and citations of deaths from starvation, oral histories with those who were alive during this time of hardship offer visceral glimpses of famine-related deaths in communities across Uzbekistan. Respondents recalled that the first indication of trouble was that many Kazakhs were arriving in their communities, fleeing hunger. Xurram (b. 1920), from Qashqa Daryo, said, "I remember that in 1933, there was famine, and a number of Kazakhs came to our kolkhoz and stayed because they had nothing to eat. They stayed five or six months and then returned to their homes."[34] Abdullo F.'s (b. 1919) recollections were similar: "In the famine . . . it began with Kazakhs coming. Their land had all dried up, so they came to Uzbekistan, driving herds of cattle."[35] A Bukhara Province dehqon, Fayzi (b. 1915), said: "In 1933 a lot of people came from Kazakhstan, because of famine. Between *vabo* [typhus] and ocharchilik, many of them died in our villages."[36] A. K. (b. 1907), from Tashkent Province, noted: "The famine started in Kazakhstan. The Kazakhs then came here, to our streets. The more that came, the worse it got, and many of them died."[37] Other respondents mentioned desperate Kazakhs selling their daughters for food or abandoning children.[38] The Swiss traveler Ella Maillert, taking a mail train in Xorazm late in 1932, saw "tattered Kazakhs" camped on goods wagons, one with a baby who "supports itself on thin sticks of legs. . . . There is no flesh on its little backside." She wrote: "Have they escaped from some totally abandoned region? Will they perish from hunger?"[39] Archival sources document that some Kazakhs went to Uzbekistan to seek aid during Kazakhstan's famine years.[40]

Interviews show that Uzbek dehqons also died in the famine. At least 6 of the 130 respondents mentioned members of their families dying either of hunger or typhus in 1933. Halil (b. 1917) spoke of drought in his Bustonliq grain-growing kolkhoz: "The famine lasted a long time. My father was a victim of it; he died here. He told me to care for the family, so I would bring home bread or *zo'gora* [corn bread]." He noted that they started planting potatoes the next season, in 1934, a point I return to later.[41] Narzi (b. 1921) remembered that in her grain-growing village there was "nothing to eat, so we were forced to eat unripe apples and apricots. People died in that famine. One of my younger brothers died; he became ill, and there was no remedy."[42] Fayzullo (b. 1909), who had joined the local kolkhoz in wheat-growing Qashqa Dayro Province, said, "My father was in Samarkand, and he died of starvation."[43] Nemat (b. 1916), from a grain kolkhoz in Bukhara Province, said, "There was not enough to eat, and they gave out bread in exchange for work. People ate *kunjara* [cotton seed hulls] and died. My younger brother Pazil died."[44] From a grain-growing kolkhoz in Xorazm, Rajab (b. 1921) said, "In the famine, my father had an older brother. Nothing could be done; he died. My mother took kunjara, some bark, and made a paste out of them to feed to him."[45]

Several respondents who lived in or near cities in cotton-growing regions of the Fergana Valley remembered watching corpses of those who died being collected from the streets. Muqimjon (b. 1902), who was working at a teahouse in Margilon in 1933, recalled, "On the way to the station we saw ten or twelve corpses. Behind the teahouse we saw so many people's dead bodies. They put the corpses onto carts."⁴⁶ Hidoyatxon (b. 1919), also of Margilon, remembered, "I myself saw the dead; there were times when I went out on to the street to stare at those who were left there, dead."⁴⁷ Sharofutdin (b. 1917), from a village near Fergana City, said, "Many people would go to the oil factory and dig out kunjara, eat it, and swell up, and many of them died.... Ten people would load them on carts and take them away to bury them.... We were young kids, and we would go out to stare at this."⁴⁸ These eyewitness accounts suggest that rural people went to cities in Central Asia seeking food, just as they did across the Soviet Union. Some were Kazakh famine refugees, and some were local people.⁴⁹

Epidemic diseases often accompany famine and may be spread when famine refugees move to seek aid. Typhus accompanied the 1932–1933 Soviet famine, as recorded for Uzbekistan in archival documents and in memory.⁵⁰ Tojivoy (b. 1917), from Parkent, said, "While I was in school, in 1933, on one hand there was famine, and on the other, vabo sickness happened. It was an epidemic."⁵¹ *Vabo* can mean "plague" or "epidemic" in its loose sense, a rapidly spreading disease that kills many people, and is often defined as "cholera," but several Bukhara respondents defined it in Russian as "typhus." One of them, Ahmad (b. 1921), said, "During that famine a lot of people died from hunger, and on top of that vabo came.... It was so bad that when typhus came, there were not enough men to carry the bodies of those who had starved, and women carried the dead to the cemetery—women."⁵² Traditionally, a death procession draws all of a community's men but none of its women into roles carrying and accompanying the bier to the cemetery, where only men take part in the burial and associated prayers.⁵³ Five respondents from Shofirkon District in Bukhara, when asked about famine, immediately mentioned vabo, telling similar stories of so many deaths and not enough healthy men to bury them.⁵⁴ Typhus is spread by lice, and an outbreak in the Ivanovo textile-producing region, near Moscow, in spring 1933, led the People's Commissariat of Health to ban the use of two tons of cotton fiber from Kokand, Uzbekistan, indicating that the commissariat knew of the typhus outbreaks in Uzbekistan.⁵⁵

Memories can only be "spontaneously enlivened" while their bearers are themselves alive. Those in Uzbekistan who remembered the 1933 famine were by definition those who survived it, and their accounts here are both "memories encoded in language" that have been repeated within families and communities and "sensory memories" that are shaped by affect, pain, or shock.⁵⁶ Those who stared at the bodies of the dead as they were carted away told those stories stressing their youth, as a way of explaining to themselves and to their listeners their macabre fascination. Others recalled their own and their community's sense of shame at being unable to bury the dead with customary honor.

Views from Below: Why Was There Famine?

Collectivization created famine in the USSR: economic plans established disastrously unrealistic quotas for grain production in Ukraine and meat production in Kazakhstan, and when peasants or herders did not turn in those quotas, empowered agents of the state seized whatever they could, leaving producers to starve. Did collectivization produce famine in Uzbekistan in such a direct way? It did, in that increased government-ordered cotton quotas displaced grain from irrigated lands. For those who came from grain-intensive regions, where grain traditionally was planted on lalm-i-kor land, not irrigated land, lived experience shaped a different perspective: grain-growing dehqons mostly blamed their 1933 hunger on drought and the failure of their wheat crops. Oral histories offering community perspectives do not contradict but rather add illustration to scholarly analyses of collectivization and its consequences.

Among many interviewees from grain-growing regions of Uzbekistan, Ravshan remembered: "In 1932–33 there was ocharchilik, but it was short—only a few months until the wheat ripened. The first year, the wheat did not get enough water; people's land had been taken; they did not know what to do. The second year, there was a brief time of hunger before the wheat ripened."[57] Fayzullo (b. 1909) said: "The reason for the famine was that it didn't rain, and so the wheat farming failed. For wheat, we depend on rain. People died."[58] In 1933, harsh weather conditions in Qashqa Daryo meant that the winter wheat crop failed. Xurram (b. 1920) said that ocharchilik happened when "the fields dried out, the crops dried up—they were on *lalm-i* land, and it dried out. And some kind of insects attacked and ate up the wheat, and after that, there's no bread. Since there was no bread, we ate other things that gave us no pleasure."[59] Abdurasul saw the lack of water for wheat fields not as inevitable but as indication of kolkhoz organization problems. He was about ten years old at the time, so it is likely that this was his parents' explanation for their hardships: "The kolkhoz did not work well. It had not extended water to the wheat fields, and there was a dry spell, and the wheat dried up and did not produce, so wheat became very expensive."[60]

In the same year, grain-planting districts in Tashkent Province also experienced drought and crop failure. Abdullo Q., who at the time was a thirty-year-old member of a kolkhoz in Parkent, recalled: "There was little snow or rain, so the fields dried, and there was no harvest. There was no wheat or barley." Abdullo's grandson then added the story that Abdullo had apparently told them many times, that he had dismantled his house bit by bit, selling the wood to get food for the family.[61] Yusupboy (b. 1917), who lived in a district north of Tashkent, remembered: "There was not a good crop. It got dried out, and at that time we did not have irrigated lands to plant. We planted in the mountains. When the Lord did not give rain, and the wheat has no water, then there was no harvest.... Then there was hunger, really severe, and in the village area it was hard to find any food."[62]

In Xorazm, where wheat was usually planted on irrigated land, dehqons remembered a lack of water in the famine year but for differing reasons. Ibroyim, a teenaged kolkhoz member at the time, said, "Well, if there is no rain and not enough water, this happens. There was no water. We worked one or two months to dig a water channel and bring water."[63] Madqurbon (b. 1914) explained that famine happened "because others took our water. They used it, and none of it remained to water our land."[64] Abdullo S., who at age twelve was working outdoors as a kolkhoz herder, said: "The crops had dried out, and the government did not have anything to give us."[65]

Uzbekistan's cotton sector underwent high-speed collectivization, but individual farmers were still raising 34 percent of Uzbekistan's grain in 1932. In 1933, government agents began seizing grain in forced requisitioning. Lutfullo (b. 1919), whose elder brother inherited their father's eight hectares, told of forcible collectivization in Qashqa Daryo, with his family land taken into a kolkhoz. His explanation for the 1933 famine differed from others in his region: "We had everything, but many fled when the regional party committee seized the lands where wheat had been planted ... and because they left, a harsh famine started." In Lutfullo's region, the OGPU reported seizing hidden grain in summer and fall 1933, finding several thousand kilos in storage pits in the ground.[66] Bekmurod (b. 1907), from the same region, said, "They came and seized every gram of wheat that we raised. If you tried to hide it, they would poke through your house to find it. Our kolkhoz had only rain-fed lands, so we raised wheat, not cotton."[67] Some interviewees regarded the famine as the result of bad leadership, bad policy, or deliberate conspiracy. Yoqubjon (b. 1919) said, "In 1933, the hardship was because Uzbekistan had dirty leadership. They were trying to make the people dissatisfied with the kolkhoz and break it up. We had enough wheat for two or three years, but nonetheless they would not distribute it."[68] In contrast, Otanazar (b. 1921) argued, "The cause of all of this was not natural but artificial. It wasn't the climate but that they made quloqs of all of the boylar and the mullahs and the specialists.... The best specialists in agriculture were made into quloqs."[69]

In June 1933, Uzbekistan's Central Committee announced a temporary suspension of taxes on land that kolkhozes brought into new production, such as the new lalm-i-kor wheat fields, as well as for all kolkhozes in regions experiencing "natural disaster." At the same time, it raised tax rates up to 70 percent for remaining quloq farms. Not surprisingly, individual farmers rapidly joined kolkhozes.[70] Regardless of whether they were farming individually or for a kolkhoz, dehqons living in grain-producing regions experienced Sen's "entitlement failure" in 1933 when drought, the state policy that prioritized cotton planting in irrigated fields, and heavy requisitioning of grain from individual producers severely diminished production of their staple food.

Trade Entitlements and Lack of Entitlement

Those who raised grain knew that their crops had failed. But those who did not raise grain saw only the results in their own lives, when grain supplies did not arrive, and when prices soared, and they called this period *qimmatchilik*, "inflation," a time when the price of bread and other foods rose unexpectedly. The latter was borne out in archival records. Grain and other foods in Uzbekistan's capital, Tashkent, showed a tripling of prices: for example, a kilogram of rice cost 8.8 rubles in a Tashkent market in March 1931, but it cost 25 rubles in the summer of 1933; other foods, from beef to oil and milk, showed a similar rise in prices.[71] Those who normally purchased staple foods, such as wheat flour and bread, experienced what Sen would call "trade entitlement failure." Kolkhozes that paid cotton growers partially in grain, flour, or bread could not fulfill those payments if grain shipments did not arrive.

Respondents recalled extraordinary efforts they engaged in to obtain food by selling their worldly goods. The Soviet state established Torgsin stores to obtain gold from its own citizens, to fund its purchase abroad of industrial technology. Several respondents, such as Sharofutdin, who lived near Fergana City, remembered selling gold for food at the Torgsin store: "There was a store here, and my grandmother had one gold ring. She was given a lot for that ring at the store: rice, oil, flour."[72] Mahkam (b. 1921), who lived in a Fergana Valley border village, told of trading for food: "In 1932, during inflation a lot of our things went to the Kyrgyz. They took grain, gold, jewels, and other things, sold them to the Kyrgyz, and brought back things to survive. My father went . . . and took our gold, and he came back with fifteen or sixteen kilos of wheat."[73] A. K. (b. 1907), from a kolkhoz near Tashkent, remembered: "Many people died from hunger. If you had money, it was hard to find food. We had four cows, and I would take their milk to the [kolkhoz station] . . . but in that direction there were Russians, all of them working to build the railroad. . . . I would pay a lot of money to enter, carrying two containers. 'How much?' 'Don't give me money; give me bread.'" The bread that the Russians exchanged for his milk was Russian loaf style, distinctly foreign. "I tell myself, get what you can. I was glad to get bread."[74] Narziya (b. 1921) recalled lack of bread and inflation in her Bukhara Province community: "If we heard in the evening that we can get one kilo of flour, we would sleep outside the store on a shirt or a robe.... No one died, but we sold all our things—quilts, chests—to buy food."[75]

During a period when most of our respondents were struggling to find food, some recalled that their families had enough to eat and sometimes enough to share. Entitlement to better food supplies belonged to those who worked for the Soviet system. Umriniso (b. 1914), whose father had organized a Fergana region kolkhoz and was serving as director, said, "My father would bring wheat from the factory, and we had enough to eat, and he fed our livestock, but the people of the kolkhoz had nothing, and he would feed them porridge." She continued with lengthy stories of kolkhoz members turning to her father to beg him for bread and of one who abandoned an infant child to her father's care.[76] Saidalixon, a twelve-year-old living in Margilon City, who witnessed people dying of starvation, said, "My father was working on a construction project. I realized later that as long as they wrote down that the number of workers was increasing, they would get a larger supply of bread, and thus we did not really feel the effect of that bread famine... but my uncle, who came to our house daily to ask for part of our bread, died right across the street, poisoned by some food that he had managed to find."[77] Qurbon B. (b. 1906), who was from G'alla-Osio, a wheat-growing center that failed to produce in 1933, noted that he knew people from home were eating zo'gora (corn bread) and kunjara but that he himself had gone to the city to work, and he had enough to eat.[78] Madqurbon (b. 1914), a tractor driver, grew up on a rice-growing kolkhoz that produced poorly in 1933 due to lack of water. "My family lived well [during the famine]. I worked in mechanization, and I had both money and wheat."[79] Zulayho (b. 1916), whose father worked as a driver on their kolkhoz, said, "Our family ate rather well... and my father kept giving wheat to our neighbors, who were left with nothing."[80] Lutfullo (b. 1919), whose family's land had been seized and who was attending school in Shahrisabz, said that in the 1933 famine, "bread was divided out with a ration card. My older brother was the education inspector, and I would go and get bread from him; he was reliable in giving me bread."[81]

The Soviet system, as Wemheuer points out, created its own set of entitlements, and in 1933, this meant that the available wheat supplies went to kolkhoz chairmen, administrators, workers in favored industries, and agricultural specialists, such as tractor drivers. However, the image of entitlement is not consistent in our accounts. Fayzullo (b. 1909), whose account of tracking down fleeing quloqs ended the previous chapter, was trained as a hydrologist and worked in an expert position on his Qashqa Daryo kolkhoz. Nonetheless, as he said, his father died of starvation in Samarkand.[82] Boltaboy (b. 1914), a Komsomol member who worked with the Raykom office, described surviving by foraging: his aunt "would get up early, pick leaves, cook them, chop them up, add some flour, and make bread."[83] These accounts of hunger come from kolkhoz members and from individual farmers, from younger and older interviewees, from those who thought of themselves as mardikor and as boylar. Entitlements were unconnected to older forms of social status. Nor were entitlements reliably attached to collective agriculture.

Surviving: The Foods of Famine

Wondering what dehqons did to survive famine, we asked questions about what sorts of things they ate. Sometimes interviewers, informed by what they had learned about famine in Ukraine and Kazakhstan, asked whether people committed cannibalism or ate meat from animals that Islam considers unclean. Roviya (b. 1915), whose father abandoned his family amid the famine and whose mother took out a loan from a neighbor and started baking bread to sell, explained that those who had nothing to eat would try making bread from clover. The interviewer Komil asked, "Did people eat dog, cat, frog, or snakes?" She responded, "Our people did not eat such things. . . . Maybe Russians and Koreans would eat that in a time of hunger, but Uzbek people would not."[84] Of course, Roviya could not speak for everyone in Uzbekistan. Abdullo, who was a twelve-year-old herder, said, "I would eat dried bread. I was hungry a lot of the time. I was working minding livestock. Once our grandfather's cow died of disease, and he said to leave it outside and not eat it. Islam forbids eating meat from an animal that dies of disease. But other people took it, ate the meat, got sick, and died."[85] In none of the interviews did we hear anything about cannibalism, but we heard many stories about eating for survival: the starving resorted to consuming things that were inedible; hungry people foraged and ate things that they regarded as undesirable; and many began to eat foods that they previously rejected for cultural reasons.

The most desperate would eat animal fodder. Narziya (b. 1921) said that during the famine, "People would eat kunjara and die." Narziya's mention of kunjara was common to all regions of Uzbekistan.[86] Uzbekistan's cotton factories separated cotton fiber from seeds, which were then taken to the oil press where oil was extracted and used to pay kolkhoz members. The seed hulls, or kunjara, were fed to livestock. Many respondents said that eating kunjara led to swelling up and meant death was certain. It may be that only people who were already on the brink of death would resort to eating inedible kunjara. Those who were not quite so desperate foraged. They ate new leaves of native plants, especially *ismaloq* (*Spinacea oleracea*), other grasses, unripe fruit, mulberry paste and mulberry flour, melon seeds, mung beans, tiny turnips. Bozorxo'ja (b. 1913), from

Parkent, said, "People would go to the fields and tear off wheat and barley by hand."[87] Saidalixon (b. 1921) mentioned people gathering at the silkworm factory, pulling caterpillars from cocoons, and eating them.[88] Hayrullo (b. 1921) said, "We ate kunjara and black grasses, dried-up grasses from the field, and ismaloq and whatever else a person could get."[89]

Dehqons ate what was available to them, which included maize, but every mention of eating zo'gora (corn-bread) was disparaging. Ismoyiljon (b. 1923) said that during the famine, "I was in the second grade, and a girl was studying in the second grade.... They arranged a wedding for her.... They gave about three hundred grams of cornmeal, including a bit of meat and oil.... Then they called in two men [two witnesses], and they didn't even have any *plov*. They had three hundred grams of zo'gora.... Her father agreed to give her for that."[90] Ismoyiljon was ten years old at the time. He emphasized the girl's youth at the time of this arranged marriage, the lack of guests, and the serving of cornbread, to portray the father's utter poverty and desperation for food. Central Asian dehqons had raised maize long before the Russian conquest. Their aversion to eating it was not connected to cultural skepticism of Russian things but to its association with poverty. Maize had spread to Central Asia as fodder for livestock and that was its primary use; as in many parts of the world, "the stigma of poverty indelibly branded corn."[91]

Haram or Just Foreign? Eating Russian Bread and Potatoes

Both in the context of discussing famine and in response to another specific question about adopting potatoes, interviewees discussed Russian foods that had been new to their region and dehqons' reluctance to consume them. Ashirboy, who was about ten years old during the famine, said: "Up until [the 1933 famine], people would say, 'Cabbage is Russian,' and would not eat it. People called tomatoes 'eggplants' and said they were Russian, feared them, and did not eat them. Before then, they were used to eating only non, but during the famine *buhonka* [Russian loaf bread] showed up, and people were in serious hardship.... During the famine year, we drank tea and ate zo'gora. We took dried apples, heated them, made them into a jam, and drank that."[92] Remembering a time during the famine when buhonka was distributed at his kolkhoz, he added: "The people said, 'Russians bake those,' but finally after they looked, they recognized that the loaves had come to them through Muslim hands, and they could be eaten. And then they got used to cabbage, too, and to tomatoes and to cars and whatever else there was."[93]

Traditionally, those who baked non for sale to the public belonged to a breadbaker's guild, which had its own manual, or *risala*, for moral conduct. The baker's risala established that every step in the making of bread, from the first plowing of the field to the final sale to a customer, was to be filled with prayer, or the baker's work would be unclean.[94] People in Ashirboy's community were willing to eat foods raised or made by Muslim hands; such foods were not haram, even if they were new. Foods that were produced by Russians were suspect, and one could not be certain that they were halal. Buhonka baked by Russians certainly was not produced in accord with the morals of the baker's risala, but Ashirboy's community rationalized that the bread was delivered by Muslims, meaning that it was indeed halal and could be eaten.

Interviewees attached similar skepticism to potatoes. Interviewees from all provinces other than Tashkent said that they had not even seen potatoes before the 1930s. Everyone regarded them as Russian food, alien and potentially haram. Yoqubjon (b. 1919), from a Fergana village, told a story that his community used to illustrate their rejection of potatoes: "The tomato came later, and the potato, too. So much misunderstanding. For example, if a soldier who was fighting against the Bosmachis requested to use someone's cooking pot, then that person would ask, 'What will you cook?' And the soldier said, 'Potatoes.' And the pot's owner shouted, 'Haram,' and threw it at him. Potatoes and tomatoes were only started later."[95] Most respondents did not call potatoes haram, but they used a different way of expressing rejection: the potato and tomato were Russian.

Uzbeks use the same term for potatoes as Russians, *kartoshka*, and it is assumed that potatoes reached this part of Central Asia with Russian conquest. But a group of Tatars from the Volga region who moved to the Kokand Khanate in the 1820s and established a village, Nogai-Kurgan, near Tashkent, may have been Turkestan's original potato growers. In 1867, two years after Russia's capture of Tashkent, an observer noted that Nogai-Kurgan was the only place in the new territory producing potatoes.[96] Russians and other European colonial settlers established numerous agricultural settlements in Tashkent Province, which was where most of Uzbekistan's potato growing took place. Outside of Tashkent Province, there were only a few thousand scattered Russians in rural communities in Uzbekistan; both Russians and their preferred staple foods remained quite foreign to most rural Uzbeks until collectivization.[97]

Uzbekistan's Communist Party Chairman Akmal Ikramov set in motion an effort to feed Uzbekistan by expanding potato production, which, on the eve of collectivization, was miniscule.[98] The Ak-Kavak Experimental Planting Station in Tashkent Province began working with selecting and improving potato strains for Uzbekistan's conditions, while another institute developed strains for mountainous areas in Central Asia.[99] In 1933, in a policy designed to stimulate potato planting, potato tax rates for the collective sector were set to equal the low cotton and grain rate, much lower than for fruits, vegetables, pulses, or rice.[100] Following Ikramov's initiative, Uzbekistan's potato crop increased from 3000 ha. in 1931 to 10,800 ha. in 1932, and to 23,500 ha. in 1940, at which point potatoes equaled the planted area of all other vegetable crops combined.[101]

However, as with maize, potatoes could be used for animal fodder, and their increased availability did not mean that Uzbekistan's dehqons were interested in eating them. The kolkhoz controlled what was planted in irrigated kolkhoz fields, where priority went to raising cotton. If kolkhoz members were to adopt the potato as a hedge against food shortages by planting it in their private plots, that demanded individual knowledge and decision. Skepticism about eating them began to disappear only when dehqons began raising their own potatoes.

Abdullo S. (b. 1921), from Xorazm, illustrated his prior unfamiliarity: "When I was young, potatoes came to Khiva, and we guessed they were egg yolks. We cooked them in an outdoor fire, on the ground, and called them egg yolks. . . . Then tomatoes came, and cucumbers."[102] Berdiqul (b. 1920), from Nurota, said that in his area, "People learned about potatoes and tomatoes later from the people who came from the cities. Before, they did not know about those things. Even rich people did not know how to produce them. There were some people who did not want to eat them, because people called those vegetables Russian food."[103]

An unnamed woman respondent whose family had been exiled to Ukraine during the making of quloqs and returned to Uzbekistan later in the 1930s discussed the adoption of foreign foods in considerable detail. In Ukraine, her mother worked in a restaurant that served cabbages and potatoes. Back in Uzbekistan, she noticed that Uzbeks were not eating potatoes or cabbage. She said, "Potatoes grew under the ground, and the people did not know them. They learned about the potato in botany class, and when the potatoes bloomed, they ate the flowers, and it was sour, and they did not like it. . . . It was Russian food."[104] Like the unnamed woman who had lived in Ukraine, Ibodat (b. 1925), who grew up in a newly settled kolkhoz near Namangan, recalled that they had no idea how to plant potatoes or what part to eat. "Someone brought potatoes from some city[,] . . . planted them, the stems, and they couldn't be eaten. But then later these full-grown potatoes came out, and then people started cooking them and found out they were good to eat. I don't know when that was, 1937 or 1938."[105] In several Xorazm villages, the outsiders who spread potatoes were Germans rather than Russians. Olmajon (b. 1903) mentioned: "Some Germans settled over there, and then tomatoes and potatoes appeared, and now they are in every garden."[106]

The most common story told was that previously potatoes were unknown, but when kolkhoz members were shown how to raise and eat them, they were willing to adopt them within their own diet. Doniyor (b. 1925), from Nurota, recalled the interventions that introduced potatoes to his community: "In 1937, for the first time, potato was planted in this village. I think the government provided it. The kolkhoz planted it. Then the tomato came, but nobody knew about it, and they did not eat it.... Later, eggplant.... A special brigade leader was assigned to plant them on separate land."[107] Muhammadjon (b. 1922), from Fergana, remembered: "When they said they would plant potato for us, they did only once. Then we figured it out ourselves. Then everybody started using potatoes."[108]

Unlike Russia, Ukraine, and Belorussia, where potatoes became the central dietary starch, in Uzbekistan bread and wheat-dough products remained the primary dietary starch, followed by rice.[109] When interviewees emphasized how much they depend on potatoes now, they highlighted the potato's shift from rejected Russian thing to an item that they included in ordinary consumption. As Jenny Leigh Smith notes, potatoes had many attractions to kolkhoz members, both as collective crops and for individual garden plots: they were easy to store and long-lasting; there was no state system for refrigerating or transporting them, and they were not subject to systematic collections, so they remained for local consumption.[110] In Uzbekistan, new strains of potato appropriate to hot, arid summers could be planted after winter wheat was harvested. Collectivization had taken away dehqon endowments in land and the entitlement to most of the fruits of their labor, but potato growing offered rural Uzbeks some control over a food plant they could include in their own diet, raise to sell at market, or feed to domestic livestock.

In the early 1930s, people in some regions of the USSR, most notably Ukraine and Kazakhstan, experienced a viciously cruel famine, resulting in many millions starving to death. To point out that other regions of the USSR such as Uzbekistan did not experience that same degree of tragedy may seem unimportant, but I do so to highlight the differing contexts for and impacts of collectivization across the USSR. Amartya Sen charges that "starvation . . . is a function of entitlements and not of food availability as such."[111] In the cases he examined, in areas with capitalist systems where natural causes decreased food production, impoverished people were far more likely to starve than better-off people because they could not purchase expensive food when prices increased due to shortages. Entitlement worked differently in the USSR, where party activists hounded grain growers and herders with unsustainable requisitions, while the government directed food supplies toward industrial workers and party members. A state that had the means to move grain from surplus to shortfall regions but did not do that did not act as though all its citizens were equally entitled to food and to life.

Oral histories recalling famine and the adoption of new foods enrich a historical reconstruction of the lives of ordinary Uzbek dehqons during the Uzbek SSR's agricultural collectivization period, with details reflecting widely shared experiences that were neither the focus of government data collection nor, under conditions of censorship, of public or personal writing. In hindsight, contextualizing ocharchilik within reflections on a span of time that encompassed rapid collectivization and participation in World War II, interviewees remembered the 1933 famine as a rather brief crisis, with a muted resonance of the emotional turmoil that they must have felt seven decades earlier. Although remembrances of collectivization were continually shaped by state discourses, discussion of famine was silenced by state and party. This did not prevent people from remembering their own stories of a particular episode of unusual hunger, but they did so in the absence of any official account or dominant narrative.

Historical analyses based on thorough study of other parts of the Soviet Union make clear the direct link between forced collectivization, extreme production quotas, forced requisitioning of grain and livestock, and mass starvation. But for Uzbekistan, producer of inedible cotton and importer of grain, the lack of any research-based or politically created dominant narrative about famine is reflected in the diversity of respondent accounts of their experiences, of being entitled while people around them suffered, of eating things that were a last resort, and of witnessing desperate actions and deaths. The lack of a dominant narrative is also reflected in their varied explanations for famine, all of which arose from their situated views: though most of them mentioned drought, some additionally blamed famine on depriving quloqs of land and grain, on mendacious efforts to undermine collectivization, or simply on the mystery of missing food supplies and consequent high prices.

7
WORKING

"Memory is not a passive depository of facts, but an active process of creation of meanings."[1] So wrote the oral historian Alessandro Portelli as he analyzed the emotion-laden inaccuracies in labor union members' accounts of a strike that turned violent. Collectivization generation respondents raised or dwelled on topics that we, the interview team, had not anticipated would be of such importance to them, often with recollections that seemed surprisingly rosy. Communist Party and state discourses, spoken at kolkhoz meetings for agitation and propaganda, in houses of culture, in schools, and published in the limited media available in rural communities interpreted the collective farm, highlighting its supposedly fair evaluation of labor and pay, its modernization in the form of tractors, and improvement of agriculture by means of irrigation canal construction. Interviewees interacted with those propaganda discourses while events unfolded, in an extreme form of creating cultural or collective memory. This chapter explores four of the themes where we find rosy recollections—tractors, canals, silkworms, and payment—to tease out the ways that material changes, state discourses about those changes, and individual remembering interact, making certain moments meaningful to their narrators.

Individual stories about tractors and irrigation construction projects were so positive that a historian might dismiss them as nostalgic. Area studies scholars have defined post-Soviet nostalgia not only as "feelings of longing for or attachment to a past" that flourished in 1990s conditions of impoverishment and uncertainty but also as something appropriated by post-Soviet states to "shape a sense of affective connectedness to the past" for political goals.[2] At the time of these interviews, the post-Soviet state of Uzbekistan was busy rejecting the Soviet past rather than cultivating positive views of Stalinist changes to serve its contemporary political purposes. The oral historian Donald Ritchie does not diagnose positive memories as nostalgia; he observes that "rosy reminiscences" are common "when oral historians interview older people about their youth.... Dissatisfaction with present conditions makes the past look far better, and people's very survival can convince them that the hard times were not so bad after all."[3] I understand the memories shared in this chapter as romance, shaped in their formation by the state's cultivation of dispositions and by collectivization generation interviewees' reveling as they recalled their own youth, strength, and senses of accomplishment. When telling of tractors and canals, interviewees linked themselves to the Uzbek nation and to its modernization. They also made clear that good pay was an important element in the ways that they valued their own work experiences. In their unusually lively responses to our bland prompts about tractors or about how they were paid, interviewees imbued material changes in everyday life with meaning, defending the idea that they, the dehqons of Uzbekistan, were rational people who knew how to benefit from challenging but worthwhile changes.

Boy Loves Tractor

O'ktam was very proud of having been a tractor driver. She was the daughter of a man who, until collectivization, worked as sharecropper in Qashqa Daryo Province. O'ktam's father had joined the newly formed collective kolkhoz willingly, but he died shortly after the kolkhoz was founded. Her mother worked on the kolkhoz, and teenaged O'ktam combined school with work:

> I studied in school, and after school our teachers would take us out to work. We drove the horses. We worked like donkeys.... I finished eighth grade, and then I worked on the kolkhoz. I worked even before the end of eighth grade....
>
> The [world] war started in 1941 when we were fifteen or sixteen. Ahmedov was director of the MTS [machine tractor station] and then Bozrukov, and then they took all the young men away [to the army], and no young men were left. Then women became tractor drivers. Our kolkhoz taught nine of us women to drive. I studied for two months and then became a driver. We got on our ChTZ tractors and plowed.[4]

If O'ktam really was fifteen or sixteen in 1941, she had falsified her birth year, telling us it was 1919, and she had married before the legal age. She refused to say just how young she was when she married, stating that she was embarrassed. When the men in her village, including her husband, were conscripted, O'ktam volunteered to drive a tractor. She remembered the names of the Uzbek men who taught her this skill: "Juma To'rayev—and Tosh Fayziliyev was our mechanic. They taught us here in the village; we did not go off to the city to learn. There were nine of us women who learned and who worked together in the fields." O'ktam's tractor driving years were the first step up the kolkhoz career ladder. After the war, as a widowed mother, she worked as a brigade leader and then director of the livestock operation, and finally she became director of the kolkhoz.

When Hurshida, the interviewer, asked O'ktam, "Do you remember who drove the first tractors?" she responded, "Among the women?" Hurshida clarified, "No, among the men, who was the first tractor driver?" "I don't know that," she said. When asked what people in her village thought of the first tractors, O'ktam, like most respondents, said, "People liked tractors because they made hard work easier." Hurshida tested a myth about tractor reception, asking, "Weren't people afraid of it, as a Russian thing?" O'ktam asserted: "We women were not afraid of tractors. We drove our tractors at night; we drove them singing songs. We weren't afraid of them."

"Boy loves tractor" is a trope and a critique about Socialist realism in literature and film.[5] The 1939 Soviet film *Traktoristi* could be hailed as the exemplar of this genre: in it, the woman tractor driver Mar'iana meets the returned tank driver Klim, who wins her heart by becoming a tractor driver and joining her in fulfilling the agricultural plan.[6] O'ktam recounted her own experience, living out the patriotic image of tractor-driving women whose fame was spread by Soviet newspapers and whom the Communist Party rewarded with medals and public praise.[7]

Like other interviewees, O'ktam remembered World War II as a time of famine, when all food production was prioritized for the front, but she said, "I was a tractor driver. The MTS paid us in bread; there was a big bread bazaar. People in the village gave us honey. We did not have such a hard time."[8] Aside from her gendered lens, O'ktam's remembrances of good pay for tractor drivers, her association of tractor driving with prestige, her recollection of the names of Uzbek tractor drivers from her community and the tractor models they used, and her comments on dehqon responses to the first appearance of tractors were all common stories. Not only boys loved tractors; some girls loved them as well.

Collectivization of agriculture was supposed to be accompanied by the provision of tractors; however, as Matt Oja writes, "On the eve of the massive drive to collectivize agriculture, only an insignificant fraction of the USSR's peasants had ever even seen a tractor, much less knew how to operate, maintain, or repair one."[9] In the 1920s, the Soviet government imported tens of thousands of tractors from the United States and Great Britain, at great cost, and distributed them unequally.[10] In 1925, there were 484 tractors in Uzbekistan, owned either

FIGURE 7.1. Photo of two women tractor drivers, by the Soviet journalistic photographer Max Penson. Approximate date 1940. The women are unidentified, but they wear clothing and headwear typical of Uzbek kolkhoz women in the 1930s and 1940s. Photo licensed by Getty Images.

TABLE 7.1 Tractors in the Uzbek SSR, 1920s

YEAR	NUMBER OF TRACTORS
1924	484
1925	1,053
1926	1,200
1927	1,525
1928	2,301

Source: Aminova, *Agrarniia preobrazovaniia v Uzbekistane* (1969), 339.

TABLE 7.2 Tractors at Uzbek SSR machine-tractor stations, 1930s

YEAR	NUMBER OF TRACTORS
1930	370
1931	2,389
1932	2,801
1933	3,229
1934	5,009
1935	12,298
1936	14,589
1937	18,267

Source: *Sel'skoe khoziaistvo Uz SSR za 40 let* (Tashkent: Gosizdat Uzbekskoi SSR, 1957), 135. This chart does not account for all tractors in Uzbekistan, some of which were owned by earlier organizations or by state farms.

by the Khlopkom (Cotton Committee), which was the state-run trust that organized cotton production in Uzbekistan, or by local divisions of the People's Commissariat for Land (NarKomZem). The Khlopkom provided tractors to major cotton producing regions, while Narkomzem sent tractors to regions perceived as backward. According to the historian Rakhima Aminova, the state had political goals in its early tractor distributions: "Sending tractors to those districts had great importance from the point of view of attracting the dehqons to the side of Soviet power, and on that basis liquidating the remainders of the Bosmachi movement."[11] As numerous historians have pointed out, the Soviet Union invested comparatively little in Central Asia's industrialization; most new infrastructure and machinery in Uzbekistan was for improving agriculture.[12]

A macro-level analysis would stress the obviously colonial pattern where agricultural investment served to entrench labor-intensive cotton production and keep dehqons on the farm, but in micro-level stories told by respondents, there was genuine excitement about tractors as complex, labor-saving machines. When we asked interviewees what they remembered about the first time they saw tractors, they told stories that linked their lives to modernization. Respondents were unsurprised when interviewers offered them stereotypes about backward Uzbeks reacting to tractors with fear and calling them *Shaytan araba* (Satan's cart), an image that recurs in Soviet films. Most respondents rejected that image, insisting instead that rational dehqons recognized the value of tractors and sought to adopt them.

Hayitboy M. (b. 1910) was an orphaned mardikor who joined a farm labor collective in the cotton zone near Andijon. He claimed that tractors stirred class conflict:

> They came around 1925 or 1927. When they first came, there was a man named Mustafaqul-aka who went and studied for a month in Hoqulobod. . . . He came back driving a tractor. . . . At that time the boylar said, "Don't drive that Russian tractor." The rich men opposed it. But he came pulling a plow to help us, the poor. . . . [The rich] went around saying that it is a Russian thing and will bring a bad result. The rich never sent any [tractors]. But he plowed the land with the tractor and gave great assistance to us, the poor.[13]

Hayitboy's presentation of tractors in relationship to his own class identity and his accusation that the boylar opposed tractors reflected the politics of his whole interview. Like others, he associated tractor adoption with a local Uzbek man, whose name he still recalled seven decades later.

Other interviewees recalled a more harmonious welcome for the new machinery. Fayzi S. (b. 1915), whose father owned enough land to hire sharecroppers, remembered the first tractor that came to his village in Bukhara, and he credited an Uzbek community leader with embracing innovation:

> FAYZI: The first tractors—one of our men spoke about tractors and brought one in 1926 or 1927. That was Davlat Nazar. He brought that tractor to our village soviet and put it to work. And some Russian man drove that tractor too. He wasn't an Uzbek; he came with a tractor. Everyone, more than a thousand people, gathered, amazed, asking how the tractor goes, discussing what has happened, how high it is, and how it is plowing the fields, what it is made of—iron? It goes putt-putt and plows the land. They were amazed, and they all came to watch.
> INTERVIEWER E. R.: They were amazed, or were they also afraid?
> FAYZI: What would they fear? They all stood and watched, and all were amazed. After that they said, "It seems to be a good thing; it can do this. It works better than oxen, and it plows."[14]

Fayzi, who later joined the Komsomol, did not remember any class division over tractors. Like others quoted in this section, Fayzi rejected interviewer skepticism about dehqons welcoming the new machines.

Interviewees remembered tractors by make, with names that traced when tractors first appeared in their district. Turdiboy (b. 1921), from the Andijon region, recalled the Fordson tractors of his childhood:

> TURDIBOY: When they established the kolkhoz here, it had nothing except for nineteen members. There were no tractors. An American tractor with two iron wheels called the Fordson came from Uchqo'rg'on. There was no technology yet in Hoqulobod.... Then they put through this road, and then the American tractor came. Those who looked after large herds for the rich left. My father said, "America has given tractors to the Soviet state. It seems that bad lands that can't be plowed with oxen can be plowed by tractors. Let's go see." And then we went to see that tractor with my father, the Fordson. At that time the Soviet state did not know how to make tractors, and so they were given by other countries. Then they gave tractors to plow the fields, put the poor to work, and form the kolkhoz.
>
> MARIANNE: When was the kolkhoz founded here?
>
> TURDIBOY: That tractor came in about 1927, and so it must have been 1928–1929.... Then the Soviet state produced a tractor called John Deere with a flywheel on the side. You turned that to start it. My father said, "I've joined the kolkhoz, and it needs tractors to plow the land, so I will go and learn to drive a tractor." He went and brought a tractor from the Uchqo'rg'on regional tractor station, and he set up a tractor station in Hoqulobod. He studied and became a tractor driver on the kolkhoz. I also became a tractor driver.[15]

Turdiboy's particular focus on Fordsons as American may have been sparked by the fact that he was being interviewed by two Americans, Russell Zanca and myself. But like Turdiboy, many respondents eagerly talked tractor: makes, power, wheels, pedals, treads, starters, capabilities. Turdiboy said, "John Deere and Fordson could plow in fields that were soaked with water!" Respondents tossed out details on planters, plows, and combines. Narzi recalled the earliest, short-lived Soviet effort at mechanized cotton harvesting: "We held a hose and picked cotton with that instead of by hand. It was like a vacuum."[16] Mechanization had no effect on cotton harvesting for decades, although tractors were adopted for grain harvesting: as of the 2020s, Uzbekistan's cotton harvest still is largely handpicked.

In the 1930s, machine tractor stations dispatched brigades of tractors and tractor drivers to nearby kolkhozes to plow and plant. Normurod recalled the

MTS's work: "At that time one MTS would serve five or ten kolkhozes. They would change out the tractors and repair them, and then they would send a mechanic with five or ten tractors to one kolkhoz, and then after they planted there, they would take them away, and they would come back to complete the harvesting."[17] Kolkhozes paid the MTS according to the area plowed, planted, or harvested, and tractor drivers were paid individually in labor-day rates based on the area they plowed.[18] Archival documents and historical descriptions of the MTS often stress its failures, the breakdown of machinery, the fact that a high proportion of the MTS tractors were idled for repair at any given moment, and the pressures on MTS directors to fulfill the plan. None of that came out in interviews, not even when former tractor drivers spoke. The daily frustrations that might have fueled dissatisfaction in the 1930s disappeared in hindsight, as respondents lauded the ways that tractors lightened their work. Tractor drivers presented themselves as well-paid innovators. As Oja notes, increased pay for tractor drivers in the 1930s raised their status on the collective farm.[19] O'ktam, the above-mentioned woman tractor driver, recalled being well-fed even during the lean times of World War II. Turdiboy mentioned that during the famine, "My father was working as a tractor driver, and even when they gave nothing to kolkhoz members, they still paid tractor drivers. Because of that, our stomachs were full, and things were fine."[20]

In some places, draft animals provided the only power until the mid-1930s, when larger tractors from the Kharkov (XTZ), Kirov (KTZ), and Cheliabinsk (ChTZ) factories arrived in Uzbekistan. Ubaydullo (b. 1922), from Bukhara Province, remembered mechanization arriving later, and like others, he went into detail on capabilities: "The oxen plowed the fields. Then in 1935 or 1937 the tractor came. The tractor was called the XTZ and the Universal. The Universal made three furrows with iron and planted cotton. But the XTZ plowed the field with four furrows. At that time there were few. Anyway, you couldn't use a tractor in sesame, so they plowed with oxen and used oxen and horses to plant cotton using the planter."[21]

Baraka (b. 1916), from the same district as Ubaydullo, spoke of a tractor demonstration that persuaded dehqons of its wonders and decreased their interest in maintaining draft animals:

> BARAKA: It was the XTZ tractor. Then after that some people came, and they were so high up! They demonstrated how to plow, and everyone saw how it turned the soil over as it went along. They said, "The oxen does not rule; it is not the shah, those oxen!" And then tractors became more numerous.
>
> ULFAT: Were they afraid of the tractor?

FIGURE 7.2. Uzbek poster, man with horse and tractor (1933), by Usto Mumin: "Even after we mechanize the kolkhozes one hundred percent, it will never be possible to do agricultural work without horses, and those who look after them are still needed. We value them every day and every hour to attain our harvest."

Source: Maria Filatova and Vladimir Bobrovnikov, comps., Plakat Sovetskogo Vostoka 1918–1940: al'bom-katalog (Moscow: Izdatel'stvo Dom Mardzhani, 2011). Photo courtesy of Maria Filatova. This poster is in the public domain.

>   BARAKA: No, they were not afraid. They gave a demonstration to show how it plowed, and the people sat and watched the show, how it plowed the field and how it could pull.[22]

Ruzim (b. 1919), whose father held out against collectivization into the mid-1930s, said that after tractors began arriving in Xorazm, dehqons began to demand them:

>   RUZIM: At that time, the people plowed and planted using oxen, horses, or donkeys. But when that power was insufficient or when people did not have that livestock, they went and made demands and brought [tractors] back to open new fields and to plant.
>   KOMIL: Who were the first tractor drivers?
>   RUZIM: A man named Oqyoz came from the center, and from here the first drivers were Yoquba Niyozova, Normat Buva, and Dovlat Jintik.
>   KOMIL: Was there opposition when the tractor drivers first brought tractors here?

> RUZIM: There were people who said that plowing this way would ruin the fields.[23]

The names that Ruzim recalled seven decades later were typical for Uzbek and other indigenous Central Asian women and men. Although early 1930s archival documents show that machine tractor stations, which served as depots for surrounding kolkhozes, employed many Russians, respondents remembered Uzbek tractor drivers, not Russians.[24] When interviewers asked if the first tractor drivers were Russians, most interview respondents asserted that they were "local," "our own," "Uzbeks." Nurmurod H. said, "Our tractor drivers were our own, from our people.... My older brother drove a tractor, and I joined up with my older brother and learned to drive."[25] The discourses about dehqon rationality and Uzbek drivers seem connected in their stories. It was not simply the tractor's obvious utility that made it an object of desire. The Uzbek tractor driver made the tractor acceptable, and tractor talk provided a moment when respondents emphasized the competence and skill of Uzbek tractor drivers who became local heroes.

Interviewers asked whether dehqons rejected tractors as evil or foreign. After Ahmed U. (b. 1919) gave a detailed description of the KTZ tractors that came to his kolkhoz in 1936, the interviewer Ulfat asked: "What kind of attitude did the people show toward the tractors? Did they welcome them happily, or did they reject it as 'Satan's machine'?" Ahmed responded, "Oh, they said, 'Satan's machine,' and other things, but after they saw how it could serve them, they all wanted it."[26] Most of the respondents were familiar with that characterization of Uzbek dehqon attitudes toward mechanization, and they countered it with their own narrative of acuity. As Rashid Sh. Put it, "After it started plowing, everyone came around, and they wanted it; everyone agreed to it and knew it was an improvement."[27]

However, several respondents told stories about rejection of the tractor. Hidoyatxon (b. 1919) recalled a kolkhoz director who, for the ten years he was in charge, refused to allow tractors on his kolkhoz. "He said that the tractor is a Russian thing from the city.... Right up until he died, he never sent a tractor into the field. After he died there was a new director who got them."[28] Tuloev (b. 1921) also recalled voices that opposed tractors:

> TULOEV: [Young men from our village] went off to study in 1931, and immediately after that, they brought the tractor. They organized the MTS and then studied there.... The MTS didn't help the dehqons, but then here there was this big dehqon, and he went to the MTS and got a tractor for harvesting. He went to ask the *domla* [Muslim teacher] about this, and the domla said that the wheat was *makruh* [not recommended by Islamic law]. He said that wheat from a place

> where a tractor worked was haram [forbidden]. Then the government found out the domla and shot him.
>
> KOMIL: When was this?
>
> TULOEV: This was in 1932–33. . . . If you told the domla, "I worked my land [with a tractor]," he would say, "Are you driving that Russian thing?" I think he said it was makruh. And then the government hunted down the domlas.
>
> KOMIL: After it was declared makruh, did they abandon the harvest?
>
> TULOEV: Of course they harvested it! The people did not have enough, and they would not leave so much as a stalk in the field. Wherever it came from, they would gather it to make bread.[29]

In Tuloev's recollection, the MTS could not or did not provide enough tractors to meet demand; it was corrupt, prioritizing influential people. He was a child, ten or eleven years old, when tractors, collectivization, and famine disrupted accepted ways of life in his Parkent grain-growing village, pitting the modernizing, mechanizing tractor users against the local domla, who, Tuloev coldly recalled, was brutally suppressed. Tuloev, who referred to the local boylar as "cheats and swindlers," told of religious resistance to tractors as an illustration that enemies of the kolkhoz and the MTS workers were out of touch with ordinary dehqons, who needed and wanted tractors.

In contrast with Tuloev's account, Ernazar (b. 1923) remembered that people in his Qashqa Daryo village used religious ideas to support tractor adoption when the ChTZ arrived in the mid-1930s: "Whoever brought the tractor from wherever it came also showed how it worked, and then there were a lot of curious rumors: 'It seems a tractor has come. The tractor is interesting. If you sit on it, God will forgive your sins.' I heard rumors going around like that, claiming [the tractor] had Allah's power."[30] Together, these stories of rejecting tractors as makruh and arguing that they were demonstrations of God's power suggest that tractors disrupted cultural ideas. Interviewees from the collectivization generation who emphasized how quickly dehqons recognized the tractor's advantages were young at that time, and they may have downplayed their elders' discomfort with this innovation.

Aliqul (b. 1916) took pride in his role as a tractor driver for his Namangan kolkhoz, framing his desire to drive the new machines with an Islamic ethic that erased any potential contradiction between religion and modernization:

> We became owners of technology. . . . I went and drove all kinds of tractors. . . . I only stopped driving recently. I got up on those very large tractors. We have an old saying: "A good intention is half the deed." I was a young boy, and my older brother was working on the kolkhoz.

And at that time, the ChTZ tractor came.... The first tractors were very small. We drove those. And then after we had driven those, new larger ones developed, and [the kolkhoz] owned very large tractors. The big tractor was called a ChTZ.... It was very tall, had a very loud sound, and I said, "When I am big enough, I'll drive this one too."... I went to Chirchiq and studied for three months after coming back from the war.... When I returned, I could drive the big tractors too. I got my desire. I had said, "When I am grown, I'll drive those." That is what I wished from Allah. He granted me that, and I say that you should wish from Allah for what you desire.[31]

Almost every respondent had something to say about their first encounter with tractors, and they spoke of the machines as an unmitigated good. Other aspects of collectivization received much more varied and critical retellings, but in recalling tractors, even the tractor drivers did not dwell on problems that must have accompanied the adoption of this new machinery.[32] Instead, interviewees remembered that their communities welcomed tractors because they made hard work easier. Establishing that Uzbeks drove tractors seems to have been part of this celebratory attitude: these mechanical wonders that came to Uzbekistan as American or Russian were mastered by Uzbeks, and this hastened their acceptance on newly formed, turbulent kolkhozes.

Digging Canals

The prevalence of romantic recollections about tractor adoption challenged our Soviet-legacy images of dehqon fear in the face of change, but their rosy images of the hard labor of canal construction replicated and adapted well-publicized Soviet-period accounts of the building of the Great Fergana Canal. We asked general questions about water management before collectivization, when the work of local irrigation canal maintenance had been a traditional dehqon obligation, and that question led more generally to stories about irrigation and struggles to obtain water. Rashid (b. 1917) talked about the labor of maintaining irrigation systems: "Before the kolkhoz, the *mirob* [irrigation manager] assigned the work of keeping the *ariqs* [small channels from the main canal to the fields] clean and digging them. The work was divided out by so many meters per day per person. There was no law forcing people to do the digging, but they did it because otherwise there was nothing to drink."[33] When we asked questions about water, many respondents recalled irrigation work, including ariq maintenance and watering the fields, as one of many tasks they undertook on collective farms.

Boltoboy cited it as the reason he left the kolkhoz: "I was an orphan, and I worked digging ariqs. When I couldn't stand slogging in the mud, I went away to study."[34]

Rustam described unusually challenging irrigation conditions in his area of Navoiy Province, where land was watered by an underground channel and well system, the *qariz*. Dehqons had to maintain underground channels, and a waterwheel lifted water to surface: "Each qariz had one brigade leader, with forty to one hundred men working at that qariz. That would be enough for planting at least one hundred hectares of wheat.... In order to keep the water flowing, you had to do *hashshar* twice a day, to bring the water from the head to down here at the foot, and then men would go in [underground, in the qariz channel] and move the mud around."[35] Most kolkhozes had ariqs, small surface-water channels that demanded constant and labor-consuming maintenance, but that did not require the qariz's daily mass effort. Respondents thought of irrigation-related work as some of the heaviest labor on the kolkhoz, meriting higher pay.[36] But some respondents instead remembered extraordinary times when they dug major canals by hand.

Canal building was freighted with ideology. From the late 1930s to the 1950s, Uzbekistan's leadership chose to build large new canals through mass mobilization for hand labor, calling this mode "people's construction."[37] The most storied such project, the Great Fergana Canal, built by the labor of "160,000" kolkhoz members in "40 days" in 1939, showed up spontaneously in the narratives of respondents from Fergana Province.[38] The project itself had been presented to a mass public across the USSR, in film, newspaper, and other kinds of celebratory media coverage.[39] Uzbekistan launched many other canal construction projects as well, and interviewees from other provinces shared some of the images that are associated with the Great Fergana Canal, with an Uzbek nationalist ideological framing. At the same time, they emphasized payment: these "people's construction" canal projects brought in extra income.

Yo'ldashev (b. 1923), a teenager who was working for the kolkhoz at the time, recalled what other kolkhoz members told him about building the Great Fergana Canal, describing it a short-term assignment that took them away from their usual farming tasks for several weeks:

> The 1930s were not good years, but 1939 was a very good year. In that year, the canal and the big train both came here; they were built. And that year was extraordinarily prosperous.... There was bread and meat and enough everywhere. Many people worked on the canal, men and women. The women dug, carrying caddies, to make the canal. They didn't pay a monthly wage but a labor-day. It was something like three so'm [rubles] per day, or was it two or ten? ... If you carried ten loads of dirt, that was one labor-day.... At that time, I was on the kolkhoz,

and I was the *tabelchi* [field recorder] for a work brigade, so I couldn't go, but everyone else went.⁴⁰

One of those women who worked on the Great Fergana Canal was Qumriniso (b. 1920), who recalled:

> I walked a long way to get there, and one of my shoes was torn. It was the long way through the hills. It was difficult for people. When they were thirsty, they would ask for something to drink. Men dug out the rocks, some women loaded them on a hand caddy, and the rest transported them. We slept there while we worked. We ate whatever they made for dinner with zog'ora [cornbread]. The food was mostly noodles and millet soup. *Osh* [made of rice and lamb] was rare. The kolkhoz used carts to transport people to work on the Fergana Canal. They assigned a specific place to dig when we went there.

The interviewer, Zavqiddin, had heard about the Great Fergana Canal project as oppressive and rather like enslavement. Building on Qumriniso's description of the unimpressive food, he asked whether people were worked to death. Qumriniso replied: "I did not see people dying from this labor." She then shifted to a more positive image: "While we were working on the Fergana Canal, the artists Halima Nosirova and Tamara-xonum came to perform. It was shown on TV."⁴¹ Of course, there was no TV at the time; Qumriniso was referring to images familiar from later TV broadcasts for proof of this remarkable occasion, when Uzbekistan's leading actress and dancer performed for the canal-digging masses. Qumriniso did not clarify whether she watched Uzbekistan's two most famous women performing artists while she was assigned to canal work. Her allusion to their performances is an instance of the way that a national narrative about the project intersects with memory, prompting her to subordinate her own toil to an iconic moment in Uzbek culture. She was not alone in doing so.

Everyone in Uzbekistan knew that Usmon Yusupov, first secretary of Uzbekistan's Communist Party (1937–1950), championed the Great Fergana Canal project and that Uzbekistan's best-known performers presented concerts to the laborers. Fergana Valley kolkhoz members brought up those associations, whether they had been participants in the dig or not. Hamid (b. 1922), from Marg'ilon, recalled: "There was a big competition. People danced the Oxunboboyev dance, and the incomparable performers Tamara-xon, Mukaram-xon, [and] Lutfi-xon performed." The interviewer, Shahnoza, pressed him: "But I heard that many people perished under duress on this project." Hamid responded with his eyewitness view: "Not true! I was in seventh grade, and I went and watched. Quite the opposite. In the morning they would slaughter sheep—they kept sheep nearby, and they would hang them up, and the fat flowed!"⁴²

Interviewers could gain no traction for the view that building the Great Fergana Canal was oppressive. Tursunboy, who was about eighteen when he participated in the canal-building project, reiterated that storied national episode: "I participated in the canal construction. They came and put on a performance right in the village where I lived. The canal passed right by us. Oxunboboyev came and Usmon Yusupov, and they built a fire and played the drum and had a concert right in our village. The canal was not a hardship; it was good for the kolkhoz. They paid a wage to those who worked on the canal." The interviewer, Hurshida, asked: "Didn't people suffer from the heat, working morning until night?" Tursunboy responded: "A doctor would go around, they would carry them to each village on a stretcher, and the doctor would treat them. And if someone got a fever or a headache, they would be treated right away with medicine. . . . No one suffered too much. They gave out all kinds of food to the workers. Those who were working on it lived well. Those who didn't work on it were jealous."[43]

Some respondents recalled various canal-building projects undertaken from the 1930s through the 1950s, and their stories, so interwoven with national discourses from that time, portrayed the onerous labor of canal digging in tones of pride. Zulayho (b. 1916) said that before collectivization, her dehqon father irrigated their fields using a waterwheel, and when Zulayho was a child, driving animals to turn the waterwheel was her task. "We had little water, so how could we plant rice? If you have good water, there is rice," she said. After they were forced to join a kolkhoz, she said, "A canal brought water from the river to us. I participated in digging the canal from near Polvon. . . . Then they brought in these iron machines to dig. Many people from my household worked on the canal; everyone from the kolkhoz was taken there. Every kolkhoz designated people for it; we were digging it for our benefit. I don't know what year that was. I was about seventeen or eighteen years old, and I worked carrying a hand caddy."[44] With the influx of water, her kolkhoz began planting rice. Zulayho linked canal construction to easier irrigation and with starting to consume rice, the most desired food.

Sanamjon (b. 1913), also from Xorazm Province, went further than Zulayho with her positive memory of canal building. "We dug that deep canal; I had my baby daughter with me. We called it Xitoy Canal. I liked going out to dig it; it was a good thing, and I was young. It brought water during the planting season, in March and April; we could water the fields. The kolkhoz paid us expense money for digging the canal, and they gave out grain and paid a labor-day. They would give four so'm for the children when I worked." This strongly positive view of toil was not characteristic of Sanamjon's memories of kolkhoz work, about which she commented: "There was no choice: you could not say, 'We will not work.' We were driven out to work with the donkeys and the horses. . . . These conditions still remain in my head even though I am ninety years old. I had a baby in 1946, and when I went to breastfeed this baby, [the brigade leader] came and beat me for leaving without permission."[45] She spoke of canal digging as a distinct contrast to the coercion of her everyday labor, focusing on the extra money that she earned and on resulting water for her kolkhoz.

Hayrullo (b. 1921), whose family held out against the kolkhoz until 1936, spoke of canal construction with a long-term perspective. Discussing his grain and herding kolkhoz in Qashqa Daryo, he detailed the difference made by a canal project:

> Back then the kolkhoz raised wheat, barley, flax, sesame, [and] melons and put the produce in its storehouses. We did not have cotton then—that came later, probably after 1953 or 1954. Back then, we would plant crops on one side of the canal one year and herd animals on the other side, and then the next year, we would plant on the other side and herd on this side. There was never enough water until we were linked to the main canal from the Amu Daryo, and then things improved. That was after the war, during Rashidov's period. Before that, water was a problem. When it rained, fields would become green. If there was water in the Maymanoq River or the Qamashi, we would work for twenty days to direct water to our fields. But in the summertime, there was no water at all. If you planted too late, you did not get a crop at all.[46]

Tojivoy (b. 1917), who spearheaded the construction of a canal in Parkent District in 1942, spoke of it as his most important accomplishment:

> In 1942 I worked as a leader of the Bozsuv canal project, bringing water from the Fergana Mountains. Two thousand men dug the canal in the Xovos Desert. I had two thousand men working from six a.m. until six p.m., digging dirt, carrying it out. The people of Parkent should be recognized as having extraordinary strength. They had one non to eat per day and perhaps some soup. We worked on the canal without full stomachs. One day I was told that important people like Usmon Yusupov were coming.... We decided to extend our section of the canal to Pskent by the time he arrived. We got up extra early to work. The workers included seven hundred women. We had music played by Zulfi the *surnai* player. Usmon-aka was impressed that our workers from the Parkent region, the most impoverished, hungry region, achieved this. He called us the Front Brigade and wrote down that so many tons of rice and macaroni should be delivered to us.[47]

Soviet propaganda valorized Uzbekistan's canal projects in imagery that respondents associated with their own lives, but post-Soviet historians examine these projects through a critical lens. Julia Obertries writes: "The 'people's construction' campaign was an ideal way to present the manual work of peasants as something that was in line with the regime's grand project of 'building socialism.'" Publicizing images of dancers and musicians at the job site diverted attention from the absence of mechanization, while the high profile and mass involvement allowed many specialists and bosses to advance their careers.[48] Christian Teichmann contextualizes Tajikistan's 1931 Vakhshstroi project, creating a main irrigation canal, through comparison to the Belomor Canal project in Russia where thousands of Gulag prisoners died or to Magnitogorsk, an example of Soviet "shock construction." The Vakhsh Canal was built in an area that its engineers thought of as isolated; it was distant from sources of building supplies, food, and populations of potential workers, and it relied for several years on constant recruitment. "Despite massive food shortages and an epidemic of malaria, new people continually arrived in the valley," with 20,000 or so households resettled to the area between 1930 and 1937.[49] Maya Peterson draws on official descriptions of the Great Fergana Canal project, which state that 160,000 "collective farm workers had worked forty-five days to move sixteen million cubic meters of earth" to build the 270 km canal, in a project that glorified human labor. The propaganda of the time claimed that kolkhoz workers volunteered for these canal projects due to their high level of labor consciousness, and Peterson, following through on the idea that voluntary meant unpaid, reasons that kolkhoz workers "owed the state a set number of labor hours."[50] Collective farmers, Peterson writes, were unfree labor, a captive population forced to dig a canal on this people's construction project.

The words of interviewees differ from the evaluations of critical history. The national story about canal building in Uzbekistan shaped respondent self-images, fostering links between their own hard work and a heroic narrative that lauded the Uzbek nation's sacrifices for improvement. Propaganda that mobilized Komsomol youth and workers to voluntarily join Soviet construction projects constructed individuals' ways of thinking about the importance of their work, and oral histories conducted decades later have shown that, in some cases, these narratives endured.[51] The workers on the Great Fergana Canal were not volunteers; their kolkhozes assigned them to their digging stints. But respondents recalled experiencing that labor in ways that were sufficiently positive, in terms of food, pay, and recognition, such that they were not disillusioned. It is important to stress that work on the Great Fergana Canal was not enslavement; nor was it unpaid: it was fundamentally different from being sent to the Gulag to labor on the Belomor Canal until one died. Kolkhoz members were unfree, in that they had no choice as to whether their brigade would be assigned to work on a canal, any more than they could choose whether to plant and pick cotton.[52] But interviewees who worked on these canal projects recalled those episodes as different from their everyday drudgery, as a time apart that linked their own lives to a celebrated Uzbek national episode.⁵³ Those whom we were interviewing had been young and strong, a factor that surely influenced their interpretations of their labor. Beyond their national romanticism, they also presented themselves as pragmatic about canal projects: canal digging was a change from their everyday work that paid extra, and it provided them with the enduring material benefits of improved irrigation.

Collective Work with Individual Pay

How much and in what form kolkhoz members were paid was a topic of very detailed memory. In the early 1930s, a time when kolkhozes formed and fell apart, the ability to pay members for working was critical to a kolkhoz's continuation. A low rate of daily pay did nothing to attract the middle and wealthy dehqons whom some agitators hoped to convince to join the kolkhoz with their lands and their livestock. Zulayho (b. 1916), who was a teenaged girl when she started working for the kolkhoz, put it this way: "When we worked, we were paid a labor-day; for a day they would give you some wheat, something like that. If not, why would you keep working?"⁵⁴

Rajab (b. 1912) said that he began working on his middle dehqon father's farm near Bukhara when he was fifteen years old, and he joined the kolkhoz at age eighteen. The kolkhoz took most of his family's land and an ox, leaving the family with their orchard, a garden plot, and most of their livestock:

> The kolkhoz paid a wage, but it was not a monthly salary. We had *patta*, little slips of paper. If you did two labor-days' worth of work, you received two. The state paid according to what you delivered, 100 percent or 80 percent [of your quota]. The state always paid in money and also paid in flour, oil, and tea.
>
> We did not have rest days on the weekend at the beginning.... People worked every day. They went out to the fields at eight a.m. or sometimes five a.m. for planting. They went out to work at leveling the fields, and women went out too at five a.m. or the very latest at eight a.m. The kolkhoz gave out hot food at noon. There were cooks out in the field who prepared the food and delivered it to each brigade—that was during planting. It was not free. They calculated the cost against people's earnings. Each received so much meat, so much bread, and it was all written down and signed.

The interviewer, Hurshida, asked Rajab, "Honored father, were there differences between the way you worked on your own land before entering the kolkhoz and the work you did on the kolkhoz?" He responded with attention to how they earned their living: "Of course, there were differences. Before the kolkhoz, on our own land we planted only wheat, sorghum, and melons, and whatever we earned for that year came from those. There was no other income. After forming the kolkhoz and planting cotton, then we earned a lot of money."[55] Rajab, like many other respondents, described work on the kolkhoz not only as a loss of an individual farmer's autonomy in decision-making and use of time but also as a shift from the self-sufficiency of grain farming to the cash-based cotton economy, accompanied by continuous calculations of earnings and immediate pay for labor.

The payment system that he mentioned, handing out small pieces of paper, stamps, or tokens for each unit of labor, was a temporary approach that the Kolkhoz Center, the organization that sent agitators to rural areas to set up collective farms, implemented during the pell-mell collectivization drive in 1930. Many interviewees recalled collecting those small pieces of paper and taking them to the kolkhoz storehouse, where they were paid in food products. Fayzi (b.1915), who had worked with his middle dehqon father farming individually, said:

> All our land went to the kolkhoz, a tiny kolkhoz. At the beginning, for the days when we did kolkhoz work, there was a thing called a patta, a little piece of paper, and you might get a whole one, a half, or a quarter, depending on how much work you completed. "You, come here, do this task for half of a labor-day or this for a whole labor-day," and they would tear it off and put it in your hand. You would collect them all, and at the end of the month, for however much work you had done, the kolkhoz would give you either wheat or something else, maybe oil; you would take them to the bookkeeper, who would figure it up, paying for each labor-day.[56]

This effort to measure labor fairly and pay immediately was not without its problems. Ravshon (b. 1920) said, "A patta had a number on it, but your name was not written on it. The director's friends could make a living by visiting him and stealing patta out from [where he stored them] under the cushions."[57] The Kolkhoz Center directed kolkhozes to stop using patta and to adopt a more complex system, assigning a tabelchi (field recorder) to each work brigade.[58] The kolkhoz thus created an entirely new set of workers, low-ranking tabelchis, who needed enough literacy and numeracy to write down names and labor-days. A very large number of the interview respondents began working for their kolkhoz in the 1930s, as young boys, in the role of tabelchi.

Yo'ldashev (b. 1923) was an orphan from a prosperous family. One of his maternal uncles was the kolkhoz bookkeeper; he arranged work for twelve-year-old Yo'ldashev in the coveted role of tabelchi, where the boy started to become aware of the kolkhoz's expenses: "When I was young, there were lots of bosses, five or ten drivers, and below each head was a storage keeper, a cashier, a head tabelchi, a bookkeeper. That could add up to thirty bookkeepers, all of them in the kolkhoz director's office." The thousands of tiny kolkhozes formed in Uzbekistan between 1930 and 1933 underwent consolidation, reducing the numbers of directors. "When their numbers decreased, money for the people increased; it got somewhat better." Yo'ldashev used a folk saying to emphasize that those who had control over the kolkhoz income tended to pay themselves first: "If the wages are your father's, you spend them on yourself. [The administrators] consumed everything, and the people had no money."[59]

Work was measured in units called labor-days, which corresponded to a discrete accomplishment: so many meters of cotton weeded, so many cows milked, or so many tenths of a hectare planted, no matter how much time that labor actually demanded, more or less than a day. The kolkhoz director, who controlled how pay was disbursed, as well as brigade leaders, technical personnel, and tractor drivers, earned higher labor-day rates than ordinary kolkhoz workers. After the crop was sold to the state and the kolkhoz calculated its expenses, including work-season labor pay, and its gain or loss, any "profit" was divided out to members based on their aggregate labor-days and was paid, according to interviewees, either in sacks of wheat or in cash. In an annual accounting, the labor-day had a monetary value, with differing rates in different areas of the USSR.[60] In 1933, the average kolkhoz household in Uzbekistan, which might include one to three working members, earned 303 labor-days; this increased to 490 in 1937. Because some kolkhoz members were earning 2 labor-days per actual day, while others earned half of a labor-day, the statistics do not provide a clear picture of how much time any member worked for the kolkhoz versus how many days they spent doing other things, but there were entire months in wintertime when kolkhoz members earned no labor-days at all.[61]

Some of the collectivization generation respondents spoke in ways that suggested they had internalized the definition of fairness manifested in the labor-day payment system: that those who worked more or took on harder tasks should be paid more. Hayitboy, who was orphaned as a young child and began working on a Namangan region kolkhoz as a teen, said: "On the kolkhoz people would work, and they would be paid every ten or fifteen days. If they did not receive money, they were given food. They were taken care of and lived neither poor nor rich but in the middle." He remembered improving conditions and pay in the 1930s: "Before the war we were paid in money on the kolkhoz, every five days. It was good. And we took food from the storehouse, and they also sold food. I earned well. I could fulfill a day and a half or two labor-days in one day. And they paid me accordingly. If they paid three so'm for one labor-day, then I could get four and a half so'm for a day, and multiply that by five."[62] Hayitboy was referring to a time when he was a young man, when he regarded earning twenty-two rubles for five days' work as a good income. To an urban worker for whom the average wage in 1934 was more than thirty rubles per week, Hayitboy's kolkhoz income would have seemed small.[63]

Tursunboy (b. 1921), whose father had been a mardikor near Margilon, described kolkhoz payment as an improvement over laboring in the gates of the wealthy:

> One cannot say it was all good or all bad; there were all sorts of experiences. One person now had a better life and could live like a rich person, but there were also the poor in those times too. Those who worked well earned a good rate. If you didn't work, your wages reflected that. Our family was in the middle in what we earned.
>
> It was better than how we lived in the time of working for the rich man.... The rich man would pay whatever he wanted to. He could give a lot to one and little to another. But those who entered the kolkhoz had things distributed equally. And people earned their pay according to how much they worked and what was recorded in their work record.... And during the time of the rich, they paid once a year.[64]

Tursunboy, like many other respondents from mardikor families, emphasized that pay was fair and was regularly distributed, and this was a basis for a positive assessment of the kolkhoz.

Abdullo S. (1921), whose wealthy family joined the kolkhoz under threat of dekulakization, depicted the life of the collective farm as impoverished, compared with the good life that preceded it:

> Until the time of collectivization, a worthwhile dehqon farmed his own land. The government would divide out to him a known amount of land. Then after the kolkhoz was formed ... I still planted on my own land even though it was a kolkhoz. The kolkhoz had certain fields, and we were forced to plant those. From the time this kolkhoz was formed until about 1960, it did not earn decent money. The government did not pay money.... They would give wheat for cotton, and not even flour. They gave cotton cloth, soap, sesame, tea, oil. They would measure out the cotton cloth to the centimeter to pay according to labor-day.... It was not enough income to live on, and so those people who needed money would leave the kolkhoz and go to work as guards.... Those who could get an [internal] passport would go; those without passports would run off and return.[65]

Whether pay was fairly distributed was not at issue; Abdullo S. spoke with resentment at being forced to labor for the kolkhoz, at working for payment in kind rather than owning the harvest, and at working for what he considered a pittance.

Rustamov (b. 1923), who worked with his father on a kolkhoz in the Namangan region, responded to a question about payment with recollections of poor compensation for driving a horse-drawn plow. "I would guide that horse in the evenings, and for that I was paid one and a half non. And if I worked in the daytime, they paid one non for that as well. So working day and evening, I could earn two and a half non. One person could eat that all up. . . . At home there was my stepmother. . . . We would divide it out: this for you, this for me." Rustamov and his interview companion Turdiboy recalled the early years of the kolkhoz as oppressive, focusing on the famine. But Turdiboy recalled improvement: "By 1937–1938, the kolkhoz had very good harvests. People lived well. I remember that there were banners hung on the streets that read: 'Let every person breakfast on cream, honey, and eggs,' and below that was written 'Stalin.'"

Rustamov added, "At that time, they paid a salary and a labor-day. But because there was theft on the kolkhoz, not everyone was paid with food to eat. If people had not betrayed each other, everything would have been fine."[66]

Uzbekistan's grain harvest was unusually productive in 1939, leaving a strong impression on Abdullo F. (b. 1917), who remembered that year's payment on his wheat- and cotton-growing kolkhoz in Qashqa Daryo:[67]

> In the first years, there was payment, but I don't know whether it was in money, because our uncles and fathers worked. They were paid by the labor-day, in wheat, which might go up to five kilos [of wheat per labor-day] at the end of the year, if the work went well. If not, three kilos or two kilos. But in 1939 there was lots of wheat, so much that we could not even harvest it all. I remember that in 1939 everyone got five kilos per labor-day or five and a half. People couldn't even take it all home and store it. The brigade leaders wrote up a list, went house to house, saying, "Won't you take some wheat?"[68]

Some respondents from various regions of Uzbekistan recalled that year's good fortune, contrasting 1939 both with earlier, leaner years and with the World War II years that respondents widely associated with hunger. Abdullo F., who became a teacher and stopped working for the kolkhoz, judged that "collectivization was better than what preceded it. Collective agriculture had leadership and development. . . . It awakened people who fed themselves, received technology for plowing, planted wheat, made storehouses, and were paid for their labor."[69]

Collectivization generation respondents who remembered the kolkhoz's elaborately individualized pay systems chose what to reminisce about, either focusing on moments that were highly remunerative or thinking of the leanest of times, when daily payment came in the form of bread. Their recollections were deeply informed by the most basic ideology of collectivization: that by uniting their lands, dehqons would improve the lives of all. However, their ways of evaluating work and payment on the kolkhoz were almost anti-ideological. It seems to me that, having lived through the Soviet decades and Uzbekistan's rejection of the Soviet experiment, interviewees who were being questioned by members of the post-Soviet generation defended themselves as rational actors, choosing to recall episodes of rewarding pay that justified their rosy views of kolkhoz life or reviewing times of misery pay to support their critical evaluations of rural transformation.

Women's Work

> INTERVIEWER E. R.: Did you work morning to evening when you were a girl?
>
> SHAROFAT (B. 1922): Early in the morning, at seven or eight, my father would say, "My dear children, leave the house, go look after the cattle, prune the cotton, and get working." Back then I placed first in fulfilling the harvest.
>
> E. R.: Did you participate in cotton planting when you were a girl?
>
> SHAROFAT: Yes, and I also was very good at picking cotton. My mother did not let me go out on the street, but we went to the cotton.
>
> E. R.: Was there a difference between going out with your mother to work on your land and working for the kolkhoz?
>
> SHAROFAT: Yes, however much cotton that you picked, the kolkhoz would measure it and pay you money, and after they sold it, they would account for your work and pay cash.[70]

Cotton picking was considered lighter work, and archival documents from the 1930s reveal that women carried out most of the cotton harvest, while political leaders tried to shame men into harvesting cotton or to lure them with higher pay than what they could earn in the equivalent time on other kolkhoz tasks.[71] An emphasis on piecework, paying each participant in kolkhoz labor according to productivity, led to "the achievement of a significant strengthening of labor discipline, with a much lower degree of non-appearance for work by members of the kolkhoz, compared with last year," judged the Commission for Overseeing Measures for Organization of Labor, in 1931. The same commission noted that women were observed doing most of the cotton picking but that "when labor books are distributed and labor-days are recorded, many instances of gross

TABLE 7.3 Russian Empire / USSR silk textile production and export, selected years 1913–1937

	1913	1928/29	1932	1938
Silk fabric production, thousand meters	42,000	9,600	21,500	58,900
Silk fiber exports, tons	2,074	971	5272	109
Silk fabric exports, thousand meters	9	3	27	173

Note: Typically, Uzbekistan produced more than 60 percent of the USSR's raw silk.
Sources: *Narodnoe Khoziaistvo SSR 1913–1955, Kratkii Statisticheskii sbornik*, table starting p. 36. *Vneshniaia torgovlia SSSR 1918–1940*. See also I. A. Fat'ianov, "K novym tempam v shelkovostve v Srednei Azii," *Sredneaziatskii Shelk* 7–9 (1929): v–ix. On Uzbekistan as the dominant sericulture republic, see I. A. Vil'nit, "Organizatsiia shelko-zagotovitel'noi kampanii v 1929 g.," *Srednei Aziiatskii Shelk* 4–6 (1929): 285–287.

violations are appearing, when women's labor-days are not accounted, and on some kolkhozes, labor booklets are not given to women."[72]

Women respondents did not compare their earnings to men's earnings, but they were just as loquacious about working and earning as men were. We asked about what kinds of work they usually performed, and they mentioned planting, mounding up, pruning, weeding, and picking cotton; planting and weeding grain; planting, tending, and harvesting rice; and raising silkworms. We asked whether women and men worked together or did the same kinds of work on the kolkhoz. Most of the women respondents said that men and women worked equally, but men's responses were more varied. The final section of this chapter contrasts two men's accounts of sericulture with a woman's account, to illustrate the gendering of memories.

Uzbekistan was consistently the Soviet Union's largest producer of silk cocoons, and traditionally hatching and feeding silkworms and harvesting the cocoons from dried-out mulberry stems was women's work, while children and the elderly were involved in cutting and carrying mulberry leaves from the trees. Soviet sericulture's New Economic Policy–period restoration paralleled cotton's transformation in the 1920s, from private enterprise to government trust, before its complete nationalization under the First Five-Year Plan goal of silk autarky.[73]

In the early 1930s, kolkhozes all over Uzbekistan were assigned annually increasing quotas for cocoon production. Sericulture nonetheless remained a household enterprise, even on the collective farm, where households made contracts to take larvae, and they raised silkworms in one of the rooms of their house.[74] Although raising silkworms had long since gone from artisanal to factory scale in Europe and Japan, in Central Asian collective farms it retained its household-based, artisanal features, producing family income on the basis of the amount and quality of cocoons rather than on a labor-day wage basis.[75]

Abduqayum (b. 1916) spoke of sericulture as an unwanted burden. He said that mulberry trees were planted on his collective farm north of Tashkent after its formation in 1930: "They gave them [silk worm eggs] to people who had joined the kolkhoz, and they received only a payment; they took care of them in their houses, and they did not have the room for it—only three rooms, and in one of them you have to take care of silkworms."[76] Another man from the same region, Ashurboy (b. 1923), recalled:

> Before collectivization we raised silkworms; at that time it was for ourselves. And then they founded the regional directorate, and we turned them in there. If you turned in your cocoons, they might pay you in two or three meters of velvet cloth.... After the kolkhoz formed, they forced women to raise silkworms; every woman was kept busy raising them. They turned over the cocoons, to be made into silk and velvet. They were not paid in money; they were given wheat, or oil if the kolkhoz had any.[77]

A woman from the same district, Qimmat (b. early 1900s), evaluated sericulture and pay differently. She said that raising silkworms was her main task on the kolkhoz:

> From the beginning of the kolkhoz, we kept silkworms for the government. The government made rich people into quloqs and took away their houses. We raised the silkworms in those houses. [She names the quloq owners.] There were Hojimat, Ergash, and Adash. Their wives—Norbuvi, Sharofat, To'ychi—and I raised silkworms for several years.... There were many mulberry trees.... The kolkhoz did not plant them. We got [leaves] from households near Bostan Lake. We would leave in the morning to find the mulberry leaves and return at night. We were given a cart to bring them home. The silkworm season was four, five months at that time. We made a living like that. They gave us money. They paid well.[78]

Qimmat never explicitly stated that her husband was taken away as a quloq, but she implied it in her association with other wives of quloqs and by noting that she was responsible for providing for her children. Qimmat's comments about sourcing the mulberry leaves to feed her silkworms point to one change from pre-kolkhoz artisanal sericulture. Traditionally, those who wanted to raise silkworms owned mulberry trees on their own land or else rented from mulberry tree owners the right to cut stems. Kolkhoz land appropriation and kolkhoz plantings of mulberry orchards meant that Qimmat relied on the kolkhoz to assign the source of leaves and the means to transport them.[79] The gendered difference between these accounts was common across interviews: men frequently scorned women's work as not worth the effort or denounced it as oppressive, while women often talked about their own earnings with pride.

Women's rate of kolkhoz membership was lower than men's rate, a fact that troubled Raykom officials and economic planners who pressured kolkhoz directors to sign up women. Some collective farms organized women's artels for silk production, which may have been a way to satisfy the official demand that women be enrolled as kolkhoz members. Yorbobo described women's kolkhoz work as a concession made by the male kolkhoz members:

> When the kolkhoz was first founded, women did not participate, except in the case where they had no one to provide for them. The kolkhoz members recognized that they needed work, so they let them work. My mother would raise silkworms or during harvest would pick cotton or would dry raisins, but at that time the women did not go out and work in the fields.... Back then their work was seasonal. They were not supposed to show their faces, so when they went out into the field, they would cover up in a scarf.[80]

These interviews were undertaken in a time when Soviet period discourses about the importance of women's employment had long since evaporated and when Uzbek cultural leaders, including the highest-ranking women in the Republic of Uzbekistan's government, consistently stressed that women's most important work was in the home, as wife, daughter-in-law, and mother.[81] Men respondents often echoed these views, which may have been their feelings all along, either expressing pity that women were forced to work outside the home or claiming that women were primarily housewives who only worked during cotton harvest. A few male respondents praised women, especially their mothers, for their kolkhoz labor and earnings, and some claimed that women and men were equal on the kolkhoz. Women, including O'ktam, the tractor driver; Sanamjon and Zulayho, who recalled canal construction; Sharofat, who picked cotton; and Qimmat, with her silkworms, chose rosier ways of recalling their own labor on the early kolkhoz, giving their working lives meaning through connection to narratives of national development and emphasizing the importance of their own earnings.

Soviet collectivization imposed a template on rural Uzbekistan, creating a single organizational pattern where regional administrators told kolkhoz directors the plans they had to fulfill, machine tractor stations and agronomists expanded cotton planting and imposed the measured furrows demanded by tractors, brigade leaders directed each kolkhoz member's labor, tabelchis wrote down labor-days, women were assigned to raise silkworms, and dehqons, both men and women, became a rural proletariat, working for wages. As a result of that uniformity, interviewees from seven provinces remembered work and payment in the same ways, though their evaluations and emotions varied. Agitators had tried to convince dehqons to join kolkhozes by telling them that their lives would improve, and the political discourses that saturated kolkhoz events, public events, and schooling insisted to them that kolkhoz life was better than individual farming. Respondents evaluated whether their lives had improved as they reminisced about the kinds of crops they grew, modes of payment, whether they raised silkworms, whether women worked on their kolkhoz, and tractors—addressing those themes because of the questions we asked. They addressed other topics spontaneously, such as digging canals and work as a tabelchi, and they did not allude to other things that we might have expected, based on what we know of the 1930s: they did not talk about shock workers, Stakhanovites, heroes of labor, socialist competition, or speeding up the plan. Several who had worked as directors of a kolkhoz mentioned increasing per hectare productivity, but collective work did not lead to collective pay, and the uniformity of early kolkhoz experience did not stimulate memories centered on the collective.

The state's dominant role in meaning making is most evident in recollections of canal construction: those who talked about canal building drew on the propaganda events that rendered back-breaking manual labor as an Uzbek national triumph. However, "the memory of the group is not identical to that of the individual within it."[82] Collectivization generation interviewees, having lived through identical, cohort-producing events, chose what to recall as they made sense of their own lives and justified their choices to a much younger audience, the interviewers. Even when talking of digging a canal by hand, respondents departed from national myths about volunteerism by stressing how well the work had paid, and they resisted interviewer interpretations of people's construction as oppression, a view implying that the respondent must be lying or a fool. Interviewees from the collectivization generation recalled their early working lives in ways that highlighted suffering or injustice or that blocked out hard times and focused on good ones. Interviewers, expecting accounts of bad times, focused their skepticism on the most positive aspects of narratives.[83] When making sense of their own working lives in the coercive conditions of a 1930s kolkhoz, many respondents insisted to their younger, urban interviewers that they were not to be pitied as collectivization's victims or dupes: either they saw collectivization's harmful results and found a way out, or they were strong and clever enough to have earned a good living on the kolkhoz.

8

ORPHANS

"Orphans occupied a special place in Soviet attitudes toward children. The theme of orphanhood . . . was closely connected to the project of creating a generation of new people," writes Mehmet Kaşikçi, in his study of Kazakh orphans during the period of Stalin's rule.[1] Sovietization of rural Uzbekistan transformed the ways that dehqons worked the land, changed the entire structure of ownership and leadership, and swiftly expanded rural education by opening new schools and End Illiteracy courses. This chapter examines the impact of those transformations on orphans, as reflected in the stories told by interviewees.[2] Over the course of 120 interviews, we learned that more than forty interviewees had lost their father during childhood (birth to age fifteen).[3]

The prevalence of orphanhood among respondents initially surprised me, although comparisons with other premodern societies suggest that high rates of orphanhood were common worldwide before the widespread provision of modern medicine.[4] As our interviewees told us, modern medicine in the form of a clinic or a doctor's office first made an appearance in their villages after collectivization. Mothers died in childbirth, parents died of disease, and there were also high rates of child mortality. Additionally, as previous chapters have shown, the decades when interviewees were children were a violent time. Fathers were killed in fighting between Bosmachis and Reds, were arrested as quloqs, or abandoned families to flee across borders.

Through a focus on orphan stories, this chapter brings to the fore the ways that the kolkhoz exploited child labor, turned mothers into workers and providers, and altered traditional norms of care. Soviet orphanages did not become the solution for many of Uzbekistan's rural orphans, but newly founded rural schools opened career doors to them. Life trajectories among orphaned respondents illustrate shifts in sources of social status: as collectivization brought agricultural innovation and government institutions to rural Uzbekistan, orphans tapped into success by becoming teachers and rising through the kolkhoz administration. On kolkhozes, the lives of orphans came to look like those of nonorphans.

Interviewees Who Were Orphaned

Many interviewees whose stories are featured in previous chapters were orphans. Those born in the prerevolution cohort told remarkably similar stories about how they lived after losing parents. Qurbon A. (b. 1908), the novcha who rebelled against the boylar during land reform (chapter 1), was orphaned at age ten; he gained land in land reform, and the kolkhoz encouraged him to become a teacher. Abdurashid (b. 1905), who watched while Bosmachis fought against Red forces in his Fergana village (chapter 2), was orphaned as a child; he made a living as a hired herder until land reform provided him with land. Hayitboy (b. 1910) was orphaned at age ten; having been the comfortable son of a butcher studying in the local Qur'an school, he then worked in the gates of the rich until land reform (chapter 3). He recalled with pleasure earning two labor-day's pay for a day of work on a Namangan kolkhoz (chapter 7). Musaxon (b. 1910), orphaned in childhood, was so enthusiastic for collectivization that he became an agitator in his Fergana Valley village (chapter 4). Among the older cohort, the path from orphanhood to mardikor seemed almost inevitable, while land reform and collectivization were transformative.[5]

Life courses were more varied for the younger cohort orphans, as this chapter demonstrates. Much has been written about orphaned and abandoned children in the early Soviet years: their steeply rising numbers drove the revolutionary Soviet government to establish children's homes, *detskiie domy*, residential facilities that raised not only orphans but also children whose parents temporarily or permanently relinquished them. Nascent Soviet social welfare institutions experimented with utopian ideas about rearing children away from the ostensible selfishness of the family and infusing the young with Communist norms of shared ownership.[6] Historical research about orphans understandably relies on institutional records from orphanages or government agencies.[7] Alan Ball's illuminating study of the scale of orphanhood and abandonment in the first decades after the revolution and Soviet welfare strategies to deal with those trends begins with records from institutions.[8] Laurie Bernstein draws on legal documents and court cases to elucidate the concepts that informed Soviet laws. The Soviets first banned adoption due to an absolute preference for state-supported care in a children's home and then allowed adoption after orphanages became overwhelmed.[9] Wendy Goldman discusses the factors such as family breakdown and impoverishment that led to the NEP-period crises of *bezprizornost'*, wherein massive numbers of orphaned and abandoned children tried to survive in Russia's urban streets and the state's welfare agencies struggled to find solutions.[10] Andrew Stone writes of "the orphans of Stalin's revolution" in the 1930s, drawing on evidence about and from orphaned and abandoned children, including children of purge victims and kulaks who were raised in children's homes. Arguing that the Communist Party continued to embrace the idea of re-making children through communal living and education away from their communities, Stone explores orphan subjectivity through autobiographical writings, eliciting the ways that orphans tried to embody Soviet values and the dominance of the motif of a "happy Soviet childhood."[11]

In studies that focus on Central Asia, Kaşikçi's archival research reveals that children who were orphaned or abandoned during the collectivization famine in Kazakhstan suffered extreme hunger and death in children's homes, at rates so severe that commissions reporting on their conditions called them "catastrophic."[12] Zuhra Kasimova examines Uzbekistan's response to the thousands of displaced orphans and abandoned children who arrived in Tashkent from other parts of the USSR during World War II. Rather than try to house them in orphanages, Uzbekistan's first secretary, Usmon Yusupov, appealed to families to take them in to their homes.[13]

The orphan stories in this chapter offer a different way of learning about orphan life trajectories than what archive-based scholarship reveals. A search in institutional records about orphans in early Soviet Uzbekistan would not address the lives of most Uzbek children who were fatherless or fully orphaned, because they were neither abandoned nor placed in children's homes. Evidence about the lives of orphaned children in rural Uzbekistan before and during collectivization was an incidental outcome of this oral history project: interviewees mentioned parental loss when identifying their parents or in connection with some episode in their early life.

Uzbeks use the term *yetim* (from Arabic, "orphan") to refer to a child whose father died or whose parents both died.[14] Loss of their father placed the child in a liminal position. Before collectivization, widows who did not remarry struggled to provide for children, and widows who remarried often left children from their deceased husband to kin care; a new husband rarely agreed to provide for stepchildren.[15] In Central Asian tradition, Islamic ethical norms favored providing for orphaned children through guardianship rather than adoption. Central Asian orphans were traditionally raised by kin, and as interviewee stories show, they were expected to work from an early age.

When interviewers followed up on orphanhood mentions, they asked social questions, about who raised the interviewee or how they survived, but not personal questions, such as how it felt to lose a parent. The evidence from the transcripts allows for a degree of comparison among the usual patterns of orphan lives before collectivization, after collectivization, between those who were raised by kin and those who were raised in Soviet institutions, between boy and girl orphan lives, and between orphan and nonorphan childhood on kolkhozes. Those comparisons show one of the many ways that the kolkhoz, when combined with the Soviet school, was a leveling institution.

Older Cohort Orphans

In 1922, Bekmurod (b. 1907) was orphaned when Red Army soldiers shot his father. In Bekmurod's version, Bosmachis shot at Red forces: "At that time, people were out working, but if someone shot at them [the Reds], they named everyone Bosmachis, and they shot eighteen people, some of them who were riding donkeys or walking or going to the bazaar.... Among them, my father was shot and killed." Bekmurod said that he was fourteen or fifteen when his mother was left with four children to raise:

> I went to work in someone's gates. I plowed, herded sheep, harvested wheat ... to provide bread for my brothers and mother.... I worked two years for G'ofurboy.... He would plant a lot of wheat, and he was a stingy man. We would work all day, and then at night we would sleep in his guest room. And for working morning to night, he would give two us two little rounds of non. Or if he gave us stew, he would not provide non.... Out of five bags of wheat [harvested for G'ofurboy], Chayir-aka [the manager] would get one. From five that Chayir-aka received, he would give me one.... That continued until some of my relatives came in 1926 and said they would take me and marry me to one of their orphan daughters.
>
> After I married, everything that I had acquired was spent on the wedding, and we had nothing left, so again I went to work in someone's gates. I built walls, made scythes, worked as a mardikor in the village until a school opened. It was 1926.... A young man named Azizov studied in the Samarkand Pedagogical Institute.... He was sent to the

TABLE 8.1 End Illiteracy enrollment, Uzbek SSR

YEAR	URBAN	RURAL	TOTAL
1922	5,600	400	6,000
1925	11,300	8,400	19,700
1930	66,200	304,400	370,600
1931	83,800	526,200	609,000
1932	91,600	615,400	707,000
1933	87,200	607,800	695,000
1934	63,400	455,900	519,300
1935	43,800	371,000	414,800
1939	34,800	497,200	532,000

Note: In Russian, these courses were called Likbez (Eradicating Illiteracy). In Uzbek, they were known as Savodsizlik Bitsin (Let Illiteracy End) or by their abbreviation, SB.
Source: Kul'turnoe stroitel'stvo SSSR Statisticheskii Sbornik, section 2, "Nachalnoe i Srednee Obshchee Obrazovanie," table 24.

village to end illiteracy.... I thought to myself, "Maybe I should go and study, and then I can be a complete person."[16] I would go in the evenings, two kilometers, after I had plowed with oxen all day.... After two months I was partially literate. I could write in the Latin alphabet.... Then he told me to try writing a letter of greeting to relatives. He wrote it for us on the board. We learned to write a letter of greeting. Then he said, "Now you need to learn how to write an *ariza* [complaint, petition]."... After that he said, "You need to learn to write a *spravka* [attestation, permission]."... Then he showed us the form that a *qaror* [decision, order] should take. After we had studied for four months, he wrote us a certificate, and then after that, the poor in our village took wheat seed from the boylar and established a shirkat.[17]

Until his father's untimely death, Bekmurod expected a future of working with his father, herding the family's sheep. Instead, at age fifteen, he started working as a mardikor. When the Communist Party used land reform to activate mardikors against boylar, Bekmurod and the other mardikors formed a collective to plant wheat. He seamlessly wove together his story of changing fortune, from orphan and mardikor, to student in the End Illiteracy class learning the forms that everyday Soviet bureaucracy required, to seizing land and grain from the boylar.

Bekmurod highlighted his own agency as he narrated his rise from mardikor to Soviet boss, justifying his own ruthlessness in defense of the kolkhoz. In the 1930s, he joined the kolkhoz, but opponents broke it up, and everyone took their property and returned to individual farming. Eventually taxes on individual farming increased severely so that "by 1935 everyone joined the kolkhoz." Bekmurod told a long story, in which the regional administration offered him a post as director of the village council, and he responded that he would take the post only if he was empowered to expel kolkhoz members. "I said, first of all, the man who founded Oktyabr kolkhoz in Qayrog'och has accepted all sorts of bad people who butchered the cattle that were seized from the rich and consumed them, and the same for oxen and sheep, and they have no labor-day books." Finally, Bekmurod said, the district leadership agreed to his conditions. He expelled and replaced those whom he thought were stealing, and, he said, "eighteen or twenty men were all taken into custody and imprisoned." Ulfat, the interviewer asked, "Why were they imprisoned?" Bekmurod declared: "From the beginning of the kolkhoz, they had been living by dividing and consuming everything it had. . . . When quloqs were finished off, the kolkhoz took their livestock. But they [the kolkhoz members] had consumed it all; nothing was left. They were all imprisoned, and they were sentenced to ten, eight, five, or four years." Although he defended his own role in arresting enemies of the kolkhoz, Bekmurod also said that when the village began to make quloqs, "people here turned against each other, and herders were made into quloqs instead of the rich. . . . Novchas were made quloqs; such injustices happened . . . and in 1935 people who had not fulfilled the plan were arrested." Bekmurod wanted to target the right people as quloqs—the ones whom he selected, not novchas or mardikors, such as he had been.

Ulfat asked him: "Were people's conditions here better after the kolkhoz formed, or did they become worse?" Bekmurod asserted, "After the kolkhoz was formed? Making a living was difficult; people suffered a lot. When I became the director of the kolkhoz, a labor-day was worth one-and-half so'm, and people earned one ton from the harvest. Before I had been the director for a year, the labor-day equaled three and a half so'm plus two kilos of wheat, and then in the second year, one labor-day rose to eleven so'm. I got harvests of more than thirty centners of cotton per hectare; the kolkhoz improved." Bekmurod went on to become district Communist Party secretary. He spoke without any hint of regret. On the contrary, he was the hero of his own life story, rising from the lowest social status as an orphan and a mardikor, fighting the battle against kolkhoz saboteurs, bringing prosperity to his community. In his case, the Soviet inversion of rural power was complete.

Orphan stories from the older cohort of men, those born before 1917, followed consistent patterns. Those alluded to in previous chapters and above—Hayitboy, Qurbon A., Abdurashid, Musaxon, and Bekmurod—became servants to their relatives or to strangers, working in the gates of the rich. Land reform and access to Soviet education changed their life trajectories. Bekmurod reached the pinnacle of the kolkhoz order. Hayitboy, Qurbon A., and Musaxon obtained land in land reform, began school in adulthood, and became teachers. Abdurashid (b. 1905), orphaned at age six, said: "When I was young, on the streets they gathered all the orphans and took them to Namangan, to an orphanage, but they did not take me. In the orphanage, children became literate. I became a herder."[18] After working for relatives as child and teenager, Abdurashid joined an unsuccessful kolkhoz that provided him with a very poor living. Boltaboy (b. 1914), completely orphaned, was raised by his father's third wife. He came from a wealthy household, attended the old-style maktab when he was a child, and after his father died, he went to a Soviet school. He worked on the kolkhoz as a tabelchi and became a teacher. Orphans were not alone in working in the gates of the rich; youths whose fathers were poor also became mardikors, as reflected in accounts from this volume.[19] Sovietization of rural communities did not turn every orphan or poor mardikor into a successful Soviet kolkhoz member, but it offered many of them new opportunities.

Fates varied for orphaned girls from the older cohort: their pre-collectivization lives did not show the uniformity seen among the male orphan mardikors; nor was the impact of Sovietization so obvious. O'g'ilxon (b. 1914), whose father was killed by Bomachis, had a traditional education, learning the Qur'an and prayers from an otin; she was cared for by her uncle until she married at age eighteen. Halimaxon (b. 1911) lost both of her parents when she was four years old; she did not explain who took care of her, but she never attended school, and her guardian arranged for thirteen-year-old Halimaxon to marry a fifty-year-old widower. Both women lived in the city of Marg'ilon; as adults, they worked for a few years in the textile industry. Azizaxon (b. 1914) lost her father to rural violence when she was seven. Her uncle supported her life in the city, making sure that she acquired a modern, Soviet education, and she became a teacher after graduating from the Fergana Pedagogical Institute.[20] Widowed mothers were almost entirely absent from the stories of the older generation of orphans; none mentioned relying on a working mother for support.

The Soviet school is mentioned in most of the stories that are told in this chapter. When mass collectivization began in 1930, Uzbekistan's rural schools doubled in number, rural school pupil enrollments more than doubled, and figures for adult students in rural End Illiteracy courses skyrocketed. Uzbeks and other Central Asians constituted almost the entire enrollment in End Illiteracy courses, where Uzbek was also the dominant language of instruction.[21] Various respondents noted that, due to this demand, they taught literacy courses while they were still students in primary or middle school.

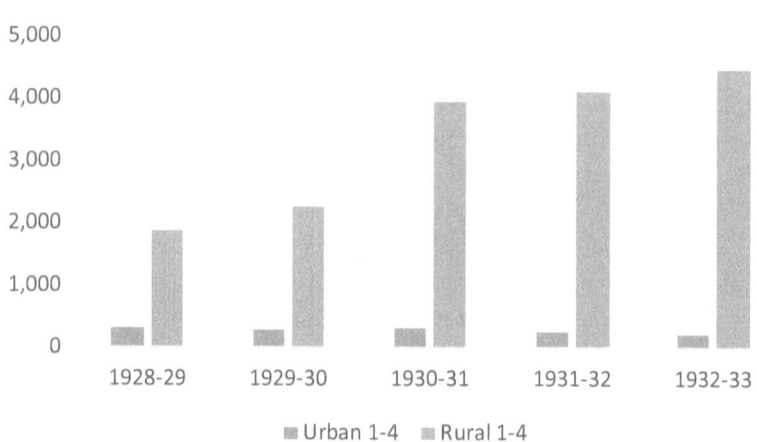

FIGURE 8.1. Primary schools, Uzbek SSR, 1928–1939. Source: *Kul'turnoe stroitel'stvo SSSR Statisticheskii Sbornik*, section 2, "Nachal'noe i Srednee Obshchee Obrazovanie," table 1. http://istmat.org/node/22545.

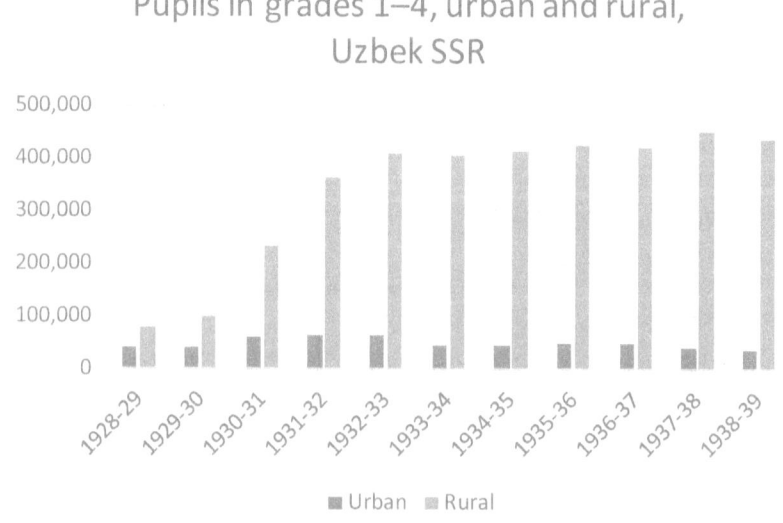

FIGURE 8.2. Primary school enrollments, Uzbek SSR, 1928–1939. Source: *Kul'turnoe stroitel'stvo SSSR Statisticheskii Sbornik*, section 2, "Nachalnoe i Srednee Obshchee Obrazovanie," table 1.

Collectivization Generation Orphans: Joining the Kolkhoz

Collectivization and the spread of rural education changed patterns of life, affecting almost all the interviewees who were born after 1917. Both men and women who had been orphaned consistently mentioned working on the kolkhoz in childhood and earning their own wages. It should be noted that so did most of the interviewees from their cohort; it is apparent that kolkhozes of the 1930s made extensive use of child labor. Unlike the older cohort orphans, orphans from the younger cohort attended school as children. Those who were fatherless often talked about widowed mothers who supported them by working on the kolkhoz.

Born in 1920, Xoji explained that his mother died when he was a baby, and his father died before the kolkhoz was founded. He was taken in by his aunt's family; they joined a kolkhoz in 1932. By that time, Xoji had finished several years of Soviet school, and his education was useful to the kolkhoz:

> XOJI: When I was eleven or twelve, I worked as a tabelchi, and in the evenings I would drive the oxen with a plow.... The teachers came from Bukhara.... I was only in second grade, but I had good literacy, and I had also learned Russian.
>
> HURSHIDA: Where did you learn Russian? While working on the kolkhoz?
>
> XOJI: Around 1932 or 1933, and I was working on the kolkhoz. I would go to Bukhara and take small things to sell, like onions and cabbage, and that was where I learned it.
>
> HURSHIDA: What age were you when you joined the kolkhoz, and what work did you do?
>
> XOJI: I was twelve.
>
> HURSHIDA: Who made you join the kolkhoz, or did you do it because you wanted to?
>
> XOJI: It was my own choice. I went to school, and then I entered the kolkhoz. They made me a tabelchi for a work brigade. I worked here as a tabelchi for ten years.... I also drove the horses and plows, the planter, worked in cotton.
>
> After Xoji gave a lengthy description of the kind of work the tabelchi did, Hurshida asked him how he learned to do it.
>
> XOJI: I went to school and learned it. I went to the office and got a form to fill in.... I wrote down what each person was doing, and I would turn in the chart to the office every five days and then distribute pay.

HURSHIDA: How much did you earn as a tabelchi?
XOJI: Me? Sixty so'm per month.
HURSHIDA: When children worked, were they paid for their labor in cash?
XOJI: Yes, they would get cash if they worked.

Xoji continued his schooling, completing grade seven. Regarding joining the kolkhoz, he said: "Although I was young, I was smart and knew that those people who joined the kolkhoz had better lives."[22] Xoji spoke with pride that he was able to use his skills, earn his own pay, and become a kolkhoz member at such a young age. He did not say much about his path in adulthood, other than that service in the military took him across the Soviet Union.

Narzi (b. 1921) said that her father died when she was nine years old:

> In the village he had no land; he was very poor and had no conditions for work, so he left and went to the city. . . . He died in the city. . . . It must have been about 1930. After we went back to the village, my mother did all kinds of service for people, worked, earned money to raise us, and we were very poor. We didn't have bread to eat or clothing to wear, but in spite of that, my mother, the poor thing, worked, doing service for everyone in order to take care of us.
>
> Then when the kolkhoz was formed, my mother was the first to enter the kolkhoz. After my mother started working, I entered under her wings, and I started to work on the kolkhoz. . . . Teenagers who worked were given a labor book. We were credited with our own work and paid in our own bread. . . .
>
> I joined the kolkhoz at age twelve. I worked in the cotton fields, planting. . . . Then we picked it by hand, carried it, turned it over to the state. . . . Especially for us Komsomol members, we would study for half a day and then work half a day in the cotton, and in the evenings, we would do things like make lamps for the kolkhoz, gather fodder—we worked all day long.[23]

Narzi explained why she started working at such a young age: "All of us had to work; there was no other way; otherwise, we would not have had full stomachs." Later in the interview, Hurshida asked about attitudes toward the kolkhoz. "My mother was very happy," said Narzi. "Because whether you did a little work or a lot of work, you could be satisfied with the money that you earned from your labor." As an adult, Narzi took on kolkhoz leadership roles.

Ubaydullo (b. 1922) said, "Poor people joined the kolkhoz. . . . After my father died in 1929, we—my mother, sister, and brother—joined the kolkhoz, because we were poor." His mother worked in cotton fields, grew vegetables, and cooked for workers on a reservoir-construction project. Like other orphans, Ubaydullo was young when he started kolkhoz work: "When I was seven, I took care of our cow. I joined the kolkhoz with my mother when I was twelve, and I worked in the cotton field. When I was fourteen, the kolkhoz gave us ten cows. The director ... told my mother that I had to take care of those cows.... My mother told them that I was only fourteen, and they said I was not too young, and children were capable of working." Ubaydullo herded the cows and cut fodder for them, his mother milked them, and together they made butter and dried yogurt balls for the kolkhoz. "The kolkhoz gave us a plan, and we turned those things according to plan."[24] Like others in his cohort, both orphans and nonorphans, he worked and attended school, completing the seventh grade; later he left the kolkhoz.

O'ktam, (b. early 1920s) the tractor driver, said that her father worked as a novcha on the lands of the rich and acquired some land of his own when he married: "I was a child of my father's third wife. The previous wives' children did not live, and after they all died, he took my mother as a wife. My mother was left widowed with two children when he died.... He lived until I was nine years old.... I was orphaned." Hurshida asked, "How did you make a living?" O'ktam answered: "My mother worked in the kolkhoz daycare, and then she became someone in the kolkhoz administration. She became the director of the daycare, and eventually she became the director of the village council." O'ktam started working for the kolkhoz at age thirteen or fourteen, while she was in school, and soon her mother arranged a marriage for her. "How old were you?" asked Hurshida. "I'm embarrassed to say," O'ktam responded and would not answer. Her husband was called up to the army, and she became a wartime tractor driver: "We had hardly started our life together when he died in the army."[25] Widowed young, she provided for her daughter by working for the kolkhoz. O'ktam followed in her mother's footsteps, eventually becoming the director of a kolkhoz.

In Xoji's, Narzi's, Ubaydullo's, and O'ktam's stories, the kolkhoz took the place of the boylar as the institution that provided orphans with a living. Rather than joining the ranks of the mardikors, orphans became kolkhoz members in their early teens, earning their labor-days and meeting their need for food. However, their stories differed substantially in that the older cohort resented the boylar, but the younger cohort tended to regard the kolkhoz as a savior. Girls and boys worked part-time and studied part-time. Some of the younger cohort orphans highlighted their continued dependency on their widowed mothers, who joined the kolkhoz to support their children.

Laboring Orphans

Although some orphaned interviewees depicted their teen years as a time when the kolkhoz provided them with tools for success in the form of Soviet schooling and their own labor-day book, other interviewees of the same generation told stories of misery that echoed the rancor of the older cohort of mardikor orphans. Oqquzi, who was born in a boylar household around 1920 in Qashqa Daryo, explained that his father died in 1924:

> OQQUZI: We became very poor, eventually, and went to live with my maternal uncle, on the Kommuna kolkhoz. That was in about 1930.
> ULFAT: So in 1930 they took all of your property and left you with nothing?
> OQQUZI: They took everything. After they took our land, we left, and then they burned everything. We went [to the Kommuna kolkhoz] because our maternal uncle was there. We had nothing to eat, nothing to wear. . . . The rich had individual farms, and the poor had the kolkhoz. The poor made plans for the rich. . . . They raised the taxes to force [the rich] to join the kolkhoz. . . . My uncles built us a house. There was still individual farming, and I drove oxen and a plow. . . . Then my uncles became kolkhoz members. They had about twenty hectares. . . . All the boylar joined the kolkhoz. . . . I became a kolkhoz member around 1931 when I was about twelve. I drove pairs of oxen and horses. My uncle still had a couple head of livestock, and I looked after them. You do not know what difficulties we had on the kolkhoz, from the time we moved there until the war.

Oqquzi described kolkhoz life as miserable: quloqs remained under threat of arrest; payment was poor. Later in the interview, Ulfat raised a question about schooling.

> ULFAT: Honored father, which school did you study in? Did you go to school in those times?
> OQQUZI: I could say that I never went to school, but I did finish an evening course.
> ULFAT: Wasn't there any school before the war?
> OQQUZI: In those times there was a school, but in short, my uncle refused to let us go to school because we were orphans.[26]

Barred by his uncle from school, Oqquzi's depiction of his teenage years laboring on the kolkhoz scarcely differed from the ways that older cohort orphans talked of working in the gates of the rich. Sovietization brought him no transformative benefits.

Rajab (b. 1917) said that his parents died when he was a small child, and he was raised by his sister and rich brother-in-law, who employed "five or six chorikors," including Rajab's older brothers. "I worked for my brother-in-law. I grew up in his gates." Rajab attended school through the third grade. "They held meetings to tell the people to form a kolkhoz. Before that, I herded my brother-in-law's livestock. Then he died, and I went to work on the kolkhoz. . . . I planted cotton, did irrigation; the kolkhoz took all of the livestock that I had herded." He said that he joined the kolkhoz "because there was nowhere else to work, but what supplies we got on the kolkhoz. It was good!" He described being paid in clothing, boots, money, and hot food. He compared the two experiences of work: "Working on the kolkhoz . . . people worked from morning to night, women too. When people had their own land, they also worked from morning to night. But on the kolkhoz, if you did not fulfill your quota, then the tabelchi would not record any labor-day for you."[27] Rajab's appreciation for kolkhoz food supplies was not enough to make him love kolkhoz labor; he left permanently when he entered the military in 1939 and fought in the Finland War.[28]

G'aybullo (b. 1920) depicted pre-kolkhoz work and kolkhoz work as equally oppressive. His father, who had owned only a little land, died before collectivization, and young G'aybullo went to work for a rich man. "I harvested wheat; I fed the cattle; we drove the donkey to grind grain. . . . The rich man's wives would bake bread, and we would eat it. We would work in the fields, and our food was our share." His widowed mother also worked "for the rich man. The rich man would give her something, clothing, food. . . . She would do laundry, make dough, look after children. . . . They did not pay money; they gave food." G'aybullo and his mother joined the kolkhoz in 1932: "I was twelve. They brought us silkworms [to raise] . . . and then we all planted cotton." His mother died when G'aybullo was fifteen: "We stayed in our own house. I had five sisters. They made me the household head." He described work on the kolkhoz as never-ending.

> We would sleep in the fields, work in the daytime, sleep only a little at night. We would eat millet. . . . As soon as the dawn broke, they would raise the flag. "Come on, millet is ready; food is ready." Later the brigade leader would signal lunchtime. A bowl of millet and some cornbread, and we would eat for half an hour and then again: "Get up, work." We would work until sunset and then millet again or macaroni. . . . We had no days of rest. We could only take time off with the brigade leader's permission.

G'aybullo said that he went to school until fourth grade, but then their school was closed, "and everyone worked," though after some time, the school reopened. "We didn't learn anything." After his military service, G'aybullo returned to work on the kolkhoz.[29]

Qumriniso (b. 1920) said that her father was a poor dehqon who worked in the gates of the rich. The interviewer Shahnoza asked whether her mother had earned their living, for instance, by sewing or weaving. "No, as I said, we came from a poor family; we didn't have those things at home. My father died in hardship." When he died, she and her brother started working on the kolkhoz. "Women softened the ground, while men watered the crops. They worked separately. . . . My brother watered crops, and we carried cotton on a hand caddy." She remembered the pay as "sacks of grain, wheat or maize." When asked if she had gone to school, Qumriniso said, "I turned out to have a small brain. One year I went a few times, but I couldn't learn the letters. I thought I wouldn't learn them even if I kept going to school, and then I grew up, and they arranged a marriage for me."[30] She told about the hardships of wartime, recalling giving birth after a morning of work in the field. After the war, she said, "I had no other opportunity but to work in the field and come home. If you study, you can do other things, but because I hadn't studied, I didn't know anything else."

Ismoyiljon (b. 1923) was not born to a dehqon, and his childhood links to a kolkhoz were tenuous. His artisan father died when he was four. His mother made her living by spinning cotton thread: "A man or woman could spin two hundred grams in one day. If you could sell that for three to six so'ms, you could live on that. That is how my mother provided for us until she died in 1936. After that, I had to provide for myself." Ismoyiljon's older brothers, who had no background in farming, went to newly reclaimed land near Andijon to find work. "In 1932, I was very young. . . . We would go to the kolkhoz, carry water, bring tea. My older brothers entered the kolkhoz. There was some temporary work. . . . I came here and worked for three or four years, and then I went to the city." After his father died, Ismoyiljon's older brothers tried sending him to an old-style school. "I went for one day and refused to go back. . . . After the kolkhoz was created, I went to school there, the new-style school. Everyone was there, children, women, young married brides and grooms. No one talked about different ages. I studied through fourth or fifth grade, but then there was no more opportunity to study." Ismoyiljon did not identify himself as a kolkhoz member; he left the kolkhoz for the army when he was conscripted for the Finland War, and after that he worked in the city.[31]

Rajab, Oqquzi, and G'aybullo all had similar experiences to the older cohort of orphans, working for the rich or for their relatives. Neither Oqquzi nor

Qumriniso went to Soviet school, and Qumriniso had to work on the kolkhoz for her own living rather than even partially depending on her widowed mother, who did not join the kolkhoz. Ismoyiljon told of working for the kolkhoz in much the same way that the others spoke about working for their relatives. Most of them joined kolkhozes, but none of them shared Xoji's or Narzi's enthusiasm for the kolkhoz or for Soviet schools, which had done little to transform their lives.

Quloq Children

Across the Soviet Union, dekulakization deprived hundreds of thousands of children of their fathers. Children of kulaks often were placed in children's homes.[32] However, as noted in chapter 5, quloq fates varied widely: many quloq men were not exiled with their families; they were imprisoned or shot, leaving behind wives and children. Among interviewees for this project, several children whose fathers were made quloqs told of impoverished mothers struggling to provide for them and turning to the kolkhoz to earn a living. Abdurasul (b. 1922) said that his father joined the kolkhoz, but in 1932, he was made a quloq: "My father was arrested and imprisoned for two years. They took his livestock, all the sheep and even our horses, and our land.... Our lives changed while Father was in jail. Mother had to find work, and our maternal uncle helped us get on our feet.... I started working at age ten, while my father was in prison." Abdurasul's father was released from prison in 1933, and he returned to the kolkhoz. When talking about quloqs, Abdurasul commented, "Their children were treated badly, not admitted to schools or allowed to go to meetings." The interviewer Hurshida asked, "You were a quloq child. Did you go to school?" He responded: "I went when I was nine or ten, to the kolkhoz school.... I almost finished the seventh grade, but I was called up from the Komsomol to the army in 1938. Four boys and four girls from our school entered the Komsomol. While I was in school, I also worked on the kolkhoz, picking cotton, helping my mother and father, irrigating."[33] Abdurasul's discussion of school seems contradictory: If schools did not admit quloq children, how was it that he not only went to school but joined the Komsomol? Abdurasul said that the "really rich boylar" were exiled to Siberia; their wives and children were not admitted to the kolkhoz. His father was not one of the "really rich," and he had joined the kolkhoz voluntarily, before he was arrested and stripped of his assets. Abdurasul's experience of fatherlessness and of being a quloq's son were temporary, but during that interlude, he started working as a child laborer for the kolkhoz.

Tursunoy (b. 1924) was orphaned when "my father was made a quloq and taken away . . . to Tashkent. . . . My father became ill and then died." Her family remained on a kolkhoz near Andijon, and she said:

> When my younger brothers were small and my mother was trying to raise seven children, it was hard time. I worked on the kolkhoz from age twelve or thirteen. . . . In the 1930s when I worked, I earned twelve so'm per month. . . . We had our assigned area; two of us worked together and planted rice and tried to survive. I didn't hide a single so'm; my mother depended on me. . . . My mother raised ten children and suffered, working on the kolkhoz. She worked in the day, came home at night, sewed clothing on the sewing machine, looked after us.[34]

Tursunoy, like many orphaned respondents, emphasized her own sense of responsibility as well as her mother's labor. While working for the kolkhoz, Tursunoy also attended school for seven years, until 1940. Although she recalled her mother's kolkhoz work as suffering, she also remembered singing with other girls while they worked in the fields: "It made harvesting wheat more interesting. . . . Now the young people don't sing while they work. Just get done and leave."

Roviya (b. 1922) said that her father's craft was building doors and windows and that until collectivization, her mother and her father's other wife were housewives. In 1927, her mother unveiled and started working in a textile craft shop. After the kolkhoz formed, "My mother and I became kolkhoz members, and my father did as well. He continued his trade, and I followed my mother to the cotton fields. . . . I don't know whether she went of her own accord or was forced." During the famine, Roviya said: "My father left us, saying, 'I cannot take care of my wife and children.' There was nothing left for us. So then one of our neighbors told me, 'You sell bread. I will sell you five kilos of flour. Take it to your mother, and make the bread, bring it, and tomorrow you will have six kilos. . . . Within five days you can pay off your debt.' So we started our breadmaking. My mother baked it and gave it to me to sell in the bazaar." Roviya's father eventually returned, but he was arrested in 1936 and again in 1938. "Our father was imprisoned, and some others were shot, for example, the director of the kolkhoz. . . . My father and fifteen others were cleared."[35] She did not have fond memories of the kolkhoz or much to say about working there, other than recalling her mother's extraordinary effort to support her. She finished eighth grade and left the kolkhoz to work as a cashier.

Ernazar (b. 1923), from a grain-growing kolkhoz in Qashqa Daryo, said:

> I started to work labor-days at age twelve. I went to work on the kolkhoz in March 1936. . . . My father had died after he was imprisoned, and I was left with my mother and my grandmother. . . .

> My grandfather and father did not join the kolkhoz; they were arrested, made quloqs. Our possessions were taken, right down to the mattresses. My father had no brothers. My grandmother was old. My mother had three small children. One of her brothers, my uncle, took care of us, provided for us bit by bit.... People who themselves saw hardship brought us provisions. My mother did not join the kolkhoz....
>
> At the time, I was in school. Our kolkhoz, Holliq, had opened a one-room school. We studied all together for several years, and neighboring kolkhozes also opened schools, and then a commission came to sort us out by abilities and put us in classes.[36]

Ernazar said that his uncle found work for him as a kolkhoz tabelchi; his wages may have been important to his family's livelihood. Ulfat asked him whether he had been excluded from school or insulted as the son of a quloq. Ernazar responded, "No, people around here did not say things like that. The government did, but local people didn't say anything like that. On the contrary, they expressed their compassion." He studied through the seventh grade. "There was a thing for the people called End Semi-Literacy, End Illiteracy, and even I gave lessons there to grownups when I was a young kid." After serving in World War II, Ernazar returned to work on the kolkhoz.

Children of quloqs became fatherless for reasons different from those of other orphans on kolkhozes. More intimate interviews than those we conducted might have elicited some of the ways that this politically driven victimization informed their senses of self or their attitudes toward the Soviet state.[37] In the broader outlines of this comparison, though, their lives were much the same as those of any other orphans on the kolkhoz, shaped by Soviet schooling, by mothers who became their providers, and by their own need to start working from an early age.

State Support for Orphans

Several orphan accounts focused on the role of Soviet institutions other than the kolkhoz, such as Soviet boarding schools for orphans and the army. Madrim (b. 1919) told of the ways that his widowed mother used Soviet schools as a resource for support:

> My father died when I was five years old, and I was left to my mother's care. She had difficulty providing, so when I was very little, she placed me in a kindergarten, where they raised me. After I finished the kindergarten, she gave me to a school. It was a showplace elementary school organized by the cotton factory, through fourth grade.... After that my

mother joined the kolkhoz, became a member, and was able to earn her living. When she started working on the kolkhoz, I was somewhat literate, and they made me a tabelchi. I worked as a kolkhoz member, doing the accounts, for two years, and then they organized a school for kolkhoz youth in the regional center, a boarding school. I went there to study . . . and then they opened a seven-year school here, and I studied there.

With the aid of the kindergarten and showplace elementary school, Madrim's mother was able to support him until his early teen years, when he started working as a kolkhoz tabelchi. Madrim described the boarding school that he attended briefly as one that "took in orphan children who had no father or mother. It would give them clothing, food, a place to sleep, and would teach them." Madrim finished school back on the kolkhoz, but he did not spend his life in kolkhoz work; he became a teacher and a school director.[38]

Abdullo F. (b. 1919), whose father died fighting the Reds and whose mother died when he was an infant, told of being raised by his artist uncle, the man who made a portrait of Oxunboboyev. Abdullo described working in his grandfather's cotton fields before collectivization, and he told of his temporary exclusion from school as the son of a quloq (chapter 5). He gave a colorful account of leaving his community in about 1932 to attend a boarding school for orphans.

> Do you know about Qaymoqul Haqqulov? . . . [He wore] a white shirt like the ones Uyghurs wear; around his waist was a silk handkerchief, on his head a *do'ppi*, and he had a beautiful mustache.[39] . . . He had studied somewhere and was a progressive teacher, a man who could tell black from white. He had a fourth-grade education. He had finished a six-month [teaching] course but only in Arabic, not in the Latin alphabet. He came to us carrying two suitcases with military clothing and something like navy caps. He fooled us all. . . . What do children understand? [He told us,] "We will give you sugar, and there will be a big feast for you—come!" All of us changed into these clothes. . . . We didn't know what was going on, but we got into four carts and headed off to Guzor. He didn't ask permission from our fathers; he just said, "I'm taking the children."

As promised, the children were served a feast while en route to the boarding school, which was located in a village near Tashkent, far from Abdullo's home in Qashqa Daryo.

> There was a children's home, for children without parents. . . . We had a hard time. The river rose and washed out the bridge, carts were

supposed to bring us fresh food, but we were left hungry for a week, and we really suffered. Our teachers taught us to write a letter to the Central Executive Committee. We did not understand what that was or who its secretary was, but they dictated the letter, and we sent it. Not fifteen days later, Akmal Ikramov [first secretary of the Communist Party of Uzbekistan] . . . came to our school. He saw our desks and dormitories and cooking pots and that there was almost nothing to eat. He said he would direct the Education Ministry to send us back home, and in less than a month, I was back in Guzor.

I attended the kolkhoz school and earned a ten-year education in seven years, in the Latin alphabet. A commission gave students the right to teach elementary classes. There was the End Illiteracy program, teaching illiterate people to read, making women and men literate regardless of age, whoever wanted to study. So I became a teacher.

While I was in school, we were given an invitation: you should learn agricultural life in the summer, how to plant cabbage, vegetables, how to work in the cotton, so we were helping in the cotton when the Bosmachis came.[40]

Abdullo F.'s early life was remarkably studded with appearances by important Uzbek leaders who played roles in his journey from orphaned child of an opponent of the Soviet state to Soviet teacher. Unlike many of the orphans from rural communities, Abdullo apparently spent little of his youth working on the kolkhoz. Although his residence in a boarding school for orphans was brief, as was Madrim's, their stories and two that follow indicate that the Education Ministry of the Uzbek SSR actively sought to enroll orphaned children in children's homes and boarding schools, even though only a fraction of orphaned children were enrolled in those institutions.

Ravshan (b. 1920) was sent to a children's home, and he linked his decision to join the army to his orphan status. His wealthy, influential father was killed in a battle against the Reds when he was a baby, and his mother also died. He was raised by one of his father's other wives and then by an aunt. His kin joined a kolkhoz, giving up their own land and the land that Ravshan inherited from his father. He talked of the work he performed as a child on the kolkhoz: "We transported loads with donkeys. Others would load the donkey, and we would drive it, and taller children would unload it. We were twenty children, and there were twenty donkeys." His aunt died, and he was sent to a boarding school for orphans, graduating after seven years in 1938.

I was appointed as a teacher to a district in Surhon Daryo. I did not have any kin there. When the army began conscripting eighteen-year-olds,

> I applied. They did not accept me, but I told them that I did not have any home or kin, so I wanted to join. They wanted a consent form from my relatives. I told them I did not have any; I alone was left from my mother and father. They accepted me, and we went to the Finland War. I went to the army when I was seventeen. The political officer would go around to villages searching for the fatherless and motherless, and when he found someone like you, he would take them. They gave clothing, food, a place to sleep, education. I had finished two years of the teacher's institute, but before I could start working, I entered the army.[41]

Of the many respondents who were orphaned, only Ravshan and G'anijon spent most of their childhood in children's homes. G'anijon (b. 1920) recalled: "In 1930, I went to the Fergana children's home. When my father died in 1927, my grandmother had difficulty raising four children, so I was sent there. I was raised in the children's home, then studied at the workers' school, and then at the institute. In 1939, the war started, and I was conscripted." G'anijon did not mention what had become of his mother or why his siblings were left to their grandmother's care. The interviewer Shahnoza asked him, "Were you the only child from your family who was raised in the children's home, or did the others go as well?"

> G'ANIJON: They were left with my grandmother. My older sister was given in marriage, and my older brother started working for the kolkhoz. The youngest was born after my father died and was left to my grandmother's care.
> SHAHNOZA: Did you ever return to your grandmother's care?
> G'ANIJON: No, as I said, after I went to the children's home, I studied ... and then I went to the army, and I was wounded, second-class invalid.... After my father died, my grandmother struggled to raise the children, and then in 1930 she started working in the textile factory. It had a place to raise children, and after giving me to the state children's home, she was able to get on with her life as she chose.[42]

G'anijon believed that orphans like himself were specifically targeted for conscription for the Finland War. The interviewer Shahnoza tried to learn whether the children's home where he was raised housed Russian children as well as Uzbeks, but he took the conversation in a different direction: "Everyone who had been in the children's home went to the army. In the army, half of them perished, died. And now . . . my beloved friends are gone." Later he added that he had been enrolled in the preparatory course for the Institute of Physics and Mathematics when "the war started. . . . After the Finland War started, within one year, all of the guys at the institute were called up to the army." G'anijon had begun life in a village with a poor dehqon father, but his orphanage and military experience redirected the course of his life, and he entered the regional administration.

Each of these interviewees portrayed the orphan's relationship to the state somewhat differently. Abdullo, who had been taken in by an uncle whom he called his father, suggested that school personnel manipulated orphan children, luring them to enroll in state boarding schools, and their kin had no choice but would not have approved. Madrim spoke of his mother choosing to put her fatherless son in a succession of institutions that he evaluated positively. G'anijon noted that his grandmother chose to send him but not his younger brother to the children's home. G'anijon believed that the military singled out orphans for conscription, while Ravshan made himself the agent, recalling that he insisted to army recruiters that he should be allowed to join because he had no parents.

Although most of the orphaned interviewees remained with their kin, attended schools in their villages, and became the youngest members of the kolkhoz, state institutions removed a few of them from kolkhoz life. Madrim and Abdullo spent only a short time in state boarding schools, but those experiences were enough to redirect them: they did not become young kolkhoz members. G'anijon found community among his boarding school peers and pursued higher education, while Ravshan, also estranged from his natal village, turned to the army for a sense of belonging.

Widowed Mothers

We did not ask respondents to talk about deaths of family members, and neither did we follow up with questions concerning how those deaths affected them emotionally. Like Bekmurod, some mentioned the death of a parent to explain its effect on their daily life circumstances. Some orphaned respondents had lost both parents, others had lost only their fathers, and some did not lose their father to death but rather because of arrest, abandonment, or divorce. In all of these circumstances, loss of a father had negative implications for their lives. A few from the older cohort remarked that relatives appropriated property that should have been their inheritance. One implication that they rarely stated directly was the orphan's loss of social status. Bekmurod, above, mentioned that he was able to marry only when his kin found him an appropriate mate, another orphan. Most orphaned respondents talked about the more obvious implications of the loss of father as provider. They spoke of struggles to survive and about starting to work early in life—among the older cohort, working in the gates of the rich, and among the younger, working for the kolkhoz. The older cohort respondents did not recall mothers who found ways to provide for them, but collectivization and other economic changes apparently changed that pattern. Younger cohort orphans spoke of remaining with widowed mothers who earned a living and provided for their children.

Two women respondents mentioned their own experiences as widowed mothers working for the kolkhoz. Zulayxo (b. 1916) had worked on her father's land before collectivization, and she started working on the kolkhoz as a teenager, planting cotton and driving camels. She was one of the respondents who had positive memories of digging canals (chapter 8), but more generally she described "working like a dog" on the kolkhoz. She said: "In the 1940s all the young men left for the army. Our son Baxtiyor was two years old in 1940. His father went into the army and served for three years. He was killed and left there. . . . I didn't marry again, and I have one living son." She had borne three sons, but only one of them survived infancy. That son became a locally famous artist, and Zulayxo was proud that she had been able to support his drawing lessons. "He studied with hardship. He would go to study with three so'm [to live on] for a week. He walked all the way to Urganch. . . . When they paid me for working on the kolkhoz, I sent him money. What could you do back then?"[43]

Olmajon (b. 1903), who after her mother died had worked with her father in the gates of the rich, said that she married at age twenty-eight. "I was the only daughter . . . and the father of my children was nine years younger than me. His mother was a widow, and my father married her. My father's wife had died, so although I was older than him [her betrothed], they married us. We had two sons and two daughters." Her explanation of her marriage, unusual in terms of her age and the fact that she was the older spouse, alluded to her status loss. Without a mother and having worked as a laborer, a cart driver, Olmajon was not thought of as a desirable, protected, young virgin, to be sought after for an arranged marriage; instead she was given in marriage to another half orphan. Olmajon and her husband became kolkhoz members. "After six months, my children's father became the director. . . . I was pregnant, but I said I would help him. They made me into the keeper of the storehouse for the kolkhoz." She bore two sons and two daughters, but the sons and a daughter died in childhood, and only one daughter survived to adulthood. Her husband was conscripted in 1942. During the war, "my children's father was on a commission in Saratov, at a hospital, when it was bombed, and he never came home." Olmajon did not remarry; she worked on the kolkhoz and provided for her daughter. She proudly spoke of her work record, of tasks ranging from driving a tractor to increasing the rice yield, and of prizes that she won.[44]

Collectivization turned orphaned boys into kolkhoz laborers rather than mardikors who worked for the rich. Widowed and abandoned mothers and teenaged, orphaned girls also became kolkhoz laborers. Thus, I argue, collectivization provoked a shift in ideas and practices about how a shattered family should survive. It was not the shift that Soviet ideologues imagined, with orphans and abandoned children raised in children's homes. Instead of relinquishing sons to work in the gates of the rich and daughters to the mercies of relatives or to early marriage or readily turning over children to Soviet children's homes, widowed mothers joined the kolkhoz as workers, supporting their children with their own labor. Children who were orphaned were also supported by kin on the kolkhoz, until they were twelve years old or so, old enough, in kolkhoz terms, for work. More than state institutions like the children's home or the boarding school, the kolkhoz itself became an institution of social welfare and self-help for rural Uzbek society's most precarious members. It was not an altruistic institution: interviewees from the post-1917 cohort, whether orphaned or not, alerted us to the system's extensive use of child labor. But for many of the orphans of the collectivization generation, the kolkhoz, combined with the Soviet Union's commitment to mass public education, created a new realm of possibilities for careers and livelihoods.

Conclusion
A GENERATION, A TIME, AND REMEMBERING

Across Uzbekistan, respondents who were interviewed for the Oral Histories of Collectivization Project in 2001 to 2004 recalled the local violence that birthed the Soviet order in rural communities in the 1920s and 1930s. As this book's analysis of their accounts showed, each dehqon responded to Communist Party initiatives from their own position within the rural economy and family, kin, and village networks. They spoke as enactors and victims of pro-Soviet and anti-Soviet violence, of banditry, and of the seizures and dispossessions that took place from 1925 until the early 1930s, moments that I understand as constitutive of their identities and of their ex post facto explanations of their actions. Our interviews took place at a time when the state no longer actively fostered positive recollections of collectivization, as it had done until the late 1980s; nor was the state silencing those recollections and fostering their opposite through a politics of retribution.

In the early 2000s, when respondents were sharing their accounts of collectivization, Uzbekistan was undergoing a slow, lurching path toward decollectivization, one where farms that were ostensibly jointly owned by their former members but that were in fact controlled by former collective-farm directors or by other locally powerful politicians leased some of their fields to would-be entrepreneurial small landholders. The government of Uzbekistan, unlike some of its neighboring countries, did not have a strong ideology or legal framework to undo collectivization or to fully privatize land, and the leasing system itself was repeatedly revised, making landholding quite tenuous. This semiprivatization introduced new forms of social stratification in Uzbekistan's rural communities.¹ However, the collectivization generation members whom we spoke with, born between 1903 and 1925, were retired before 1991. Unlike Gail Kligman and Katherine Verdery's oral history respondents who recalled Romania's 1950s collectivization during a time of post-Communist privatization, respondents to our research in Uzbekistan were not directly involved in or significantly affected by de-collectivization, which in any case was a tepid, gradual process.² In Romania, privatization gave tangible importance to recollections about which land one's family had owned, as those memories, combined with documents, provided grounds for restitution.³ Within that oral history project, one of the researchers, Liviu Chelcea, observed that among forty-three respondents from one region, "some who came from poor families . . . skipped rapidly over the collectivization period, whereas rich peasants talked longer and in more detail about it."⁴ Interviewees in Uzbekistan faced no similar pressure: regardless what claims they made in the 2000s about past family holdings, nothing they said was in any way related to whether they or their children would become owners of private land.

Post-Communism brought reckonings in many places, such as excluding former Communist Party members from government or certain kinds of work or releasing the identities of secret police informers, as was the case in the former East Germany. In many countries, an overt state-led reckoning with the Communist past encouraged discourses of victim and perpetrator, creating a political atmosphere where self-identified victim stories became important to the reconstruction of a national history and where people who believed they would be labeled as perpetrators would have chosen not to tell their stories or to substantially revise their stories. After independence in 1991, Uzbekistan banned the Communist Party, with the party's leading members forming a new national political party in place of the former structure. Although there was a period of lively public discussion and relative press freedom during perestroika (1986–1991), which continued for a short time after independence, the reckoning that interested the leaders of Uzbekistan's government was anticolonial rather than anti-Communist per se. Uzbekistan's leaders had no desire to investigate Communist Party members' misdeeds in any time since Stalinism, though there was and remains a commitment to exploring Soviet episodes, such as dekulakization or mass political repression in the 1930s or the cotton scandal of the 1980s, with a focus on Uzbekistan's people as victims and Russians or "Soviets" as perpetrators and colonizers.⁵ In Uzbekistan, the Communist Party archive, which became an important source for post-Soviet historical and political revision in other countries, was open to researchers only until 1992, and then it was closed again. Since that time Uzbekistan's government has admitted researchers to Communist archive collections for very specific purposes that can contribute to decolonization, such as Shamutdinov's research on political repression in the 1930s, but most of the documents, especially the personnel files, remain off limits to researchers.

Uzbekistan's leadership determined from the start of independence that there would be no accusations that Communism was criminal and no denunciation of former party members. For respondents to the Oral Histories of Collectivization Project, there was neither threat nor benefit to recalling their own roles or their family's positions as activist mardikors or dispossessed quloqs, and respondents from both of those positions could be equally loquacious in recalling their own gains or losses. Their stories linger on actions that in more politicized post-Communist situations would likely have been silenced, such as episodes of tracking down Bosmachis, entering quloq homes to seize their possessions, or deciding who would be excluded from their kolkhoz. In the early 2000s, Uzbekistan was politically repressive in many ways, but attention to history focused on building up a glorious pre-Soviet past rather than on a thorough reevaluation and rejection of the Soviet period.

There have been many post-Soviet projects that elicit remembering of the Soviet past, some of which feature a nostalgia that may seem incomprehensible in light of the Soviet system's violence. In the words of the historian Serguei Oushakine, "Nostalgia for things Soviet is usually construed as a deliberate or implicit denial of the present. But it also is perceived as a revisionist project of rewriting history, as a postcommunist censorship of sorts aimed at making the complex and troubling past more user-friendly."[6] Most citizens in ex-Soviet Central Asian countries experienced such a wrenching destruction of their economic circumstances in the first years of independence that they bitterly compared with the relative stability and prosperity of their lives in the 1970s and 1980s. By the time that we conducted these interviews, Uzbekistan's government's reimposition of Soviet-style cotton quotas resulted in rural underemployment, poverty, and a rising trend of rural youth migrating to Russia to work. Interviewing rural retirees in their homes, we witnessed that some were living quite comfortably, while others appeared to be suffering from poverty. When asked a final question about their own opinion of collectivization, many reflected on a trajectory of hard times in the 1930s and 1940s, improving material conditions in the 1950s, and salaries that bought them as much meat as they could eat in the 1970s and 1980s. In the 1990s, incomes were so small and prices for meat so high that many households consumed meat only once or twice a month, and comments that compared the present with the past often focused on meat. Pensioners were aware of, but somewhat cushioned from the economic issues that beset younger generations. Most lived in houses that they had built long ago (most rural Uzbeks lived in privately built and privately owned houses, not apartment buildings), often with their adult children, and paying pensions had been prioritized by President Karimov, even when paying workers' salaries was delayed. The contrast between a troubled present and a stable past emerges when they expressed their pride in their own working lives on the kolkhoz at a time when the kolkhoz had no investment and was being dismantled, as well as in their positive if joking references to prosperity under "Padishah" Brezhnev, and their emphasis on growing pay and increasingly abundant food in the 1930s.

In a much earlier study of the ways that one Uzbek woman, Saodat Shamsieva, told her life story, I was able to compare narratives about her life in the 1920s and 1930s that she told in different political moments—during de-Stalinization, during perestroika, and after independence—to analyze some of the ways that she shifted her interpretation of the events of her life. The events she told of did not change, but she presented her motivations in becoming an emancipated Uzbek woman as more pragmatic and individually driven when she was no longer composing for the explicit goal of supporting a Communist Party narrative of emancipation.[7]

The materials for this book do not offer the evidence for that sort of fine-grained analysis of individuals' reappraisals of their own lives. We engaged with each respondent only once, and we did not ask them for documents or other materials about themselves. Neither did we try to document the veracity of their individual biographies or of the details of their accounts. The shared elements in these oral history narratives from members of the same generation living in different regions of Uzbekistan, and the correspondence of mundane details to documents from the time, persuade me to assess their accounts as truthful in the sense that they are subjective renderings of things that really happened. Their accounts represent a spectrum of experiences and recollections of experiences that were common among dehqons of the collectivization generation.

The archival records that we use as historians of the Soviet Union are freighted with problems. These stem not only from the ordinary human proclivity to present what we do in the best possible light and to impose coherence but more importantly from a profoundly fear-inducing state apparatus that levied extreme punishments on kolkhoz directors and regional leaders for nonfulfillment of ever-changing plans and for expressing ideas that might be acceptable one day and deemed treasonous the next. A reflection of the effect of such fear is found in the thinning of the files of the Central Asia Bureau: while folders of documents related to collectivization in 1931 are abundant and produce wildly differing impressions of success or disaster, folders from 1933 contain far fewer documents, and these tend to be less narrative, as though their writers were convinced that presenting statistics without discussion or filing absolutely minimal reports might be the safer approach.[8] At the same time, the archival collections for the

1920s and early 1930s are overwhelming in their scope and detail, convincing the dedicated researcher that every important thing that could be known is found there. However, the veracity of every kind of document, especially statistical items such as the data sets that show harvest figures, have provoked deep skepticism. I use such items anyway, although they likely present exaggerations, because those Soviet-produced, flawed records are the only ones that exist. They give a sense of trends and of the scope of change that collectivization brought about. Many historians work with archival documents about Central Asia in a deconstructionist way, examining the power of Soviet ideology to articulate, record, and thus limit and construct what was thought then and what we can know about it now, making a study of the past into a study of discourse and representations. Others work with archival collections in a postcolonial, against-the-grain way, teasing out "silences," highlighting what they regard as the truths that slipped past the limitations of ideology, and taking as credible only those records that can be read to reveal the destructiveness of the Soviet system and the gaps between aspirations and outcomes.

This large-scale oral history project had a different purpose than either a fine-grained analysis of ego accounts or a rigorous archival study. Oral historians seek to give voice to the past. As the oral historian Adrienne Edgar notes, "Oral history plays a crucial role in investigating everyday life and family history in the Soviet Union, where . . . rigid censorship ensured that many aspects of life were never discussed in print."[9] I emphasize the multiple voices and standpoints of many dehqons who were witnesses to and participants in agricultural collectivization in the 1930s. Rather than summarizing and aggregating, which in my view is to speak over the narrators, I have tried to translate their words with faithfulness to their ways of expressing themselves and to select sections from one or several interviewee accounts that are unique in expression and representative of what numerous speakers said on specific themes. Finding commonalities among responses from collectivization generation interviewees across seven provinces and multiple communities allows me to reconstruct some of their experiences of a series of transformative moments, focusing on what they articulated as significant, the ways that they perceived and evaluated events and their own participation in them, or the effects of events on themselves and their families. In other words, this is a traditional use of historical methods, using interviews as primary sources from which to construct a grounded understanding of everyday life, examining moments of change through the retrospective lenses of dehqons from Uzbekistan.

This meant paying attention to nuances that may seem trivial. For example, no one spoke of their spouse by given name; nor did they refer to a spouse with the party-approved term from 1920s emancipation discourse, "life partner" (*turmush o'rtoq*). I translated Xusenboy's reference to his wife, *kampir*, as "my old lady," both because that is accurate and because his use carried the same jovial and scoffing connotations as that phrase does in English.[10] I adhered to Olmajon's reference to her husband using the phrase *bolalarim otasi*, "the father of my children," a locution that both men (*onasi*, "their mother") and women use that highlights their status as parent while respectfully avoiding the utterance of a spouse's given name.[11]

Seemingly small distinctions that respondents made when talking about cotton, between g'oza and paxta, carried enormous economic and labor-related implications. Although cotton was not a new crop in the provinces of Uzbekistan that had previously belonged to Bukhara and Khiva, the labor demands and rhythms for the g'oza that dominated those regions were far less intensive than for the paxta that was planted in the Fergana Valley. Collectivization, which put planting decisions into the hands of the state, turned dehqons who had grown g'oza or wheat into planters of paxta, and it forced paxta planters in the Fergana Valley to devote even more irrigated land and labor time to cotton. Uzbekistan's cotton output increased swiftly in the 1930s. That increase in output had to correlate to a dramatic shift in the ways that members of dehqon households expended their own energy, with every additional ton of the paxta harvest representing men, women, and children who, in some cases for the first time, spent springtime in planting, pruning, and weeding and autumn handpicking cotton. That observation, supported by data on the increase in labor-days between 1933 and 1937, is a result of aggregated readings of many transcripts.[12] Individuals talked about this labor shift in terms of their own lives, either recalling when they started planting paxta in the 1930s or remembering cotton-related tasks among the kinds of work they performed in their youth, in days divided between school and kolkhoz labor.

The distinction that respondents made between Bosmachi and Qurboshi raised questions about the politics of memory. There was no moment when *Bosmachi* was not a political term, given the Red Army's efforts, beginning in 1918, to attach a word that traditionally meant raider and bandit to the Qurboshi-led militant groups who violently opposed the Bolshevik takeover of Central Asia. A Soviet depiction of Bosmachis as fanatical enemies of the people shaped history writing, fiction works, and films through most of the Soviet period, but a total revision in post-Soviet Uzbekistan rejected the term *Bosmachi* and hailed the Qurboshis as fighters for national liberation.[13] Respondents' ways of talking about Bosmachis or Qurboshis cast remembrance of violent raids on their own communities in one of those frames. One might charge that respondents' individual memories were so overwritten by dominant national narratives that the most interesting thing to be learned from their stories is the construction of myth. This, however, would be to view memory as initially correct and then corrupted by subsequent interactions, and that is not my view. Social experiences of the sort that narrators were recalling were never separable from the conversations that accompanied them. Umriniso (b. 1914), who came from the epicenter of the Bosmachi or Qurboshi movement and who spoke of these groups using the term *Bek*, told of childhood experiences of hiding with her mother from the Beks, being shot at by the Beks, being entreated for food by the Beks, and discussing the Beks and their activities repeatedly after the fact. Umrinoso recalled that family members connected those various episodes to her father's militia record of service to the Soviet state and to gendered fears of rape and kidnap. Her stories intersected with and supported the standard Soviet anti-Bosmachi version of history, but that version did not overwrite her memories. Rather, her memories were coconstructed in the moment of events, shaped in violent and frightening interactions with hostile raiders and in what were probably emotionally charged conversations with family members, and her stories also evolved in engagement with state discourses. Women and men who were at the receiving end of bandit actions had repeatedly recalled those episodes throughout the sixty years of Soviet rule, connecting their own moments of terror to propaganda about anti-Soviet Bosmachis. Through a close reading and comparison among these varied accounts, I conclude that these experiences and their shadows in memory reflect a fundamental aspect of gendered life. Women had been raised in awareness that their vulnerability to rape was a personal danger, in that they could be subjected to painful sexual violence as well as to kidnapping for marriage, and this vulnerability posed a danger to family honor that could cause shame and the disruption of parent-arranged marriage, with all of its household economic and status implications.

The sixty or so interviewees who responded to our prompt asking them about Bosmachis made clear that their judgments about Bosmachis or Qurboshis, whether they thought of them as violent raiders or as anti-Soviet heroes, were related not only to the state's stagnant and then rapidly changed politics but to widely differing experiences that they had lived and rendered into shared memories together with their natal families and close kin. The stories shared by those who said that their kin participated in Qurboshi-led militant groups, with attestations that Qurboshis only fought the "Soviets" and never harmed ordinary people, were utterly incommensurate with the stories told by those who were victims of violent raids and who called their attackers Bosmachis. Respondents who rejected the word that we interviewers used, *Bosmachi*, consciously referring to Qurboshis instead, carried personal and family stories that contradicted the Soviet version of events. Accounts of engagement in the Qurboshi movement burgeoned after independence, encouraged by an atmosphere critical of Soviet colonialism and seeking a heroic foundation for national history, in which the evil anti-Soviet Bosmachis were reconstructed as Qurboshi heroes of failed national liberation.

The research we did was far more focused on social class issues than on nationality or colonialism. The formation of national republics and the Soviet practices of nationality affected lives in ways that were more implicit than explicit in these interviews. I alluded to those in instances when an interviewee recalled collectivization-related decisions to move across a border, such as Avez, whose family moved permanently from Turkmenistan to Uzbekistan to escape their quloq label, or Ahmed, whose grandfather moved from to Tajikistan for a few years for the same reason, before returning to Marg'ilon.[14] We asked questions about interactions with people of other nationalities at two points in the interviews. We asked about Russians when trying to understand who agitated for and organized their kolkhoz, and we asked a more general question about whether other people moved into their villages during collectivization. Many respondents noted Russian and Tatar specialists, such as doctors or teachers, who appeared in their communities after the kolkhoz formed, and some gave detailed recollections of the forced resettlement of Koreans to nearby villages or of wartime displaced Ukrainians or deportees from the Caucasus. Their strong declarations in response to questions about who organized the kolkhoz, with numerous respondents exclaiming, "No Russians came!" and emphasizing "our own Uzbeks" as the kolkhoz founders, provoked me to seek out archival documentation that indeed confirms their view and leads me to a rather different conclusion than what Sarah Cameron makes about Kazakh plenipotentiaries who forced the disastrous collectivization of Kazakh nomads. Conrad notes that the empowered activists who were sent from regional centers to carry out confiscation of the bais in 1928–1930 were Kazakhs but were alien to the communities they were collectivizing. She writes, "The participation of Kazakh plenipotentiaries in the confiscation campaign gave them a role and a stake in the regime's programs."[15] In our interviews, respondents who recalled the activists and agitators for collectivization were sometimes remembering their own actions and frequently those of their fathers or uncles. Land reform, I argue, had given tens of thousands of dehqon households a stake in the regime's programs for transforming agriculture and rural communities, and cooperatives that distributed advances for cotton planting drew them into the planned economy and displaced the boylar from their role as lenders. Building on a base of land reform recipients and members of planting, purchasing, and labor cooperatives, collectivization in rural Uzbekistan did not rely primarily on outsider plenipotentiaries. Respondents like Qurbon A. or Sharofutdin became local activists or leaders who joined efforts with Communist Party members from the regional centers to organize their community's first kolkhoz.[16] Unlike what then transpired in Kazakhstan, where the newly collectivized herders starved or fled, in Uzbekistan most of the collectivized dehqons stayed, survived, and saw their kolkhozes increase in size and membership as more local dehqons joined, succumbing to inducement or to threat.

Taking credit for creating the kolkhoz was a more dominant motif in interviews than was assigning blame for creating the kolkhoz. This is in part a result of selection: we went to rural communities where early members of kolkhozes were still living. Some interviewees were people who had left the kolkhoz, moved to the city, or pursued a nonfarm career in their village, but most of them had been involved with their kolkhoz for a lifetime, as indeed were most rural Uzbeks and other Central Asians of their generation. We were not hearing from people who would have been collectivization's strongest critics: dehqons who were shot for their opposition, whose voices no one can hear; those who were permanently exiled outside of Uzbekistan, like those interviewed by Rustambek Shamsutdinov in the late 1990s; or people who left the Soviet Union, like the Bukharan Jews whom Thomas Loy interviewed in the 2000s or the WWII prisoners of war who told their stories to the Harvard Interview Project in the 1950s.[17] Freed from the Soviet-period politics of praising Russian elder brothers and the Communist Party for providing backward Central Asians with progress, many interviewees took the credit for collectivization for themselves, recalling local Uzbek or other Central Asian kolkhoz directors by name. Even in the changed atmosphere of post-Soviet Uzbekistan, where collectivization was officially regarded as part of Soviet colonialism, many of the men and women interviewees who had spent their entire lives living in and working for a collective farm and who, at the time we interviewed them, were living on the pensions that had first been granted to kolkhoz members in 1953, frequently spoke about the founding and growth of their kolkhoz as their accomplishment, even when they also discussed hardships.

I forced the reader to learn certain Uzbek words, such as *dehqon* or *boylar*, to emphasize the scope of meanings that are not easily encompassed by a standard translation of "peasant" or "wealthy person." A deconstruction of the written language of propaganda—a term that I use here as a shorthand for the Communist Party's political communication with the masses—might convince us that there was no such thing as social class until Bolshevik agitators introduced concepts differentiating rich from poor peasants. If that were so, the elderly who lived through that change should have used Bolshevik class terms. Notably, when discussing positions of dependence, interviewees used words and phrases that preexisted Soviet rural transformation, such as *novcha*, one of many terms for hired farm laborer, and the pervasive phrase "working in the gates of the rich." Some of the terms that they used do not appear in Uzbek-language print propaganda or archival reports, although they may have moved from common usage into the oral propaganda of Uzbek agitation speeches, for which we lack records. Such terms are important for understanding how dehqons regarded their relative social positions and the lenses that shaped their reception of the explicitly Bolshevik division of dehqons into poor (*kambag'al*), middle (*o'rta xol*), and rich (*boylar, quloq*). The sedimentary layering of respondents' uses of words that signified social statuses and economic relations serves as a marker of Sovietization, a deliberately transformative process that some of our respondents engaged with intentionally, merging their marked status as chorikor into the new politically empowered grouping of the *kambag'allar*. The Sovietization of status and class terms is most distinctive as the multifaceted boylar were politically identified as *mushtumzo'r*, a direct translation of *kulak*, the Bolshevik euphemism for "oppressor," and then the word *kulak* entered the Uzbek language and the lives and worldviews of dehqons through a violent process: making quloqs.

Survivor stories almost inherently concern coping strategies. One in ten respondents identified themselves as coming from quloq families, and their recollections provide evidence of the broad-ranging consequences of this violent key to the collectivization process. It is not news to note that many who were made quloqs were shot or taken away to prison; that was the experience that Ernazar related about his father.[18] Others were exiled with their households to places within Uzbekistan: Abduqodir related his father's dispossession and the family's construction of a new life in SAZLag imprisonment at Bekabod.[19] Similar accounts about Soviet dekulakization are abundant in histories, memoirs, and works of fiction.[20] What is somewhat different from other works that specifically focus on exiled or imprisoned kulaks is that we were not looking for kulaks. Instead, experiences of being made quloq emerged within scattered interviews, drawing attention to broader impacts of this violent policy on lives of those who were not exiled or imprisoned. Interviewees told of their family's either successful or unsuccessful efforts to evade being made quloqs, such as by redistributing land to chorikors or by fleeing to Tajikistan. Some focused on the consequences of becoming orphaned, abandoned, or socially labeled as a quloq. Even as kolkhozes became established and collective ownership and labor rapidly became the norm for Uzbekistan's dehqons, making quloqs continued in repeated waves, posing an ongoing and seemingly irrational or at least unpredictable threat not just to the holdouts against collectivization but also to those who had joined kolkhozes. While the Communist Party and its local enforcers carried out top-down plans with numerical quotas for dispossession and arrest, respondents told stories about quloq making that reflected decades of trying to find rational explanations for the seemingly random selection of targets, for unpredictable fates and outcomes, for death and exile, or for moving, making appeals for protection, reinvention, reliance on kin, or making peace with the kolkhoz.

I chose to put stories from respondents who participated in quloq making together with stories of those who were victimized. Dekulakization forced its surviving victims who remained in their own communities to grapple with many challenges, one of which was how to tell a coherent and self-protective account during the decades of Stalin's repression and how to revise that narrative in an atmosphere of increasing freedom. In contrast, those who told of participating in ferreting out quloqs used forms of storytelling that demonstrated that they had internalized the party's class categories, though in language that had local roots. For example, Bozorxo'ja's self-ascription as a chorikor and discussion of who was a quloq reflected his engagement with party discourses that vilified the boylar and enhanced the standing of people like him.[21] Although national histories in independent Uzbekistan no longer employed those Soviet ideologies, these rural respondents did not change their own stories. Faced with challenges about the morality of dispossessing quloqs from their slightly younger neighbors (the veterans' representatives) and the questions of the much younger interviewers, a few respondents actively resisted new interpretations that would have undermined their own moral position, which echoed Soviet-period evaluations of dekulakization: there were real quloqs who deserved their fate, but mistakes were made. Following the historian Pierre Nora's observation about history and memory, here history and memory are opposed: critical knowledge of collectivization coming from scholarly studies that emerged after independence differed from the living memories of many interviewees.[22]

Putting these quloq-maker recollections into a chapter with their opposite, victims of quloq making, is problematic: Shouldn't the victims be allowed to tell their stories without the perpetrators' counterpoints? Dehqons or boylar who were denounced as quloqs, dehqons who denounced others as quloqs, and people who observed these processes all lived together in the same villages. Ongoing interactions among them were shaped by the state but also by their own interactions in their communities and by the limited forms of agency that their own stories reflect. Oral history lends itself to much clearer moral statements when the historian chooses to focus solely on victim stories or to frame every story as a version of victimhood. I am reluctant to call any interviewee a "perpetrator." Not one of them was an inventor of the Stalin revolution from above, and none had significant power over the lives of others in the 1920s or 1930s. The closest to a "little Stalin," to use Sergei Abashin's description of a regime-supporting local leader, was Bekmurod, who openly recalled his efforts to exclude kolkhoz members whom he deemed corrupt and who voiced no regret over their arrest.[23]

Any oral history is an individual's version of life, a version that they might tell differently on a different occasion but one that is inherently inclined toward self-justification. Like many other interviewees who eventually moved into positions of leadership, Bekmurod told of his own agency. Orphaned as a teenager and forced by that circumstance to work in the gates of the rich, his account featured his choice to join with other land recipients in a work collective and his bargain with the district administration for the right to kick saboteur members out of the kolkhoz. Everyone whom we interviewed, whether they presented stories of victimhood or agency or both, had lived among family and in community where there was ongoing interaction over such stories. Exiled quloqs returned home, and other dispossessed quloqs remained in their communities. Interviewees from such families had to deal with neighbors who may have participated in their dispossession, and their accounts reflect a defensiveness, emphasizing their family's industriousness or their charity toward the poor. Youths who joined enthusiastically in the party-led assault on neighbors, exposing stores of grain or reporting community members who kept Qur'ans or spinning wheels, became adults who either defended their youthful actions, as Bozorxo'ja did, or spoke of them with some chagrin, as Turdiboy did.[24] Placing those accounts in juxtaposition to each other offers a way to highlight the interactive, communal, and social outcomes in everyday life of radical policies imposed from above.

From these interviews, we see the ways that collectivization produced immediate, memorable effects in everyday life. What was memorable? Interviewees dwelled on some themes that the state framed with its propaganda, such as the coming of tractors or building canals, bridging their own experiences with romantic national narratives of Uzbekistan's hard-earned progress. They also brought up experiences that were never mentioned at all in public discourse, such as famine or child labor. Respondents recalled the mundane workings of the kolkhoz, its invention of such new roles as tabelchi, the payment systems that made them feel exploited or accomplished, and the ways that families, including broken families, interacted with this new socioeconomic institution. They also talked about other impacts on daily life that I have discussed elsewhere, such as the pressures they felt against their practice of Islam and the disappearance of mullahs, who fled, were arrested, or hid their identities.[25] In other parts of interviews that are undiscussed in this volume, interviewees recalled wartime hardships as more severe than those of collectivization, and some mentioned the 1950s as the time when kolkhoz life finally began to improve. They reflected on the relative lack of change that the kolkhoz brought to their housing, village amenities, and clothing, but they were surprisingly specific about changing foodways, detailing many fruits and vegetables they began to grow and consume in the 1930s.

Interviewees talked about the 1930s from their individual perspectives, but these were structured by their class-based experiences. The project's focus on a mass, social process leads to a wealth of social, generational memory. Aleida Assmann, a scholar of communicative and cultural memory, writes: "Structures of relevance and frames of reference can change dramatically over the course of a lifetime, so what was once important can gradually become unimportant."[26] Thus memory is communicative and social, and generations share experiences and understandings of the world. "If one takes this sociological approach to generations seriously, the abstract unity of a historical epoch and its social memory can then be differentiated into different memories that are immersed in experience. . . . A remembrance is alive only insofar as a past is made present within a familiar context by means of conversation or verbal exchange."[27] The "highly divergent memories" of members of Uzbekistan's collectivization generation who existed side by side but were from diverse communities offer an account of Stalin's rural revolution and its varied effects on the everyday life of dehqons, bringing their cohort's memories to life in a post-Soviet context where nothing is the same.

Why did this system survive? Recent studies of collectivization in Ukraine and Kazakhstan make clear that the Soviet systems endured under Stalin's leadership through brute force and terror. In this Uzbekistan-based research, many respondents emphasized that they joined collective farms against their will, in response to threats and pressures, in accounts that resonate with post-Soviet critical analysis of collectivization. But in many other accounts, I see evidence of support for the Soviet system from below. Soviet efforts to cultivate the loyalty of society's more marginalized people are strongly reflected in the stories of those who identified themselves as orphans or mardikors. They judged the Sovietization of rural Uzbekistan not through a big-picture or postcolonial perspective and certainly not through a Lev Kopelev–style disillusionment with the violence of Communism.[28] Interviews with dehqons from the collectivization generation who were not critics of the Soviet project but who spoke from their own class-based standpoints that had developed over decades of involvement with kolkhozes reveal their enduring identity with the collective farm as a place where they invested their labor and from which they said they had benefitted. The Soviet system relied not only on coercion but also on the millions who, like these interviewees, continued to hope that Communism would improve their lives and who at least occasionally saw evidence of promised improvements.

Appendix A
ORAL HISTORY INTERVIEWEES

TABLE A.1 Bukhara interviewees

BUKHARA	GIVEN NAME, SURNAME INITIAL	YEAR OF BIRTH	MALE	FEMALE	DISTRICT	LANGUAGE IF OTHER THAN UZBEK
1	Nurmurod H.	1921	x		G'ijduvon	
2	Ne'mat B.	1916	x		G'ijduvon	
3	Ahmed U.	1921	x		G'ijduvon	
4	Rashid Sh.	1917	x		G'ijduvon	
5	Sa'dullo R.	1920	x		Shofirkon	
6	Rajab Sh.	1912	x		Shofirkon	
7	Baraka Ra.	1921	x		Shofirkon	
8	Ravshan H.	1920	x		Shofirkon	
9	Baraka Ro.	1916	x		Shofirkon	
10	Narziya J.	1921		x	Shofirkon	
11	Fayzi S.	1915	x		Shofirkon	
12	Ubaydullo M.	1922	x		Shofirkon	
13	G'aybullo Sh.	1920	x		Buhoro	Tajik
14	Qurbonberdi J.	1921	x		Buhoro	
15	Avez J.	1921	x		Buhoro	
16	Interview failed					
17	Xojimurod M.	1916	x		Buhoro	
18	Sharofat B.	1922		x	Buhoro	
19	Qurbon B.	1906	x		Buhoro	
20	Xoji A.	1920	x		Buhoro	
Total			17	2		

TABLE A.2 Fergana/Marg'ilon interviewees

FERGANA/ MARG'ILON	GIVEN NAME, SURNAME INITIAL	YEAR OF BIRTH	MALE	FEMALE	DISTRICT	LANGUAGE IF OTHER THAN UZBEK
1	Hamid U.	1922	x		Marg'ilon	
2	Obidjon M.	1924	x		Marg'ilon (urban, trade)	
3	Saidalixon M.	1921	x		Marg'ilon (urban)	
4	Musaxon T.	1910	x		Marg'ilon (urban)	
5	Ahmadxon T.	1920	x		Marg'ilon	
6	Halimaxon M.	1911		x	Marg'ilon	
7	Tursunboy Y.	1921	x		Marg'lon	
8	Muqumjon J.	1902	x		Marg'ilon	
9	Hidoyatxon S.	1919		x	Marg'ilon	
10	Faizixon T.	1917		x	Farg'ona (Vodil)	
11	Yoqubjon B.	1919	x		Farg'ona (Vodil)	
12	Mahkam T.	1921	x		Farg'ona	
13	G'anijon M.	1920	x		Farg'ona	
14	Qumriniso R.	1920		x	Farg'ona	
15	Umriniso M.	1914		x	Farg'ona	
16	O'g'ilxon M.	1914		x	Farg'ona	
17	Muhamadjon I.	1920	x		Farg'ona	
18	Eminjon X.	1920	x		Far'gona	
19	Safarali P.	1914	x		Farg'ona	
20	Sarafutdin Q.	1911	x		Farg'ona	
Total			14	6		

APPENDIX A

TABLE A.3 Namangan interviewees

NAMANGAN	GIVEN NAME, SURNAME INITIAL	YEAR OF BIRTH	MALE	FEMALE	DISTRICT	LANGUAGE IF OTHER THAN UZBEK
1	Yo'ldashev and wife Tursunoy S.	1923 1924	x	x	Hoqulobod/ Norin	
2	Hayitboy M.	1910	x		Uchqurg'on	
3	Sotibaxon M.	1920		x	Namangan (urban)	
4	Mavluda U. and friend Ibodat I.	1920 1925		x x	Yangiobod	
5	Aliqul I. and wife To'falda I.	1916 1925	x	x	Hoqulobod/ Norin	
6	Yo'lchivoy A.	1922	x		Quvasoy, then Norin	
7	Ismoyiljon N.	1923	x		Yangiobod	
8	Interview failed					
9	Abdurashid R.	1905	x		Xo'jobod, Baliqchi	
10	Interview failed					
11	Tursunoi O.	1903		x	Namangan area	
12	Rustamov and Turdiboy T.	1921 1922?	x x		Namangan area	
Total			8	6		

TABLE A.4 Navoiy interviewees

NAVOIY	GIVEN NAME, SURNAME INITIAL	YEAR OF BIRTH	MALE	FEMALE	REGION	LANGUAGE IF OTHER THAN UZBEK
1	Karimtosh A.	1926	x		Nurota	
2	Berdiqul B.	1920	x		Nurota	
3	Jumagul Y.	1924		x	Nurota	
4	Zulfiya H.	1917		x	Nurota	
5	Razoqbobo B.	1917	x		Nurota	
6	Zumrat Sh.	1921		x	Nurota	
7	Doniyor E.	1925	x		Nurota	Tajik
8	Rustam M.	1912	x		Nurota	
9	Bozorova	1910?		x	Nurota	Tajik
10	O'rozboy D.	1907	x		Nurota	Mixed Tajik/ Uzbek language
Total			6	4		

APPENDIX A

TABLE A.5 Qashqa Daryo interviewees

QASHQA DARYO	GIVEN NAME, SURNAME INITIAL	YEAR OF BIRTH	MALE	FEMALE	REGION OF CHILDHOOD / OF INTERVIEW	LANGUAGE IF OTHER THAN UZBEK
1	Ernazar S.	1923	x		Kaspi/Qarshi	
2	Abdurasul E.	1922	x		Qoraquch/Qarshi	
3	Lutfullo A.	1919	x		Qarshi	
4	O'ktam A.	1919		x	Katta Novqat, Shahrisabz	
5	Oqquzi B.	1922	x		Chorvog', Shahrisabz	
6	Zaynab X.	1922		x	Dukchi, Shahrisabz	
7	Qurbon A.	1908	x		Mo'minobod, Shahrisabz	
8	Xurram X.	1920	x		Panji, Kitob	
9	Rajab H.	1917	x		Hayrobod, Kitob	
10	Yorbobo N.	1922	x		Quyeqboy, Kitob	
11	Qarol M.	1922	x		Yakkabog'	
12	Bekmurod Sh.	1907	x		Yakkabog'	
13	Aslon R.	1922	x		Koson	
14	Barno J.	1922	x		Koson	
15	Temir X.	1920	x		Qumariq, Koson	
16	Hayrullo Sh.	1921	x		Mug'lon, Koson	
17	Halil F.	1905	x		Maymanoq, Koson	
18	Abdullo F.	1919	x		Katta Qishloq, Qarshi	
19	Narzi A.	1921	x		Bukhara/Qarshi	
20	Fayzullo R.	1909	x		Shahrisabz	
Total			18	2		

TABLE A.6 Tashkent interviewees

TASHKENT	GIVEN NAME, SURNAME INITIAL	YEAR OF BIRTH	MALE	FEMALE	REGION	LANGUAGE IF OTHER THAN UZBEK
1	Bozorxo'ja U.	1913	x		Parkent	
2	Tojivoy D.	1917	x		Xisorak, Parkent	
3	Sattor A.	1923	x		So'qoq, Parkent	
4	Parda B.	1915	x		So'qoq, Parkent	
5	B. Xoldarova	1896		No count	No transcript, failed	
6	M. Tuloev	1921	x		Parkent	
7	Abdullo Q.	1902	x		Parkent	
8	Qimmat T.	1906		x	Bo'stonliq	
9	Xudoybergen R.	1922	x		Bo'stonliq	
10	Xalil A.	1917	x		Bo'stonliq	
11	K. Xudoybergenov	1916	x		Bo'stonliq	
12	Yusubboy H.	1917	x		Bo'stonliq	
13	Nabi E.	1920	x		Bo'stonliq	
14	Umrqul X.	1919	x		Bekobod	
15	Xusenboy A.	1919	x		Bekobod	
16	Abduqodir P.	1916	x		Oyim/ Bekobod	
17	Aziza I.	1914		x	Marg'ilon/ Tashkent	
18	Qudratilla R.	1922	x		Tashkent (urban)	
19	I. Rahimov	1922	x		Olmazor/ Tashkent	
20	Abdurauf H.	1920	x		Tashkent	
21	S. Muhammajonov	1921	x		Tashkent	
22	A. Komilov	1907	x		Tashkent	
23	Melivoy A.	1918	x		Uchqurg'on, Namangan/ Tashkent	
24	Ashurboy P.	1923	x		Bo'stonliq/ Tashkent	
Total			21	2		

TABLE A.7 Xorazm interviewees

XORAZAM	GIVEN NAME AND SURNAME INITIAL	YEAR OF BIRTH	MALE	FEMALE	REGION	LANGUAGE IF OTHER THAN UZBEK
1	Elposho Y.	1937		x	Xorazm (urban)	
2	Otanazar M.	1921	x		Xorazm (urban)	
3	Sidiq U.	1921	x		Khiva	
4	Boltaboy K.	1914	x		Khiva	
5	Ibroyim K.	1917	x		Urganch	
6	Yo'ldosh S.	1918	x		Urganch	
7	Madrim A.	1919	x		Gurlan	
8	Ra'jab Q.	1921	x		Gurlan	
9	Zulayho A.	1916		x	Xazorasp	
10	Sayidabdullo	1922	x		Xazorasp	
11	Roviya A. and B. (husband)	1926 1920?	x	x	Xonqa	
12	Abdullo S.	1922	x		Qo'shko'pir	
13	Madqurbon J.	1914	x		Qo'shko'pir	
14	Jumagul I.	1915		x	Shovot	
15	Ruzim I.	1919	x		Shovot	
16	Rahimajon S.	1924		x	Yangiariq	
17	Olmajon X.	1903		x	Yangiariq	
18	Sanamjon M.	1913		x	Bog'ot	
Total			12	7		

TABLE A.8 Overall interviewees

	MEN	WOMEN	NUMBER OF INTERVIEWS WITH TRANSCRIPTS
Bukhara	17	2	19
Marg'ilon	14	6	20
Namangan	8	6	10
Navoiy	6	4	10
Qashqa Daryo	18	2	20
Tashkent	21	2	23
Xorazm	12	7	18
Total interviewees (125)	96	29	120

Note on failed interviews: we began an interview, but the respondent either could not respond adequately or could not be heard adequately.

Appendix B

QUESTIONNAIRE

We started with a less-developed questionnaire, but the research group eventually came up with a very thorough questionnaire to make sure that interviews addressed similar topics. Interviewers did not use every question. Interviewers treated questions as thematic prompts. They did not necessarily address topics in the order of these questions. The questions here appear to be yes-no questions, but interviewers often asked about the theme in a more open-ended way, and their mention of the topic of the question prompted new directions. Interviewers sometimes followed up in directions that the interviewee took, which might mean that the interviewee raised themes rather than the interviewer. The interview assistant kept track of what had been covered in an interview and sometimes added questions. Although questions about new foods do not appear in this questionnaire, they were regularly asked, as were questions about mosques and religious practice.

1. When were you born?
2. Where were you born?
3. What is your nationality (*millat*)?
4. What was your father's nationality?
5. What was your mother's nationality?
6. When did you move to the place you live now, and why?
7. How many of your ancestors (father, grandfather) can you name?
8. What was your father and grandfather's way of making a living (*kasb*)?

APPENDIX B

9. Did your ancestors pass down an occupation from long ago, something that you continued, or was their occupation lost at some point?
10. What can you remember about land reform?
11. If you heard about land reform, did your family have additional/excess (ko'shimcha) land?
12. If your family received additional land in land reform, where was that, and how many tanobs?
13. What effect did land reform have on your family's property?
14. In land reform, was there someone whose land was given to your family, or on the contrary, did your family divide its land out to someone else?
15. Before collectivization began, did your family have its own property (planted fields, gardens)?
16. Before collectivization where was your family's land located, and can you remember what kinds of things were planted there?
17. Before collectivization, to whom did you pay land and water taxes?
18. What form did land and water taxes take (money, wheat, cotton, etc.)?
19. Did you ever hear about the Rabzemles Union? [This question, about a union mainly for forest workers, was asked in the Tashkent region, but no one ever responded that they knew about it, and the question was dropped].
20. What do you remember about the Qoshchi Union? [Union of plowmen—this prompt did elicit specific responses among some older respondents.]
21. What do you remember about your family's necessary equipment and tools before collectivization? Did you have these (mill, oil press, yoke, weaving loom, spinning wheel, etc.)?
22. Before collectivization, what kinds of livestock were in your family's care, and how many (sheep, cows, horses, camels, etc.)?
23. Before collectivization, how was a family's inheritance divided out? [This theme was asked in the Tashkent and Fergana regions but usually late in the interview if at all.]
24. What kinds of things were divided as inheritance?
25. Who primarily received inheritance and what shares (older son, younger son, older daughter, younger daughter)?
26. What do you remember about first hearing about collectivization?
27. What was the name of your kolkhoz?
28. Who was the first director of the kolkhoz, what nationality, from where?
29. How many households made up the kolkhoz at first?

30. What kind of attitudes did people express toward the collectivizing process (disagreement, agreement, fear, surprise, etc.)?
31. If people disagreed with collectivization, how did they show that?
32. What do you remember about people's thoughts on collectivization?
33. What kind of actions did collectivization start with (seizing the land or livestock from the rich, giving some opportunities, land to the poor)?
34. Who were the people who played an active role in collectivization, at the very beginning (local Bolsheviks, Russians, educated people, the poor, etc.)?
35. What forms did that kind of action/activism take?
36. Do you remember when Russians first appeared here?
37. When collectivization started, were the boylar completely stripped of everything, or were they left with some things?
38. What kinds of conditions did the state make to get people to join the kolkhoz?
39. Were there agitators and propagandists, and if so, who were they, from where, and what did they do?
40. During the time of collectivization, what kinds of punishments did the state's opponents receive (prison, exile, shooting, forced resettlement, etc.)?
41. What were the qualifications/demands for joining the kolkhoz?
42. Were there people who did not want to join the kolkhoz? Who hid their property and livestock? What was done to them?
43. In your village did people talk openly to each other about collectivization? How much did they trust each other?
44. What do you know about quloqs and dekulakization (*quloqlashtirish*)? [They responded with *quloq kilish*, "making quloqs."]
45. Whom did the government consider to be quloqs?
46. If there were people who were taken from your village as quloqs, do you know what their fate was?
47. If someone from your close relatives was made a quloq [here we borrowed their term, *quloq kilingan*], what was their fate?
48. What did the government do to quloqs?
49. Was the Bosmachi movement connected to the process of dekulakization?
50. Were there people who disagreed with collectivization who voluntarily joined the Bosmachis?
51. What kind of influence did collectivization have on the Bosmachi movement?
52. Did any of your relatives or family members rise up against collectivization?

53. In collectivization, did everyone participate/work together, or did women work separately from men?
54. What kind of participation/work did young children do in the time of collectivization?
55. Do you remember people saying, "There's no other possibility / Nothing else can be done" [expressing that collectivization is an irresistible fate]?
56. When the kolkhoz formed, what kinds of work were done?
57. When did tractors first appear on the kolkhoz?
58. What do you remember about the MTS's (Machine Tractor Station) actions?
59. What do you remember about agronomists' initiatives?
60. When the kolkhoz was first organized, the people who were taking leading roles came from what nationalities?
61. At the time of collectivization, did women cover up in *paranji* [Uzbek veiling robe], or had they thrown it off? If they threw it off, when was that?
62. What attitudes did people show toward women removing paranjis?
63. What kind of work did you do on the kolkhoz?
64. What were the differences between the way you worked on the kolkhoz and what you did (before) on your own family's land?
65. In general, after the kolkhoz was founded, did life become harder or easier? Were living conditions improved, or did they worsen?
66. On the kolkhoz, was there a difference in work that men did versus work that women did, or was everyone forced to do the same work?
67. Before collectivization, were women doing the kind of work they did in the time of collectivization, or were they just housewives?
68. During collectivization, what kinds of new public buildings were built (stores, clinics, schools, clubs, libraries, etc.)?
69. What do you remember about difficult times on the kolkhoz?
70. During collectivization was there famine (ocharchilik) among the population, and if there was, how long did it last?
71. During collectivization what kinds of crops were planted? What kinds of cattle raising was started?
72. Before collectivization, what kinds of crops did you raise?
73. Did your first kolkhoz later merge with others, and if so, what was the new kolkhoz called?
74. Did people keep wearing the same kinds of national clothing and headwear as they wore when collectivization began? Or did they start wearing new forms of dress and footwear?

75. After collectivization, did new people move to your kolkhoz? Did the kolkhoz reclaim (*o'zlashtirish*) new fields? What kind of new infrastructure was built?
76. Did your family build a new house during collectivization?
77. During collectivization did you study at a new school? How many grades did you attend?
78. How did attitudes toward collective property change among people?
79. What is your overall view of collectivization?

Appendix C

GLOSSARY OF UZBEK TERMS USED IN THIS WORK

ariq: a small irrigation channel that intermittently brings water from the main canal to the fields.

artel: a workers' collective. Some respondents used this term from Russian; others used the Uzbek term *shirkat*. In the 1920s, artisans, craftworkers, and agricultural laborers were encouraged to form such collectives.

atala: a porridge of flour and water.

Bek: a title referring to the leadership of armed groups; respondents used it interchangeably with *Qo'rboshi*, but they also used it to refer to state-organized militia leaders.

Bosmachi: bandit, raider, and the pejorative name that the Soviet government pinned to armed Central Asian militants who fought against Soviet power. Other authors use the Russified spelling *Basmachi*. *See also* Qo'rboshi.

boylar: (pl.) the rural wealthy, the rich. I avoid the singular (*boy*) because of the obvious confusion that would cause in an English-language text. Other scholars use the Russian spelling, *bai*, or a Turkish spelling, *bay/bey*.

buhonka: Uzbek version of the Russian word *bukhanka*, "loaf," for Russian style bread, *khleb*.

chorikor: sharecropper; a tenant who raised crops and paid the landowner with a share of the crop. *Chor* indicates "one-fourth," but shares retained by the sharecropper ranged from one-fourth to one-half of the crop. *See also* yarimchi.

dehqon: one who tills the land, either as an owner of the land or as a worker on someone else's land; an agriculturalist.

domla: in Islamic education in Uzbekistan, a male teacher for the beginning levels of instruction at a maktab. Uzbeks also referred to their local mullah as domla.

eshon: a Muslim preacher or the leader of a Sufi group.

g'oza: Central Asian strain of *Gossypium herbaceum* cotton, with short fibers, growing in pods that must be dried and broken open.

halal: pure, acceptable for use or consumption in Islamic codes of behavior.

haram: impure, unacceptable, or forbidden for use or consumption in Islamic codes of behavior.

hashshar: work on shared community projects, such as ariq maintenance or housebuilding; in theory hashshar was voluntary, but social expectations made refusal difficult.

imam: Muslim preacher, often associated with a large "Friday" mosque, more influential than the mullah or domla who led a small local mosque. Soviet anti-religious measures often named imams as their target.

kambag'al: poor, a description of a dehqon household that owned little or no land; equivalent to Russian *bedniak*.

Kambag'allar Uyushmasi: Union of the Poor, a soviet organization for hired laborers and sharecroppers.

ketmon: a very large-headed hoe, the primary implement for fieldwork and a key symbol of the Central Asian dehqon used in collectivization-related imagery.

kishlak: village, rural settlement in the agricultural zones of Central Asia. *See the Uzbek version*, qishloq.

kulak: Russian, "fist"; a politicized label for wealthy peasants. *See* quloq.

lalm-i kor: dry land, unirrigated land, rain-fed land; also known as *bahori-kor* (planted in spring) and in Russian as *bogara*.

kunjara: seed hulls, the remainders from pressing cotton seeds to extract oil. Used as fodder for animals, kunjara was the last resort for human consumption in the context of famine.

maktab: school. Respondents differentiated between *diniy maktab*, a traditional religious school providing basic Islamic education, and the Soviet maktab that provided a modern, Soviet curriculum.

makruh: not acceptable, not recommended, in Islamic code of behavior.

manap: a title for Kyrgyz tribal chieftains.

mardikor: a hired rural laborer, "day worker." *See also* novcha.

millat: nation, nationality.

mirob: the traditional overseer of a local irrigation network, who regulated flows, collected fees, and organized maintenance.

ocharchilik: famine; a dramatic decline in food availability due to war, drought, or other events.

oqsoqol: village elder (lit., "white beard").

o'rta xol: middle condition, a description for a dehqon household with adequate resources to support itself; translation of Russian *sredniak*.

non: wheat bread, usually round with a flattened center, baked in a clay oven. The Russian term for *non* is *lepioshka*, "flat cake."

novcha: a hired farm worker.

osh: food. The word can refer specifically to plov, or it can refer to any meal.

otin: in Islamic education, a woman teacher who usually taught literacy and basic knowledge of Islam to girls.

patta: a token used for tallying labor-days for payment on newly organized kolkhozy.

paxta: cotton fiber; also used as the generic name for *Gossypium hirsutum* (American upland) strains of the cotton plant.

plov: a dish of meat and rice. In the 1920s, most dehqons thought of it as a festive treat rather than as everyday food.

qariz: underwater system for channeling water from mountain sources to lowland fields.

qazi: a judge, trained in a madrasa to adjudicate cases on the basis of Shariah law (Russian, *kazi*; Arabic, *qadi*).

qimmatchilik: inflation.

qishloq: rural community or village of sedentary farmers and herders. A qishloq might have few tens of households, a mosque, and a teahouse, or it might be significantly larger. When collectivization began, some qishloqs saw the formation of multiple small kolkhozes.

Qo'rboshi: commander. Before the revolution, the term was used for Central Asians who were leaders of local militias, appointed by the Russian Turkestan Administration. Qo'rboshis became leaders of militant guerrilla groups who fought against the Red Army.

Qoshchi: one who drives the pair of oxen and plow; the name for a Bolshevik-created agricultural labor organization.

quloq: rural landowner who was deemed to be wealthy and was targeted for dispossession; borrowed from Russian *kulak*.

risala: a Muslim treatise for a guild, defining how to fulfill the guild's tasks in a halal (pure) way.

shirkat: a collective of workers. *See* artel.

so'm: the Uzbek term for the main unit of money, the ruble.

tabelchi: field recorder for kolkhoz labor; usually a young, literate boy who recorded how much work each member of a work brigade accomplished.

tanob: measure of land, varying from one-sixth to one-fourth hectare.

tiyin: a coin equal to one-hundredth of a s'om (ruble); a kopeck.

vabo: epidemic disease. In some cases, it is used to mean typhus.

yakka xo'jalik: individual husbandry, with that term indicating both ownership of land and cultivation; the term that respondents used retrospectively to name the rural economic order before collectivization.

yarimchi: sharecropper, in Xorazm, from the term meaning "one-half."

yer islohoti: land reform, the term most commonly used in print and in speech for the land redistribution that took place in the 1920s. Although legal documents called for "land and water reform," in practice land, not water, was subject to redistribution.

yetim: (1) orphan or fatherless child; (2) hired herder.

yigit: young man, warrior, member of a Bosmachi group of raiders or of a Qo'rboshi-led guerrilla group.

xizmatchi: servant.

zog'ora: corn bread, a food looked down on as something to eat when there is nothing else available.

Notes

INTRODUCTION: COLLECTIVIZATION GENERATION

1. Qashqa Daryo 7, Qurbon A., b. 1908, near Sharisabz. Interviewed in 2003. I use the initial letter of his surname, A, to differentiate him from another interviewee, Qurbon B., a practice for cases when interviewees shared names. Translations are the author's work.

2. Seymour Becker, *Russia's Protectorates in Central Asia: Bukhara and Khiva, 1865–1924* (Cambridge, MA: Harvard University Press, 1968); Alexander Morrison, *The Russian Conquest of Central Asia 1814–1907: A Study in Imperial Expansion* (Cambridge: Cambridge University Press, 2021).

3. Qashqa Daryo 7, Qurbon A., b. 1908.

4. Donald Raleigh, "'On the Other Side of the Wall, Life Is Even Better': Travel and the Opening of the Soviet Union; The Oral Evidence," *Ab Imperio* 4 (2012): 373–399.

5. Among the regional variations for farm laborer in the Uzbek language, the most common term that we encountered in interviews was *mardikor*, but *novcha* was used in Qashqa Daryo and *korranda* in parts of Bukhara.

6. Jeff Sahadeo, *Russian Colonial Society in Tashkent, 1865–1923* (Bloomington: Indiana University Press, 2007), 209; Julia Obertreis, *Imperial Desert Dreams: Cotton Growing and Irrigation in Central Asia 1960–1991* (Göttingen: V&R unipress, 2017), 142–143. Central Asians did not have any practice of the annual commemoration of a birthday. State-run birth registry offices first opened in rural regions in the 1930s.

7. Adeeb Khalid, *Making Uzbekistan: Nation, Empire, and Revolution in the Early USSR* (Ithaca, NY: Cornell University Press, 2015), chap. 4.

8. Elections for local village committees began in some places in 1922 but in others, especially in former Bukhara lands, only after the national delimitation of the Uzbek Soviet Socialist Republic, which was announced in November 1924. Rossiiskii Gosudarstvennyi Arkhiv Sotsial'no-Politicheskoi Istorii (RGASPI) fond. 62, opis. 2, delo. 290. Documents housed in Russian and Uzbek state archives are presented in this standard format: abbreviated name of archive, followed by the specific fund (fond), the finding list (opis), the file (delo) and pages (listy). This document is a report of the commission investigating *kishlak* and *aul*, late 1925. The same commission spearheaded land reform. RGASPI f. 62, op. 2, d. 279, l. 51, November 1925, lists the members of this committee.

9. RGASPI f. 62, op. 2, d. 279, ll. 48–50, late 1925, lists the exact categories to be dispossessed; l. 57 notes that the Uzbek Communist Party Kurultai issued two decrees on November 30, 1925, nationalizing land and making land-water reform official policy.

10. The party commission investigating villages in Uzbekistan noted that in the Bukhara region, the traditional village leaders, generally wealthy landowners, had carried out village committee elections to ratify their own leadership and were typically recognized by earlier village-leadership terms, such as *amin*. RGASPI f. 62. op. 2, d. 290, ll. 27–28. Bosmachis and quloqs are subjects of later chapters.

11. In a collection of the memoirs of collective farmers, setting fire to the other side's assets comes up in accounts about the Soviet versus Bosmachi struggle. Jamol Sharopov, ed., *Unutilmas Xotiralar (O'zbekiston qishloq xo'jaligi veteranlarning xotiralari)* (Tashkent: Mehnat, 1990).

12. Qurbon A.'s formal education was very limited; he may have been appointed school director on the basis of membership in the Communist Party, a pattern visible in education data from Uzbekistan for 1938. *Kul'turnoe stroitel'stvo SSSR Statisticheskii Sbornik* (Moscow: Gosplanizdat, 1940) 88, sec. 2, table 20, http://istmat.org/node/22545.

13. Marianne Kamp, Russell Zanca, and Elyor Karimov, "Collectivization in Uzbekistan: Oral Histories." Sponsored by a grant for collaborative research from NCEEER (2002–2004), and grants from the University of Wyoming (faculty grant-in-aid, 2002–2003), this collaborative project began in 2001 and ended in 2004. The Yosh Olimlar (Young Scholars) society of the Academy of Sciences of Uzbekistan was headed by Elyor Karimov and the researchers Komiljon Kalonov (sociologist), Shahnoza Madaeva (philosopher), Hurshida Jabbarova (historian), Ulfat Abdurasulov (historian), Zavqiddin Gadoev (philosopher), and E. R. Xalilov.

14. Oral History Association Principles and Best Practices Guidelines, October 2018, https://www.oralhistory.org/principles-and-best-practices-revised-2018/.

15. Elizabeth Tonkin, *Narrating Our Pasts: The Social Construction of Oral History*, Cambridge Studies in Oral and Literate Culture 22 (Cambridge: Cambridge University Press, 1992).

16. Marianne Kamp, *The New Woman in Uzbekistan: Islam, Modernity, and Unveiling under Communism* (Seattle: University of Washington Press, 2006); Timur Dadabaev, "Power, Social Life, and Public Memory in Uzbekistan and Kyrgyzstan," *Inner Asia* 12 (2010): 29.

17. Marianne Kamp, "Uzbek and Soviet on the Collective Farm," in *Erinnerungen nach der Wende: Oral History und (post)sozialistische Gesellschaften*, ed. Anke Stephan and Julia Obertreis (Essen: Kalrtext Verlag, 2009), 233–242.

18. Twelve interviewees were from urban artisan or intellectual families, and they had little direct engagement with collectivization. The team interviewed one scholar who was much younger than the cohort, born in 1937. These interviews are included in the archive, but I make little reference to them in this book.

19. Viktoria Semenova, *Sotsial'naia dinamika pokalenii: problema i real'nost'* (Moscow: Rosspen, 2009), 140, 156–186.

20. Seth Bernstein, *Raised under Stalin: Young Communists and the Defense of Socialism* (Ithaca, NY: Cornell University Press, 2017). Bernstein's analysis focuses on those who joined the Komsomol, or Communist Youth League. Only a small number of our interviewees mentioned joining the Komsomol.

21. James Pennebaker and Amy Gonzales, "Making History: Social and Psychological Processes Underlying Collective Memory," in *Memory in Mind and Culture*, ed. Pascal Boyer and James Wertsch (Cambridge: Cambridge University Press, 2009), 175.

22. To date, there is no published breakdown of Soviet World War II forces by nationality, though a reckoning of the known dead, by nationality, puts deaths of soldiers identified as Uzbeks at 117,000. M. V. Filimoshin, "Liudskie poteri vooruzhennykh sil SSSR," *Mir Rossii* 4 (1999): 92–101. Uzbekistan's public monuments approximate 1.5 million, out of a population of 6.5 million, were mobilized for military service in the war. During the war years, ethnic Uzbeks constituted about 4.1 million of Uzbekistan's population of 6 million, and Uzbek men of conscription age (eighteen to forty-three during the years 1941–1945) may have numbered as many as 1 million, meaning 10 percent or more of those Uzbeks who were of the conscription-age cohort died on the front.

23. Their stories contrast with representations of Uzbeks and other Central Asians in recent historiography about World War II, which has featured skepticism that Central Asians served loyally or willingly. See, for example, Roberto Carmack, *Kazakhstan in World War II: Mobilization and Ethnicity in the Soviet Empire* (Lawrence: University of Kansas Press, 2019), chaps. 1 and 2; Paul Stronski, *Tashkent: Forging a Soviet City*

(Pittsburgh: University of Pittsburgh Press, 2010), chaps. 4 and 5; Moritz Florin, "Becoming Kyrgyz through War: The Kyrgyz and the Great Fatherland War," *Kritika: Explorations in Russian and Eurasian History* 17, no. 3 (2016): 495–516. The Soviet journalist Vassily Grossman's wartime diaries show that those prejudicial views of Uzbeks and Central Asians were rife among non–Central Asian troops. Vasily Grossman, *A Writer at War: Vasily Grossman with the Red Army 1941–1945*, ed. and trans. Antony Beevor and Luba Vinogradova (New York: Pantheon, 2006). A comprehensive account, Feodor Sinitsyn, *Sovetskaia natsiia i voina: Natsional'nyi, vopros v SSSR 1933–1945* (Moscow: Tsentrpoligra, 2018), similarly relies on archives reflecting the views of Russian military officers. In World War II, some of the tens of thousands of Central Asians who became POWs joined Nazi Germany's Turkestan Legion. Some who survived and remained in the West wrote accounts that justified their actions through reflection on collectivization and other Soviet brutalities. Those nonmainstream individuals shaped Cold War Western historiography of Soviet Central Asia and post-Soviet Uzbekistan's history writing as well. Baymirza Hayit, who emerged from that POW experience to become a historian in West Germany, wrote works that became foundational to Western Cold War–period understandings of Central Asia. Other accounts with similar renderings include Stephen L. Crane, *Survivor of an Unknown War* (Greenwich, CT: Diane Books, 1999); Enver Atayli, *A Dark Path to Freedom: Ruzi Nazar from the Red Army to the CIA* (Oxford: Oxford University Press, 2017); and some from the Harvard Interview Project on the Soviet Social System.

24. Timur Dadabaev, *Identity and Memory in Post-Soviet Central Asia: Uzbekistan's Soviet Past*, (Abingdon, UK: Routledge, 2016); Timur Dadabaev and Hisao Komatsu, eds., *Kazakhstan, Kyrgyzstan, and Uzbekistan: Life and Politics during the Soviet Era* (London: Palgrave Macmillan, 2017).

25. Soviet policy in Central Asia as malicious, destructive, imperialist, and so on is the consistent evaluation found in Western scholarship since the early Cold War years, beginning with work by Baymirza Hayit, *Turkestan im XX Jahrhundert* (Darmstadt: Leske, 1956); and Richard Pipes, "The Muslims of Soviet Central Asia: Trends and Prospects" (part 2), *Middle East Journal* 9, no. 3 (1955): 295–308; through to the volume from the end of the Cold War, William Fierman, ed., *Soviet Central Asia: The Failed Transformation* (Boulder, CO: Westview, 1991). Soviet scholars who read Western scholarship dismissed any criticisms as "bourgeois falsification." Post-Soviet archive-based research on Central Asia tends to add to the judgment that Soviet control was disastrous, with these serving as two examples: Beatrice Penati, "The Reconquest of East Bukhara: The Struggle against the Basmachi as a Prelude to Sovietization," *Central Asian Survey* 26, no. 4 (2007): 521–538; Christian Teichmann, "Wildscapes in Ballyhooland: Shock Construction, Soviet Colonization, and Stalinist Governance," *Cahiers du Monde Russe* 57, no. 1 (2016): 221–246; Botakoz Kassymbekova, *Despite Cultures: Early Soviet Rule in Tajikistan* (Pittsburgh: University of Pittsburgh Press, 2016).

26. Kathy Davis, "Intersectionality as Buzzword: A Sociology of Science Perspective on What Makes a Feminist Theory Successful," *Feminist Theory* 9, no. 1 (2018): 68.

27. As discussed in Susan Hekman, "Truth and Method: Feminist Standpoint Theory Revisited," *Signs: Journal of Women in Culture and Society* 22, no. 2 (1997): 345; Donna Haraway, "Situated Knowledges: The Science question in Feminism and the Privilege of Partial Perspectives," *Feminist Studies* 14, no. 3 (1988): 575–599.

28. Hekman, "Truth and Method," 345.

29. That Soviet rule in Central Asia was colonial is articulated most forcefully by Botakoz Kassymbekova and Aminat Chokobaeva, "On Writing Soviet History of Central Asia: Frameworks, Challenges, Prospects," *Central Asian Survey* 40, no. 4 (2021): 483–503; and in Douglas Northrop, *Veiled Empire: Gender and Power in Stalinist Central Asia*

(Ithaca, NY: Cornell University Press, 2004); and Madina Tlostanova, *Gender Epistemologies and Eurasian Borderlands* (New York: Palgrave MacMillan, 2010).

30. Obertreis, *Imperial Desert Dreams*, 34–35.

31. Alieda Assmann, "Transformations between History and Memory," *Social Research* 75, no. 1 (2008): 65.

32. Pierre Nora, *Realms of Memory: Rethinking the French Past*, vol. 1, trans. Arthur Goldhammer (New York: Columbia University Press, 1996); Sue Campbell, Christine Koggel, and Rodney Jacobsen, *Our Faithfulness to the Past: The Ethics and Politics of Memory* (Oxford: Oxford University Press, 2014).

33. See also Marianne Kamp, "Three Lives of Saodat: Communist, Uzbek, Survivor," *Oral History Review* 28, no. 2 (2001): 21–58.

34. Alessandro Portelli, "What Makes Oral History Different," in *The Oral History Reader*, 3rd ed., ed. Robert Perks and Alistair Thomson (Abingdon, UK: Routledge, 2016), 67.

35. Raleigh, "'On the Other Side,'" 376–377.

1. INEDIBLE HARVEST

1. Bukhara 19, Qurbon B., b. 1906.

2. Qurbon first went to Bukhara around the year 1920. Following Russia's withdrawal from World War I, Austro-Hungarian and Ottoman prisoners in Central Asia were freed to make a living; they were gradually repatriated from Turkestan and Bukhara. Khalid, *Making Uzbekistan*, 80, 154. POW accounts include Austrian Fritz Willfort, *Turkestanishe Tagebuch: Sechs Jahre in Russische-Zentralasien* (Vienna: Wilhelm Braumüller, 1930); Mehmet Arif Ölçen, *Vetluga Memoir: A Turkish Prisoner of War in Russia 1916–1918*, trans. Gary Leiser (Gainesville: University Press of Florida, 1995). There were 200,000 POWs in Russia's Turkestan Military District; Alon Rachamimov, *POWs and the Great War: Captivity on the Eastern Front* (London: Bloomsbury, 2002), 95.

3. Maya K. Peterson, *Pipe Dreams: Water and Empire in Central Asia's Aral Sea Basin*, Studies in Environment and History (Cambridge: Cambridge University Press, 2019). Benjamin Loring, "'Colonizers with Party Cards': Soviet Internal Colonialism in Central Asia, 1917–39," *Kritika: Explorations in Russian and Eurasian History* 15, no. 1 (2014): 77–102. Olaf Caroe, *Soviet Empire: The Turks of Central Asia and Stalinism*, 2nd ed. (London: St. Martin's, 1967).

4. Elizabeth B. Brite and John M. Marston, "Environmental Change, Agricultural Innovation, and the Spread of Cotton Agriculture in the Old World," *Journal of Anthropological Archaeology* 32 (2013): 39–53. Discussion of premodern Central Asian cotton production and export is found in Richard W. Bulliet, *Cotton, Climate, and Camels in Early Islamic Iran* (New York: Columbia University Press, 2009); Stephen F. Dale, "Silk Road, Cotton Road or . . . Indo-Chinese Trade in Pre-European Times," *Modern Asian Studies* 43, no. 1 (2009): 79–88; Edward H. Schafer, *The Golden Peaches of Samarkand: A Study of T'ang Exotics* (Berkeley: University of California Press, 1985); V. V. Bartol'd, "Khlopkovodstvo v Srednei Azii," in V.V. Bartol'd, *Sochinenie* Tom II, Chast' 2, (Moscow: Isdatel'stvo Nauka, 1964; originally published in 1925), 437–448.

5. Valijon Turgunbaev, "Znachimost' khlopovykh produktov vo vneshnei torgovle stran Srednei Azii do 60-х godov XIX veka," *Molodoi Uchenyi* 6, no. 6 (2015): 549–551.

6. V. I. Iuferev, *Khlopkovodstvo v Turkestane* (Leningrad: Akademia Nauk SSSR, 1925), 15; Scott Levi, *The Rise and Fall of Khoqand, 1709–1876: Central Asia in the Global Age* (Pittsburgh, PA: University of Pittsburgh Press, 2017), 27n35. Levi documents the rising value of Kokand raw cotton exports to Russia in the mid-1800s. On the Kokand Khanate's expansion of irrigation, see Akira Ueda, "The Demographic and Agricultural

Development of the Kokand Oasis in the Russian Imperial Era: Nomad Immigration and Cotton Monoculture," *Central Asian Survey* 38, no. 4 (2019): 510–530.

7. Giorgio Riello and Prasannan Parthasarathi, eds., *The Spinning World: A Global History of Cotton Textiles, 1200–1850*, Pasold Studies in Textile History 16 (Oxford: Oxford University Press, 2009); Sven Beckert, *Empire of Cotton: A Global History* (New York: Vintage, 2014).

8. Seymour Becker, *Russia's Protectorates in Central Asia 1865–1924* (Cambridge, MA: Harvard University Press, 1968), 88–97, 100–104. Iuferev, *Khlopkovodstvo*, describes g'oza in terms of fiber length and quality (21–22) and the introduction of American upland cotton (27).

9. Morrison, *Russian Conquest*, 135–137.

10. Beckert, *Empire of Cotton*, 54.

11. Levi, *Rise and Fall of Khoqand*, 243–244.

12. Stuart Thompstone, "Russian Imperialism and the Commercialization of the Central Asian Cotton Trade," *Textile History* 26, no. 2 (1995): 233–258, 251–254.

13. Marianne Kamp and Mariana Markova, *Muslim Women of the Fergana Valley: A 19th Century Russian Ethnography* (Bloomington: Indiana University Press, 2016), 99–100, 164.

14. Peterson, *Pipe Dreams*, 134–140.

15. David Brophy, *Uyghur Nation: Revolution and Reform on the China-Russia Frontier* (Cambridge, MA: Harvard University Press, 2016), 44.

16. Thompstone, "Russian Imperialism," 235–236.

17. Beatrice Penati, "The Cotton Boom and the Land Tax in Russian Turkestan (1880s–1915)," *Kritika: Explorations in Russian and Eurasian History* 14, no. 4 (2013): 741–774; Iuferev, *Khlopkovodstvo*, 53–54; Muriel Joffe, "Autocracy, Capitalism, and Empire: The Politics of Irrigation," *Russian Review* 54 (1995): 365–388. R. Kh. Aminova, *Agrarnaia Politika Sovetskoi Vlasti v Uzbekistane (1917–1920 gg)* (Tashkent: Izdatel'stvo Akademii Nauk, 1963), 60.

18. John Whitman, "Turkestan Cotton in Imperial Russia," *American Slavic and East European Review* 15, no. 2 (1956): 190–205; M. N. Veksel'man, *Rossiiskii monopolisticheskii i inostrannyi kapital v srednei azii. Konets XIX- nachalo XX vek* (Tashkent: Fan, 1987), 143.

19. Iuferev, *Khlopkovodstvo*, 55–56. From 1888, raw cotton could travel by train and then ship, via the Caspian, and then by boat or train to the Moscow-region factories.

20. Sahadeo, *Russian Colonial Society*, 120–122.

21. Thompstone, "Russian Imperialism," 238–239, 251.

22. A. V. Stolitskogo, ed., *Khlopkovodstvo v SSSR* (Moscow: Biuro Pechati, 1926), 28–32, 75–76. In 1914, Fergana had 150 factories with 750 gins for removing seeds from paxta. By comparison, in 1917, Bukhara had 24 cotton factories, with 182 machines designed to break open g'oza, and 43 gins.

23. The Hungry Steppe Project, an effort at colonial investment in irrigation expansion and cotton production, received tremendous attention in imperial Russia's agricultural press and left plenty of records for historians to comb through. M. Iu. Iunuskhodzhaeva, *Iz istorii zemlevladeniia v dorevoliutsionnom Turkestane (na materialakh khoziaistva kniazia N. K. Romanova)* (Tashkent: Fan, 1970); Obertreis, *Imperial Desert Dreams*, 85–89; Peterson, *Pipe Dreams*; Ian Matley, "The Golodnaya Steppe: A Russian Irrigation Venture in Central Asia," *Geographical Review* 60, no. 3 (1970): 328–346; Joffe, "Autocracy, Capitalism, and Empire." Beatrice Penati points out that there was much written about the plans for this project, but not much came to fruition. Penati, "Cotton Boom." Records regarding the vast majority of agriculturalists, the Uzbeks, and their projects are nowhere near as

abundant, and thus Russian colonizers, while very few in number and having minimal impact on the real work of farming in Russian Central Asia, garner an unrepresentative share of historians' attention.

24. On prosperous Central Asian cotton merchants, see Sahadeo, *Russian Colonial Society*, 154–155.

25. Akmal Bazarbaev and Chloé Drieu, "The 1916 Uprisings in Jazzish: Economic Background and Political Rationales," in *The Central Asian Revolt of 1916: A Collapsing Empire in the Age of War and Revolution*, ed. Aminat Chokobaeva, Chloé Drieu, and Alexander Morrison (Manchester: Manchester University Press, 2020), 75–76. Rylov, "Predislovie," in *Materialy ob obsledovaniiu kochevogo i osedlago tuzemnago khoziaistva i zemlepolzovaniia v Amu-Dar'inskom otdele Syr Dar'inskoi oblasti* (Tashkent: Tipo-Lit Il'ina, 1915), ii–iii.

26. *Materialy po izucheniu khoziaistva osedlago tuzemnago naseleniia v Turkestanskom Krae: Sartovskoe khoziaistvo v chimkenskom uezd Syr-Dar'inskoi oblasti* (Tashkent: V. M. Ilina, 1912), 69. See also Babajanov's commentary on the relevant hadith, which was cited in fatwas by pro-land-reform ulama. Bakhtiyar Babajanov and Sharifjon Islamov, "Shari'a for the Bolsheviks? Fatvas on Land Reform in early Soviet Central Asia," in *Islam, Society, and States across the Qazaq Steppe (18th–early 20th Centuries)*, ed. Niccoló Pianciola and Paolo Sartori (Vienna: Verlag der Österreichischen Akademie der Wissenschaften, 2013), 255–256. Babajanov interprets "dead lands" as those that have never been previously cultivated, but other interpretations attributed to the second caliph ʿUmar suggest instead that dead land was defined as abandoned and unused for three years. See also Hélène Carrère d'Encausse, *Islam and the Russian Empire: Reform and Revolution in Central Asia* (London: Tauris, 1988), 9, referring to Bukhara, where dead holdings are interpreted as those that have fallen out of cultivation; they reverted to the emir as *amlak* (state land) for redistribution, to become the private land (*mulk*) of the cultivator.

27. R. Kh. Aminova, ed., *Istoriia Uzbekskoi SSR*, vol. 2 (Tashkent: Tarix va arxeologiya instituti, 1967–1968), 50–51, referring to the 1886 code, statutes 255–262. Morrison, *Russian Conquest*, 110–125. This is a simplified explanation. As Penati describes it, there were in fact many uncertainties about landownership, and the colonial administration was perplexed as to how to levy taxes. Penati, "Cotton Boom."

28. The Russian Military Administration seized farmed lands around Andijon in revenge for Dukchi Ishon's 1898 uprising and around Jizzakh in retribution for the 1916 uprising. These had limited effect on landownership, resulting in settlement by a few thousand Russian agriculturalists, but immense political effect as a display of colonial power. Larger numbers of Russian agricultural settlers established farms in areas near Tashkent. Peterson, *Pipe Dreams*.

29. Agricultural census data cited in A. M. Iuldashev, *Agrarnye otnosheniia v Turkestane (konets XX–nachalo XIX vv)* (Tashkent: Uzbekistan, 1969), 182; A. Kh. Valiev, *Polozhenie dekhanstva Fergany v kontse XIX–nachale XX vekov* (Tashkent: Fan, 1958), 13; Morrison, *Russian Conquest*, 211.

30. Tashkent 16, Abduqodir P., b. 1916, Bekabod.

31. A. M. Iuldashev, *Agrarnye otnosheniia v Turkestane*, 175–184, 199. Whether debt-related land consolidation was driven entirely by cotton was subject to debate; the historian M. Iu. Iuldashev argued that the same process was underway in early twentieth-century Khiva, where paxta had made only small inroads. M. Iu. Iuldashev, *K istorii krest'ian khivy XIX veka* (Tashkent: Fan, 1966), 15, 37–38, 56.

32. Sven Beckert, "Emancipation and Empire: Reconstructing the Worldwide Web of Cotton Production in the Age of the American Civil War," *American Historical Review* 109, no. 5 (2004): 1434.

33. Valiev, *Polozhenie*, 34.

34. Carrère D'Encausse, *Islam*, 37–45. Peterson notes that Bukhara's mode of taxation discouraged adoption of *Gossypium hirsutum*. Peterson, *Pipe Dreams*, 137. But that evidence is from 1908 and does little to explain why g'oza persisted until collectivization.

35. Becker, *Russia's Protectorates*, 76. Russian subjects could settle on the right bank of the Amu Darya, which became part of Amu-Darya District, Syr Darya Province. A group of Mennonites from Russia's heartland negotiated with the Khan of Khiva and settled on land within the khanate in 1883. Fred Belk, *The Great Trek of Russian Mennonites to Central Asia, 1880–1884* (Scottsdale, AZ: Herald, 1976).

36. N. I. Noskov, "Zemledelie," in Glavnoe Upravleniie Zemleustroistva i Zemledeliia. Pereselencheskoe Upravlenie, *Materialy o obsledovaniiu kochevogo i osedlago tuzemnago khoziaistva i zemlepol'zovaniia v Amu-Dar'inskom otdele Syr'-Dar'inskoi oblasti*, Vyp 1 (Tashkent: Tipo-Lit Il'ina, 1915), 231–232, 267.

37. Xorazm 5, Ibroyim K., b. 1917, Urganch.

38. Xorazam 18, Sanamjon M., b. 1913.

39. Xorazam 12, Abudullo S., b. 1921, Ko'shko'pir.

40. This was a change: at the time of the Arab conquest, dehqon meant owner of large holdings and village head. Richard N. Frye, *The History of Bukhara*, translated from a Persian abridgement of the Arabic original by Narshakhi (Cambridge, MA: Mediaeval Academy of America, 1954), 7–8.

41. Russian translation of *Dehqonchilik*, Mikhail Gavrilov, trans. and ed., *Risoliia sartovskikh' remeslennikov': izsledovanie predanii musulmanskikh tsekhov'* (Tashkent: Tipografiia pri kantseliarii generalgubernatora, 1912), 54–57. There are many hadith that call for wearing cotton clothing and some that prohibit Muslim men from wearing pure silk clothing.

42. There is extensive scholarship on Islamic law regarding ownership of farmed lands, taxation, sharecropping, and tenancy. Hanafi juristic thought is the most relevant to pre-conquest Central Asia. Baber Johansen argues that developments in Hanafi land law shifted the tax burden from owner to sharecropper in a way that made owners prefer offering sharecropping arrangements over renting land. Baber Johansen, *The Islamic Law on Land Tax and Rent: The Peasants' Loss of Property Rights as Interpreted in the Hanafite Legal Literature of the Mamluk and Ottoman Periods* (London: Croom Helm, 1988).

43. Namagan 6, Yo'lchiboy A., b. 1922.

44. Fergana 13, G'anijon M., b. 1920, Marg'ilon.

45. Xorazm 13, Madqurbon D., b. 1914.

46. Tashkent 1, Bozorxo'ja U., b. 1913.

47. Tashkent 2, Tojivoy D., b. 1917.

48. Namangan 5, Aliqul I., b. 1916.

49. Bukhara 17, Hojimurod M., b. 1916.

50. Lidiia Kunakova, *Zemel'no-vodnaia reforma v Uzbekistane, 1925–1929 gg.* (Frunze: Mektep, 1967), 209–211. Adrienne Edgar describes the Turkmen *sanashlik* form of collective land ownership in similar terms. Adrienne Edgar, *Tribal Nation: The Making of Soviet Turkmenistan* (Princeton, NJ: Princeton University Press, 2006), 176–178. The late Peterson, drawing on descriptions of communities near Samarkand in the 1880s and on Edgar's description, misattributes this shared ownership of land to Turkestan more generally. Peterson, *Pipe Dreams*, 55–56.

51. Qashqa Daryo 17, Halil F., b. 1905.

52. Tashkent 23, Melivoy A., b. 1918.

53. Xorazm 17, Olmajon, b. 1903.

54. Iuferev, *Khlopkovodstvo*; Whitman, "Turkestan Cotton," 201, 203.

55. Chokobaeva, Drieu, and Morrison, eds., *The Central Asian Revolt*. On the exceptional role of Turkmen forces in Russia's military, see Ovez A. Gundogdyev, *Boevoi put'*

tekinskogo konnogo polka (1914–1918) (Ashkhabad: Turkmenskaia gos. izdat. sluzhba, 2012).

56. Dina Amanjolova, "Nekotorye problem izucheniia istorii vosstaniia 1916 g. v Srednei Azii," *Rossiiskaia Istoriia* 1 (2017): 125–138, offers numbers on demonstrations, on deaths, and on sentences and outlines the changing interpretations of the uprising, from a Soviet-period emphasis on class struggle to a post-Soviet emphasis on ethnonational conflict. Marco Buttino, "Central Asia 1916–1920: A Kaleidoscope of Local Revolutions and the Building of the Bolshevik Order," in *The Empire and Nationalism at War*, ed. Eric Lohr et al. (Bloomington, IN: Slavica, 2014), 109–135, 114.

57. Sahadeo, *Russian Colonial Society*, 180; Niccolò Pianciola, "Scales of Violence: The 1916 Central Asian Uprising in the Context of Wars and Revolutions (1914–1923)," in Chokobaeva, Drieu, and Morrison, *Central Asian Revolt*, 169–190. Manchester, UK: Manchester University Press, 2020.

58. Aziz Niallo (a.k.a. A. V. Stanishevskii), "Ocherki Istorii revoliutsii i grazhdanskoi voiny v Kirgizii i Srednei Azii," in *Basmachestvo*, ed. S. A. Shumov and A. R. Andreev (Moscow: Eksmo, 2005; originally published in 1941), 88.

59. Sahadeo, *Russian Colonial Society*, 185; Aaron Retish, *Russia's Peasants in Revolution and Civil War: Citizenship, Identity, and the Creation of the Soviet State 1914–1922* (Cambridge: Cambridge University Press, 2008).

60. R. Abdullaev and S. S. Agzamkhodzhaev (Ag'zamxo'jaev), *Turkestan v nachale XX veka: k istorii istokov natsional'noi nezavisimosti* (Tashkent: Shark, 2000), 48.

61. Qashqa Daryo 20, Faizulla R., b. 1905.

62. Qashqa Daryo 7, Qurbon A., b. 1908.

63. Sahdeo, *Russian Colonial Society*, 191.

64. A. V. Stolitskogo, *Khlopkovodstvo SSR*, 49–50.

65. Abdullaev and Ag'zamxo'jaev, *Turkestan*, 48–49; on the commercial control and underwriting of Central Asian cotton by Russian banks, see Thompstone, "Russian Imperialism."

66. Stolitskogo, *Khlopkovodstvo SSR*, 51–54, 64.

67. Much has been published on this topic: for example, Ian Campbell, *Knowledge and the Ends of Empire: Kazak Intermediaries and Russian Rule on the Steppe, 1731–1917* (Ithaca, NY: Cornell University Press, 2017); Steven Sabol, *"The Touch of Civilization": Comparing American and Russian Internal Colonization* (Boulder: University of Colorado Press, 2017); Steven Sabol, *Russian Colonization and the Genesis of Kazak National Consciousness* (New York: Palgrave, 2003); Daniel R. Brower, *Turkestan and the Fate of the Russian Empire* (London: Routledge, 2003); and Sarah I. Cameron, *The Hungry Steppe: Famine, Violence, and the Making of Soviet Kazakhstan* (Ithaca, NY: Cornell University Press, 2018).

68. "Mindontsy v XVIII–nachale XX v. Istoriia meniaiushchegosia samosoznaniia," chap. 2 in Sergei Abashin, *Natsionalizmy v Srednei Azii, v poiskakh identichnosti* (St. Petersburg: Alettiia, 2007), 63–64.

2. BOSMACHI STORIES

1. Marg'ilon 16, O'g'ilxon, b. 1914. Her name means "son," followed by a feminine ending.

2. Madaminbek, a shortened version of Muhammad Aminbek Ahmad o'g'li (d. 1920). Mansurxo'ja Xo'jayev, *Shemuhammadbek Qo'rboshi* (Tashkent: Sharq, 2008), 20–22. This volume is an important contribution to Uzbekistan's new history of the Qo'rboshis as national liberators.

3. Ayat ul-Kursi, from al-Baqarah, Qur'an 2:225, which includes the words "Neither drowsiness nor sleep overtakes Him. To Him belongs whatever is in the heavens and on earth."

4. O'g'ilxon names two of the leaders of Fergana Valley Bosmachi groups, Shermuhammad Bek and Madamin Bek. O'g'ilxon first identified Nurhon as *opa* (elder sister) and then as *og'ay-opa*, or cousin, in this context. O'g'ilxon's reference to Turkestan is unclear: she may have meant eastern Turkestan or the city of Turkestan in southern Kazakhstan.

5. Shahnoza used the word *ziyoli*, meaning "well-educated," used similarly to the Russian word *intelligentsia*. Uzbekistan's President Karimov officially rehabilitated Madamin Bek in 1998, and new descriptions emphasized his Islamic learning. Qahramon Rajabov, *Madamin Bek (risola)* (Tashkent: Abu Matbuot Konsalt, 2011).

6. This sort of description appears in Abdullaev and Agzamkhodzhaev, *Turkistan v nachale*.

7. Accounts of Bosmachi raids were ubiquitous in the 1920s Uzbek press, and the Uzbek-language women's journal *Yangi Yo'l* emphasized their violence against women and girls. See, for example, Rafiqova, "Tog' qizi," *Yangi Yo'l* 9 (1927): 12–13; Xosiyat Tillaxonova, trans., "Tun urgutlari. O'tgan kunlardan," *Yangi Yo'l* 9–10 (1929): 5. Translations by Marianne Kamp on the database Women and Social Movements in Modern Empires since 1820, https://alexanderstreet.com/products/women-and-social-movements-modern-empires-1820

8. Violent abduction for rape and marriage preexisted the revolution in Central Asia, was the focus of legal prohibitions in the 1920s, and was identified by the Women's Division of the Communist Party as a factor that contributed to family unwillingness to allow teenaged daughters to go outside the home to attend school. Kamp, *New Woman in Uzbekistan*, 66–74, 112–119; Edgar, *Tribal Nation*, 254–256. Kidnapping for marriage, whether violently or as a consensual ruse, was a social practice unrelated to Bosmachi raids, and it has become widespread in independent Kazakhstan and Kyrgyzstan. Cynthia Werner, "Women, Marriage, and the Nation-State: The Rise of Non-Consensual Bride Kidnapping in Post-Soviet Kazakhstan," in *The Transformation of Central Asia*, ed. Pauline Jones-Luong (Ithaca, NY: Cornell University Press, 2004), 59–89. In post-2010 Osh, Kyrgyzstan, fear of violent abduction in a context of intercommunal violence drove a resurgence in early marriages, argues Aksana Ismailbekova. Aksana Ismailbekova, "From Endogamous Marriage to Ethnicity: Uzbek Community Survival Strategy after the 2010 Conflict in Osh," *Anthropology and Archeology of Eurasia* 58, no. 3 (2019):134–154.

9. For example, Tashkent 8, Qimmat T., b. 1906, said that the Bosmachis were Kazakhs; Xorazm 11, Roviya A., b. 1922, identified the Bosmachis as Turkmen.

10. Khalid, *Making Uzbekistan*; Saidakbar Agzamkhodzhaev, *Istoriia Turkestanskoi Avtonomii (Turkiston Muxtoriyati)* (Tashkent: Toshkent Islom Universiteti, 2006); Abdullaev and Ag'zamxo'jaev, *Turkestan v nachale*, 61–95.

11. Adeeb Khalid, *The Politics of Muslim Cultural Reform: Jadidism in Central Asia* (Berkeley: University of California Press, 1998), 245–279; Buttino, "Central Asia 1916–1920."

12. Madamin Bek's decision to negotiate with the Soviet side led to his execution by Ko'r Shermat and Halxo'ja. Abdullaev and Agzamkhodzhaev, *Turkestan v nachale*, 217–224. It also made his 1998 rehabilitation an easier case than that of other Bosmachis. Buttino details the makeup of Red forces. Buttino, "Central Asia 1916," 121. Abdullaev and Agzamhodjaev, *Turkestan v nachale*, 164–225, details the events of 1917, the unfolding of the Kokand Autonomy, and the war between Qo'rboshis and the Reds. Beatrice Penati writes that the Soviets used periodic amnesties for Bosmachi fighters and paid local volunteers to join Red Army forces. Penati, "Reconquest," 523–526.

13. Abdullaev and Agzamkhodzhaev, *Turkistan v nachale*, 368–371.

14. Edgar, *Tribal Nation*; Becker, *Russia's Protectorates*.

15. Opposition to the Red Army even included a 1922 attempt by the leader of the Ottoman triumvirate, Enver Pasha, who had slipped the noose of British justice for his role in the Ottoman annihilation of the Armenians and made his way into the nascent Soviet Union, to turn the Bosmachi struggle into his own career relaunch. Eugene Rogan, *The Fall of the Ottomans: The Great War in the Middle East* (New York: Basic Books, 2015), 306–308. Some historians have taken Enver's presence in Central Asia on the side of the Bosmachis as an indication of shared pan-Turkist ideas. Some historians have transported Turk/Armenian enmity into discussion of the Turkestan Autonomy and civil war in Central Asia, portraying "Dashnaks" as key elements in the fall of Kokand and the spread of violent disorder in Fergana Valley.

16. Buttino, "Central Asia 1916–1920," 124–128; Penati, "Reconquest."

17. Sahadeo, *Russian Colonial Society*, 212–214.

18. On the messiness of this term and the difficulties it causes for understanding the early Soviet years in Central Asia, see Sergei Abashin, "Sem' kratkikh tezisov o 'basmachestve,'" Central Asian Analytical Network, April 17, 2020, https://www.caa-network.org/archives/19045. Bosmachism, defined as combining plundering and building resources to challenge a political order, resembles the fifteenth- and sixteenth-century term *qazaqliq*, which Joo-Yup Lee defines as political vagabondage. Joo-Yup Lee, "The Political Vagabondage of the Chinggisid and Timurid Contenders to the Throne and Others in Post-Mongol Central Asia and the Qipchaq Steppe: A Comprehensive Study of Qazaqlïq, or the Qazaq Way of Life," *Central Asiatic Journal* 60, nos. 1–2 (2017): 59–95.

19. N. A., "Laqlaqa qotillari sud mahkamasida," *Yer Yuzi* 8 (1926): 14–15.

20. N. F. Karimov and R. T. Shamsutdinov, eds., *Repressia 1937–1938 gg. Dokumenty i materialy*, vol. 4, *Zhertvy bol'shogo terrora iz Uzbekistana* (Tashkent: Sharq, 2008). All the Bosmachi names were Central Asian; Russians in this repression list who were accused of murder were not designated as Bosmachis. The series of volumes publishes brief notices naming each of the individuals who were shot or exiled during Stalin's 1937–1938 purge, a repression that fell primarily on members of the Communist Party. At the same time, there was also an operation for "the repression of former kulaks, criminals, and anti-Soviet elements."

21. Urban and village housing in Marg'ilon and elsewhere in Central Asia consisted of houses built of mud brick, surrounded by courtyard walls, adjoined to the neighboring house. Sleeping on the rooftop was a way to stay cool in the summer, but when Bosmachis came, their sound would have alerted those sleeping outdoors, who could escape across neighboring rooftops or into neighboring courtyards.

22. Fergana/Marg'ilon 8, Muqimjon J., b. 1902.

23. Terms varied widely. In his interview, Namangan 9, Abdurashid R., b. 1905, used *bek* to refer to government soldiers who were of Central Asian ethnicities and *yigit* to refer to the young fighters in a Qo'rboshi-led unit.

24. Fergana 15, Umriniso M., b. 1914.

25. Fargana 6, Halima-xon M., b. 1911.

26. Xorazm 9, Zulayho A., b. 1916.

27. Nurota 9, Bozorova (only family name recorded, birth year missing, interview content suggests born in late 1910s). One of the best-loved Soviet films set in Central Asia, *Beloe Sol'ntse Pustyni* (Mosfil'm, 1970), features Red Army soldiers fighting Bosmachis to free kidnapped women.

28. Marg'ilon 9, Hidoyatxon S., b. 1919. Women interviewees who talked about hiding from Bosmachi raids that took place in later years, from the mid-1920s to the 1930s, included Farg'ona 14, Qumriniso R., b. 1920; Bukhara 10, Narziya J., b. 1921. Bukhara 18, Sharofat B., b. 1922, did not see Bosmachis, but her father told her about their raids and kidnapping of girls. Qashqa Daryo 4, O'ktam A., b. 1919, was told by her parents that her

father sent her pregnant mother to the city to prevent kidnapping, after Bosmachis seized another pregnant woman in her village. Qashqa Darya 19, Narzi A., b. 1921, said Bosmachis attacked her kolkhoz in the 1930s, murdered the director, and had unmentionable relations with his wife.

29. Qashqa Dayra 4, O'ktam A., b. 1919, or maybe a couple of years later based on evidence in her story.

30. Xorazm 11, Roviya A, b. 1922, who said her father took his two wives and fled from Turkmen Bosmachi; Bukhara 18, Sharofat B., b. 1922.

31. Two men: Bukhara 20, Xoji A., b. 1920, said Bosmachis murdered his father in 1932; Tashkent 11, Abduqayum X., b. 1916, told of his grandfather's murder at Bosmachi hands; one woman, Tashkent 17, Azizaxon I., b. 1914, said that Bosmachis murdered her father when he, a Muslim judge, tried to adjudicate their inheritance dispute.

32. Under *paranji*, Fergana 18, Eminjon, b. 1920; cemetery, Namangan 12, Rustamov, b. 1921; Navoiy 2, Berdiqul B., b. 1920; tandir, Qashqa Daryo 18, Abdullo F., b. 1919; and Bukhara 20, Xoji A., b. 1920; hole, QD 9, Rajab H,, b. 1917 and QD 5, Oqquzi B., b. 1916.

33. Tashkent 2, Tojivoy D., b. 1917, said his brother was robbed at knifepoint; Bukhara 11, Faizi S., b. 1915, was beaten and robbed by Bosmachis; Qashqa Daryo 16, Hayrullo S., b. 1921, hid and watched while Bosmachis stole his grandparents' horses.

34. Bukhara 3, Ahmad U., b. 1921. It is possible that Ahmad was engaged or married at fifteen or sixteen.

35. Farg'ona 18, Eminjon H., b. 1920.

36. Navoiy 8, Rustam M., b. 1912, p. 3. He used a term that our transliterators found unfamiliar and represented as *shaharbozlik*, but I think that it was *shohidbozlik*, an Uzbek or Persian term for "pederasty" (along with *javonbozlik, bachchabozlik*).

37. Qashqa Darya 17, Halil F., b. 1905. Penati discusses Ibrahim Bek's taxation of areas in Tajikistan. Penati, "Reconquest," 530–531.

38. His village became the site of economic data collection in 1925, by the Karp commission, and is described in detail in the collection *Sovremenniy Kishlak*, volumes 1 and 6, about which more is said in the next chapter.

39. Namangan 9, Abdurashid R., b. 1905, Baliqchi District.

40. Abdullaev and Ag'zamxo'jaev, *Turkistan v nachale*, 371, citing archive documents, write, "On 21 December 1922, Shermuhammedbek with a contingent of 800 men and 3 artillery guns managed to overrun the Soviet garrison in Xo'jaobod"—though it must be noted there were several communities with that name near Andijon, so it is not certain that this is the same battle Abdurashid described.

41. Fergana 10, Fayzixon T., b. 1917; Tashkent 8, Qimmat T., b. 1906.

42. Farg'ona 20, Sharafutdin Q., b. 1911.

43. National-territorial delimitation in 1924 and the conducting of the 1926 census forced Central Asians to specify their identities within a state-imposed grid of possibilities; as is discussed briefly in the next chapter, those processes and the benefits that being Uzbek in Uzbekistan conferred made identifying as Uzbek a strategic choice for people like Sharafutdin.

44. Navoiy 10, O'rozboy D., b. 1908.

45. Bukhara 8, Ravshan H., b. 1920.

46. Fergana 3, Saidalixon M., b. 1921.

47. Qashqa Daryo 18, Abdullo F., b. 1919.

48. Tashkent 12, Yusupboy H., b. 1917; Nabi E., b. 1920 in a village near Yusupboy's village, told the same story about the murder of a district Communist Party member, but unlike Yusupboy, he disapproved of Bosmachism.

49. Fergana 10, Fayzixon T., b. 1917.

50. Bukhara 19, Qurbon B., b. 1906.

51. Bukhara 15, Avez J., b. 1912.
52. Marg'ilon 3, Saidalixon M., b. 1921.
53. Sergei Abashin, *Sovetskii Kishlak: Mezhdu kolonializmom i modernizatsii* (Moscow: Novoe Literaturnoe Obozrenie, 2015), 137–38, 155–57.
54. Xorazm 10, Sayidabdullo A., b. 1926.
55. Qashqa Daryo 12, Bekmurod Sh., b. 1907. His story is told in chapter 8.
56. Xorazm 4, Boltaboy K., b. 1914.
57. Abdullaev and Agzamkhodzhaev, *Turkestan v nachale*, 241.
58. Fergana 8, Muqimjon J., b. 1902.
59. Abdullaev and Agzamkhodzhaev, *Turkestan v Nachale*, 535–536.
60. Bukhara 18, Sharofat B., b. 1922.
61. Tashkent 21, Muhammadjonov, b. 1921.
62. L. E. Bliakher and I. F. Yarulin, "Kto takie basmachi? Sovetskoe mifotvorchestvo i stigmitizatsiia grazhdanskoi voiny v Srednei Azii," *Politiia* 2, no. 81 (2016): 109–123.
63. Some examples where authors seem to take these Qo'rboshi defense claims at face value: Abdullaev and Ag'zamxo'jaev, *Turkestan v nachale*; Komilludin Abdullaev, *Ot sintsiana do khorasana: Iz istorii sredneaziatskoi emigratsii 20 veka* (Dushanbe: Irfon, 2009); R. Shamsutdinov and A. Ishakov, *Andijon tarixdan lavhalar* (Tashkent: Sharq, 2013), 266–286; M. Juraev, editor, *O'zbekiston Soviet Mustamlakachiligi Davrida*, vol. 2 of *O'zbekiston Yangi Tarixi* (Tashkent: Sharq, 2000), 83–113, 195–213.
64. It is hard to document Bosmachi numbers. An important framer of the pro-Bosmachi story, one who claims that nearly every able-bodied man in the Fergana Valley initially fought on the rebel side against the Red Army, was the historian Baymirza Hayit, a native of the Fergana Valley who was captured by the Germans in World War II, becoming a participant in the Nazi anti-Soviet Turkestan Legion. He made his career as an anti-Soviet historian of Central Asia in postwar West Germany, writing first about the Kokand Autonomy in his 1950 doctoral dissertation and publishing his interpretation of Bosmachis as national liberators at an opportune time to influence post-Soviet nationalist history writing in Uzbekistan. Baymirza Hayit, *Basmatchi: Nationaler Kampf Turkestans in den Jahren 1917 bis 1934* (Cologne: Dreisem Verlag, 1992). In an interesting and complex analysis of the politicized myth of Bosmachism, Bliakher and Yarulin, "Kto takie basmachi?," deem this the "view from below."

3. LAND REFORM

1. Namangan 2, Hayitboy M., b. 1910. Interviewers: Russell Zanca and Marianne Kamp.
2. *Vabo* means an epidemic disease, or typhus. In interviews that connected vabo to starvation, "typhus" might be the correct translation. Hayitboy's parents died in 1918, and he does not mention hunger as a related issue: it may be that they died of the Spanish flu. A respondent from Qashqa Daryo mentioned that twelve of his father's brothers, all of them farming together, died in rapid succession of epidemic disease. Qashqa Daryo 15, Temir, b. 1920. The 1918 flu epidemic is not documented for Central Asia.
3. Namangan 2, Hayitboy M., b. 1910.
4. Although titular nationals, such as Azerbaijanis and Uzbeks, were minorities in the Russian-dominated USSR, they were majorities in their republics, where they could experience violence and discrimination but could also enact violence and marginalization against minorities within their republics. Krista Goff, *Nested Nationalism: Making and Unmaking Nations in the Soviet Caucasus* (Ithaca, NY: Cornell University Press, 2021), 5–6.
5. Party membership by nationality in Institut Istorii Partii pri TsK KP Uzbekistana, *Kommunisticheskaia partiia Uzbekistana v tsifrakh: Sbornik statisticheskikh materialov*

1924–1977 (Tashkent: Uzbekistan, 1979). The proportion of Uzbek members among all party members increased to constitute the majority until the 1937 purge and then rose to a permanent majority following World War II.

6. Myra Marx Ferree, "Inequality, Intersectionality, and the Politics of Discourse: Framing Feminist Alliances," in *The Discursive Politics of Gender Equality: Stretching, Bending, and Policy-Making*, ed. E. Lombardo, P. Meier M. Verloo. (London: Routledge 2009), 87–88. While historians of the USSR generally understand nationality as the basis of identity and discrimination, as opposed to race, recent scholarship has highlighted the racialization of identity in the later Soviet decades: Jeff Sahadeo, *Voices from the Soviet Edge: Southern Migrants in Leningrad and Moscow* (Ithaca, NY: Cornell University Press, 2019); Adrienne Edgar, *Intermarriage and the Friendship of Peoples: Ethnic Mixing in Soviet Central Asia* (Ithaca, NY: Cornell University Press, 2022). Botakoz Kassymbekova notes that race was one of the concepts deployed when determining who would be considered Uzbek and who would be named as Tajik; Kassymbekova, *Despite Cultures*, 56.

7. Khalid, *Making Uzbekistan*; Francine Hirsch, *Empire of Nations: Ethnographic Knowledge and the Making of the Soviet Union* (Ithaca, NY: Cornell University Press, 2005); Abashin, *Sovetskiĭ Kishlak*.

8. From 1924 until 1936, the Uzbek SSR had noncontiguous boundaries: it extended from Andijon in the east through Bukhara in the west and then added Xorazm as an island of Uzbekistan surrounded by the Karakalpak region of the Kazakh ASSR on its east and north, and by the Turkmen SSR in the south and west. Xorazm's exclave status ended when Karakalpakstan was added to Uzbekistan as an autonomous oblast in 1936, making Xorazm contiguous with the rest of Uzbekistan. To the outrage of those who hoped for a large and prosperous Tajik republic, the predominantly Tajik-speaking cities of Bukhara and Samarkand were included in Uzbekistan. Kirill Nourzhanov and Christian Bleuer, *Tajikistan: A Political and Social History* (Canberra: Australia National University Press, 2013). The less populated mountain lands of the Bukhara People's Republic were designated as the Tajikistan ASSR, subordinate to Uzbekistan until 1929.

9. According to the 1926 census, Uzbekistan's rural population minus the provinces that became Tajikistan numbered 3,225,945, among which were 40,335 Russians, Ukrainians, and Germans. Kazakhstan and Kyrgyzstan were both recognized as SSRs, or union republics, in 1936, at which point the Karakalpak Oblast was transferred from Kazakhstan to Uzbekistan.

10. Tsentral'noe Statisticheskoe Upravleniia, Vsesoiuznaia Perepis' Naselenii (Moscow: TsSU Soiuza SSSR, 1928–1932), vol. 15, table. Volume 15 includes a thorough representation of Khujand's population by urban/rural, ethnicity, age, and so on but does not include a detailed breakdown for the Tajik ASSR.

11. The total population for the Uzbek SSR, including the subordinate Tajik ASSR, was 5,275,000. Although Khujand Province (pop. 206,600) belonged to the Uzbek SSR in 1926, it was reassigned to Tajikistan when the latter's status changed from Autonomous SSR to SSR in 1929. For purposes of clarity in discussing Uzbekistan's population during mass collectivization, which began after the Tajik ASSR's status changed, I have chosen to exclude Khujand and the Tajik ASSR from the census data for Uzbekistan.

12. One of the best-known proponents of irredentist claims is R. M. Masov, *Istroiia Topornogo razdeleniia* (Dushanbe: Irfan, 1991). Cold War–period Western arguments about the national-territorial delimitation often built on arguments made by the exiled politicians Mustafa Shokay and Zeki Validi Togan, to discredit the Central Asian boundaries as a mendacious Soviet divide-and-rule strategy; see, e.g., Pipes, "Muslims of Soviet Central Asia"; Michael Rywkin, *Moscow's Muslim Challenge* (London: Routledge, 1982). Scholars who adhered to that view were surprised that the newly independent states of Central Asia did not choose to give up their independent identities and unite. Scholarship

revisiting the creation of the map of Central Asia in a less partisan mode based in archival research includes Hirsch, *Empire of Nations*; Nicholas Megoran, *Nationalism in Central Asia: A Biography of the Uzbekistan-Kyrgyzstan Border* (Pittsburgh, PA: University of Pittsburgh Press, 2015); Madeleine Reeves, *Border Work: Spatial Lives of the State in Central Asia* (Ithaca, NY: Cornell University Press, 2014); Khalid, *Making Uzbekistan*.

13. Hirsch, *Empire of Nations*; Nourzhanov and Bleuer, *Tajikistan*.

14. Table 3.2 is based on the All-Union Population Census 1926, vol. 15, table 4, data from pages 13–48.

15. "Census, Map, Museum," chap. 10 in Benedict Anderson, *Imagined Communities: Reflections on the Origin and Spread of Nationalism* rev. ed. (London: Verso, 2006).

16. Abashin, *Natsionalizmy v Srednei Azii*, 36–71.

17. Peter Finke, *Variations on Uzbek Identity: Strategic Choices, Cognitive Schemas and Political Constraints in Identification Processes*, Integration and Conflict Studies, vol. 7 (New York: Berghahn Books, 2014).

18. Bukhara 3, Ahmed U., b. 1923.

19. Tashkent 15, Xusenboy A., b. 1919.

20. Navoiy interviews 5, 7, 8, 9, 10.

21. Qashqa Daryo 3, Lutfullo U., b. 1919.

22. Cameron, *Hungry Steppe*, 70–96.

23. Some of these accounts of migration appear in Marianne Kamp, "Where Did the Mullahs Go? Oral Histories from Rural Uzbekistan," *Die Welt des Islams* 50, nos. 3/4 (2010): 503–531. Such accounts also appear in Artemy Kalinovsky, *Laboratory of Socialist Development: Cold War Politics and Decolonization in Soviet Tajikistan* (Ithaca, NY: Cornell University Press, 2018).

24. Sheila Fitzpatrick, "The Bolshevik Invention of Class: Marxist Theory and the Making of 'Class Consciousness' in Soviet Society," in *The Structure of Soviet History: Essays and Documents*, ed. Ronald Suny (Oxford: Oxford University Press, 2014), 172–186.

25. Richard Lorenz, "Economic Basis for Basmachi Movement in the Farghana Valley," in *Muslim Communities Reemerge: Historical Perspectives on Nationality, Politics, and Opposition in the Former Soviet Union and Yugoslavia*, ed. Andreas Kappeler, Gerhard Simon, and Gerog Brunner (Durham, NC: Duke University Press, 1994), 277–303, misreads his source, writing that "the average sector of the population employed in the [cotton] industry ... in the Fergana Valley reached 57 percent" before the revolution. But then he notes that industrial cotton enterprises such as gins employed only 30,000 workers.

26. An argument that Adrienne Edgar made in *Tribal Nation*.

27. Ronald Suny, *The Soviet Experiment: Russia, the USSR, and the Successor States* (Oxford: Oxford University Press, 2011), 53–58.

28. Chokobaeva, Drieu, and Morrison, *Central Asian Revolt*; Brower, *Turkestan and the Fate*; Cameron, *Hungry Steppe*; Aminova, *Agrarnaia politika sovetskoi vlasti*.

29. On the topic of state approaches to organizing regions and surveying landholdings, see Beatrice Penati, "Adapting Russian Technologies of Power: Land-and-Water Reform in the Uzbek SSR 1924–1928," *Revolutionary Russia* 25, no. 2 (2012): 187–217. On the numbers in districts, see the All-Union Population Census 1926, vol. 15, table 10, 144ff.

30. Qashqa Daryo 7, Qurbon A., b. 1908.

31. Namangan 5, Aliqul I., b. 1916.

32. Initial reports that shaped the course of land reform were published in the journals *Narodnoe Khoziaistvo Srednei Azii* (Agriculture in Central Asia) and *Bulletin Tsentral'noi Statisticheskoi Upravlenii Uz SSR* (Bulletin of the Uz SSR Central Statistical Directorate). Documents and analyses were published in a multivolume set under the title *Sovremennyi kishlak Srednei azii (sotsial'no ekonomicheskii ocherk)* edited by I. V. Karp and N. K. Suvlov (Tashkent: Izdaniia Sred Az Biuro TsK VKP [b], 1927).

33. K. A. Shuliak, Chapter 2 of *Sovremenniy Kishlak*, Volume 5:5–12, 91–97. Data for the Balikchi region show a sharp drop in population for 1920, during the Bosmachi struggle, but a rapid rise in 1924, along with a sharp rise in planted land. Dehqons who had been displaced or uncounted in wartime conditions had returned.

34. Shuliak, *Sovremenniy Kishlak*, 5:133; Stoklitskogo, *Khlopkovodstvo SSR*, 71.

35. Shuliak, 5:33.

36. Qashqa Daryo 15, Temir X., b. 1920. Other accounts of large family holdings or *paykals* included Bukhara 8, Bukhara 11, Bukhara 12, Qashqa Daryo 3, Qashqa Daryo 5, Qashqa Daryo 11, Qashqa Daryo 18.

37. Xorazm 17, Olmajon X., b. 190.

38. Namangan 2, Hayitboy M., b. 1910.

39. O'zRMDA, f. 62, op. 2, d. 279, l. 48–50, "Osnovnye polozheniia po likvidatsii netrudovykh xoziaistv po iz'iatiiu zemel" (Basic regulation on liquidating nonworking farms by seizing lands), 1925, secret project. Although some historians refer to this process as land-and-water reform, most Party documents, and most conversations with those who remembered, referred to *zemreform* (Russian) or *yer islohoti* (Uzbek), leaving out water. It was not that water was unimportant, but land was the quantifiable element in means of production. Redistribution was based solely on how much land dehqons owned, not on any concept of water rights.

40. Assertions reiterated in the Uzbekistan Communist Party and Central Committee declarations and resolutions repeatedly from 1927 through mid-1929. Examples from the published collection of Party documents: R. Kh. Abdullaeva, editor, *Kommunisticheskaia Partiia Uzbekistana v rezoliutsiiakh s'ezdov i plenumov TsK*, vol. 1, 1925–1937 (Tashkent: Uzbekistan 1987); Third S'ezd, of KP Uz, 1927, pp. 330–331, 350–358; TsK KP Uz Second Plenum, Feb–March 1928, p. 390; TsK KP Uz Fourth Plenum, Dec 1928, 424–425, 456–457. A shift in emphasis to the socialized sector over individual farming takes place in October 1929. TsK KP Uzbekistan Third Plenum, 464–466.

41. Qashqa Daryo 15, Temir X., b. 1920.

42. Tashkent 2, Tojivoy D., b. 1917.

43. Reports on land reform for 1926, Tash Oblast: RGASPI, f. 62 op 2 d. 562, ll. 6–7.

44. Marg'ilon 5, Ahmad T., b. 1920.

45. "Those who gave a third or a fourth"; this was Hidoyat-xon dodging the word *chorikor* which literally translates as 'working for a quarter share.' Fergana 9, Hidoyat-xon S., b. 1919.

46. Stoklitskogo, *Khlopkovodstvo*, 79.

47. Tashkent 11, Abduqayum X., b. 191.

48. March 23, 1926: RGASPI, f. 62 op 2 d. 562, ll. 93–101.

49. Namangan 6, Yo'lchivoy A., b. 1922.

50. Namangan Filial of O'zRMDA, new f. 14 (old f. 13, ed. khr. 48) Ispolkom Nam. Gor. I Rai Soveta Rabochikh Dekhanskikh i Kras. Armei. Deputatov, 1925–1930, pp. 11–12 Zhelanie Grazhdan ob ostavlenie im zemel' i o nepravel'nykh otobrannykh u nikh zemliakh [Citizen wishes concerning land they abandoned and lands wrongly seized from them].

51. Fergana 11, Yoqubjon B., b. 1919.

52. Among the state-supported rural cooperative groups was the *meliorativnoe tovarishchestvo*, or land reclamation comradeship. Turning unfarmed land into irrigated fields goes by a misleading term in English (land reclamation) and in Russian: *osvoenie*, "appropriation," or *meliorizatsia*, "amelioration"; Xo'ji's Uzbek term was *ochilish*, "opening."

53. Bukhara 20, Xoji A., b. 1920.

54. Xorazm 5, Ibroyim K., b. 1917. The size of a tanob varied across Uzbekistan; Ibroyim's father's five tanobs may have been anything from one hectare to two hectares.

55. Fargana 15, Umriniso, b. 1914.

56. Tashkent 14, Umrqul X., b. 1919. His name means "slave of Umar."

57. Babajanov and Ismailov, "Shari'a for the Bolsheviks?" The fatwas opposed sharecropping as un-Islamic. In the twentieth century there appeared many conflicting Shari'a based arguments as to whether Islam endorses or opposes private property with respect to agricultural land and as to whether sharecropping is an approved way for making productive use of land.

58. O'zRDMA, f. 301, op. 1, d. 232, ll. 17, 22–23, "O sotsialnom sostave chlenov pravlenii melioritivnykh tovarishchestv po Okrugom i Respublike," October 1927.

4. AGITATING FOR THE KOLKHOZ

1. Much of this chapter is based on Marianne Kamp and Russell Zanca, "Recollections of Collectivization in Uzbekistan: Stalinism and Local Activism," *Central Asian Survey* 36, no. 1 (2017): 55–72. Examples of studies that highlight mobilization include Mary Buckley, *Mobilizing Soviet Peasants: Heroines and Heroes of Stalin's Fields* (Lanham, MD: Rowman and Littlefield, 2006); Stephen Kotkin, "Modern Times: The Soviet Union and the Interwar Conjuncture," *Kritika: Explorations in Russian and Eurasian History* 2, no. 1 (2001): 111–164; Stephen Kotkin, *Magnetic Mountain: Stalinism as Civilization* (Berkeley: University of California Press, 1997); Cameron, *Hungry Steppe*; Suny, *Soviet Experiment*.

2. O'zRMDA, f. 196, op. 1, d. 64, ll. 23–32, December 2, 1930. The report is missing at least one page at the beginning. Documents from the 1920s and 1930s in Uzbek Arabic script are often cataloged in archive finding aids as "Arabic" with no further description or name; I found this one simply because it was included in a larger folder of documents from the Kolkhoz Center.

3. Niccolò Pianciola, "The Collectivization Famine in Kazakhstan, 1931–1933," *Harvard Ukrainian Studies* 25, nos. 3/4 (December 2001): 237–251; Niccolò Pianciola, "Towards a Transnational History of Great Leaps Forward in Pastoral Central Eurasia," *East/West: Journal of Ukrainian Studies* 3, no. 2 (June 2016): 75–116; Lynne Viola, *Peasant Rebels under Stalin: Collectivization and the Culture of Peasant Resistance* (Oxford: Oxford University Press, 1999); Lynne Viola et al., eds., *The War against the Peasantry, 1927–1930: The Tragedy of the Soviet Countryside* (New Haven, CT: Yale University Press, 2005); Andrea Graziosi, *Stalinism, Collectivization, and the Great Famine* (Cambridge, MA: Ukrainian Studies Fund, Holodomor Series, 2009); Moshe Lewin, *Russian Peasants and Soviet Power: A Study of Collectivization* (London: Allen & Unwin, 1968); Sheila Fitzpatrick, *Stalin's Peasants: Resistance and Survival in the Russian Village after Collectivization* (Oxford: Oxford University Press, 1994); Christian Teichmann, *Macht der Unordnung: Stalins Herrschaft in Zentralasien 1920–1950* (Hamburg: Hamburger Edition, 2016).

4. Buckley, *Mobilizing Soviet Peasants*, 327.

5. Dmitrii Verkhoturov, *Stalinskaia Kollektivizatsiia: Bor'ba za khleb* (Moskva: Veche, 2019), 229–230.

6. C. J. Storella and A. K. Sokolov, *The Voice of the People: Letters from the Soviet Village, 1918–1932* (New Haven, CT: Yale University Press, 2012), 292–299; Robert. W. Davies, *The Socialist Offensive: The Collectivization of Soviet Agriculture 1929–1930* (London: Macmillan, 1980), 39–60; Anne Applebaum, *Red Famine: Stalin's War on Ukraine* (London: Allen Lane, 2017); James Hughes, *Stalinism in a Russian Province: A Study of Collectivization and Dekulakization in Siberia* (London: Macmillan, 1996).

7. Teichmann, *Macht der Unordnung*, 122–125; *Piatiletnii plan narodno khoziaistvennogo stroitel'stva SSR* (Moscow: Plannovoe Izdatel'stvo, 1930), 2:385; plan to increase gross cotton harvest in the USSR from 718,000 tons (1928) to 1,690,000 tons (1932) and net production from 215,000 to 525,000 tons.

8. Teichmann cites summer 1929 Politburo claims that the USSR was importing more than 40 percent of the raw cotton for its textile mills and that if cotton independence was not achieved, the USSR would be expending a hundred million rubles annually on cotton. Teichmann, 122–123. Vneshtorg [the Soviet foreign trade division] data on annual imports of cotton showed the USSR increasing its imports of cotton from 1923 onward and importing 157,000 tons at a cost of 577,000 rubles in 1927. Overwhelmingly, that cotton was imported from the United States; other sources were China, Turkey, Iran, and Egypt. *Vneshniaia torgovlia SSSR, 1918–1940: Statisticheskii obzor* (Moscow: Vneshtorgizdat, 1960). At the same time that the USSR was increasing cotton imports, production of cotton within the USSR was also rising dramatically. In addition, the USSR was expanding its exports of finished cotton cloth: major purchasers were China and Iran.

9. *Piatiletnii plan*, 2:343.

10. Oxunboboyev, "Paxta problemasi haqida: O'zbekiston SSR sho'rolar markazii ijroya komitetining 2-sessiyasida qilingan doklad 1929 yil 3 Oktiabr," published in *Qizil O'zbekiston* 8 (October 1929); republished in Yo'ldosh Oxunboboyev, *Tanlangan Asarlar* (Tashkent: O'zbekiston nashriyoti, 1985), 89.

11. Davies, *Socialist Offensive*, 155–194; Stephen Kotkin, *Stalin: Waiting for Hitler, 1929–1941* (New York: Penguin, 2017), 35–36.

12. TsK VKP(b), "O tempe kollektivizatsii i merakh pomoshchi gosudarstva kolkhoznomu stroitel'stvu," January 5, 1930. This document has been reproduced many times; one online version of the text can be found at http://www.gumer.org/bibliotek_Buks/History/Article/temp_koll.php.

13. On the 1929 purge of nationalists, Khalid, *Making Uzbekistan*, 371–378; M. Jo'rayev, editor, *O'zbekiston Yangi Tarixi*, 2:320–322. "Postanovlenie isponitel'nogo biuro tsentral'nogo komiteta kommunisticheskoi partii (bol'shevikov) Uzbekistana 'o plane kolkhoznogo stroitel'stva na 1929-/30 g,'" dated November 27, 1929, republished in Dilarom A. Alimova, ed., *Tragediia Sredneaziatskogo kishlaka: kollektivizatsiia, raskulachivanie, ssylka*, vol. 1 (Tashkent: Shark, 2006), doc. 1, 26–27.

14. "Postanovlenie isponitel'nogo," 27.

15. Teichman argues that "the real winners of land reform were not simple peasants who lived in poverty and landlessness, but the countless Uzbek state employees who worked in agricultural cooperatives, land commissions, or local government agencies." Teichman, *Macht der Unordnung*, 76. Joining an artel did not make those newly landed dehqons into employees of state cooperatives; this is an overestimation of the meaning of cooperation in late 1920s Uzbekistan. Most cooperatives were associations of dehqons who gained seed credit as a group but who individually made contracts to produce cotton on their minimal or newly acquired land. Many cooperatives were groups who formed work brigades to do specialized tasks on a temporary basis for local boylar. Some cooperatives undertook land reclamation together. They earned money in the same ways as did dehqons who were not in cooperatives, by raising and selling their crops or by contracting with the rich; none were state employees.

16. Sheila Fitzpatrick, "On the Question of Social Support for Collectivization," *Russian History* 37 (2010): 156.

17. On commission members, see "Iz protokola no 108," December 5, 1929, in Alimova, *Tragediia Sredneaziiatskogo*, vol. 1, doc. 2, 33. On speeding up to 75 percent, see "Vystupleniia G. N. Kaminskogo," December 14, 1929, in Alimova, vol. 2, doc 3. Regions for total and mass collectivization were named in February 1930.

18. *Qizil O'zbekiston*, January 5, 1930. The decree is signed by the Soviet Central Executive Committee chair, Oxunboboyev, by the chairman of Uzbekistan's People's Commissars, Fayzulla Xo'jaev, and by the Executive Committee's deputy secretary, Tanilskii.

19. O'zRMDA, f. R-95, op. 2, d. 186, l. 8–10, "Svodka o khode kollektivizatsii, obobshestvlen ... ploshadei i rabskota, na 10/10/1931." Total figures: 888,467 rural households in Uzbekistan; of those, 486,937 collectivized, or 66 percent. The fact that 63 percent of irrigated lands and 53 percent of dry lands were included in collective farms suggests that those who remained outside the kolkhozes tended to be owners of larger dryland holdings.

20. Isabelle Ohayon, *La sédentarisasion des Kazakhs dans l'URSS de Staline: Collectivasation et changement social* (Paris: Massioneuve & Larose, 2006) Cameron, *Hungry Steppe*; Pianciola, "Towards a Transnational History"; Niccolò Pianciola, "Stalinskaya 'ierarkhiya potrebleniya' i velikii golod 1931–1933 gg. v Kazakhstane," *Ab Imperio* 2 (2018): 80–116.

21. Kassymbekova, *Despite Cultures*; Botakoz Kassymbekova, "Humans as Territory: Forced Resettlement and the Making of Soviet Tajikistan," *Central Asian Survey* 30, nos. 3–4 (2011): 349–370; Stéphane Dudoignon and Christian Noack, eds., *Allah's Kolkhozes: Migration, De-Stalinisation, Privatization, and the New Muslim Congregations in the Soviet Realm (1950s–2000s)* (Berlin: Klaus Schwarz Verlag, 2015).

22. Viola et al., *War against the Peasantry*; Viktor Kondrashin, *Golod v SSSR 1929–1934*, 3 volumes, (Moscow: Mezhdunarodnyi fond demokratiia, 2012); Viktor P. Danilov et al., *Tragediia sovetskoi derevni: kollektivizatsiia i raskulachivanie: dokumenty i materialy v 5 tomov 1927–1939* (Moscow: Rossiiskaia Polit. Entsiklopediia, 1999–2006).

23. There were plenty of exceptions. Quloqs were forcibly resettled and ordered to reclaim unfarmed lands, a subject addressed in the next chapter. Zeev Levin describes an effort to turn urban Jews from Samarkand into grape farmers outside of the city, a project that failed. Levin, *Collectivization and Social Engineering: Soviet Administration and the Jews of Uzbekistan* (Leiden, Netherlands: Brill Academic, 2015). Dam and canal building opened arid lands to farming, as in a project near Andijon that resettled six thousand households in the early 1930s; several interviewees told of their families moving to that newly opened district because they saw potential improvement to their livelihoods: Namangan 4, Mavluda U., b. 1921, and Ibodat N., b. 1925; Namangan 6, Yolchivoy A., b 1922; Namangan 12, Turdiboy T., b. 1921.

24. Among the rural population, 9 percent were not dehqons; they were nomadic or sedentary herders. Figures from January 1932 Svodka, O'zRMDA R95, op. 2, d. 186, ll. 21–23.

25. Examples of reference to strengthening or improving kolkhozes can be found in every issue from November 24, 1929, onward, such as a story with the headline "Kolxoz qurilishining va bundai so'ng vazifalari," in *Qizil O'zbekiston*, November 24, 1929; "Qishloqda sosializm sektorini kuchaytirimiz," *Qizil O'zbekiston*, November 25, 1929.

26. "Qishloqlardag'i siyasatimizning eng asasiy paytlari," *Qizil O'zbekiston*, December 8, 1929.

27. Articles on kolkhozes being organized: *Qizil O'zbekiston*, December 13, 1929; December 17, 1929; December 20, 1929; quotation from *Qizil O'zbekiston*, December 22, 1929.

28. "Ommavi kolektivlash," *Qizil O'zbekiston*, January 28, 1930.

29. Xorazm 17, Olmojon X., b. 1903.

30. Fergana 15, Umriniso, b. 1914.

31. As of 1926, there were 161,000 dehqon members of credit cooperatives, and the number grew rapidly over the next three years. K. Yusupov, *Agrarye otnosheniia v Uzbekistane v periode stroitel'stva sotsializma* (Tashkent: Fan, 1977), 95–96. O'zRMDA R-95, op. 1, d. 1794, l. 181, Uzbekpakhtasoiuz, "Raspredelenie beniatskogo fonda v sezone 1929–1930 roda." 597,000 households planted cotton; of those, 133,000 who planted less than 0.5 ha. received these advances, as did 57,600 households planting more than 0.5 ha.

32. The Baliqchi region in the Fergana Valley gained agricultural credit through co-ops for the first time in 1925, with 80 percent in-kind distribution of advances, including flour; using credit to undermine the boylar's influence is explained. *Sovremennyi kishlak srednei azii (sotsial'no ekonomicheskii ocherk)*, 5:91–97, 135–139. Before land reform, the wealthy were able to obtain advances from the Khlopkom. *Sovremennyi kishlak*, vol. 6, Isfara region, 51.

33. A. Itkich, "Khlopkovodcheskie kooperatsiia Uzbekistana i ee perspektivy," *Narodnoe Khoziaistvo Srednei Azii* 1 (1929): 97–100. In 1925–1926, Uzbekistan produced 397,000 tons of cotton, of which 89 percent was delivered to state purchasing points, and 11 percent stayed in the private market. In 1928–1929, Uzbekistan raised 559,000 tons of cotton, of which 93 percent was delivered to government cotton purchase points. Agricultural credit increased cotton production and eliminated a private market. A. F. Volotkin, "Osedaniie khlopka v Uzbekistane," *Biulleten' Tsentral'nogo Statisticheskogo Upravleniia Uzbekskoi SSR*, no. 23 (1930): 46.

34. RGASPI, f. 62, op. 2, d. 2134, l. 5, on precise amounts of grain for distribution; l. 46, Zelenskii's correspondence and speeches on collectivization, 1930. Data on uprisings: Rustambek Shamsutdinov, *Qishloq fojeasi: Zhamoalashteirish, quloqlashtirish siyosati va uning fojeali oqibatlari* (Tashkent: Sharq, 2001), 125–163; "Iz postanovleniia Sredazbiuro TsK VkP(B) direktiva Ts KP(b) U zot 10.III-30 r. 'Ob ispravlenii oshibok, dopushchennykh pri provedenii kollektivizatsii'. 10 Marta 1930," republished in *Tragediia Sredneaziattskogo Kishlaka*, vol. 1, doc. 42, 149–152.

35. "Partisan": Sharofutdin may have meant that Isayev served in a pro-Soviet militia fighting against Bosmachis.

36. Fergana 20, Sharofutdin Q., b. 1911.

37. Fergana 4, Muxaxon T., b. 1910.

38. Navoiy 2, Berdiqul B., b. 1920.

39. Namangan 12, Turdiboy T., b. 1921.

40. Navoiy 8, Rustam M., b. 1912.

41. Qashqa Daryo 15, Temir X., b. 1920.

42. Qashqa Darya 17, Halil F., b. 1905.

43. Regressive taxes, heavier for the poor than for the rich: O'zRDMA, f. 86, op. 2, d. 118, l. 2.

44. Tax rates on kolkhoz members' private plantings ranged from 7 to 33 percent; on individual farm profits, up to 33 percent. Kolkhozes that brought dry land into production, with a specific mention of Kazakh kolkhozes, were supposed to be tax-free for four years. Sovnarkom Uz SSR decision 44/138, June 5, 1933: O'zRDMA, f. 86, op. 10, d. 118, l. 197, 210, 218, 226–228.

45. In assessing recent scholarship on collectivization in Russia, the historian Viktor Zemtsov writes: "In our view, the main explanation that the rural population wound up in kolkhozes and sovkhozes should be sought in the physical and economic sphere. On the one hand, there were announcements of tax privileges for the kolkhozes and their members, and on the other, the levying of ever-increasing tax weights on individual farmers." Zemtsov, *Stalinskaia epokha: Ekonomika, repressii, industrializatsiia 1924–1954* (Moscow: Veche, 2018), 13.

46. O'zRMDA, f. 196, op. 1, d. 49, l. 24. Yusupov, *Agrarnye otnosheniia*, 140–141. Rakhima Aminova shows that Uzbeks made up 89 percent of the trained plenipotentiaries. R. Kh. Aminova, *Osushshchestvlenie kollektivizatsii v Uzbekistane (1929–1932)* (Tashkent: Fan, 1977), 200. On the 25,000ers, see Lynne Viola, *Best Sons of the Fatherland: Workers in the Vanguard of Soviet Collectivization* (Oxford: Oxford University Press, 1989).

47. Institutions such as Uzbeksovkhozkhlopka, Uzbekbrliashu, Uzbkolkhoztsentr, and Narkomfin employed mostly nonnatives in 1932, according to a report on nativization. O'zRDMA, f. 86, op. 10, d. 42, ll. 39–41.

48. Qashqa Dayro 12, Bekmurod Sh., b. 1907.

49. Qashqa Daryo 18, Abdullo F., b. 1919.

50. Bukhara 11, Fayzi S., b. 1915.

51. Qashqa Daryo 9, Rajab H., 1917.

52. O'zRMDA, f. R-95, op. 1, d. 2252, l. 3, Vseuzbekskii Komitet Sodeistviia Tekstilkhlopok, "Svedeniia kolichestve prebyvshykh brigad iz tsentra dla provedeniia vesenei posevknoi kampanii." Undated but filed with other documents from February 1930.

53. O'zRMDA, f. R-95, op. 1, d. 2252, ll. 24–25ob, Brigada No. 1 Seropukhovskogo ... 14/III/1930. The brigade included 4 mechanics, one tractor driver, one film operator, one doctor, and two others.

54. Bukhara 3, Ahmad U., b. 1921.

55. O'zRMDA, f. R-95, op. 1, d. 2252, l. 3, Vseuzbekskii Komitet shows 20 workers from Tver' were deployed to G'ijduvon and Novaia Bukhara in winter 1930.

56. Bukhara 8, Ravshan, b. 1920.

57. Some of them may have been effective agitators, but archival documents from the 1930s preserve what went wrong rather than noting successes. Examples: O'zRMDA, f. 196, op. 1, d. 44, ll. 106, 126, 138–141.

58. Boltaboy used the word *mahalliy*, which I translate as "local," but it could also be translated as "native." In Uzbek, it means "from the neighborhood," and it is only used to designate someone or something indigenous to Central Asia.

59. Xorazm 4, Boltaboy K., b. 1914.

60. Xorazm 4, Boltaboy K., b. 1914. Letters from some of the several hundred 25,000ers who went to Uzbekistan confirm the point that due to lack of knowledge of Uzbek language, they had difficulty accomplishing the kinds of tasks they thought they had volunteered to do. O'zRMDA, f. R-95, op. 1, d. 2252, ll. 27–27ob, letter from a brigade leader in the Bulungur region, Samarkand Province, March 14, 1930; l. 35, from a 25,000er in the Ikramov region, Tarariq village soviet, Arabxon kolkhoz, March 12, 1930.

61. O'zRMDA, f. R-95, op. 1, d. 2252, l. 93–94, "Hleb sentir ra'isi Tajiyev tarafidan qisqacha daklanavi zapiska," March 18, 1930 (in Latin Uzbek).

62. O'zRMDA, f. R-95, op. 1, d. 2252, l. 36, an incomplete section of a general report on the work of 25,000ers in Uzbekistan, from March 19, 1930, notes that of the fourteen brigade members sent to Xorazm, not one had been to a kolkhoz at all. A similar account from an Ivano-Vozensensk worker who was sent to Yakkobog', Qashqa Daryo: O'zRMDA, f. R-95, op. 1, d. 2252, ll. 70–71, February 28, 1930.

63. Cameron, *Hungry Steppe*, 105.

5. MAKING QULOQS

1. J.V. Stalin, "K voprosam agrarnoi politiki v SSSR: rech' na konferentsii agrarnikov-marksistov 27 Dekabria 1929 g.," subsection 5 "O prirode kolkhozov," republished on https://www.marxists.org/russkij/stalin/t12/t12_10.htm.

2. Lewin, *Russian Peasants*. Buxoro 15, Avez J., b. 1920.

3. On collectivization, see Kotkin, *Stalin*, chap. 1; Viola, *Peasant Rebels under Stalin*; Viola et al., *War against the Peasantry*.

4. Baxtiyor Rasulov, *O'zbekiston kollektivlashtirish jarayonidagi siyosi qatag'onlar va surgun qilingan dehqonlar ahvoli* (1929–1959) (Tashkent: Sharq, 2012), 18–22. Uzbek has a consonant that is pronounced forward in the mouth as [k] and in the back of the mouth as [q]. The word *quloq* means "ear"; the adoption of this Russian term created a homophone.

5. *Qizil O'zbekistan*, December 22, 1929.
6. O'zRMDA, f. 196, op. 1, d. 64, ll. 23–32, December 2, 1930.
7. Zelenskii, "Iz postanovleniia sredazbiuro TsK VKP (B) 'o meropriiatiiakh v sviazi s likvidatsiei kulachestva kak klassa'," January 28, 1930, published as doc. 110 in *Tragediia Sredneiaziatskogo Kishlaka* (hereafter *Tragediia SAK*), 1:311–316.
8. Navoiy 10, O'rozboy, b. 1907; Tashkent 7, Abdullo Q., b. 1902; Qashqa Daryo 20, Fayzulla R., b. 1909. A sample of one hundred men named as quloqs and deported to Ukraine in 1931 shows that the average age of someone who was arrested as a quloq was forty-seven. In the sample, ages ranged from sixteen to seventy-six, but most were in their thirties to fifties and headed households that included several "work-capable" younger members. "Kharakteristiki kulatskikh khoziaistv, podlezhashchikh vyseleniiu v iuzhnye raiony Ukrainy i severnogo Kavkaza po Andijanskomu raiony iz st. gor. Andizhana"; original is O'zRMDA, f. 58, op. 7, d. 252, ll. 77–78, signed Orekhov and Bezverkhov, published as doc. 261, *Tragediia SAK*, 2:56–89.
9. Rakhima Aminova's series of studies of collectivization comes from this period, although some were not published until later. Aminova, *Agrarnaia politika Sovetskoi*; R. Kh. Aminova, *Agrarnaia preobrazovaniia v Uzbekistane v gody perekhoda Sovetskogo gosudarstvo k NEPu* (Tashkent: Fan, 1965); R. Kh. Aminova, *Agrarnaia preobrazovaniia v Uzbekistane nakanune sploshnoi kollektivizatsii, 1925–1929* (Tashkent: Fan, 1969); Aminova, *Osushchestvleniie kollektivizatsii v Uzbekistane*. In the early 1960s, Aminova was in Moscow, working with the revisionist historian V. P. Danilov; see Danilov, ed., *Ocherki istorii kollektivizatsii sel'skogo khoziaistva v soiuznikh respublikakh: sbornik statei* (Moscow: Gospolizdat, 1963). After independence, Aminova published a somewhat revised view of collectivization: R. Kh. Aminova, *Vozvrashchaias' k istorii kollektivizatsii v Uzbekistane* (Tashkent: Fan, 1995). Danilov edited the massive document collection *Tragediia Sovetskoi Derevni: Kollektivizatsiia i raskulachivania: dokumenty i materialy v 5 tomakh, 1927–1939*, which is the model for *Tragediia Sredneiaziatskogo Kishlaka*.
10. In 2001, Uzbekistan's government commissioned the creation of the Museum in Memory of the Victims of Repression (Qatag'on Qurbonlar Xotirasi); it opened in 2002. New histories include Rustambek Shamsutdinov, *O'zbekistonda sovetlarning quloqlashtirish siyosati va uning fojeali oqibatlari* (Tashkent: Sharq, 2001); Shamsutdinov, *Qishloq fojeasi*; Rustambek Shamsutdinov, *O'zbekiston Tarixi* (Tashkent: Sharq, 2013); D. A. Alimova, editor, with Shamsutdinov, *Tragediia Sredneaziiatskogo kishlaka: Kollektivizatsiia, reskulachivaniia, ssylka 1929–1955: Dokumenty i materialy (3 volumes)* (Tashkent: Sharq 2006); Shamsutdinov, *Shimolii Kavkaz surgundagi yurtdoshlar qismati* (Tashkent: Sharq, 2005). A three-volume history of Uzbekistan denotes the entire Soviet period as *mustabid* (tyranny): Hamdan Sodiqov and Nazrulla Jo'rayev, *O'zbekiston Sovet mustamlakachiligi davrida* (Tashkent: Sharq, 2011).
11. Sulton Boyvachcha, or Sulton, "son of a rich man."
12. Tashkent 1, Bozorxo'ja U., b. 1913.
13. Bukhara 4, Rashid Sh., b. 1917.
14. "O likvidatsii baiskikh khoziaistv v Iangi-Iule," February 3, 1930, g. Chinaz, as reported by Alek. Rogov, RGASPI, f. 62, op. 2, d. 2138, ll. 9–15, published as doc. 114, *Tragediia SAK*, 1:324–331. Similar reports from other Tashkent regions follow in *Tragediia SAK*, 1:333–357.
15. "O likvidatsii baiskikh khoziaistv v Iangi-Iule," *Tragedia SAK*, 1:327.
16. "Direktiva I. V. Stalina vsem partorganizatsiiam 'ob opasnosti uvlecheniia raskulachivaniem v ushcherb kollektivizatsii," January 30, 1930, published in *Tragediia sovetskoi derevnii: kollektivizatsiia*, 2:131, and as doc. 12, *Tragediia SAK*, 1:56–57.
17. Zelenskii, "Telegramma Okruzhkom Party Baltaevu," January 30, 1930, FO AAP RUz, f. 110, op. 1, d. 468, ll. 18–20, published as doc. 14, *Tragediia SAK*, 1:57–59.

18. The estimate was suspiciously precise, not supported by other data. "Zapiska po priamomu provodu. Vneocherednaia opersvodka iz Tashkenta," March 15, 1930, arrived at 2:10, totally secret. To Moscow OGPU, Evdkokimov, D'iakov, Zaporozhets, from Karutskii. TsA FSB RF, f. 2, op. 8, d. 3, ll. 244–247, published as doc. 55, *Tragediia SAK*, 1:198–201.

19. "Svodka massovykh vystuplenii dehkhanstva za fevral' po Uz SSR," March 12, 1930, totally secret, RGASPII, f. 62, op. 2, d. 2141, ll. 62–75, published as doc. 51, *Tragediia SAK*, 1:176–187.

20. J. V. Stalin, "Dizzy with Success: Concerning Questions with the Collective-Farm Movement," originally published in *Pravda*, March 2, 1930, English translation on https://www.marxists.org/reference/archive/stalin/works/1930/03/02.htm.

21. "Iz postanovleniia TsK KP(b) Uzbekistana ot 4 Marta 1930 g," FO AAP RUz, f. 110, op. 1, d. 468, ll. 25–33, published as doc. 33, *Tragediia SAK*, 1:117–127.

22. "Dynamika kollektivizatsii Ferokruga" (for January 1 to March 20, 1930), FO AAP Respublika Uzbekistana, f. 109, op. 1, d. 974, ll. 3–4, published as docs. 63 and 64, *Tragediia SAK*, 1:221–222.

23. Zelenskii, "Iz postanovleniia TsK KP(b)," doc. 33, *Tragediia SAK*, 1:117–127.

24. "Zapiska po priamomu provodu," March 20, 1930, totally secret, reported to Moscow OGPU by Karutskii, TsA FSB RF, f. 2, op. 8, d. 3, l. 265, published as doc. 58, *Tragediia SAK*, 1:207–209. Figures are a collection from across Central Asia. The Uzbekistan figures do not include Tashkent, Zarafshan, or Surhon Daryo Provinces, meaning that the totals should be significantly higher. Fergana Province provided no breakdown for its 164 arrestees.

25. Tashkent 16, Abduqodir P., b. 1916. "Chasing in the *uloq* game," a polo-style competition where teams try to carry a goat carcass to a goal. Played across Central Asia and Afghanistan, the game has many names, such as *buzkashi*.

26. Tashkent 16, Abduqodir P., b. 1916.

27. Postanovlenie soveta Nar Kom Uz SSR, "O priznakakh kulatskikh khoziaistv, v kotorykh podlezhit primeneniiu kodeks zakonov o trude UzSSR i o poriadke ucheta takikh khoziaisv," April 6, 1930, TGA RUz, f. 837, d. 311, ll. 80–82, published as doc. 132, *Tragediia SAK*, 1:376–379.

28. Tashkent 16, Abduqodir P., b. 1916.

29. Tashkent 16, Abduqodir P., b. 1916.

30. Storella and Sokolov, historians of collectivization in Russia, offer some validation for this view in letters to the editor of *Krestianskaia Gazeta*. One such letter discussed those who were voluntarily joining kolkhozes, where some of the new kolkhoz members voiced the view that if the kolkhoz broke up, "we'll get to keep the property." Storella and Sokolov, *Voice of the People*, 230.

31. Tashkent 16, Abduqodir P., b. 1916, interviewed in Bekobod. A *ketmon* is a very wide, deep hoe. A millionaire kolkhoz was one that was on productive land, that began with more resources than others, and that received unusual attention from the Kolkhoz Center, such as priority tractor use.

32. An archival record includes mention of a 1930 demonstration in Oyim, where "61 were arrested, among them 29 leaders." "Zapiska," published as doc. 51, *Tragediia SAK*, 1:189.

33. He used the word *podachi*, herders who collected livestock from a number of households to take them to graze while their dehqon owners were busy farming. How many head of livestock constituted "wealth" varied by region.

34. Qashqa Daryo 2, Abdurasul E., b. 1922.

35. Qashqa Daryo 1, Ernazar A., b. 1923.

36. Navoiy 10, O'rozboy D., b. 1907 or 1908—he was uncertain.

37. Margilon 5, Ahmad T., b. 1920.
38. Marg'ilon 5, Ahmed T., b. 1920. For discussion of other cases of flight to Tajikistan from this oral history project, see Kamp, "Where Did the Mullahs Go?"
39. Khiva 12, Abdullo S., b. 1920.
40. The 1937–1938 Kulak Operation has received less attention than the Party Purge of the same period. More than 700,000 "kulaks, criminals, and other anti-Soviet elements" were arrested, and half of them were sentenced to be shot. Nicholas Werth, "The NKVD Mass Secret Operation No. 00447 (August 1937–November 1938)," https://www.sciencespo.fr/mass-violence-war-massacre-resistance/en/document/nkvd-mass-secret-operation-n-00447-august-1937-november-1938.html#title4. Records of 3,644 of those who were arrested in Uzbekistan's Kulak Operation in December 1937 are found in Rustambek Shamsutdinov, *Repressiia 1937–1938, Dokumenty i Materialy Vyp 4, Zhertvy bol'shogo terrora iz Uzbekistana 1937 god, Dekiabr'* (Tashkent: Sharq, 2008). Of them 392 were sentenced to death; most of them were accused of murder or Bosmachism. The freed numbered 34; the rest were sentenced to eight or ten years of imprisonment or exile in a special settlement.
41. Bukhara 15, Avez J., b. 1921.
42. Bukhara 5, Sa'dullo R., b. 1920.
43. Shamsutdinov, *Qishloq fojeasi*, 203–215. The quota for all Central Asia (not including Kazakhstan) was 6,000 households. The actual tallies were Turkmenistan, 430 households, 2,332 persons; Tajikistan, 737 households, 3,003 individuals; Kyrgyzstan, 708 households, 3,850 individuals.
44. Shamsutdinov, 220–241.
45. "Kharakteristiki kulatskikh khoziaistv," published as doc. 261, *Tragediia SAK*, 2:56–116.
46. Rasulov, *O'zbekiston kollektivlashtirish*, 307–314. Sovkhoz names and locations of places designated for the special resettlement and detention of kulak exiles in the Uzbek SSR's SAZLag: Bauman, in Bulungur; Dalvarzin, in Bekobod; Norin, in Norin; Oxunboboyev, place not stated; Jizzakh sovkhoz, in Jizzakh; Nizhnii Khan, in Pskent; Boyovut, in Mirzacho'l; Angor, in Ikramov; Xazorbog', in Denov; Narpay, in Narpay; Ikromov, in Norin; Savai, in Jalaquduk.
47. Tashkent 16, Abduqodir P., b. 1916.
48. Abduqodir's father had sixteen children by his two wives, but most of them had died in childhood, Abuqodir said. Some were apparently adults who initially stayed in the Oyim region but who later "followed us" to Dalvarzin.
49. Akrihin, a form of Mepacrinum, a synthetic replacement for quinine, was developed in Soviet pharmacy labs in the early 1930s and distributed for use in treating malaria in 1935. https://ru.wikipedia.org/wiki/%D0%9C%D0%B5%D0%BF%D0%B0%D0%BA%D1%80%D0%B8%D0%BD
50. He meant after the sovkhoz was given tractors.
51. Rasulov, *O'zbekiston kollektivlashtirish*, 310. In the next year, 1933, when fewer quloqs were sent to special settlements, the OGPU recorded 3,469 deaths and 15,790 escapes.
52. Tashkent 16, Abduqodir P., b. 1916.
53. Teichmann, *Macht der Unordnung*.
54. Shamsutdinov's volume listing the names and accusations of all those who were arrested in the December 1937 Kulak Operation in Uzbekistan includes nine women's names out of the 3,644 total. Of those nine women, eight were Russian, and one was Tatar from Kazan; they were not arrested as kulaks but for theft, murder, or counterrevolutionary propaganda. Shamsutdinov, *Repressia*, vol. 4.
55. Qashqa Daryo 18, Abdullo F., b. 1919.

56. Qashqa Daryo 18, Abdullo F., b. 1919.

57. For example, Hamid, the son of a middle dehqon whose mother was an activist on the village soviet, praised Stalin for reining in the troikas that arrested and tried quloqs. Marg'ilon 1, Hamid U., b. 1922.

58. Tashkent 7, Abdullo Q., b. 1902.

59. Sidiq explained that an oxun (akhund) is an educated man with a degree higher than that of a mufti.

60. Xoraxm 3, Sidiq U., b. 1907.

61. Rasulov, *O'zbekiston kollektivlashtirish*, 270, 309–310.

62. Shamsutdinov, *O'zbekistonda sovetlarning*, 12. The 880,000 figure comes from early 1930s sources, which may include all rural households, whether or not they performed dehqon labor; Rasulov seems to be using an estimate of dehqon households from the late 1920s.

63. Totals varied from 10,000 to 14,000 with the same documents also noting that at least as many of these "special resettlers" escaped as remained in their places of settlement. See, e.g., "Svedeniia o bezhavshikh i zaderzhannykh spetspereselentsakh za 1930, 1931, 1932 i 1933 gg," and doc. 318, "Glavnoe upravelenie lageriami OGPU Tov. Koganu, Spravka o kolichestve s/p po kraim i oblastiam," published as doc. 311, *Tragediia SAK*, 2:209, 215.

64. Baxtyar Babadjanov's research in a small village, Xo'jaobod, in the Fergana Valley, shows that dozens were exiled as quloqs but then returned from exile in 1939. Bakhtyar Babadjanov, "The Economic and Religious History of Kolkhoz Village: Khojawot from Soviet Modernization to the Aftermath of the Islamic Revival," in *Allah's Kolkhozes: Migration, De-Stalinisation, Privatization, and the New Muslim Congregations in the Soviet Realm (1950s–2000s)*, ed. Stephane Dudoignon and Christian Noack (Berlin: Klaus Schwarz Verlag, 2014), 202–264. Tashkent 16, Abduqodir P., remained and built his career in Dalvarzin rather than returning the Oyim region after his family's sentence expired.

65. Olivier Roy presents continuity of village leaders as the norm, in *The New Central Asia: The Creation of Nations* (London: Tauris, 2000); and Kathleen Collins assumes such continuities in *Clan Politics and Regime Transition in Central Asia* (Cambridge: Cambridge University Press, 2006). Sergei Abashin demonstrates this kind of continuity in a Tajik community, in *Sovetskii Kishlak*.

66. Qashqa Daryo 20, Faizulla R., b. 1909.

67. Bukhara 8, Ravshan H., b. 1920.

68. For a typical example, see O'zRDMA, f. 86, op. 10, d. 849, ll. 2–8 (1933) and 127–133, (1935), records of the commission reviewing cases wherein dehqons are placed under special individual taxation and dehqons appealed for reconsideration.

6. FAMINE

1. When I first visited Uzbekistan in 1991, my host family (Dilarom Alimova and Sagdulla Bag'ramov) told me that respect for bread is shown in these ways: non is torn by hand (rather than cut) and shared with all at the table; bread cannot be thrown away; rather, leftovers should be placed outside on a clean raised surface for the poor; and when bread falls to the ground, you pick it up, brush it off, touch it to your forehead, and kiss it.

2. This chapter is adapted from a previously published article. Marianne Kamp, "Hunger and Potatoes: The 1933 Famine in Uzbekistan and Changing Foodways," *Kritika: Explorations in Russian and Eurasian History* 20, no. 2 (2019): 237–267. O'tkir Hoshimov, "Non—Iymon," *Toshkent Haqiqati*, July 1, 1983. In the 444 days when Leningrad was besieged by German forces, some 600,000 Leningraders died, primarily of starvation.

3. Tashkent 6, M. T., b. 1921, Parkent region.

4. M. T. said *osh*, a word that often means plov, a dish of rice and meat, but it can simply mean "food" or "a meal." Other interviewees were more precise, mentioning *atala*, a porridge made from flour and water, as one of the foods that sustained them during this time of hunger.

5. Tashkent 6, M. T., b. 1921, Parkent region.

6. Amartya Sen, *Poverty and Famines: An Essay on Entitlement and Deprivation* (Oxford: Oxford University Press, 1981).

7. K. Sh. Shaniiazov, "O traditsiionoi pishche Uzbekov," in *Etnograficheskoe izuchenie byta i kul'tury Uzbekov*, ed. Kh. Ziioev (Tashkent: Fan, 1972), 96–118; Nancy Rosenberger, *Seeking Food Rights: Nation, Inequality, and Repression in Uzbekistan* (Boston: Wadsworth/Cengage, 2012), 42–44; Russell Zanca, "Fat and All That: Good Eating the Uzbek Way," in *Everyday Life in Central Asia*, ed. R. Zanca and J. Sahadeo (Bloomington: Indiana University Press, 2007), 178–197; R. R. Nazarov, "Natsionnal'naia kukhnia Uzbekistana: traditsii i innovatsii," in *Istoriia iedy i traditsii pitaniia narodov mira*, ed. A. V. Pavlovskaia et al. (Moscow: Tsentr po izucheniiu vzaimodestviia kul'tur, 2016), 172–183.

8. Sen, *Poverty and Famines*, 39, 41, 50, 56.

9. Amartya Sen, "Famines," *World Development* 8 (1980): 617.

10. Felix Wemheuer, *Famine Politics in Maoist China and the Soviet Union* (New Haven, CT: Yale University Press, 2014), 151.

11. Sen, *Poverty and Famines*, 45.

12. From 253,000 tons in 1925 to 549,000 in 1928; data not broken out by republic, but it is likely that most of this grain went to Uzbekistan. M. Shatunovskii and S. Zashuk, "Khlebofurazhnyi balans Srednei Azii," *Narodnoe khoziaistvo Srednei Azii* 1 (1929): 78–81.

13. RGASPI, f. 62, op. 2, d. 2089, l. 74, "O pribytie khleba v srednei azii." In 1933, at the end of the First Five-Year Plan, 51.8 percent of Uzbekistan's cultivated land was planted with grain crops, and 38.8 percent, with "technical" crops, meaning cotton. *Sotsialisticheskoe stroitel'stvo SSSR: Statisticheskii ezhegodnik* (Moscow: TsUNXhU Gosplana SSR, 1934), 178–179, table 35.

14. For specific data for Shahrisabz grain productivity decline in 1933, see AP RF, f. 3, op. 40, d. 88, ll. 96–98, published as doc. 43 in Kondrashin, *Golod*, 3:95–96. Ikramov pointed to this reduced productivity in an appeal to Stalin for additional grain. "Dokladnaia zapiska rukovodstva Uzbekistana I.V. Stalinu," November 30, 1933, or later, AP RF, f. 3, op. 40, d. 90, ll. 122–123, published as doc. 156 in Kondrashin, *Golod*, 3:217–219. A study by G. N. Vinogradov points out that some districts significantly decreased grain cultivation and increased cotton and shows the decrease in per hectare productivity of grain in 1932 and 1933. Vinogradov, "Irrigatsia v doline Kashka-dar'I," *Trudy Sredneaziiatskogo nauchno-issledovatel'skogo instituta irrigatsii* 29 (1935): 47–48, 50.

15. On these estimates, see Shatunovskii and Zashuk, "Khlebofurazhnyi balans Srednei Azii," 79.

16. Gosplan estimated Uzbekistan's grain harvest at 72 percent of the multiyear average. *Sotsialisticheskoe stroitel'stvo 1934*, 204–205, table 45, and 206–207, table 46.

17. Per hectare productivity in 1932, 5.7 centners; in 1933, 6 centners; in 1934, 11 centners. "Posevnaia ploshchad', urozhainost', i obshchie razmery urozhaia vsekh zernovnikh kul'tur po vsem kategoriiam khoziaistv v 1913, 1938, 1932–1944," http://istmat.org/node/46315. Tables for grain production in Central Asia 1930s, original source from 1945, RGAE, f. 1562, op. 2, d. 1409, ll. 1–193, 11. Such variability is not unusual; it can be seen in rain-fed, dryland wheat crops in the US west as well.

18. M. W. Williams and V. G. Konovalov, "Central Asian Temperature and Precipitation Data, 1879–2003," USA National Snow and Ice Data, 2008, https://nsidc.org/data/g02174/versions/1. Precipitation timing and form, not indicated in the database, are

important. Winter mountain precipitation that falls as rain, not snow, leads to irrigation shortfalls in spring and summer.

19. RGASPI, f. 62, op. 2, d. 2013, l. 93.

20. RGASPI, f. 62, op. 2, d. 2157, l. 285, April 19, 1931.

21. Kondrashin, *Golod*, 2:193–198, 250, 257, 262, 267–268.

22. "Shifrotelegramma sekretaria TsK KP(B) Uzbekistana A I Ikramova I V Stalinu o prodovol'stvennoi pomoshchi neurozhainym rayonam," March 6, 1933, published as doc. 379 in Kondrashin, *Golod*, 3:463.

23. Sarah Cameron, "The Kazakh Famine of 1930–1933: Current Research and New Directions," *East/West: Journal of Ukrainian Studies* 3, no. 2 (2016): 117–32; Niccolò Pianciola, "Famine in the Steppe: The Collectivization of Agriculture and the Kazakh Herdsmen, 1928–1934," *Cahiers du Monde Russe* 45, no. 1/2 (2004): 137–191.

24. Viktor Kondrashin, *Khlebozagotovitel'naia politika v gody pervoi piatletki i ee rezult'taty (1929–1933 gg.)* (Moscow: Politicheskaia Entsiklopediia, 2014), 159, 161.

25. R. Kh. Aminova, "Agrarnye preobrazovaniia v Uzbekistane 20x godov," *Obshchestvennye Nauki v Uzbekistane* 9 (1989): 38.

26. Shamsutdinov, *O'zbekistonda sovetlarning quloqlashtirish siyosati*, 7.

27. M. Juraev et al., eds., *O'zbekiston yangi tarixi, ikkinchi kitob*, 366, citing RTsXIDNI, f. 122, op. 4, d. 3421, ll. 17–20; and f. 17, op. 5, d. 640, ll. 74–75.

28. "Spravka nachal'nika sektora naseleniia," March 31, 1934, RGAE, f. 1562, op. 329, d. 132, ll. 56–66, published as doc. 499 in Kondrashin, *Golod*, 3:594–608. ZAGS is the abbreviation in Russian for Registry Office for Citizen Life Events.

29. Bukhara 4, Rashid Sh., b. 1917, G'ijduvon.

30. "Dokladnaia zapiska zamestitel' nachal'nika otdel naseleniia, March 14, 1937, AP RF, f. 3, op. 56, d. 15, ll. 62–68, published as doc. 514 in Kondrashin, *Golod*, 3:646.

31. "Pokazateli demograficheskogo krizisa v period goloda," in Kondrashin, *Golod*, 3:751.

32. *Vsesoiuznoe perepis' naselenie* SSSR 1939 g., table showing rural population in Uzbekistan. Immigration increased urban population more than rural population in the 1930s, though urban populations also show a nadir at age five. Previous censuses in Central Asia show "clustering," meaning overrepresentation, at ages five and ten, making the low number at age five here more striking. The 1939 census was not published in full. The website *Demoskop Weekly* (www.demoscope.ru) published the archived tables that breakdown population distribution, including this one, from RGAE, f. 1562, op. 366, d. 604. https://www.demoscope.ru/weekly/ssp/sng_age_39.php. Wheatcroft uses similar data from Saratov to point toward a "natality crisis" related to famine in 1921, p. 337. S. G. Wheatcroft, "Famine and Epidemic Crises in Russia, 1918–1922: The Case of Saratov," *Annales de démographie historique*, Mères et nourrissons (1983): 329–352.

33. For example, the "Hunger Winter" of 1944, when Dutch food supplied was suddenly reduced by war, may have killed only 20,000 people directly from starvation, in a population of 12,000,000, but left other long-lasting physical effects. L. H. Lumey and F. W. A. Van Poppel, "The Dutch Famine of 1944–45: Mortality and Morbidity in Past and Present Generations," *Social History of Medicine* 7, no. 2 (1994): 229–246.

34. Qashqa Daryo 8, Xurram X., b. 1920.

35. Qashqa Daryo 18, Abdullo F., b. 1919.

36. Buxoro 11, Fayzi S., b. 1915.

37. Tashkent 22, A. K., b. 1907.

38. Tashkent 14, Umrqul X., b. 1919. A similar story is told in Guljanat K. Ercilsun, "Famine in Kyrgyzstan in the 1930s and 1940s," in *Kazakhstan, Kyrgyzstan, and Uzbekistan: Life and Politics during the Soviet Era*, ed. T. Dadabaev (London: Palgrave, 2016), 34–52.

39. Ella Maillert, *Turkestan Solo: One Woman's Expedition from the Tien Shan to the Kizil Kum* (London: William Heinemann, 1938), 268–270.

40. Kazakhs migrating to "Central Asia" or Uzbekistan: "Spetssvodka sekretno politicheskogo otdela ogpu SSSR o khode khlebozagotovok i otkochevkakh v kazakhstane," December 7, 1932, published as doc. 161 in Kondrashin, *Golod*, 2:245–247. No earlier than July 10, 1932: "Spetssvodka GPU Aktiubinskoi oblasti o prodovol'stvennykh zatrudnenniiakh," published as doc. 526 in Kondrashin, *Golod*, 1:135–139. I first became aware of Kazakh flight to Uzbekistan in 1992, when a Kazakh friend from Tashkent took me to the village in Tashkent Province where her father was raised. Aset Nuritov was brought to Uzbekistan as a child, fleeing the famine in Kazakhstan; he became a historian who wrote about collectivization.

41. Tashkent 10, Halil A., b. 1917. His region, Bustonliq, was transferred from Kazakhstan to Uzbekistan in 1952; to be accurate, he was recalling famine in Kazakhstan.

42. Qashqa Daryo 19, Narzi A., b. 1921, near Qarshi.

43. Qashqa Daryo 20, Fayzullo R., b. 1909.

44. Bukhara 2, Nemat B., b. 1916.

45. Xorazm 8, Rajab Q., b. 1921.

46. Fergana 8, Muqimjon A., b. 1902, Margilon.

47. Fergana 9, Hidoyatxon S., b. 1919, Margilon; Fergana 3, Saidalixon, b. 1921, Margilon; Xorazm 8, Rajab Q., b. 1921, similar story.

48. Ferbana 20, Sharofutdin Q., b. 1910s.

49. Harvard Project on the Soviet Social System, Widener Library, Harvard University, last reviewed March 31, 2021, schedule B, vol. 8, case 252, p. 3. Interview with an Uzbek, b. 1914, who deserted the Soviet Army during World War II and was living in Germany in 1951. http://hcl.harvard.edu/collections/hpsss/index.html tells a similar story about Kazakhs dying on the streets in Stalinabad, Tajikistan, in 1932.

50. "Spetssoobshenie sekretno-politicheskogo otdela OGPU SSSR ob epidemicheskie zabolevaniiakh," July 27, 1933, secret report included 306 cases of typhus and 86 of typhoid for Uzbekistan, published as doc. 325 in Kondrashin, *Golod*, 2:434–435.

51. Tashkent 2, Tojivoy D., b. 1917, Parkent.

52. Bukhara 3, Ahmed U., b. 1921.

53. Based on my observation of these processions in visits to Uzbekistan over thirty years and on what Uzbek friends have told me about death rituals.

54. Bukhara 5, Sa'dullo R., b. 1921; Bukhara 7, Baraka R., b. 1921; Bukhara 8, Ravshan H., b. 1920; Bukhara 10, Narziya J., b. 1921; Bukhara 11, Fayzi S., b. 1915.

55. "Spetssoobshchenie ekonomicheskogo upravleniia OGPU SSSR ob epidemii sypnogo tifa v Ivanovskoi promyshlennoi oblasti," May 22, 1933, published as doc. 488 in Kondrashin, *Golod*, 2:605–606.

56. Aleida Assmann, *Shadows of Trauma: Memory and the Politics of Postwar Identity* (New York: Fordham University Press, 2016), 16, 106–107.

57. Bukhara 8, Ravshan H., b. 1920, Shofirqon District.

58. Qashqa Daryo 20, Fayzullo R., b. 1909.

59. Qashqa Daryo 8, Xurram X., b. 1920.

60. Qashqa Daryo 2, Abdurasul E., b. 1922.

61. Tashkent 7, Abdullo Q., b. 1902, Parkent.

62. Tashkent 12, Yusupboy H., b. 1917, Xo'jakent, a district transferred from Kazakhstan to Uzbekistan in the 1950s.

63. Xorazm 5, Ibroyim K., b. 1917.

64. Xorazm 13, Madqurbon J., b. 1914.

65. Xorazm 12, Abdullo S., b. 1921.

66. Qashqa Daryo 3, Lutfullo U., b. 1919, p. 16. "Zapiska po primomu provodu nachanl'nika ekonomicheskogo otdela," September 27, 1933, totally secret, published as doc. 97 in Kondrashin, *Golod*, 3:158–160.

67. Qashqa Daryo 12, Bekmurod Sh., b. 1907.

68. Fergana 11, Yoqubjon B., b. 1919, Vodil. There were substantial storage places for seed grain all over the Soviet Union, including in Uzbekistan.

69. Xorazm 2, Otanazar M., b. 1921.

70. O'zRMDA, f. 86, op. 10, d. 118, ll. 195–227, pp. 196–197, 201, 218. Decrease in grain planting by individual farmers: *Sotsialisticheskoe stroitel'stvo SSSR*, tables 36–28, pp. 180–185.

71. "Dynamicheskie tablitsy TsUNKhU Gosplan SSSR ucheta bazarnykh tsen na sel'skokhoziaistvennet produkty i predmety potrebleniia po 31 gorodu SSSR za 1913-1936 gg.," RGAE, f. 1562, op. 12, d. 1918, ll. 31–61. This archival document, from the Russian State Archive of the Economy, is republished on the website *Istoricheskii Materialy* (www.istmat.org), which provides a massive collection of statistical and historical documents, published and archival, from the Soviet period: https://istmat.org/node/48622. Maillert witnessed the lack of bread and high market prices in Bukhara in fall 1932 but much greater abundance and cheap prices in Turt Köl, Karakalpakstan. Maillert, *Turkestan Solo*, 256–257, 284–285.

72. Fergana 20, Sharafutdin Q., b. 1911. On Torgsin stores, see Elena Osokina, *Zoloto dlia industrializatsii: TORGSIN* (Moscow: Rosspen, 2009).

73. Fergana 12, Mahkam T., b, 1921.

74. Tashkent 22, A. K., b. 1907.

75. Bukhara 10, Narziya J., b. 1921.

76. Fergana 15, Umriniso N., b. 1914.

77. Fergana 3, Saidalikhon M., b. 1921, Margilon.

78. Bukhara 19, Qurbon B., b. 1906, Galla-osio.

79. Xorazm 13, Madqurbon J., b. 1914.

80. Xorazm 9, Zulayho A., b. 1916.

81. Qashqa Daryo 3, Lutfullo U., b. 1919.

82. Qashqa Daryo 20, Fayzullo R., b. 1909.

83. Xorazm 4, Boltaboy K., b. 1914.

84. Xorazm 11, Roviya A., b. 1921.

85. Xorazm 12, Abdullo S., b. 1921.

86. Bukhara10, Narziya J., b. 1921. Kunjara or kunjala appears in discussion of famine in 52 of 120 interviews, everywhere except Nurota, which was a grain and herding region that had no cotton gins in 1933. A factor that makes cotton seed hulls less digestible by humans than other seed hulls is that a considerable amount of cotton fiber clings to every seed after ginning.

87. Tashkent 1, Bozorxo'ja U., b. 1913.

88. Silkworm story from Fergana 3, Saidalixon M., b. 1921, Margilon.

89. Qashqa Daryo 16, Hayrullo Sh., b. 1921.

90. Namangan 7, Ismoyiljon N., b. 1923. Plov, a rice and meat dish, was the standard for festive occasions. "In the past, plov was the food of the wealthy. Ordinary people prepared it only as a festive dish." Shaniiazov, "O traditsiionoi pishche Uzbekov," 105.

91. Arturo Warman, *Corn and Capitalism: How a Botanical Bastard Grew to Global Dominance*, trans. Nancy L Westrate (Chapel Hill: University of North Carolina Press, 2003), 125. The diffusion of maize to Central Asia is hard to trace. Uzbeks call it *Makkajuhori*, or "the sorghum of Mecca." It was raised in Bukhara in the early 1800s, and it was grown as an ordinary crop in the Fergana Valley in the 1870s, and perhaps long before that.

92. Tashkent 24, Ashurboy P., b. 1923. In Uzbek, the term for Russian bread is the borrowed Russian term for loaf, *bukhanka*. In Russian, Uzbek bread (non) is called *lepëshka*, using a Russian word that means "flat cake."

93. Tashkent 24, Ashurboy P., b. 1923. Others also said tomatoes were Russian food. Fergana 3, Saidalixon M., b. 1921, Margilon.

94. Gavrilov, *Risolia sartovskikh remeslennikov*, 47.

95. Fergana 11, Yoqubjon B., b. 1919, Vodil.

96. Rinat Shigabdinov, "Nogai-Kurgan—pervyi Tatarskii aul v Uzbekistane," *Idel-Idel'* 5 (2018): 100–103, http://idel-rus.ru/nogaj-kurgan-pervyj-tatarskij-aul-v-uzbekistane/ Nazarov. "Nationnal'naia kukhnia" points out when certain foods first appeared but not whether or when Uzbeks began to eat them.

97. R. R. Alieva explains the very low number of Russian settlers outside of Syr Darya Province. R. R. Alieva, "Iz istorii obrazovaniia Russkikh posolkov v khodzhentskom uezde," *Nomai Donishgoh* 3, no. 52 (2017): 15–22.

98. Potatoes were planted on 2,900 desiatinas out of Uzbekistan's 1.7 million planted desiatinas. Tsentral'noe statisticheskoe upravleniie SSSR, *Osnovnye elementi produktsiia sel'skogo khoziaistva SSR* (Moscow: Izdanie TsSU SSSR 1928), 36–37, 55. In 1925 potato production in the Russian Soviet Federative Socialist Republic (RSFSR) provided 19 *poods* (304 kilos) per capita as human food and 606 kilos per head of livestock as fodder. For Uzbekistan and Turkmenistan: 6.5 kilos per capita and 16 kilos per head of livestock.

99. V. S. Sudorgin, "Tsvetite, sady," in *Istoria Kolkhozov i Sovkhozov Uzbekistana*, ed. R. Kh. Aminova (Tashkent: Mekhnat, 1989), 409; S. M. Busakov, "The Problems of Potato Breeding," *American Potato Journal* 13, no. 9 (1939): 235–252.

100. Tax Tables for Kolkhozes, 1933, O'zRDMA, f. 86, op. 10, d. 118, ll. 226–228. The tsarist administration had set Turkestan's taxation rates for cotton equal to those for grain, to stimulate cotton planting, and both were traditionally taxed at lower rates than most other crops, a practice that continued in the 1920s and 1930s. Penati, "Cotton Boom."

101. *Sel'skoe khoziaistvo SSR. Ezhegodnik 1935*, part b, "Rastenovodstvo" (Moscow: Selxozgiz, 1936), 469, table 331. *Posevnye Ploshadi SSSR* (Moscow: Gos Stat Izdat, 1957), 1:52–53. This was not a lasting pattern. After World War II, Uzbekistan grew fewer potatoes and greatly expanded other vegetables.

102. Xorazm 12, Abdullo S., b. 1921.

103. Navoiy 2, Berdiqul B., b. 1920, Nurota; similar, a Russian thing, Fergana 18, Eminjon H., b. 1920.

104. Tashkent 18, wife of Qudratillo R.; b. 1924. We failed to record her name.

105. Namangan 4, Ibodat N., b. 1925; similar, Xorazm 4, Boltaboy K., b. 1914.

106. Xorazm 17, Olmojon X., b. 1903.

107. Navoiy 7, Doniyor E., b. 1925. Jenny Leigh Smith, *Works in Progress: Plans and Realities on Soviet Farms, 1930–1963* (New Haven, CT: Yale University Press, 2014), 79–83, describes the ways that the Soviet state expanded potato cultivation and peasant advantages in potato growing.

108. Fergana 17, Muhammadjon I., b. 1922.

109. Shaniiazov, "O traditsiionoi pishche Uzbekov," 99–102.

110. Smith, *Works in Progress*, 80–83.

111. Sen, *Poverty and Famines*, chap. 1.

7. WORKING

1. Portelli, "What Makes Oral History," 54.

2. Otto Boele, Boris Noordenbos, and Ksenia Robbe, "Introduction: The Many Practices of Post-Soviet Nostalgia: Affect, Appropriation, Contestation," in *Post-Soviet*

Nostalgia: Confronting the Empire's Legacies, ed. Otto Boele, Boris Noordenbos, and Ksenia Robbe (Milton Park, UK: Taylor & Francis, 2019), 7.

3. Donald Ritchie, *Doing Oral History*, 3rd ed. (Oxford: Oxford University Press, 2015), 19.

4. Qashqa Daryo 4, O'ktam A., b. 1919, according to documents. Several internal references in her interview suggest she may have been born in 1924 or so. Among those born before 1932 in Uzbekistan, passport-recorded birth date and actual birth date often differed, sometimes by years. ChTZ were tractors produced by the Cheliabinsk Tractor Factory, starting in 1933.

5. Katerina Clark, *The Soviet Novel: History as Ritual*, 1st ed. (Chicago: University of Chicago Press, 1981).

6. Description of *Traktoristi* is based on Sofia Bargan, "'Traktoristi': traktor i tank—brat'ia-bliznetsi," accessed September 6, 2011, http://www.nashfilm.ru/sovietkino/4346.html.

7. M. A. Akhunova, ed., *Uzbekskaia SSR v gody velikoi otechestvennoi voiny (1941–1945)*, vol. 1 (Tashkent: Fan, 1981), 176–183.

8. Qashqa Daryo 4, Oktam A., b. 1920

9. Matthew Oja, "Traktorizatsiia as Cultural Conflict, 1929–1933," *Russian Review* 51 (1992): 345.

10. Dana Dalrymple, "American Technology and Soviet Agricultural Development, 1924–1933," *Agricultural History* 40, no. 3 (1966): 187–206. From 1925 to 1931, the USSR purchased tens of thousands of American-made Fordson, Case, Farmall, John Deere, and International Harvester tractors. Ford contracted with the Soviets to build tractor manufacturing factories. In 1929, the Krasnyi Putilovets factory in Leningrad began producing thousands of tractors based on the Fordson model, and by the early 1930s, Soviet-produced tractors ended the need for imports. David E. Greenstein, "Assembling Fordizm: The Production of Automobiles, Americans, and Bolsheviks in Detroit and Early Soviet Russia," *Comparative Studies in Society and History* 56, no. 2 (2014): 259–289.

11. Aminova, *Agrarnye preobrazovaniia v Uzbekistane*, 332–334, 339.

12. For example, Loring, "'Colonizers with Party Cards'"; Kassymbekova, *Despite Cultures*; Peterson, *Pipe Dreams*.

13. Namangan 2, Hayitboy M., b. 1910. He remembered accurately. In 1925 Hoqulobod had an agricultural station that rented out four tractors. *Sovremennyi kishlak Srednei azii*, 30.

14. Bukhara 11, Fayzi Si., b. 1915.

15. Namangan 12, Turdiboy, b. 1921, interviewed with Rustamov. Respondent pronunciations of the American tractor names confused me initially: Tarzan, Parzon, Jondar, Parmall.

16. Qashqa Darya 19, Narzi A., b. 1921. A laborer had to hold and direct each hose; it offered little if any improvement in efficiency. In 1937, the USSR had 1,283 mechanical cotton harvesters, of which 427 were at machine tractor stations in Uzbekistan. *MTS po vtoroi piatletke*, (Moscow: Gosplanizdat, 1939), 54, table 27, https://istmat.org/node/22524. In 1932, the Soviets manufactured 2,196 cotton harvesters but no more until the 1950s. *Narodnoe Khoziaistvo SSSR 1913–1955*, Kraktii Statisticheskii Sbornik, RGAE, f. 1562, op. 33, d. 2310, ll. 1–250. A. D. Dadabaev, *Uzbekskii Khlopok* (Tashkent: Uzbekistan, 1973), drawing of vacuum harvester on p. 46. On Uzbekistan's choice for handpicking, even when combines became available, see Shoshana Keller, "The Puzzle of Manual Harvest in Uzbekistan: Economics, Status, and Labour in the Khrushchev Era," *Central Asian Survey* 34, no. 3 (2015): 296–309.

17. Bukhara 1, Nurmurod H., b. 1921, G'ijduvon.

18. The rates were differentiated by tractor type. "Postanovleniia sredazbiuro TsK VKP (b) 'ob oplate Traktoristov MTS,'" February 28, 1934, published in *Pravda Vostoka*, March 12, 1934, and republished in R. Kh. Aminova, ed., *Organazatsionno-khoziaistvennoe ukreplenie kolkhozov Uzbekistana (1933–1940). Sbornik dokumentov* (Tashkent: Uzbekistan, 1983), doc. 20, pp. 79–80.

19. Oja, "Traktorizatsiia," 348.

20. Namangan 10, Rustamov and Turdiboy T., b. 1922.

21. Bukhara 12, Ubaydullo M., b. 1922, Shofirkon District.

22. Bukhara 9, Baraka R., b. 1916, Shofirkon District.

23. Xorazm 15, Ruzim I., b. 1919. The drivers had common Uzbek names; one was a woman. He also recalled the names of several MTS activists, an Uzbek and Russian.

24. For example, an October 1933 list of personnel for an MTS in Alti-Ariq (Fergana Valley) showed thirty-five names that are likely Russian or European and twenty-six that are likely Uzbek or other Central Asian. O'zRMDA, f. R-213, op. 6, d. 7, ll. 132–133. Other similar files, with similar evidence, in ll. 92–94 and ll. 107–108. A 1932 resolution criticized many administrative organs in Uzbekistan, including the Kolkhoz Center, with inadequate levels of *korennizatsia*, meaning "nativization." O'zRMDA, f. 86, op. 10, d. 42, ll. 39–41.

25. Bukhara 1, Nurmurod H., b. 1921.

26. Bukhara 3, Ahmed U., b. 1921, G'ijduvon District.

27. Bukhara 4, Rashid Sh., b. 1917.

28. Fergana 9, Hidoyatxon S., b. 1919. Hidoyat-xon's father was one of the boylar who fled across the border, while her mother, a Communist Party activist, became a kolkhoz director.

29. Tashkent 6, M. Tuloev, b. 1921

30. Qashqa Daryo 1, Ernazar S., b. 1923.

31. Namangan 5, Aliqul I., b. 1916.

32. Management and labor differ in attitudes to delays. For a kolkhoz director, tractor breakdowns meant difficulties in fulfilling plowing plans, but for kolkhoz members, they provided time off. When we started interviewing in Namangan Province in 2001, I learned from one of the sons in our host family, who was working in the former kolkhoz's wheat harvest, that he and his fellow workers preferred their old Soviet grain combines to the newly purchased Case combines, which were too reliable. When the Soviet-made combine broke down, as it did that day, he and his fellow workers each filled a sack with grain and took it home—the sort of unaccounted and unofficial payment that a worker would see as a benefit, while the manager viewed it as a loss. Archival records from kolkhozes almost by definition reflect management attitudes.

33. Bukhara 4, Rashid Sh., b. 1917, G'ijduvon.

34. Xorazm 4, Boltaboy K., b. 1914, Khiva.

35. Navoiy 8, Rustam M., b. 1912. Qariz, or qarez, systems were used in parts of southern Turkmenistan, Iran, and Xinjiang as well. They are a remarkable adaptation that allowed the irrigation of desert regions, and their demise is frequently lamented. Those laments rarely give thought to the immense amount of human labor required to keep a qariz operating.

36. On the ordinary toll of labor to maintain canals, see Obertries, *Imperial Desert Dreams*, 201–208. Obertries overestimates the amount of time required to do canal work by interpreting "labor-day" as the same as "day of labor." "Labor-day" was a rate of pay, not a measure of time expended.

37. Maya K. Peterson discusses this people's construction approach to creating irrigation infrastructure in *Pipe Dreams*, chap. 6. See also Obertries, 211–222.

38. Coverage of the canal project in Russian-language Soviet press in 1940 claimed instead that the northern Fergana canal was built by kolkhoz members in four months,

while the southern Fergana canal was built in three and a half months. G. Rizaev, *Sotsialisticheskoe sel'skoe khoziaistvo Uzbekistana* (Tashkent: Uzbekistan, 1978), 47–48, citing *Pravda*.

39. Examples of that coverage can be found on the website Seventeen Moments in Soviet History, http://soviethistory.msu.edu/1939-2/great-fergana-canal/.

40. Namangan 1, Yo'ldashev, b. 1923.

41. Fergana 14, Qumriniso R., b. 1920.

42. Fergana 1, Hamid U., b. 1922, Marg'ilon.

43. Fergana 7, Tursunboy Y., b. 1921, Marg'ilon.

44. Xorazm 9 (Hazarasp), Zulayho A., b. 1916.

45. Xorazm 18 (Bog'ot), Sanamjon M., b. 1913.

46. Qashqa Daryo 16, Hayrullo Sh., b. 1921, Kasbi.

47. Tashkent 2, Tojivoy D., b. 1917, Parkent.

48. Obertries, *Imperial Desert Dreams*, 217–220.

49. Teichmann, "Wildscapes in Ballyhooland," 231, 242. The Gulag Belomor project has the most attention from historians. Recent work includes Cynthia Ruder, *Making History for Stalin: The Story of the Belomor Canal* (Gainesville: University of Florida Press, 1998); Julie Draskoczy, *Belomor Criminality and Creativity in Stalin's Gulag* (Brighton, MA: Academic Studies, 2014). Mieka Erley writes about Soviet representations of the building of the Kara-Kum Canal in Turkmenistan, in "'The Dialectics of Nature in Karakum': Andrei Platonov's *Dzhan* as the Environmental History of a Future Utopia," *Slavic Review* 73, no. 4 (2014): 727–750.

50. Peterson, *Pipe Dreams*, 308–317. The late Obertries documents that some materials for canal building resulted from prison labor but does not provide evidence that prisoners were among those digging the canal. *Imperial Desert Dreams*, 219.

51. For example, Komsomol girls who volunteered to go to Siberia in the 1930s. Elena Shulman, *Stalinism on the Frontier: Women and State Formation in the Soviet East* (Cambridge: Cambridge University Press, 2012); workers at Magnitogorsk, whom Stephen Kotkin interviewed, in Kotkin, *Magnetic Mountain*; builders of the Nurek Dam, Kalinovsky, *Laboratory of Socialist Development*. In contrast, records from the 25,000ers in the early 1930s reveal their disillusionment: Viola, *Best Sons*.

52. The term "unfree labor" comes from Peter Kolchin's seminal work, *Unfree Labor: American Slavery and Russian Serfdom* (Cambridge, MA: Belknap, 1987), which gave historians of the Soviet period an analysis that highlights the similarities between kolkhoz labor and serfdom.

53. Seth Bernstein interprets the Communist Party's efforts to attract masses of young people into the Komsomol and involve them in socialist construction as a way to "forge reliable, pliant subjects rather than self-reflective historical actors." S. Bernstein, *Raised under Stalin*, 7.

54. Xorazm 9, Zulayho A., b. 1916.

55. Bukhara 6, Rajab Sh., b. 1912.

56. Bukhara 11, Fayzi S., b. 1915.

57. Bukhara 8, Ravshon H., b. 1920.

58. O'zRMDA, f. R-196, op. 1, d. 118, ll. 63–65, Kolkhoztsentr, "Vsem kolkhoztsentram soiuznykh respublik kolkhozsoiuzam avtonomnykh respublik, kraev i oblastei," July 21, 1931.

59. Namangan 1, Yo'ldashev, b. 1923. Some kolkhoz directors were removed and charged with crimes when complaints came in that they collected pay without working. O'zRMDA, f. R 86, op. 10, d. 182, ll. 140–142, "O'zbekistan Markazi Ijraya Qomitasini Hayat Rayasatija, V Oltirish, 1933." As with all such claims and charges in archival files from the 1930s, we are left wondering whether directors acted corruptly, or kolkhoz

members were using their denunciation abilities to attack the director, or regional officials were justifying personnel changes.

60. The cash value of a labor-day increased year to year in Uzbekistan. In 1933 it was 75 kopeks per labor-day; in 1935, it was 3.75 rubles. Average annual kolkhoz household income rose accordingly, from 230 rubles in 1932 to 2,564 rubles in 1936. Rizaev, *Sotsialisticheskoe sel'skoe khoziaistvo Uzbekistana*, 84–85. In the Kuban region, a labor-day paid 40 kopeks in 1933 and 1.80 rubles in 1937. M. A. Gal'tsin, *Istoki kolkhoznoi posedevnosti (na materialakh iug Rossii 1930-x godov)* (Novocherkassk: LIK, 2018), 155.

61. Rizaev, *Sotsialisticheskoe sel'skoe khoziaistvo Uzbekistana*, 84–85, citing party archive documents.

62. Namangan 2, Hayitboy M., b. 1910.

63. TsUNKhU Gosplana SSSR, *SSSR v tsifrakh 1935 g.* (Moscow: Soiuzorgotchet, 1935), "Srednei-godovaia zarabotnaia plata rabochikh i sluzhashchikh po otrasliam truda v 1928–1934 g," 168–169, http://istmat.org/files/uploads/19822/sssr_1935_trud.pdf. Examples: MTS worker average annual pay in 1932 was 844 rubles versus construction pay, which was 1,509 rubles. There was improvement in the wage gap in 1934, when the MTS worker averaged 1,207 and the construction worker, 1,994. These statistics seem to include only those agricultural workers who earned a salary; they do not include the pay that kolkhoz member workers earned.

64. Fergana 7, Tursunboy Y., b. 1921.

65. Xorazm 12, Abdullo S., b. 1921. In 1932, the Soviet state issued internal passports to urban people and industrial workers that enabled them to move about freely, but until 1953, kolkhoz members were granted a passport only under exceptional circumstances. After Stalin's death, passports were issued to kolkhoz members, providing them with possibilities for leaving the farm.

66. Namangan 12, Rustamov, b. 1921. Rustamov was interviewed with his friend Turdiboy, whose experiences paralleled his but from a poor dehqon class perspective.

67. On wheat harvests in Uzbekistan in the 1930s: Tables for grain production in Central Asia 1930s, original source RGAE, f. 1562, op. 2, d. 1409, ll. 1–193, p. 11. Found on http://istmat.org/node/46315.

68. Qashqa Daryo 18, Abdullo F., b. 1919, but maybe in 1917.

69. Qashqa Daryo 18, Abdullo F., b. 1917.

70. Bukhara 18, Sharofat B., b. 1922. Interviewer E. R. Xalilov.

71. O'zRMDA, f. R-196, op. 1, d. 118, l. 84, "Normy oplaty truda progressivnoi sdel'shchine po sboru khlopka v uborki guza-pai," associate director of the MTS, Tashmatov. The 1931 rates: one labor-day for 16 kilos of cotton bolls; 3.25 labor-days for 52 kilos. Typically bosses thought of women as picking faster than men did, but men's efficiency came from carrying heavier loads, thus not repeatedly leaving the field for the weighing station, as my friends who picked cotton in the 1980s told me. Rates for picking go'za, the Central Asian cotton boll picked in its husk, were lower: one labor-day for picking 70 kilos. Clearing cotton stalks (*g'oza poyi*) paid one labor-day per tanob, or per 0.2 hectare. Kolkhoz members retained g'oza poyi for their own use as cooking fuel.

72. O'zRMDA, f. R-196, op. 1, d. 118, ll. 148–152, "Postanovlenie komissii ispolneniia pri SNK Uz.SSR po voprosu o proverke meropriiatii po organizatsii truda v kolkhozakh," September 12, 1931, 149. A report from Marg'ilon, December 1930, lamented the slow tempo of cotton harvest in this (final) year when individual farms planted 85 percent of the cotton, but collectivization raised questions about who bore the responsibility for picking and for paying the laborers. The author, Lisitsin, blamed the slow tempo on that uncertainty and on "an old but not yet outlived tradition that men should not pick cotton." O'zRMDA, f. R-196, op. 1, d. 64, ll. 125–127, Lisitsin, "Margelanskii Raikolkhozsoiuz," December 14, 1930.

73. V. F. Kulachenko, "Shelkovyi rynok Srednei Azii," *Srednei Aziiatskii Shelk* 7–9 (1929): 344–359; K. A. Bekotserkovskaia, "O chastnom grenazhe v Srednei Azii," *Srednei Aziiatskii Shelk* 4–6 (1929): 124–127.

74. Fergana 15, Umriniso M., b. 1914, described in detail the process by which women incubated silkworm eggs, carrying them in a small cotton sack under their armpits, and then fed the larvae with mulberry leaves. Bukhara 1, Nurmurod H., b. 1921, explained that there was a time when his kolkhoz paid wages for sericulture, it was collectivized, but then it again became private, based on a contract.

75. For comparison, see Tessa Morris-Suzuki, "Sericulture and the Origins of Japanese Industrialization," *Technology and Culture* 1 (1992): 101–121. For a Chinese comparison in Wuxi, where household-based sericulture was a lucrative addition to household income from the 1870s through the 1920s, see Li Zhang, "Net Per Capita Income in Rural Wuxi, 1840s–1940s," *Journal of the Economic and Social History of the Orient* 3 (2014): 291–325. Shakers in nineteenth-century South Union, Kentucky, raised silkworms in larger silk houses with women members of the commune collectively providing the labor to feed them. Jonathan Jeffrey and Donna Parker, "A Thread of Evidence: Textiles at South Union, Kentucky," *Register of the Kentucky Historical Society* 94, no. 1 (1996): 33–58.

76. Tashkent 11, Abduqayum P., b. 1916, G'azalkent.

77. Tashkent 24, Ashurboy P., b. 1923, Hojakent.

78. Tashkent 8, Qimmat T., birth year unknown, but her granddaughter estimated that she was more than one hundred years old at the time of the interview in 2003.

79. V. O. Aratov, "Arendnye Otnosheniia v shelkovodstve," *Za Rekonstrukstiiu Shelkovodstva* 1–2 (1931): 100–107.

80. Qashqa Daryo 10, Yorbobo N., b. 1922, Kitob.

81. Marianne Kamp, "Gender Ideals and Income Realities: Discourses about Labor and Gender in Uzbekistan," *Nationalities Papers* 33 (2005): 403–422.

82. Anna Green, "Can Memory Be Collective?," in *The Oxford Handbook of Oral History*, ed. Donald Ritchie (Oxford: Oxford University Press, 2011), 103, 106.

83. Central Asians who were captured by Germany in World War II and who defected to the German side, joining the Turkestan Legion, had many reasons to make sense of their own past by remembering those elements of life under the Soviets that would justify their action—their treason. Interviewers for the Harvard Project on the Soviet Social System, like ours, were expecting to hear very negative accounts of life in the USSR from Central Asians (and all others whom they interviewed), and they subjected rosy accounts to skepticism.

8. ORPHANS

1. Mehmet Volkan Kaşikçi, "Growing Up Soviet in the Periphery: Imagining, Experiencing, and Remembering Childhood in Kazakhstan, 1928–1953" (PhD diss., University of Arizona, 2020), 28.

2. This chapter includes some sections from a previously published chapter: Marianne Kamp, "Kinship and Orphans: Rural Uzbeks and Loss of Parents in the 1920s and 1930s," in *The Family in Central Asia: New Perspectives*, ed. Sophie Roche (Berlin: KSV, 2017), 242–269.

3. Based on incomplete data, forty-four had lost their father. We did not ask, "Were you orphaned?" And some interviewees may not have known or may not have mentioned it.

4. In many premodern European societies, up to 40 percent of all children lost at least one parent before they reached the age that their society recognized as adulthood. See, for example, David Vassburg, "Orphans and Adoption in Early Modern Castilian Villages," *History of the Family* 3, no. 4 (1998): 441–458.

5. Qashqa Daryo 7, Qurbon A., b. 1908; Namangan 9, Abdurashid, b. 1905; Namangan 2, Hayitboy, b. 1910; Fergana 4, Musaxon, b. 1910.

6. Alan Ball, *And Now My Soul Is Hardened: Abandoned Children in Soviet Russia, 1918-1980* (Berkeley: University of California Press, 1994); Laurie Bernstein, "The Evolution of Soviet Adoption Law," *Journal of Family History* 22, no. 2 (1997): 204-226.

7. Scholarship on orphanhood, worldwide, is abundant, but oral history research is rare. In an oral history study of orphanhood from the perspective of the orphan rather than the institution, Alain Bideau, Guy Brunet, and Fabrice Foroni traced the fates of a cohort of orphans and half orphans who were born between 1901 and 1925 and orphaned by age ten in France, where adoption was illegal until 1923. Alain Bideau, Guy Brunet, and Fabrice Foroni, "Orphans and Their Family Histories," *History of the Family* 5, no. 3 (2000): 315-325, esp. 322-324.

8. Ball, *Now My Soul*.

9. Bernstein, "Evolution of Soviet Adoption."

10. Wendy Z. Goldman, *Women, the State, and Revolution: Soviet Family Policy and Social Life, 1917-1936* (Cambridge: Cambridge University Press, 1993).

11. Andrew Stone, "Growing Up Soviet? The Orphans of Stalin's Revolution and Understanding the Soviet Self" (PhD diss., University of Washington, 2012).

12. Kaşikçi, "Growing Up Soviet."

13. Zuhra Kasimova, "Uzbek Wartime Adoptions on Display: Multinational in Form, Socialist in Content?," presentation at the Inner Asian and Uralic National Resource Center, Indiana University, Bloomington, February 2020, part of her dissertation. Other discussions of wartime orphans in Uzbekistan are found in Roberta Manley, *To the Tashkent Station: Evacuation and Survival in the Soviet Union at War* (Ithaca, NY: Cornell University Press, 2009); and Stronski, *Tashkent*. During World War II, Uzbekistan became known across the USSR as a refuge for Soviet citizens displaced by war, and many Uzbek families took in war orphans. Accounts were widely publicized, through the Soviet Uzbek poet G'ofur G'ulom's wartime poem "Sen yetim emassan" (You are not an orphan) and newspaper articles featuring Uzbek families who took in orphans; through a 1963 film about one of those families; and through a sculpture in a central Tashkent square.

14. In many societies, any child whose father died is considered an orphan, even if the mother remains alive as a widow.

15. Kamp, "Kinship and Orphans."

16. Qashqa Daryo 12, Bekmurod Sh., b. 1907. He uses the phrase *tuzuk odam*, an expression that can mean a person who is whole, sound, healthy, upright.

17. Qashqa Daryo 12, Bekmurod Sh., b. 1907.

18. Namangan 2, Abdurashid, b. 1910. Flora Roberts writes of teachers in Khujand, Turkistan ASSR, who "picked up half-dead orphans" to enroll them in the Behbudi boarding school in 1918. Flora Roberts, "Old Elites under Communism: Soviet Rule in Leninobod" (PhD diss., University of Chicago, 2016), 91.

19. Xorazm 4, Boltaboy, b. 1914. Other examples: Qurbon B. (b. 1906), who explained the difference between g'oza and paxta (chapter 2), told of working with his father as a mardikor but running away to a school in Bukhara and becoming a teacher. Bozorxo'ja (b. 1913) worked with his father and brothers in the gates of the rich before entering those same rich men's homes to make them into quloqs (chapter 6).

20. Fergana 16, O'g'ilxon M., b. 1914. Her name means "honored son," indicating her parents' wish for a son. Fergana 6, Halimaxon M., b. 1911; Tashkent 17, Aziza I., b. 1914.

21. Data from 1938 shows that 82 percent of students in Uzbekistan's primary schools studied in Uzbek, 7.6 percent in Russian, and 5.3 percent in Tajik. *Kul'turnoe stroitel'stvo SSSR Statisticheskii Sbornik*, table 2, schools and participants; table 24, End Illiteracy; table 15, language of instruction. Education for grades five to seven expanded more slowly

to rural Uzbekistan, and by the late 1930s, middle schools with grades eight to ten were available only in cities and regional centers. Russian-language education was more prevalent for grades eight to ten. Data from New Urganch, Xorazm, 1931, showed that all of the 6,903 adults enrolled in End Illiteracy—15 to 20 percent of the population of that district—were Uzbeks. O'zRMDA, f. R-86, op. 1, d. 6795, ll. 145–146, Narodnoe Obrazovanie, Novyi Urchench 1931.

22. Bukhara 20, Xoji A., b. 1920, Shofirkon District.
23. Qashqa Daryo 19, Narzi A., b. 1921.
24. Buxoro 12, Ubaydullo M., b. 1922.
25. Qashqa Daryo 4, O'ktam A., b. 1919 or sometime in the early 1920s.
26. Qashqa Daryo 5, Oqquzi B., b. around 1920. His passport said 1916; his other documentation said 1922, and his narrative comments to being age twelve in about 1931 or 1932 would have him born in 1919 or 1920.
27. Qashqa Daryo 9, Rajab X., b. 1917.
28. Five others who were orphaned told of being conscripted in 1939 for the Finland War; this was not an experience mentioned by any nonorphans. Rajab said that he was in action in Finland only for a few days, and then in 1940, "We invaded Latvia." Tashkent 9, Xudoybergan R., b. 1922, G'azalkent, was ethnically Kazakh, and his district belonged to Kazakhstan until the 1950s. In 1939, he said, "We established the Kazakh National Cavalier division in Jambul." Others included Bukhara 8, Ravshan H., b. 1920; Tashkent 10, Xalil A., b. 1917; Namangan 7, Ismoyiljon N., b. 1923; and Fergana 13, Ganijon M., b. 1920.
29. Bukhara 13, G'aybullo S., b. 1920. G'aybullo identified himself as Tajik, and his interview was in Tajik. Although we asked questions about different ethnic groups living in a respondent's community or kolkhoz, we did not raise questions about discrimination. Neither he nor other Tajik speakers spoke of being Tajik as a disadvantage in the Uzbek republic.
30. Fergana 14, Qumriniso R., b. 1920. Qumriniso said her husband went to war, but she did not mention whether he returned.
31. Namangan 7, Ismoyiljon N., b. 1923.
32. Stone, "Growing Up Soviet?"
33. Qashqa Daryo 2, Abdurasul E., b. 1922. Many of the orphaned respondents mentioned maternal uncles as their providers.
34. Namangan 1, Tursunoy S., b. 1924, second respondent in Namangan 1 interview.
35. Xorazm 11, Roviya, b. 1922.
36. Qashqa Daryo 1, Ernazar S., b. 1923.
37. Andrew Stone, drawing on memoirs from children of the Gulag and others raised in Soviet children's homes in the 1930s, notes that those who composed their autobiographies often wanted to "restore the 'good name' of their parents through their memoir." Stone, "Growing Up Soviet?," 343.
38. Xorazm 7, Madrim A., b. 1919.
39. *Do'ppi*, an embroidered skullcap. Abdullo was describing the look that male Uzbek nationalist intellectuals, like the playwright Hamza, wore in the 1920s, combining stylish versions of dehqon clothing with an urban/military preference for mustaches.
40. Qashqa Daryo 18, Abdullo F., b. 1919.
41. Bukhara 8, Ravshan H., b. 1920.
42. Fergana 13, Ganijon M., b. 1920.
43. Xorazm 9, Zulayxo A., b. 1916.
44. Xorazm 17, Olmajon X, b. 1903.

CONCLUSION: A GENERATION, A TIME, AND REMEMBERING

1. Alisher Ilkhamov discusses the first steps in decollectivization in the 1990s. Alisher Ilkhamov, "Shirkats, Dehqon Farmers, and Others: Farm Restructuring in Uzbekistan," *Central Asian Survey* 12, no. 1 (1998): 539–560. Tommaso Trevisani explores changes in land tenure of the early 2000s and their socioeconomic implications in Xorazm Province. Tommaso Trevisani, *Land and Power in Khorezm: Farmers, Communities, and the State in Uzbekistan's Decollectivisation*, Halle Studies in Anthropology of Eurasia vol. 23 (Berlin: Lit Verlag Dr. W. Hopf, 2008). Russell Zanca portrays the collapse of collective farming in the 1990s. Russell Zanca, *Life in a Muslim Uzbek Village: Cotton Farming after Communism* (Belmont, CA: Wadsworth, 2010). On rural social stratification, see Zulfiya Tursunova, *Women's Lives and Livelihoods in Post-Soviet Uzbekistan: Ceremonies of Empowerment and Peace-Building* (Lanham, MD: Lexington, 2014).

2. Gail Kligman and Katherine Verdery, *Peasants under Siege: The Collectivization of Romanian Agriculture, 1949–1962* (Princeton, NJ: Princeton University Press, 2011).

3. Wim van Meurs, "Land Reform in Romania—a Never-Ending Story," *South-East Europe Review* 2 (1999): 117–121.

4. Liviu Chelcea, "'Here in Reviga, There Was Nobody to Wage the Class Struggle': Collectivization in Reviga, Baragan Plain (Bucharest Region)," in *Transforming Peasants, Property, and Power: The Collectivization of Agriculture in Romania, 1949–1962*, ed. Constantin Iordachi and Dorin Dobrincu (Budapest: Central European University, 2009), 400. Cited by Kligman and Verdery, who note that they did not find a similar trend among other interviews in the project. Kligman and Verdery, *Peasants under Siege*, 31.

5. This anticolonial version of history provides the thematic emphasis for Uzbekistan's Museum of Victims of Political Repression (Qatag'on Qurbonlari Xotirasi Muzeyi) in Tashkent.

6. Serguei Oushakine, "'We're Nostalgic but We're Not Crazy': Retrofitting the Past in Russia," *Russian Review* 66, no. 3 (2007): 452.

7. Kamp, "Three Lives."

8. The Central Asia Bureau was closed in 1934. Shoshana Keller, "The Central Asian Bureau, an Essential Tool in Governing Soviet Turkestan," *Central Asian Survey* 22, nos. 2–3 (2003): 281–297, 293. My impression of thinning folders comes from my 2003 research in the Central Asia Bureau collections held at RGASPI.

9. Edgar, *Intermarriage*, 7.

10. Tashkent 15, Xusenboy A., b 1919, chap. 3; Xusenboy was explaining why he calls himself Uzbek and his wife Tajik.

11. Xorazm 17, Olmajon X., b. 1903, chap. 8; she was discussing her unusual marriage to a younger man and his death.

12. Rizaev notes that in 1933 an average household earned 330 labor-days working on a kolkhoz, a tally that rose to 490 labor-days in 1937. Rizaev, *Sotsialisticheskoe sel'skoe khoziaistvo Uzbekistana*, 84–85, citing party archive documents. As explained earlier, a labor-day was a rate of pay, not a measure of time, and certain tasks that might have actually taken a day could earn two labor-days, while others might earn only half a labor-day. This makes it impossible to calculate the average time that a typical household's work-capable adults and youths put into the kolkhoz, but whatever that was in 1933, it rose by 1937.

13. Kirill Nourzhanov discusses the same process of reassessment in Tajikistan. Kirill Nourzhanov, "Bandits, Warlords, National Heroes: Interpretations of the Basmachi Movement in Tajikistan," *Central Asian Survey* 34, no. 2 (2015): 177–189.

14. Bukhara 15, Avez, b. 1920; Fergana 5, Ahmed T., b. 1920. Recollections of other community members, especially mullahs, moving to Tajikistan were rife in our interviews, and they correspond to the period when building and resettlement projects in Tajikistan

were actively seeking recruits, paying dehqons to move, and providing them with individual plots of land as inducements. Peterson, *Pipe Dreams*, 302–305.

15. Cameron, *Hungry Steppe*, 96.

16. Qashqa Daryo 7, Qurbon A., b. 1908; Fergana 20, Sharofutdin Q., b. 1911.

17. Shamsutdinov, *Qishloq fojeasi*; Thomas Loy, *Bukharan Jews in the 20th Century: History, Experience, and Narration* (Wiesbaden: Reichert Verlag, 2008); Widener Library, Harvard Project on the Soviet Social System.

18. Qashqa Daryo 1, Ernazar A., b. 1923.

19. Tashkent 16, Abduqodir P., b. 1916.

20. For Uzbekistan, the most significant works on this topic are by Rustambek Shamsutdinov. These are far too extensive to discuss, but two particularly striking accounts in English that are of interest to Central Asia scholars are Mukhamet Shayakhmetov's memoir of dekulakization and famine, *The Silent Steppe: The Memoir of a Kazakh Nomad under Stalin*, trans. Jan Butler (New York: Overlook/Rookery, 2007); and Guzel Yakhina's novel, *Zuleikha*, trans. Lisa Hayden (London: Oneworld, 2019), about dekulakization in a Tatar community and reconstructing life in exile.

21. Tashkent 1, Bozorxo'ja, b. 1913.

22. Nora, *Realms of Memory*.

23. Abashin, *Sovetskii Kishlak*; Qashqa Daryo 12, Bekmurod, b. 1907.

24. Tashkent 1, Bozorxo'ja, b. 1913; Namangan 12, Turdiboy, b. 1921.

25. Kamp, "Where Did the Mullahs Go?"

26. Assmann, *Shadows of Trauma*, 13.

27. Assman, 14, 15.

28. Lev Kopelev, *The Education of a True Believer* (New York: Harper Collins 1980).

Bibliography

ARCHIVES

O'zRMDA (O'zbeikiston Republikasi Markazii Davlat Arxivi), the Central State Archive of the Republic of Uzbekistan, Tashkent

RGASPI (Rossiiskii Gosudarstvennyi Arkhiv Sostial'no-Politicheskii Istorii), the Russian Governmental Archive of Socio-political History, formerly the Communist Party Archive, Moscow

NEWSPAPERS, JOURNALS, MAGAZINES, AND ONLINE COLLECTIONS

Bulletin Tsentral'noi Statisticheskoi Upravlenii Uz SSR

Demoskop Weekly, reproduces much of the information from the Soviet population censuses; https://www.demoscope.ru/weekly/2024/01017/index.php

Harvard Project on the Soviet Social System, last reviewed March 31, 2021, Widener Library Harvard University. https://library.harvard.edu/sites/default/files/static/collections/hpsss/index.html.

Istroicheskie Materialy, provides a large collection of statistical and political archival documents and Soviet era publications; https://www.istmat.org/ (formerly istmat.info)

Narodnoe Khoziaistvo Srednei Azii

Qizil O'zbekiston

Srednei Aziatskii Shelk

Xotira.uz [Memory.uz], Doim Yodimizdasiz Doim Minnatdormiz [We remember eternally, we are eternally grateful]; Uzbekistan official site for World War II–related memoirs

Yangi Yo'l pdfs and Marianne Kamp translations available on Social Movements in Modern Empires since 1820, https://alexanderstreet.com/products/women-and-social-movements-modern-empires-1820

Yer Yuzi

BIBLIOGRAPHY

Abashin, Sergei. *Natsionalizmy v Srednei Azii, v poiskakh identichnosti*. Saint Petersburg: Alettiia, 2007.

Abashin, Sergei. "Sem' kratkikh tezisov o 'basmachestve.'" Central Asian Analytical Network, April 17, 2020. https://www.caa-network.org/archives/19045.

Abashin, Sergei. *Sovetskii Kishlak: Mezhdu kolonializmom i modernizatsii*. Moscow: Novoe Literaturnoe Obozrenie, 2015.

Abdullaev, Kamolludin. *Ot sintsiana do khorasana: Iz istorii sredneaziatskoi emigratsii 20 veka*. Dushanbe: Irfon, 2009.

Abdullaev, R., and S. S. Agzamkhodzhaev (Ag'zamxo'jaev). *Turkestan v nachale XX veka: K istorii istokov natsional'noi nezavisimosti*. Tashkent: Shark, 2000.

Agzamkhodzhaev, Saidakbar. *Istoriia Turkestanskoi Avtonomii (Turkiston Muxtoriyati)*. Tashkent: Toshkent Islom Universiteti, 2006.

Akhunova, M.A. editor, *Uzbekskoi SSR v gody velikoi otetchestvennoi voiny (1941-1945)*, Vol. 1. Tashkent: Fan, 1981.

Alieva, R. R. "Iz istorii obrazovaniia russkikh posolkov v khodzhentskom uezde." *Nomai Donishgoh* 3, no. 52 (2017): 15–22.
Amanjolova, D. "Nekotorye problemy izucheniia istorii vosstaniia 1916 g. v Srednei Azii." *Rossiiskaia Istoriia* 1 (2017): 125–138.
Aminova, R. Kh. *Agrarnaia politika Sovetskoi valsti v Uzbekistane (1917–1920 gg)*. Tashkent: Izdatel'stvo Akademii Nauk, 1963.
Aminova, R. Kh. *Agrarnaia preobrazovaniia v Uzbekistane nakanune sploshnoi kollektivizatsii, 1925–1929*. Tashkent: Fan, 1969.
Aminova, R. Kh. *Agrarnaia preobrazovaniia v Uzbekistane v gody perekhoda Sovetskogo gosudarstvo k NEPu*. Tashkent: Fan, 1965.
Aminova, R. Kh. "Agrarnye preobrazovaniia v Uzbekistane 20x godov." *Obshchestvennye Nauki v Uzbekistane* 9 (1989): 32–39.
Aminova, R. Kh. *Osushchestvleniie kollektivizatsii v Uzbekistane (1929–1932)*. Tashkent: Fan, 1977.
Aminova, R. Kh. *Vozvrashchaias' k istorii kollektivizatsii v Uzbekistane*. Tashkent: Fan, 1995.
Aminova, R. Kh., ed. *Organazatsionno-khoziaistvennoe ukreplenie kolkhozov Uzbekistana (1933–1940). Sbornik dokumentov*. Tashkent: Uzbekistan, 1983.
Aminova, R. Kh. et al. *Istoriia Uzbekskoi SSR*. Vol 2. Tashkent: Tarix va arxeologiya instituti, 1967–1968.
Anderson, Benedict. *Imagined Communities: Reflections on the Origin and Spread of Nationalism*. Rev. ed. London: Verso, 2006.
Applebaum, Anne. *Red Famine: Stalin's War on Ukraine*. London: Allen Lane, 2017.
Aratov, V. O. "Arendnye Otnosheniia v shelkovodstve." *Za Rekonstrukstiiu Shelkovodstva* 1–2 (1931): 100–107.
Assmann, Aleida. *Shadows of Trauma: Memory and the Politics of Postwar Identity*. New York: Fordham University Press, 2016.
Assmann, Aleida. "Transformations between History and Memory." *Social Research* 75, no. 1 (2008): 49–72.
Ataylı, Enver. *A Dark Path to Freedom: Ruzi Nazar from the Red Army to the CIA*. Oxford: Oxford University Press, 2017.
Atlas Soiuza Sovetskikh Sotsialisticheskikh Respublik. Moscow: Izdaniie TsIK SSSR, 1928.
Babadjanov, Bakhtyar. "The Economic and Religious History of Kolkhoz Village: Khojawot from Soviet Modernization to the Aftermath of the Islamic Revival." In *Allah's Kolkhozes: Migration, De-Stalinisation, Privatization, and the New Muslim Congregations in the Soviet Realm (1950s–2000s)*, edited by Stephane Dudoignon and Christian Noack, 203–264 Berlin: Klaus Schwarz Verlag, 2014.
Babajanov, Bakhtiyar, and Sharifjon Islamov. "Shari'a for the Bolsheviks? Fatvas on Land Reform in Early Soviet Central Asia." In *Islam, Society, and States across the Qazaq Steppe (18th–Early 20th Centuries)*, edited by Niccoló Pianciola and Paolo Sartori, 233–266. Vienna: Verlag der Österreichischen Akademie der Wissenschaften, 2013.
Bargan, Sofia. "'Traktoristi': Traktor i tank—brat'ia-bliznetsi." Nashfilm.ru, accessed Sept 6, 2011, http://www.nashfilm.ru/sovietkino/4346.html.
Ball, Alan. *And Now My Soul Is Hardened: Abandoned Children in Soviet Russia, 1918–1980*. Berkeley: University of California Press, 1994.
Bartol'd, V. V. "Khlopkovodstvo v Srednei Azii." In V. V. Barto'ld, *Sochinenie* Tom II, Chast' 2, 437–448. Moscow: Isdatel'stvo Nauka, 1964; originally published in 1925.
Bazarbaev, Akmal, and Chloé Drieu. "The 1916 Uprisings in Jizzakh: Economic Background and Political Rationales." In *The Central Asian Revolt of 1916: A Collapsing Empire in the Age of War and Revolution*, edited by Aminat Chokobaeva, Chloé

Drieu, and Alexander Morrison, 71–94. Manchester: Manchester University Press, 2020.
Becker, Seymour. *Russia's Protectorates in Central Asia: Bukhara and Khiva, 1865–1924*. Cambridge, MA: Harvard University Press, 1968.
Beckert, Sven. "Emancipation and Empire: Reconstructing the Worldwide Web of Cotton Production in the Age of the American Civil War." *American Historical Review* 109, no. 5 (2004): 1404–1438.
Beckert, Sven. *Empire of Cotton: A Global History*. New York: Vintage, 2014.
Bekotserkovskaia, K. T. "O chastnom grenazhe v Srednei Azii." *Srednei Aziiatskii Shelk* 4–6 (1929): 124–127.
Belk, Fred. *The Great Trek of Russian Mennonites to Central Asia, 1880–1884*. Scottsdale, AZ: Herald, 1976.
Bernstein, Laurie. "The Evolution of Soviet Adoption Law." *Journal of Family History* 22, no. 2 (1997): 204–226.
Bernstein, Seth. *Raised under Stalin: Young Communists and the Defense of Socialism*. Ithaca, NY: Cornell University Press, 2017.
Bideau, Alain, Guy Brunet, and Fabrice Foroni. "Orphans and Their Family Histories." *History of the Family* 5, no. 3 (2000): 315–325.
Bliakher, L. E., and I. F. Yarulin. "Kto takie basmachi? Sovetskoe mifotvorchestvo i stigmitizatsiia grazhdanskoi voiny v Srednei Azii." *Politiia* 2, no. 81 (2016): 109–123.
Boele, Otto, Boris Noordenbos, and Ksenia Robbe. "Introduction: The Many Practices of Post-Soviet Nostalgia: Affect, Appropriation, Contestation." In *Post-Soviet Nostalgia: Confronting the Empire's Legacies*, edited by Otto Boele, Boris Noordenbos, and Ksenia Robbe, 1–18. Milton Park, UK: Taylor & Francis, 2019.
Boele, Otto, Boris Noordenbos, and Ksenia Robbe, eds. *Post-Soviet Nostalgia: Confronting the Empire's Legacies*. Milton Park, UK: Taylor & Francis, 2019.
Brite, Elizabeth B., and John M. Marston. "Environmental Change, Agricultural Innovation, and the Spread of Cotton Agriculture in the Old World." *Journal of Anthropological Archaeology* 32 (2013): 39–53.
Brophy, David. *Uyghur Nation: Revolution and Reform on the China-Russia Frontier*. Cambridge, MA: Harvard University Press, 2016.
Brower, Daniel R. *Turkestan and the Fate of the Russian Empire*. London: Routledge, 2003.
Buckley, Mary. *Mobilizing Soviet Peasants: Heroines and Heroes of Stalin's Fields*. Rowman and Littlefield, 2006.
Bulliet, Richard W. *Cotton, Climate, and Camels in Early Islamic Iran*. New York: Columbia University Press, 2009.
Busakov. S. M. "The Problems of Potato Breeding." *American Potato Journal* 13, no. 9 (1939): 235–252.
Buttino, Marco. "Central Asia 1916–1920: A Kaleidoscope of Local Revolutions and the Building of the Bolshevik Order." In *The Empire and Nationalism at War*, edited by Eric Lohr, Vera Tolz, and Alexander Semyonov, 109–135. Bloomington, IN: Slavica, 2014.
Buttino, Marco. "Economic Crisis and Depopulation in Turkestan, 1917–1920." *Central Asian Survey* 9, no. 4 (1990): 59–74.
Cameron, Sarah. *The Hungry Steppe: Famine, Violence, and the Making of Soviet Kazakhstan*. Ithaca, NY: Cornell University Press, 2018.
Cameron, Sarah. "The Kazakh Famine of 1930–1933: Current Research and New Directions." *East/West: Journal of Ukrainian Studies* 3, no. 2 (2016): 117–132.
Campbell, Ian. *Knowledge and the Ends of Empire: Kazak Intermediaries and Russian Rule on the Steppe, 1731–1917*. Ithaca, NY: Cornell University Press, 2017.

Campbell, Sue, Christine Koggel, and Rodney Jacobsen. *Our Faithfulness to the Past: The Ethics and Politics of Memory*. Oxford: Oxford University Press, 2014.
Carmack, Roberto. *Kazakhstan in World War II: Mobilization and Ethnicity in the Soviet Empire*. Lawrence: University of Kansas Press, 2019.
Caroe, Olaf. *Soviet Empire: The Turks of Central Asia and Stalinism*. 2nd ed. London: St. Martin's, 1967.
Carrère d'Encausse, Hélène. *Islam and the Russian Empire: Reform and Revolution in Central Asia*. London: Tauris, 1988.
Chelcea, Liviu. "'Here in Reviga, There Was Nobody to Wage the Class Struggle': Collectivization in Reviga, Baragan Plain (Bucharest Region)." In *Transforming Peasants, Property, and Power: The Collectivization of Agriculture in Romania, 1949–1962*, edited by Constantin Iordachi and Dorin Dobrincu, 399–422. Budapest: Central European University, 2009.
Chokobaeva, Aminat, Chloé Drieu, and Alexander Morrison, eds. *The Central Asian Revolt of 1916: A Collapsing Empire in the Age of War and Revolution*. Manchester, UK: Manchester University Press, 2020.
Clark, Katerina. *The Soviet Novel: History as Ritual*. 1st ed. Chicago: University of Chicago Press, 1981.
Collins, Kathleen. *Clan Politics and Regime Transition in Central Asia*. Cambridge: Cambridge University Press, 2006.
Crane, Stephen L. *Survivor from an Unknown War*. Greenwich, CT: Diane Books, 1999.
Dadabaev, A. D. editor, *Uzbekskii Khlopok*. Tashkent: Uzbekistan, 1973.Dadabaev, Timur. *Identity and Memory in Post-Soviet Central Asia: Uzbekistan's Soviet Past*. Abingdon, UK: Routledge, 2016.
Dadabaev, Timur. "Power, Social Life, and Public Memory in Uzbekistan and Kyrgyzstan." *Inner Asia* 12 (2010): 25–48.
Dadabaev, Timur, and Hisao Komatsu, eds. *Kazakhstan, Kyrgyzstan, and Uzbekistan: Life and Politics during the Soviet Era*. London: Palgrave Macmillan, 2017.
Dale, Stephen F. "Silk Road, Cotton Road, or . . . Indo-Chinese Trade in Pre-European Times." *Modern Asian Studies* 43, no. 1 (2009): 79–88.
Dalrymple, Dana, "American Technology and Soviet Agricultural Development, 1924–1933." *Agricultural History* 40, no. 3 (1966): 187–206.
Danilov, V. P., ed. *Ocherki istorii kollektivizatsii sel'skogo khoziaistva v soiuznikh respublikakh: sbornik statei*. Moscow: Gospolizdat, 1963.
Danilov, Viktor P. et al., eds. *Tragediia sovetskoi derevni: kollektivizatsiia i raskulachivanie: dokumenty i materialy v 5 tomov 1927–1939*. Moscow: Rossiiskaia Polit. Entsiklopediia, 1999–2006.
Davies, Robert W. *The Socialist Offensive: The Collectivization of Soviet Agriculture 1929–1930*. London: Macmillan, 1980.
Davis, Kathy. "Intersectionality as Buzzword: A Sociology of Science Perspective on What Makes a Feminist Theory Successful." *Feminist Theory* 9, no. 1 (2008): 67–85.
Draskoczy, Julie. *Belomor Criminality and Creativity in Stalin's Gulag*. Brighton, MA: Academic Studies, 2014.
Dudoignon, Stéphane, and Christian Noack, eds. *Allah's Kolkhozes: Migration, De-Stalinisation, Privatization, and the New Muslim Congregations in the Soviet Realm (1950s–2000s)*. Berlin: Klaus Schwarz Verlag, 2015.
Edgar, Adrienne. *Intermarriage and the Friendship of Peoples: Ethnic Mixing in Soviet Central Asia*. Ithaca, NY: Cornell University Press, 2022.
Edgar, Adrienne. *Tribal Nation: The Making of Soviet Turkmenistan*. Princeton, NJ: Princeton University Press, 2006.

Ercilsun, Guljanat K. "Famine in Kyrgyzstan in the 1930s and 1940s." In *Kazakhstan, Kyrgyzstan, and Uzbekistan: Life and Politics during the Soviet Era*, edited by T. Dadabaev, 34–52. London: Palgrave, 2016.

Erley, Mieka. "'The Dialectics of Nature in Karakum': Andrei Platonov's *Dzhan* as the Environmental History of a Future Utopia." *Slavic Review* 73, no. 4 (2014): 727–750.

Fat'ianov, I. A. "K novym tempam v shelkovostve v Srednei Azii." *Sredneai Aziiatskii Shelk* 7–9 (1929): v–ix.

Fedotov, A. I. *Tekstil'naia promyshlennost' SSSR*. Moscow: Tentral'noe Upravlenie Pechati VSNKh SSSR, 1926.

Ferree, Myra Marx. "Inequality, Intersectionality, and the Politics of Discourse: Framing Feminist Alliances." In *The Discursive Politics of Gender Equality: Stretching, Bending, and Policy-Making*, edited by E. Lombardo, P. Meier, and Mieke Verloo, 86–104. London: Routledge, 2009.

Fierman, William, ed. *Soviet Central Asia: The Failed Transformation*. Boulder, CO: Westview 1991.

Filatova, Maria, and Vladimir Bobrovnikov, comps. *Plakat Sovetskogo Vostoka 1918–1940: al'bom-katalog*. Moscow: Izdatel'stvo Dom Mardzhani, 2011.

Filimoshin, M. V. "Liudskie poteri vooruzhennykh sil SSSR." *Mir Rossii* 4 (1999): 92–101.

Finke, Peter. *Variations on Uzbek Identity: Strategic Choices, Cognitive Schemas, and Political Constraints in Identification Processes*. Integration and Conflict Studies, vol. 7. New York: Berghahn Books, 2014.

Fitzpatrick, Sheila. "The Bolshevik Invention of Class: Marxist Theory and the Making of 'Class Consciousness' in Soviet Society." In *The Structure of Soviet History: Essays and Documents*, edited by Ronald Suny, 172–186. Oxford: Oxford University Press, 2014.

Fitzpatrick, Sheila. "On the Question of Social Support for Collectivization." *Russian History* 37 (2010): 153–177.

Fitzpatrick, Sheila. *Stalin's Peasants: Resistance and Survival in the Russian Village after Collectivization*. Oxford: Oxford University Press, 1994.

Florin, Moritz. "Becoming Kyrgyz through War: The Kyrgyz and the Great Fatherland War." *Kritika: Explorations in Russian and Eurasian History* 17, no. 3 (2016): 495–516.

Frye, Richard N., trans. *The History of Bukhara*. Translated from a Persian abridgement of the Arabic original by Narshakhi. Cambridge, MA: Mediaeval Academy of America, 1954.

Gal'tsin, M. A. *Istoki kolkhoznoi posedevnosti (na materialakh iug Rossii 1930-x godov)*. Novocherkassk: LIK, 2018.

Gavrilov, Mikhail, trans. and ed. *Risolia sartovskikh' remeslennikov': izsledovanie predanii musulmanskikh tsekhov'*. Tashkent: Tipografiia pri kantseliarii generalgubernatora, 1912, 54–57.

Goff, Krista. *Nested Nationalism: Making and Unmaking Nations in the Soviet Caucasus*. Ithaca, NY: Cornell University Press, 2021.

Goldman, Wendy Z. *Women, the State, and Revolution: Soviet Family Policy and Social Life, 1917–1936*. Cambridge: Cambridge University Press, 1993.

Graziosi, Andrea. *Stalinism, Collectivization, and the Great Famine*. Cambridge, MA: Ukrainian Studies Fund, Holodomor Series, 2009.

Green, Anna. "Can Memory Be Collective?" In *The Oxford Handbook of Oral History*, edited by Donald Ritchie, 96–111. Oxford: Oxford University Press, 2011.

Greenstein, David E. "Assembling Fordizm: The Production of Automobiles, Americans, and Bolsheviks in Detroit and Early Soviet Russia." *Comparative Studies in Society and History* 56, no. 2 (2014): 259–289.

Grossman, Vasily. *A Writer at War: Vasily Grossman with the Red Army 1941–1945*. Edited and translated by Antony Beevor and Luba Vinogradova. New York: Pantheon, 2006.
Gundogdyev, Ovez A. *Boevoi put' tekinskogo konnogo polka (1914–1918)*. Ashkhabad: Turkmenskaia gos. izdat. Sluzhba, 2012.
Halbwachs, Maurice. *Notes on Collective Memory*. Translated, edited, and introduced by Lewis Coser. Chicago: University of Chicago Press, 1992.
Haraway, Donna. "Situated Knowledges: The Science Question in Feminism and the Privilege of Partial Perspectives." *Feminist Studies* 14, no. 3 (1988): 575–599.
Hayit, Baymirza. *Basmatchi: Nationaler Kampf Turkestans in den Jahren 1917 bis 1934*. Cologne: Dreisem Verlag, 1992.
Hayit, Baymirza. *Turkestan im XX Jahrhundert*. Darmstadt: Leske, 1956.
Hekman, Susan. "Truth and Method: Feminist Standpoint Theory Revisited." *Signs: Journal of Women in Culture and Society* 22, no. 2 (1997): 341–365.
Hirsch, Francine. *Empire of Nations: Ethnographic Knowledge and the Making of the Soviet Union*. Ithaca, NY: Cornell University Press, 2005.
Hoshimov, O'tkir. *"Non—Iymon,"* in *Toshkent Haqiqati*, July 1, 1983 . . .
Hughes, James. *Stalinism in a Russian Province: A Study of Collectivization and Dekulakization in Siberia*. London: Palgrave MacMillan 1996.
Ilkhamov, Alisher. "Shirkats, Dehqon Farmers, and Others: Farm Restructuring in Uzbekistan." *Central Asian Survey* 12, no. 1 (1998): 539–560.
Ismailbekova, Aksana. "From Endogamous Marriage to Ethnicity: Uzbek Community Survival Strategy after the 2010 Conflict in Osh." *Anthropology and Archeology of Eurasia* 58, no. 3 (2019):134–154.
Itkich, A. "Khlopkovodcheskie kooperatsiia Uzbekistana i ee perspektivy." *Narodnoe Khoziaistvo Srednei Azii* 1 (1929): 95–118.
Itogi vsesoiuznoi perepisi naseleni 1959 goda Uzbekskaia SSR. Moscow: Gosizdat, 1962. Reprint, Nendeln: Kraus Reprint, 1975.
Iuferev. V. I. *Khlopkovodstvo v Turkestane*. Leningrad: monografii izdavliaiut komissiei po izucheniiu estestvennykh proizvoditel'nykh sil SSR pri Rossiiskoi akademii nauk, 1925.
Iuldashev, A. M. *Agrarnye otnoshenia v Turkestane (konets XX–nachalo XIX vv)*. Tashkent: Uzbekistan, 1969.
Iuldashev, M. Iu. *K istorii krest'ian khivy XIX veka*. Tashkent: Fan, 1966.
Iunuskhodzhaeva, M. Iu. *Iz istorii zemlevladeniia v dorevoliutsionnom Turkestane (na materialakh khoziaistva kniazia N. K. Romanova)*. Tashkent: Fan, 1970.
Jeffrey, Jonathan, and Donna Parker. "A Thread of Evidence: Textiles at South Union, Kentucky." *Register of the Kentucky Historical Society* 94, no. 1 (1996): 33–58.
Joffe, Muriel. "Autocracy, Capitalism, and Empire: The Politics of Irrigation." *Russian Review* 54 (1995): 365–388.
Johansen, Baber. *The Islamic Law on Land Tax and Rent: The Peasants' Loss of Property Rights as Interpreted in the Hanafite Legal Literature of the Mamluk and Ottoman Periods*. London: Croom Helm, 1988.
Juraev, M. et al., eds. *O'zbekiston Soviet Mustamlakachiligi Davrida*. Vol. 2 of *O'zbekiston Yangi Tarixi*. Tashkent: Sharq, 2000.
Kaier, Christina, and Eric Naiman. *Everyday Life in Early Soviet Russia: Taking the Revolution Inside*. Bloomington: Indiana University Press, 2006.
Kalinovsky, Artemy. *Laboratory of Socialist Development: Cold War Politics and Decolonization in Soviet Tajikistan*. Ithaca, NY: Cornell University Press, 2018.
Kamp, Marianne. "Femicide as Terrorism: The Case of Uzbekistan's Unveiling Murders." In *Sexual Violence in Conflict Zones: From the Ancient World to the Era of Human*

Rights, edited by Elizabeth Heineman, 56–71. Philadelphia: University of Pennsylvania Press, 2011.

Kamp, Marianne, "Gender Ideals and Income Realities: Discourses about Labor and Gender in Uzbekistan." *Nationalities Papers* 33, no. 3 (2005): 403–422.

Kamp, Marianne. "Hunger and Potatoes: The 1933 Famine in Uzbekistan and Changing Foodways." *Kritika: Explorations in Russian and Eurasian History* 20, no. 2 (2019): 237–267.

Kamp, Marianne. "Kinship and Orphans: Rural Uzbeks and Loss of Parents in the 1920s and 1930s." In *The Family in Central Asia: New Perspectives*, edited by Sophie Roche, 242–269. Berlin: KSV, 2017.

Kamp, Marianne. *The New Woman in Uzbekistan: Islam, Modernity, and Unveiling under Communism*. Seattle: University of Washington Press, 2006.

Kamp, Marianne. "Three Lives of Saodat: Communist, Uzbek, Survivor." *Oral History Review* 28, no. 2 (2001): 21–58.

Kamp, Marianne. "Uzbek and Soviet on the Collective Farm." In *Erinnerungen nach der Wende: Oral History und (post)sozialistische Gesellschaften*, edited by Anke Stephan and Julia Obertreis, 233–242. Essen: Kalrtext Verlag, 2009.

Kamp, Marianne. "Where Did the Mullahs Go? Oral Histories from Rural Uzbekistan." *Die Welt des Islams* 50, nos. 3/4 (2010): 503–531.

Kamp, Marianne, ed., and Mariana Markova, trans. *Muslim Women of the Fergana Valley: A 19th Century Ethnography from Central Asia*. Bloomington: Indiana University Press, 2016.

Kamp, Marianne, and Russell Zanca, "Recollections of Collectivization in Uzbekistan: Stalinism and Local Activism." *Central Asian Survey* 36, no. 1 (2017): 55–72.

Karimov, Naim F., and Rustam T. Shamsutdinov, eds. *Repressia 1937–1938 gg. Dokumenty i materialy*. Vol. 4, *Zhertvy bol'shogo terrora iz Uzbekistana*. Tashkent: Sharq, 2008.

Kaşikçi, Mehmet Volkan. "Growing Up Soviet in the Periphery: Imagining, Experiencing, and Remembering Childhood in Kazakhstan, 1928–1953." PhD diss., University of Arizona, 2020.

Kasimova, Zukhra. "Hybridizing Sovietness: Modernity, Nationality, and Provinciality in Uzbekistan, 1941–1984." PhD diss., University of Illinois, Chicago, 2023.

Kasimova, Zukhra. "Uzbek Wartime Adoptions on Display: Multinational in Form, Socialist in Content?" Presentation at the Inner Asian and Uralic National Resource Center, Indiana University, Bloomington, February 2020.

Kassymbekova, Botakoz. *Despite Cultures: Early Soviet Rule in Tajikistan*. Pittsburgh, PA: University of Pittsburgh Press, 2016.

Kassymbekova, Botakoz. "Humans as Territory: Forced Resettlement and the Making of Soviet Tajikistan." *Central Asian Survey* 30, nos. 3–4 (2011): 349–370.

Kassymbekova, Botakoz, and Aminat Chokobaeva. "On Writing Soviet History of Central Asia: Frameworks, Challenges, and Prospects." *Central Asian Survey* 40, no. 4 (2021): 483–503.

Kassymbekova, Botakoz, and Christian Teichmann. "The Red Man's Burden: Soviet European Officials in Central Asia in the 1920s and 1930s." In *Helpless Imperialists: Imperial Failure, Fear, and Radicalization*, edited by Maurus Reinkowski and Gregor Thum, 163–186. Gottingen: Vanderhoek and Ruprecht, 2013.

Keller, Shoshana. "The Central Asian Bureau, an Essential Tool in Governing Soviet Turkestan." *Central Asian Survey* 22, nos. 2–3 (2003): 281–297.

Keller, Shoshana. "The Puzzle of Manual Harvest in Uzbekistan: Economics, Status, and Labour in the Khrushchev Era." *Central Asian Survey* 34, no. 3 (2015): 296–309.

Khalid, Adeeb. *Making Uzbekistan: Nation, Empire, and Revolution in the Early USSR*. Ithaca, NY: Cornell University Press, 2015.

Khalid, Adeeb. *The Politics of Muslim Cultural Reform: Jadidism in Central Asia.* Berkeley: University of California Press, 1998.
Kligman, Gail, and Katherine Verdery. *Peasants under Siege: The Collectivization of Romanian Agriculture, 1949–1962.* Princeton, NJ: Princeton University Press, 2011.
Kolchin, Peter. *Unfree Labor: American Slavery and Russian Serfdom.* Cambridge, MA: Belknap, 1987.
Kommunisticheskaia partiia Uzbekistana v tsifrakh: Sbornik statisticheskikh materialov 1924–1977. Tashkent: Uzbekistan, 1979.
Kommunisticheskaia Partiia Uzbekistana v rezoliutsiiakh s'ezdov i plenumov TsK. Vol. 1. 1925–1937. Edited by R. Abdullayeva. Tashkent: Institut Istorii Partii pri TsK Kompartii Uzbekistana 1987.
Kondrashin, Viktor. *Golod v SSSR 1929–1934.* 3 vols. Moscow: Mezhdunarodnyi fond demokratiia, 2012.
Kondrashin, Viktor. *Khlebozagotovitel'naia politika v gody pervoi piatletki i ee rezult'taty (1929–1933 gg.).* Moscow: Politicheskaia Entsiklopediia, 2014.
Kopelev, Lev. *The Education of a True Believer.* New York: Harper Collins, 1980.
Kotkin, Stephen. *Magnetic Mountain: Stalinism as a Civilization.* Berkeley: University of California Press, 1997.
Kotkin, Stephen. "Modern Times: The Soviet Union and the Interwar Conjuncture." *Kritika: Explorations in Russian and Eurasian History* 2, no. 1 (2001): 111–164.
Kotkin, Stephen. *Stalin: Waiting for Hitler, 1929–1941.* New York: Penguin, 2017.
Kulachenko, V. F. "Shelkovyi rynok Srednei Azii." *Srednei Aziiatskii Shelk* 7–9 (1929): 344–359.
Kul'turnoe stroitel'stvo SSSR Statisticheskii Sbornik. Moscow: Gosplanizdat, 1940. Published on http://istmat.org/node/22545.
Kunakova, Lidiia. *Zemel'no-vodnaia reforma v Uzbekistane, 1925–1929 gg.* Frunze: Mektep, 1967.
Lee, Joo-Yup. "The Political Vagabondage of the Chinggisid and Timurid Contenders to the Throne and Others in Post-Mongol Central Asia and the Qipchaq Steppe: A Comprehensive Study of Qazaqlïq, or the Qazaq Way of Life." *Central Asiatic Journal* 60, nos. 1–2 (2017): 59–95.
Levi, Scott. *The Rise and Fall of Khoqand, 1709–1876: Central Asia in the Global Age.* Pittsburgh, PA: University of Pittsburgh Press, 2017.
Levin, Zeev. *Collectivization and Social Engineering: Soviet Administration and the Jews of Uzbekistan.* Leiden, Netherlands: Brill Academic, 2015.
Lewin, Moshe. *Russian Peasants and Soviet Power: A Study of Collectivization.* London: Allen & Unwin, 1968.
Li, Zhang. "Net Per Capita Income in Rural Wuxi, 1840s–1940s." *Journal of the Economic and Social History of the Orient* 3 (2014): 291–325.
Lorenz, Richard. "Economic Basis for Basmachi Movement in the Farghana Valley." In *Muslim Communities Reemerge: Historical Perspectives on Nationality, Politics, and Opposition in the Former Soviet Union and Yugoslavia,* edited by Andreas Kappeler, Gerhard Simon, and Gerog Brunner, 277–303. Durham, NC: Duke University Press, 1994.
Loring, Benjamin. "'Colonizers with Party Cards': Soviet Internal Colonialism in Central Asia, 1917–39." *Kritika: Explorations in Russian and Eurasian History* 15, no. 1 (2014): 77–102.
Loy, Thomas. *Bukharan Jews in the 20th Century: History, Experience, and Narration.* Wiesbaden: Reichert Verlag, 2008.

Lumey, L. H., and F. W. A. Van Poppel. "The Dutch Famine of 1944-45: Mortality and Morbidity in Past and Present Generations." *Social History of Medicine* 7, no. 2 (1994): 229-246.

Maillert, Ella. *Turkestan Solo: One Woman's Expedition from the Tien Shan to the Kizil Kum*. London: William Heinemann, 1938.

Manley, Roberta. *To the Tashkent Station: Evacuation and Survival in the Soviet Union at War*. Ithaca, NY: Cornell University Press 2009.

Martin, Terry. "An Affirmative Action Empire: The Soviet Union as the Highest Form of Imperialism." In *A State of Nations: Empire and Nation-Making in the Age of Lenin and Stalin*, edited by Ronald Suny and Terry Martin, 67-90. Oxford: Oxford University Press, 2001.

Masov, R. M. *Istroiia Topornogo razdeleniia*. Dushanbe: Irfan, 1991.

Materialy po obsledovaniiu kochevogo i osedlago tuzemnago khoziaistva i zemlepolzovaniia v Amu-Dar'inskom otdele Syr Dar'inskoi oblasti. Vol. 1. Tashkent: Tipo-Lit Il'ina, 1915.

Materialy po izucheniiu khoziaistva osedlago tuzemnago naseleniia v Turkestanskom Krae: Sartovskoe khoziaistvo v chimkentskom uezd Syr-Dar'inskoi oblasti. Tashkent: V. M. Ilina, 1912.

Matley, Ian. "The Golodnaya Steppe: A Russian Irrigation Venture in Central Asia." *Geographical Review* 60, no. 3 (1970): 328-346.

Megoran, Nicholas. *Nationalism in Central Asia: A Biography of the Uzbekistan-Kyrgyzstan Border*. Pittsburgh, PA: University of Pittsburgh Press, 2015.

Morris-Suzuki, Tessa. "Sericulture and the Origins of Japanese Industrialization." *Technology and Culture* 1 (1992): 101-121.

Morrison, Alexander. *The Russian Conquest of Central Asia 1814-1907. A Study in Imperial Expansion*. Cambridge: Cambridge University Press, 2021.

MTS po vtoroi piatletke. Moscow: Gosplanizdat, 1939.

Narodnoe Khoziaistvo SSR 1913-1955, Kraktii Statisticheskii Sbornik, RGAE F. 1562. Op. 33, D. 2310, ll.1-250. http://istmat.org/node/36699.

Narodnoe Khoziaistvo Uzbekskoi SSR za 50 leto. Edited by Bektimirova, V. A. Tashkent: Izdatel'stvo Uzbekistana, 1967.

Nazarov, R. R. "Natsionnal'naia kukhnia Uzbekistana: Traditsii i innovatsii." In *Istoriia iedy i traditsii pitaniia narodov mira*, edited by A. V. Pavlovskaia, 172-183. Moscow: Tsentr po izucheniiu vzaimodestviia kul'tur, 2016.

Niallo, Aziz (a.k.a. A. V. Stanishevskii). "Ocherki Istorii revoliutsii i grazhdanskoi voiny v Kirgizii i Srednei Azii." In *Basmachestvo*, edited by S. A. Shumov and A. R. Andreev, 84-194. Moscow: Eksmo, 2005; originally published in 1941.

Nora, Pierre. *Realms of Memory: Rethinking the French Past*. Vol 1. Translated by Arthur Goldhammer. New York: Columbia University Press, 1996.

Northrop, Douglas. *Veiled Empire: Gender and Power in Stalinist Central Asia*. Ithaca, NY: Cornell University Press, 2004.

Noskov, N. I. "Zemledelie." In *Materialy po obsledovaniiu kochevogo i osedlago tuzemnago khoziaistva i zemlepol'zovaniia v Amu-Dar'inskom otdele Syr'-Dar'inskoi oblasti*, vol. 1, , 190-375. Tashkent: Tipo-Lit Il'ina, 1915.

Nourzhanov, Kirill. "Bandits, Warlords, National Heroes: Interpretations of the Basmachi Movement in Tajikistan." *Central Asian Survey* 34, no. 2 (2015): 177-189.

Nourzhanov, Kirill, and Christian Bleuer, *Tajikistan: A Social and Political History*. Canberra: Australia National University Press, 2013.

Obertreis, Julia. *Imperial Desert Dreams: Cotton Growing and Irrigation in Central Asia 1960-1991*. Göttingen: V&R University Press, 2017.

Ohayon, Isabelle. *La sédentarisasion des Kazakhs dans l'URSS de Staline: Collectivasation et changement social.* Paris: Massioneuve & Larose, 2006.
Oja, Matt. "Traktorizatsiia as Cultural Conflict, 1929–1933." *Russian Review* 51 (1992): 343–362.
Ölçen, Mehmet Arif. *Vetluga Memoir: A Turkish Prisoner of War in Russia 1916–1918.* Translated by Gary Leiser. Gainesville: University Press of Florida, 1995.
Oral History Association. "Principles and Best Practices." 2009. https://oralhistory.org/about/principles-and-practices-revised-2009/.
Osnovnye elementi produktsiia sel'skogo khoziaistva SSR. Moskva: Izdanie TsSU SSSR, 1928.
Osokina, Elena. *Zoloto dlia industrializatsii: TORGSIN.* Moscow: Rosspen, 2009.
Oushakine, Serguei. "'We're Nostalgic but We're Not Crazy': Retrofitting the Past in Russia." *Russian Review* 66, no. 3 (2007): 451–482.
Oxunboboyev, Yo'ldosh. *Tanlangan Asarlar.* Tashkent: O'zbekiston nashriyoti, 1985.
Penati, Beatrice. "Adapting Russian Technologies of Power: Land-and-Water Reform in the Uzbek SSR 1924–1928." *Revolutionary Russia* 25, no. 2 (2012): 187–217.
Penati, Beatrice. "The Cotton Boom and the Land Tax in Russian Turkestan (1880s–1915)." *Kritika: Explorations in Russian and Eurasian History* 14, no. 4 (2013): 741–774.
Penati, Beatrice. "The Reconquest of East Bukhara: The Struggle against the Basmachi as a Prelude to Sovietization." *Central Asian Survey* 26, no. 4 (2007): 521–538.
Pennebaker, James, and Amy Gonzales. "Making History: Social and Psychological Processes Underlying Collective Memory." In *Memory in Mind and Culture*, edited by Pascal Boyer and James Wertsch, 117–137. Cambridge: Cambridge University Press, 2009.
Peterson, Maya K. *Pipe Dreams: Water and Empire in Central Asia's Aral Sea Basin.* Studies in Environment and History. Cambridge: Cambridge University Press, 2019.
Pianciola, Niccolò. "The Collectivization Famine in Kazakhstan, 1931–1933." *Harvard Ukrainian Studies* 25, nos. 3/4 (December 2001): 237–251.
Pianciola, Niccolò. "Famine in the Steppe: The Collectivization of Agriculture and the Kazakh Herdsmen, 1928–1934." *Cahiers du Monde Russe* 45, nos. 1/2 (2004): 137–191.
Pianciola, Niccolò. "Scales of Violence: The 1916 Central Asian Uprising in the Context of Wars and Revolutions (1914–1923)." In *The Central Asian Revolt*, edited by Chokobaeva et al., 169–190. Manchester, UK: Manchester University Press, 2020.
Pianciola, Niccolò. "Stalinskaya 'ierarkhiya potrebleniya' i velikii golod 1931–1933 gg. v Kazakhstane." *Ab Imperio* 2 (2018): 80–116.
Pianciola, Niccolò. "Towards a Transnational History of Great Leaps Forward in Pastoral Central Eurasia." *East/West: Journal of Ukrainian Studies* 3, no. 2 (June 2016): 75–116.
Piatiletnii plan narodno khoziaistvennogo stroitel'stva SSR. Vol. 2. Moscow: Plannovoe Izdatel'stvo, 1930.
Pipes, Richard. "The Muslims of Soviet Central Asia: Trends and Prospects." *Middle East Journal* 9, no. 2 (1955): 147–162, part 1; 9, no. 3 (1955): 295–308, part 2.
Portelli, Alessandro. "What Makes Oral History Different." In *The Oral History Reader*, 3rd ed., edited by Robert Perks and Alistair Thomson, 48–58. Abingdon, UK: Routledge, 2016.
Posevnye Ploshadi SSSR. Vol. 1. Moscow: Gos Stat Izdat, 1957.
Privratsky, Bruce G. *Muslim Turkistan: Kazak Religion and Collective Memory.* Richmond, UK: Curzon, 2001.
Rachamimov, Alon. *POWs and the Great War: Captivity on the Eastern Front.* London: Bloomsbury, 2002.

Rajabov, Qahramon. "Bosmachilik harakatiga oid ikki hujjat." In *Tarihning noma'lum sahifalari*, vol. 2, edited by A. Hasanov and O. Vul'f, 195–245. Tashkent: O'qituvchi nashriyot, 2010.
Rajabov, Qahramon. *Madamin Bek (risola)*. Tashkent: Abu Matbuot Konsalt, 2011.
Raleigh, Donald. "'On the Other Side of the Wall, Things Are Even Better,' Travel and the Opening of the Soviet Union: The Oral Evidence." *Ab Imperio* 4 (2012): 373–399.
Rasulov, Baxtiyor. *O'zbekiston kollektivlashtirish jarayonidagi siyosi qatag'onlar va surgun qilingan dehqonlar ahvoli (1929–1959)*. Tashkent: Sharq, 2012.
Reeves, Madeleine. *Border Work: Spatial Lives of the State in Central Asia*. Ithaca, NY: Cornell University Press, 2014.
Retish, Aaron. *Russia's Peasants in Revolution and Civil War: Citizenship, Identity, and the Creation of the Soviet State, 1914–1922*. Cambridge: Cambridge University Press, 2008.
Riello, Giorgio, and Prasannan Parthasarathi, eds. *The Spinning World: A Global History of Cotton Textiles, 1200–1850*. Pasold Studies in Textile History, vol. 16. Oxford: Oxford University Press, 2009.
Ritchie, Donald. *Doing Oral History*. 3rd ed. Oxford: Oxford University Press, 2015.
Rizaev, G. *Sotsialisticheskoe sel'skoe khoziaistvo Uzbekistana*. Tashkent: Uzbekistan, 1978.
Roberts, Flora. "Old Elites under Communism: Soviet Rule in Leninobod." PhD diss., University of Chicago, 2016.
Roche, Sophie. "Maintaining, Dissolving, and Remaking Group Boundaries through Marriage: The Case of Khujand in the Ferghana Valley." In *Intermarriage from Central Europe to Central Asia: Mixed Families in the Age of Extremes*, edited and introduced by Adrienne Edgar and Benjamin Frommer, 163–200. Lincoln: University of Nebraska Press, 2020.
Rogan, Eugene. *The Fall of the Ottomans: The Great War in the Middle East*. New York: Basic Books, 2015.
Rosenberger, Nancy. *Seeking Food Rights: Nation, Inequality, and Repression in Uzbekistan*. Belmont, CA: Wadsworth/Cengage, 2012.
Roy, Olivier. *The New Central Asia: The Creation of Nations*. London: Tauris, 2000.
Ruder, Cynthia. *Making History for Stalin: The Story of the Belomor Canal*. Gainesville: University of Florida Press, 1998.
Rylov, "Predislovie." In *Materialy po obsledovaniiu kochevogo i osedlago tuzemnago khoziaistva i zemlepolzovaniia v Amu-Dar'inskom otdele Syr Dar'inskoi oblasti*, vyp. 1, 1–2. Tashkent: Tipo-Lit Il'ina, 1915.
Rywkin, Michael. *Moscow's Muslim Challenge: Soviet Central Asia*. London: Routledge, 1982.
Sabol, Steven. *Russian Colonization and the Genesis of Kazak National Consciousness*. New York: Palgrave, 2003.
Sabol, Steven. *"The Touch of Civilization": Comparing American and Russian Internal Colonization*. Boulder: University of Colorado Press, 2017.
Sahadeo, Jeff. *Russian Colonial Society in Tashkent, 1865–1923*. Bloomington: Indiana University Press, 2007.
Sahadeo, Jeff. *Voices from the Soviet Edge: Southern Migrants in Leningrad and Moscow*. Ithaca, NY: Cornell University Press, 2019.
Sartori, Paulo. "'Colonial Legislation Meets Sharia': Muslims' Land Rights in Russian Turkestan." *Central Asian Survey* 29, no. 1 (2010): 43–60.
Schafer, Edward H. *The Golden Peaches of Samarkand: A Study of T'ang Exotics*. Berkeley: University of California Press, 1985.
Sel'skoe khoziaistvo SSR. Ezhegodnik 1935. Part b, "Rastenovodstvo." Moscow: Selxozgiz, 1936.

Sel'skoe khoziaistvo Uz SSR za 40 let. Tashkent: Gosizdat Uzbekskoi SSR, 1957.
Semenova, Viktoria. *Sotsial'naia dinamika pokalenii: problema i real'nost'*. Moscow: Rosspen, 2009.
Sen, Amartya. "Famines." *World Development* 8 (1980): 613–621.
Sen, Amartya. *Poverty and Famines: An Essay on Entitlement and Deprivation*. Oxford: Oxford University Press, 1981.
Shamsutdinov, Rustambek. *O'zbekistonda sovetlarning quloqlashtirish siyosati va uning fojeali oqibatlari*. Tashkent: Sharq, 2001.
Shamsutdinov, Rustambek. *O'zbekiston Tarixi*. Tashkent: Sharq, 2013.
Shamsutdinov, Rustambek. *Qishloq fojeasi: Jamoalashtirish, quloqlashtirish, surgun: O'rga Osiyo respublikalari misolida*. Tashkent: Sharq, 2003.
Shamsutdinov, Rustambek. *Repressia 1937–1938. Dokumenty i Materialy Vyp 4, Zhertvy bo'lshogo terrora iz Uzbekistana 1937 god, Dekiabr'*. Tashkent: Sharq, 2008.
Shamsutdinov, Rustambek. *Shimolii Kavkaz surgundagi yurtdoshlar qismati*. Tashkent: Sharq, 2005.
Shamsutdinov, Rustambek, and A. Ishaqov. *Andijon tarixdan lavhalar*. Tashkent: Sharq, 2013.
Shaniiazov, K. Sh. "O traditsiionoi pishche Uzbekov." In *Etnografichekoe izuchenie byta i kul'tury Uzbekov*, edited by Kh. Ziioev, 59–89. Tashkent: Fan, 1972.
Sharopov, Jamol, ed. *Unutilmas Xotiralar (O'zbekiston qishloq xo'jaligi veteranlarning xotiralari)*. Tashkent: Mehnat 1990.
Shatunovskii, M., and S. Zashuk. "Khlebofurazhnyi balans Srednei Azii." *Narodnoe khoziaistvo Srednei Azii* 1 (1929): 78–81.
Shayakhmetov, Mukhamet. *The Silent Steppe: The Memoir of a Kazakh Nomad under Stalin*. Translated by Jan Butler. New York: Overlook/Rookery, 2007.
Shigabdinov, Rinat. "Nogai-Kurgan—pervyi Tatarskii aul v Uzbekistane." *Idel-Idel'* 5 (2018): 100–103. http://idel-rus.ru/nogaj-kurgan-pervyj-tatarskij-aul-v-uzbekistane/.
Shulman, Elena. *Stalinism on the Frontier: Women and State Formation in the Soviet East*. Cambridge: Cambridge University Press, 2012.
Sinitsyn, Feodor. *Sovetskaia natsiia i voina: Natsional'nyi vopros v SSSR 1933–1945*. Moscow: Tsentrpoligraf, 2018.
Smith, Jenny Leigh. *Works in Progress: Plans and Realities on Soviet Farms, 1930–1963*. New Haven, CT: Yale University Press, 2014.
Sodiqov, Hamdam, and Nazrulla Jo'rayev. *O'zbekiston Sovet mustamlakachiligi davrida*. Tashkent: Sharq, 2011.
Sotsialisticheskoe stroitel'stvo SSSR: Statisticheskii ezhegodnik. Moscow: TsUNXhU Gosplana SSR, 1934.
Sovremennyi kishlak Srednei azii (sotsial'no ekonomicheskii ocherk) Vypusk V, Balykchinskaia Volost (Ferganskoi oblasti Uzbeksoi SSR); Vypusk 4 Zarafshan, edited by IV Karp and N K Suvlov. Tashkent: Izdaniia Sred Az Biuro TsK VKP (b), 1927.
Stolitskogo, A. V. *Khlopkovodstvo SSR i ego perspektivy*. Moscow: Biuro Pechati, 1926.
Stone, Andrew. "Growing Up Soviet? The Orphans of Stalin's Revolution and Understanding the Soviet Self." PhD diss., University of Washington, 2012.
Storella, C. J., and A. K. Sokolov, eds. *The Voice of the People: Letters from the Soviet Village, 1918–1932*. Annals of Communism. New Haven, CT: Yale University Press 2012.
Stronski, Paul. *Tashkent: Forging a Soviet City*. Pittsburgh, PA: University of Pittsburgh Press, 2010.
Sudorgin, V. S. "Tsvetite, sady." In *Istoria Kolkhozov i Sovkhozov Uzbekistana*, edited by R. Kh. Aminova, 405–452. Tashkent: Mekhnat, 1989.
Suny, Ronald. *The Soviet Experiment: Russia, the USSR, and the Successor States*. Oxford: Oxford University Press, 2011.

Teichmann, Christian. *Macht der Unordnung: Stalins Herrschaft in Zentralasien 1920–1950*. Hamburg: Hamburger Edition, 2016.
Teichmann, Christian. "Wildscapes in Ballyhooland: Shock Construction, Soviet Colonization and Stalinist Governance." *Cahiers du Monde Russe* 57, no. 1 (2016): 221–246.
Thompstone, Stuart. "Russian Imperialism and the Commercialization of the Central Asian Cotton Trade." *Textile History* 26, no. 2 (1995): 233–258.
Tlostanova, Madina. *Gender Epistemologies and Eurasian Borderlands*. New York: Palgrave MacMillan, 2010.
Tonkin, Elizabeth. *Narrating Our Pasts: The Social Construction of Oral History*. Cambridge: Cambridge University Press, 1992.
Tragediia Sredneaziatskogo kishlaka: Kollektivizatsiia, raskulachivanie, ssylka 1929–1955. Vols. 1–3, edited by Dilarom A. Alimova. Tashkent: Shark, 2006.
Trevisani, Tommaso. *Land and Power in Khorezm: Farmers, Communities, and the State in Uzbekistan's Decollectivisation*. Halle Studies in Anthropology of Eurasia, vol. 23. Berlin: Lit Verlag Dr. W. Hopf, 2008.
TsUNKhU Gosplana SSSR. *SSSR v tsifrakh 1935 g*. Moscow: Soiuzorgotchet, 1935. http://istmat.org/files/uploads/19822/sssr_1935_trud.pdf.
Turgunbaev, Valijon. "Znachimost' khlopovykh produktov vo vneshnei torgovle stran Srednei Azii do 60-x godov XIX veka." *Molodoi Uchenyi* 6, no. 6 (2015): 549–551.
Tursunova, Zulfiya. *Women's Lives and Livelihoods in Post-Soviet Uzbekistan: Ceremonies of Empowerment and Peace-Building*. Lanham, MD: Lexington, 2014.
Ueda, Akira. "The Demographic and Agricultural Development of the Kokand Oasis in the Russian Imperial Era: Nomad Immigration and Cotton Monoculture." *Central Asian Survey* 38, no. 4 (2019): 510–530.
Valiev, A. Kh. *Polozhenie dekhanstva Fergany v kontse XIX–nachale XX vekov*. Tashkent: Fan, 1958.
van Meurs, Wim. "Land Reform in Romania—a Never-Ending Story." *South-East Europe Review* 2 (1999): 109–122.
Vassburg, David. "Orphans and Adoption in Early Modern Castilian Villages." *History of the Family* 3, no. 4 (1998): 441–458.
Veksel'man, M. N. *Rossiiskii monopolisticheskii i inostrannyi kapital v srednei azii. Konets XIX—nachalo XX vek*. Tashkent: Fan, 1987.
Verkhoturov, Dmitrii. *Stalinskaia Kollektivizatsiia: Bor'ba za khleb*. Moscow: Veche, 2019.
Vil'nit, I. A. "Organizatsiia shelko-zagotovitel'noi kampanii v 1929 g." *Srednei Aziiatskii Shelk* 4–6 (1929): 285–287
Vinogradov, G. N. "Irrigatsia v doline Kashka-dar'i." *Trudy Sredne-aziiatskogo nauchno-issledovatel'skogo instituta irrigatsii* 29 (1935): 47–50.
Viola, Lynne. *Best Sons of the Fatherland: Workers in the Vanguard of Soviet Collectivization*. Oxford: Oxford University Press, 1989.
Viola, Lynne. *Peasant Rebels under Stalin: Collectivization and the Culture of Peasant Resistance*. Oxford: Oxford University Press, 1999.
Viola, Lynne, V. P. Danilov, N. A. Ivnitskii, and Denis Kozlov, eds. *The War against the Peasantry 1927–1930: The Tragedy of the Soviet Countryside*. New Haven, CT: Yale University Press, 2005.
Vneshniaia torgovlia SSSR 1918–1940: Statisticheskii obzor. Moscow: Vneshtorgizdat, 1960.
Volotkin, A. F. "Osedania khlopka v Uzbekistane." *Biulletin' TsSU Uzbekskoi SSR* 23 (1930): 35–46.
Vsesoiuznaia Perepis' Naselenii 1926 g. [All-Union Population Census 1926] Tsentral'noe Statisticheskoe Upravlenie, Moscow: TsSU Soiuza SSSR 1928-1933. Vol. 15.

Vsesoiuznoe Perepis' Naselenie 1939 goda. [All-Union Population Census 1939] Tsentral'noe Statisticheskoe Upravleniia. Moscow: TsSU Soiuza SSSR, 1928-1932. Archival files published on website *Demoscope Weekly,* https://www.demoscope.ru/weekly/ssp/census.php.

Warman, Arturo. *Corn and Capitalism: How a Botanical Bastard Grew to Global Dominance.* Translated by Nancy L. Westrate. Chapel Hill: University of North Carolina Press, 2003.

Wemheuer, Felix. *Famine Politics in Maoist China and the Soviet Union.* New Haven, CT: Yale University Press, 2014.

Werner, Cynthia. "Women, Marriage, and the Nation-State: The Rise of Non-Consensual Bride Kidnapping in Post-Soviet Kazakhstan." in *The Transformation of Central Asia,* edited by Pauline Jones-Luong, 59–89. Ithaca, NY: Cornell University Press, 2004.

Werth, Nicholas. "The NKVD Mass Secret Operation No. 00447 (August 1937–November 1938)." https://www.sciencespo.fr/mass-violence-war-massacre-resistance/en/document/nkvd-mass-secret-operation-n-00447-august-1937-november-1938.html#title4.

Wheatcroft, S. G. "Famine and Epidemic Crises in Russia, 1918–1922: The Case of Saratov." *Annales de démographie historique* (1983): Mères et nourrissons. 329–352.

Whitman, John. "Turkestan Cotton in Imperial Russia." *American Slavic and East European Review* 15, no. 2 (1956): 190–205.

Willfort, Fritz. *Turkestanishe Tagebuch: sechs Jahre in Russische-Zentralasien.* Vienna: Wilhelm Braumüller, 1930.

Williams, M. W., and V. G. Konovalov. "Central Asian Temperature and Precipitation Data, 1879–2003." USA National Snow and Ice Data, 2008. https://nsidc.org/data/g02174/versions/1.

Xo'jaev, Mansurxo'ja. *Shermuhammadbek Qo'rboshi.* Tashkent: Sharq, 2008.

Yakhina, Guzel. *Zuleikha.* Translated by Lisa Hayden. London: Oneworld, 2019.

Yusupov, K. *Agrarye otnosheniia v Uzbekistane v periode stroitel'stva sotsializma.* Tashkent: Fan, 1977.

Zanca, Russell. "Fat and All That: Good Eating the Uzbek Way." In *Everyday Life in Central Asia,* edited by R. Zanca and J. Sahadeo, 178–197. Bloomington: Indiana University Press, 2007.

Zanca, Russell. *Life in a Muslim Uzbek Village: Cotton Farming after Communism.* Belmont, CA: Wadsworth, 2010.

Zemtsov, Viktor. *Stalinskaia epokha: Ekonomika, repressii, industrializatsiia 1924–1954.* Moscow: Veche, 2018.

Index

Afghanistan, 41, 52–53, 69, 98, 113, 120–121, 128, 139
agitation, 4, 13–14, 46, 55, 62, 70, 83–105, 108, 111, 126, 130, 152, 169, 170, 178, 180, 202, 202–211
agriculture, 15–16, 27, 35, 71, 87–88, 102, 143, 156, 209
Anticolonial, 40, 53, 55, 57, 107, 203
artel, 60–62, 75, 85, 88, 92–93, 96, 132, 177

Bosmachi, 2–8, 17, 37–58, 84, 92, 98, 105–109, 114, 125, 130, 156, 179–182, 197, 204, 207–209
boylar, 3–7, 14, 30–32, 42, 48, 61–62, 64, 73, 75, 88, 90, 102, 105–114, 117–131, 157, 162, 183, 189, 209–212
bread, wheat, 21, 45, 79, 114–115, 123, 132–133, 140, 142, 144–148, 150, 154–162, 164, 169, 174, 182, 188, 191, 194; zo'gora, cornbread, 16, 22, 140, 145, 147, 165, 191
Bukhara, 3–4, 22–29, 34, 36, 40–42, 56, 63–67, 69, 89, 97, 100, 107, 116, 124, 207, 210

census, 27, 63–68, 138–139
chorikor. See sharecropper
class conflict, 4–8, 14, 36, 59, 69, 73, 80, 87, 104–105, 111, 126, 129, 157
class differentiation, 2, 11–12, 17–18, 23, 32, 40, 42, 53, 59, 60–64, 71, 73, 81, 92, 102, 130–131, 209–214
cohort, 9–11, 19, 37, 45–46, 57, 139, 178–180, 182–192, 199–201
colonialism, 14, 16–17, 24–29, 34, 40, 63, 69, 76, 82, 106–107, 148, 156, 203–204
Communist Party, 2, 4, 17, 23, 30, 33, 37, 43, 60–61, 63–64, 69–70, 83–90, 93, 101, 105, 111–112, 127–128, 131
confiscation, 8, 13, 18, 30, 33, 46, 60–62, 68–69, 73–74, 77, 81, 95, 104–106, 110–113, 119–120, 202, 209, 211, 213
cooperative, 61, 79–82, 87, 93, 112, 209
cotton, 16–17, 21–36, 41–42, 60, 69, 71–74, 79–82, 84–96, 106–107, 119, 123, 135–136, 141–144, 156, 158, 170, 174, 177, 203–204, 207

dehqon, 2, 15–17, 23–26, 29–33, 36, 63–64, 72–74, 77, 81, 87–88, 90, 102–105, 127–128, 156, 207, 209
dependence, 3, 15, 23, 29–33, 36, 64, 70, 80–82, 189, 210
dispossession. See confiscation
dryland farming. See *lalm-i kor*

education, 22, 60–62, 66, 100, 106, 118–119, 122–126, 179, 182–199
epidemic, 3, 59, 72, 134, 137, 140–141, 168
exile, 18, 38, 47, 57–58, 61–62, 68, 75, 81–82, 100, 104–107, 112–114, 117–131, 139, 210

famine, 2–4, 13, 16–19, 34, 89, 123, 132–151, 154, 159, 162, 173, 181, 194, 213
Fergana Valley, 23–28, 35, 37–41, 44–46, 48–51, 71–72, 77, 81, 111–112, 163–168
foods, 2, 26, 35, 60, 62, 93, 95, 113, 133–151, 165–173, 191, 205, 213

gender, 13–14, 17, 37–58, 77–78, 124, 141, 153–155, 164–165, 174–178, 200–201, 208
generation, 1–2, 10–11, 37–40, 58, 81, 162–163, 171, 174, 185, 190, 205–206, 210, 213
grain, 2, 25–26, 28–29, 33–36, 64, 86–90, 95–96, 102, 127, 132–151, 161, 171–173, 192
Gulag, 107, 114, 123, 128, 168, 211

herding, 4, 21, 29–30, 33, 49, 66, 76, 114–115, 143, 146, 180, 183, 185

identity, 2–3, 11, 14–17, 23, 30–33, 51, 53, 58, 60–83, 85, 92, 94, 97, 101–102, 113, 124, 127, 130, 146, 157, 214
Ikramov, Akmal, 136, 148–149, 197
indigenous, 27, 33–34, 40, 63, 161
intersectionality, 13–14, 39, 42, 59, 62
irrigation, 6–7, 12, 19, 24, 27, 35–36, 112, 152, 163–169, 178
Islam, beliefs, 29, 38, 133, 147–148, 162, 180–181, 185; institutions, 60, 185; personnel, 4–7, 31, 38, 60–61, 73, 78, 81, 98, 112, 114, 117–118, 120–128, 143, 161–162, 185, 213

283

284 INDEX

kambag'al, 4, 7, 30–31, 60–64, 70–82, 85, 88, 91–94, 100, 102, 109, 113, 125, 129, 188, 190, 210–213
Kazakh, 8, 27, 34, 40, 50, 52–53, 66, 89, 138–140, 179, 209
Kazakhstan, 2, 18, 35, 64, 68–69, 75, 87, 90, 102, 116–122, 128, 135–138, 142, 146, 150, 209, 214
Khiva. See Xorazm
kidnap, 17, 38–40, 44–48, 53–54, 56–57, 208
kinship, 3, 6, 9–12, 14, 32–33, 45–57, 60, 70, 107, 116–126, 130, 179–201
kolkhoz, formation and characteristics, 1, 9, 60–61, 83–90, 93, 102, 106, 124, 128, 131, 145, 149
kulak. See *quloq*
Kyrgyz, Kyrgyzstan, 15, 18, 27, 34, 39–40, 51–52, 64, 66, 69, 77, 144

labor-day. See payment, labor-day
laborer. See *mardikor*
lalm-i kor, 3, 27, 32, 34, 135–136, 142–143
landownership, 2–3, 23, 25, 27–28, 30–36, 61, 63, 73, 76, 81–82, 85, 104, 115, 179–180
land reform, 5, 31, 59–82, 85, 88, 93, 102, 113, 180, 183–185, 209
lending, 18, 25–28, 30, 35–36, 61, 71, 78–80, 83–85, 87, 93, 112, 124, 209
literacy, 8, 55, 62, 99, 118, 125, 170, 179, 183, 185, 187, 195–197

mardikor, 3–7, 22–34, 70, 74–75, 77–78, 82, 116, 120, 127–131, 180–185, 204, 210, 214
memory, 2, 8–9, 12, 15–17, 37–58, 97–99, 102, 126–127, 130, 141, 151, 165, 203–213
militia, 39–40, 44–45, 51, 79, 92, 96, 98, 110, 114–115, 208

narrative, hegemonic, 12–14, 17, 32, 37–38, 56–57, 82, 104–107, 130, 152, 164–169, 178–179, 202–213
nationality, ethnicity, 17, 40–42, 45, 50–53, 63–69, 81, 85, 107, 138, 153
novcha. See *mardikor*

oral history, 1–3, 8–10, 12, 15–16, 19, 134, 203–206, 212
orphan, 3, 16, 19, 34, 49, 54, 59–60, 73, 81, 94, 98–99, 126, 130, 157, 164, 170–171, 179–201, 211–214
Oxunboboyev, Yo'ldosh, 87, 125–126, 165–166, 196

payment, labor-day, 2, 32–33, 90, 144, 152–153, 159, 164, 168–175, 178, 184, 207
peasant. See *dehqon*
poor. See *kambag'al*
post-Soviet, 12, 37, 39, 55–56, 203–204

Qo'rboshi, 17, 38–41, 44–45, 48–58, 108
quloq, 3, 18, 75, 82, 84–86, 96, 104–131, 139, 184, 193–195, 204, 211–213

Red Army, 4–7, 17, 37–44, 48, 52–56, 124, 182, 207
requisitioning, 41, 86, 143–144, 150–151
resistance, 33–34, 37–44, 52, 75–76, 85, 95–98, 111–112, 119, 120–122, 128
Revolutions (1917), 1, 4, 11, 23, 34–35, 40–41, 56, 69
Russia, 15, 26, 31, 33–35, 40, 175
Russian language, xii, 30–31, 62, 83, 92, 101, 104–105, 141, 148, 187
Russian people or things, 3–4, 25–29, 34, 40, 42, 49, 52, 62–64, 67, 69, 76, 85, 91–95, 97, 99–101, 104–106, 122–123, 130, 134, 138, 144, 146–149, 157, 161–163, 198, 203, 209–210
Russian Turkestan, 4, 16, 23–29, 33–36, 44, 69

school. See education
sharecropper, 27–33, 70–82, 90, 113–114, 127, 129–130, 211–212
silkworms, 147, 175–178
social capital, 2, 63, 68, 81
Soviet supporters, 3–4, 14–15, 17, 19, 37–38, 54, 58–62, 82, 93, 100–103, 124, 131, 208–214
Stalinism, 2, 12, 18, 83, 86–87, 90, 102–104, 107, 111–112, 117, 121–122, 126, 136, 153, 173, 179, 181, 203, 205, 212, 214
standpoint, 12–14, 51–54, 58, 62, 82, 107, 206, 214
starvation. See famine

tabelchi, 101, 165, 170–171, 178, 185, 187, 195–196, 213
Tajikistan, 41, 54, 64–65, 68, 75, 89, 117–118, 122, 138–139, 168, 209, 211
Tajik people or language, xii, 8–9, 15, 27, 29, 40, 46, 52, 65–68, 79, 139
taxation, 25–26, 29, 33, 35, 49, 79, 90, 96–98, 102, 143, 148, 183, 190
teacher, 8–9, 22, 38, 60–63, 118, 153, 180, 185, 187, 196–198

textile industry, 24–26, 33–35, 71, 141, 175
tractors, 16, 19, 86, 101, 123, 145, 152–163, 177–178
Turkestan (Kokand) Autonomy, 40
Turkmen, Turkmenistan, 40–41, 53, 55, 66, 69, 119–121, 138, 209
typhus. *See* epidemic

Uyghur, 44, 66, 92, 196
Uzbek ethnicity, identity, 50–51, 62, 107, 153, 164–169, 178–179, 203
Uzbekistan, independent, 17–18, 37, 45, 57, 107, 130, 153, 177, 201–212
Uzbek language, 55, 57, 68, 84–85, 90, 97, 100–101, 104–105, 183–186
Uzbek SSR, formation of, 4, 17, 37–41, 57, 61–69, 73, 77, 81, 197, 209

vabo. *See* epidemic
victim, 37–43, 47–58, 107–110, 140, 178, 181, 195, 202–203, 208, 212–213

war, 11–12, 33–37, 40–41, 48–51, 55–56, 59, 69, 71, 89–90, 132, 153–154, 181, 191–195
wealthy. See *boylar*
women. *See* gender
working in the gates of the rich, 31, 33, 49, 54, 59–63, 70, 72–73, 78, 80, 82, 92, 96, 100, 102, 107–108, 116, 118, 120, 172, 182–185, 191–192, 199–201, 210, 2013

Xorazm, 4, 8, 16–17, 23, 26, 28–30, 40–41, 46, 72–73, 89, 140

Yusupov, Usmon, 50, 165–167, 181

www.ingramcontent.com/pod-product-compliance
Lightning Source LLC
Chambersburg PA
CBHW021653230426
43668CB00008B/611